Great Garden
SHORTCUTS

Great Garden
SHORTCUTS

100s of All-New Tips & Techniques That Guarantee You'll
• Save Time • Save Money
• Save Work

JOAN BENJAMIN, EDITOR

Contributing writers: **Erin Hynes, Tina James, Barbara Kaczorowski, Deborah L. Martin, Susan McClure, Felder Rushing**

Rodale Press, Inc.
Emmaus, Pennsylvania

OUR MISSION

We publish books that empower people's lives.

RODALE BOOKS

Library of Congress Cataloging-in-Publication Data

Great garden shortcuts : 100s of all-new tips and techniques that guarantee you'll save time, save money, save work / edited by Joan Benjamin.
    p. cm.
  Includes bibliographical references and index.
  ISBN 0–87596–702–7 (hardcover : alk. paper)
  1. Gardening—Encyclopedias. I. Benjamin, Joan.
SB450.95.G74 1996
635'.03—dc20   95–51212

Distributed in the book trade by St. Martin's Press

2 4 6 8 10 9 7 5 3 1   hardcover

GREAT GARDEN SHORTCUTS
EDITORIAL AND DESIGN STAFF

Editor: Joan Benjamin

Contributing Editors: Fern Marshall Bradley, Deborah L. Martin, and Jean M. A. Nick

Senior Research Associate: Heidi A. Stonehill

Copy Editor: Ann Snyder

Administrative Assistants: Nancy C. Kutches and Stephanie Wenner

Editorial Assistance: Amy M. DiGiovanni and Georgia Keramas

Interior Book Design and Layout: Diane Ness Shaw

Interior Book Designers: John Lotte and Frank Milloni

Technical Artists: Robin Hepler and Maureen Logan

Interior Illustrators: Janet Bohn and Barbara Field

Cover Designer: Diane Ness Shaw

Cover Illustrator: Randall Hamblin

Studio Manager: Leslie Keefe

Manufacturing Coordinator: Melinda Rizzo

Indexer: Nan Badgett

RODALE HOME AND GARDEN BOOKS

Vice President and Editorial Director: Margaret Lydic Balitas

Managing Editor: Ellen Phillips

Art Director: Michael Mandarano

Copy Director: Dolores Plikaitis

Office Manager: Karen Earl-Braymer

If you have any questions or comments concerning the editorial content of this book, please write to:

  Rodale Press, Inc.
  Book Readers' Service
  33 East Minor Street
  Emmaus, PA 18098

CONTENTS

CONTENTS

INTRODUCTION

You've probably got one in your neighborhood. You know, one of those green-thumbed gardeners who always has the earliest tomatoes, the most beautiful flowers, and the most gorgeous lawn. And somehow they do it without spending every waking hour in their yard and garden. What's their secret? Shortcuts.

Great gardeners have developed shortcuts that help them get great results faster or with less effort. So even if they work long hours at the office or have their hands full with the kids' schedules, they still have beautiful yards and bountiful gardens—*and* the time to enjoy them. Now, you can put their tips and techniques to work with *Great Garden Shortcuts.*

That's because we went straight to the source for these tips—green-thumbed gardeners all over the country. When we pooled all of their ideas, we had hundreds of shortcuts that gardeners are actually using to get beautiful, productive gardens with less time, money, and work than ever before. Use their hard-won secrets to get great results—guaranteed!

Great Garden Shortcuts is arranged alphabetically so you can find what you need fast. Just turn to the topic you're interested in—whether it's Animal Pests, Composting, or Potatoes. You'll find new and unusual techniques you've never heard of before, but believe me, they work! Whether it's a quick trick for getting more strawberries faster, or an easy and inexpensive way to keep deer out of your garden, the shortcuts just keep on coming.

Special features make *Great Garden Shortcuts* even more useful. You'll find "Quick Fix Mixes" that give you simple recipes for everything from do-it-yourself mole repellent to perfectly preserved hot peppers. Look for tips and chores to skip under the "Just Say 'No'" heading throughout this book. (You'll be surprised at how many garden chores just aren't necessary!) Plus, turn to the "Proven Plants" recommendations that tell you at a glance which plants to use if you want great results.

You know how good it feels when you stumble across a great shortcut for staking plants, growing crops faster, or getting rid of pests—one that really works. In *Great Garden Shortcuts,* we give you a gardenful of them!

Joan Benjamin

Protect your fruits from birds by covering them with bird netting (bottom). To make a bird net cage—without breaking branches—set four or more tall stakes around each fruit bush. Put an upside-down clay pot on the end of each stake, then drape bird netting over the top. Since the pots are bigger than the holes in the net, the net will rest on the pots, instead of on the branches. You can also protect your plantings by surrounding them with reflective bird scare tape (top).

ANIMAL PESTS

2 Tricks to Baffle Birds

STEER YOUR
FEATHERED
FRIENDS AWAY
FROM RIPE FRUIT

Keep birds off your berries, cherries, grapes, and other fruits. It's easy if you know the right way to use bird netting and bird scare tape. When and how you use these deterrents make the difference between saving and losing a crop. So order netting and bird scare tape from garden supply catalogs, then use these tips to make sure they work.

Birds can't surf this net. When you protect your plants with netting, birds can't get a grip on the covered fruit. But if you just drape netting on the plant, the netting can catch on or break berry branches. Avoid this by creating a net "cage" over your plant. (See the opposite page for details.)

Cover berry bushes and fruit trees as soon as the fruit starts changing color. If you're using stakes, bury the edge of the netting so birds can't crawl under. For fruit trees or large bushes where stakes are impractical, drape the netting directly over the plant and tie it tight around the trunk of the plants so birds can't hop beneath it and get at the crop.

A flash in the…fruit trees?! Birdscare Flash Tape is made of glossy silver and red metallic polyethylene that flashes like a fire in the wind. The tape did a good job of repelling birds in United States Department of Agriculture (USDA) studies says Doug Clark, of Modern Agri-Products, a Birdscare Flash Tape supplier in Lynden, Washington. He adds that flash tape works especially well against flocking birds like starlings.

To set out the tape, put rows of 8-foot stakes around your bush or planting. Then tack or staple a roll of tape to the top of the stakes in each row. The stakes should be far enough apart so the tape can "wiggle" and flash in the wind. Birds will get used to the tape after several weeks, so don't set it out until fruit is almost ready to harvest.

1

Mulberries Keep Birds from Mauling Fruit Crops

Instead of driving birds away from your fruit plants, try luring them to something they'd rather eat—mulberries. In his southern Indiana garden, organic gardener John McMahan uses mulberry trees to keep the birds from dining on his blackberries, gooseberries, red and black raspberries, and strawberries.

Although he does nothing else to protect his berry crops from the birds, John says his fruits suffer no damage when there are fruits on the mulberries. However, since his strawberries ripen about two weeks before the mulberries, the birds have first pick of this crop. "I can tell exactly when the birds start moving to the mulberries, because they stop eating my strawberries," he explains.

John says that his technique works best if the mulberry trees are located away from sidewalks or patios where messy mulberries—and the resulting purple bird droppings—aren't welcome.

Tom Vorbeck, owner of Applesource, a supplier of rare apples in Chapin, Illinois, has also found that mulberries work for birds. Tom says that wild mulberry trees near his orchard keep the birds off his fruit. "Mulberries have a relatively long ripening season, which keeps the birds busy most of the time." However, Tom warns that birds will be looking for other sources of food if the mulberries don't come through. "We had really bad bird damage the one year when the mulberries froze out," he says.

Birds leave your berries alone when you provide them with a mulberry feast instead.

2

Flat Fence Foils Cats Fast

A FALLEN FENCE
IS THE PURRFECT
SOLUTION FOR
CATS

Keep cats out of your garden with chicken wire or decorative welded wire fencing laid flat on the ground. An upright fence isn't much of a challenge to a determined cat, but uncomfortable footing sends felines in search of softer digging surfaces, says Washington State University Cooperative Extension Service agent Holly Kennell.

Once neighborhood cats find a soft place to dig, it becomes their litter box, Holly points out. The results not only smell bad, but they can bring diseases into your garden that are contagious to people as well as other cats. And digging cats can wreak havoc on newly sown seedbeds and young seedlings. "Laying wire fencing on the soil surface puts a stop to all that," Holly says. "The cats won't even walk over it."

Lay pieces of chicken wire on the bare soil in your vegetable garden as a friendly reminder to felines to stay away. Use decorative wire in your flower beds—it comes in pieces that are easy to fit around plantings.

You can also use this unobtrusive technique to keep cats away from bird feeders—and birds. Just lay a sheet of fencing on the ground under your bird feeder. When grass or groundcovers grow up around the fence, you won't even know it's there, but tenderfooted cats will!

3

Dogs Drive Animal Pests Away

PUT MAN'S

BEST FRIEND

TO WORK

PROTECTING

YOUR GARDEN

Hungry critters and dogs don't mix. John McMahan, an organic gardener in Clifford, Indiana, says his dogs provide nearly all the animal pest control his garden needs without any help from him. Because John allows his dogs free range, he does have to tolerate some dog damage in his garden. But, he says, "at least the rabbits aren't eating my lettuce." John adds that his dogs rarely catch visiting wildlife, but they do keep rabbits, groundhogs, and other marauders moving on.

At his rural home, John is able to let his dogs patrol the property without restraint. Where neighbors and leash laws restrict your dog's movements, you can tie the dog near your garden. Or use an invisible fence and radio collar system to keep your dogs out of the garden but inside your property line. Invisible fencing (created by radio signals) lets your dog chase foraging critters away, but keeps him from getting into the veggies—or your neighbor's yard.

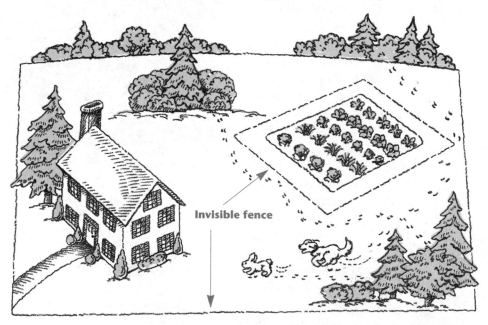

Invisible fence

Outline your garden and property with invisible fence to keep your dog out of your plants and on patrol against animal pests. Radio signals from the fence let your dog know where he can and cannot wander—he'll let pesky critters know that your garden is out of bounds.

Castor Oil Spray Chases Moles— and More—Away

Drive moles out with a castor oil repellent. A commercial castor oil spray like Mole-Med will repel eastern moles without killing them, says Glenn Dudderar, extension wildlife specialist at Michigan State University. Glenn says to thoroughly soak the area with water before and after you apply the repellent, and you'll get good mole control for at least a month.

A castor oil repellent may chase off other pests too. Glenn is now testing the product as a squirrel and chipmunk repellent and says it's kept the critters out of flower beds for about a month. Mole-Med employee Bill Reed reports that gardeners in the West are successfully controlling gophers with the product.

But Glenn notes that applying Mole-Med to an entire yard can be a pricey proposition—a pint of the concentrate sells for about $20 and only covers a 5,000-square-foot area. So he likes to save it for smaller sites where shovel-packing mole hunters are likely to do more harm than good. Glenn also cautions that Mole-Med may not repel other species of moles, and it may not be effective on sandy soils.

✎ QUICK FIX MIX

Moles-Away Spray

Here's an easy, inexpensive recipe for an effective homemade mole-repelling mix.

1 tablespoon castor oil
2 tablespoons liquid dishwashing soap
6 tablespoons water

Mix the oil and soap in a blender until the mix has the consistency of shaving cream. Add the water and blend again. In a watering can, mix 2 tablespoons of "mole mix" with 2 gallons of water. Sprinkle the mix over mole-infested yard and garden areas. Apply the repellent after a rain to make sure it soaks into the soil.

🍃 **For more information on controlling animal pests, see the Deer entry.**

ANNUALS

Turbo-Plant for Professional Results

Make annual planting simple and speedy with this expert technique, and you'll have plenty of time for other garden tasks. Each spring and fall, professional landscaper Rose Vincent of Vincent Landscapes in Austin, Texas, installs huge beds of annuals for her commercial clients. To pick up the pace, Rose has her crews use a technique she calls "turbo-planting." Here's how it works.

1 Remove all the transplants from their pots and lay the plants on their sides in a diamond pattern.

2 Make a hole just below where you've set a transplant, so you don't have to move the plant aside. To make the hole, stick your trowel into the soil to the beginning of the handgrip. Don't pull the trowel out of the ground; just draw it to the side to create a hole.

3 While holding the soil back with the trowel, use your free hand to slip the plant in the hole. Then slide the soil back into the hole, pull out the trowel, and firm the soil with your free hand.

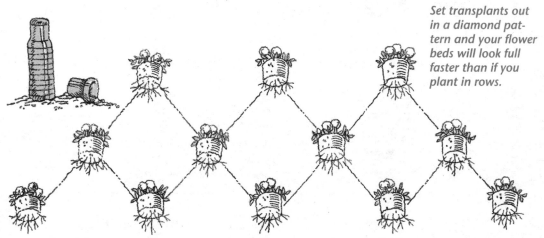

Set transplants out in a diamond pattern and your flower beds will look full faster than if you plant in rows.

Rose says that as you plant, your hands will develop a fast, natural planting rhythm. The beauty of the system is that it cuts down on the number of times you need to touch each transplant and the number of steps it takes to plant each one. Rose claims that one person can plant 80 4-inch plants in an hour using turbo techniques. You'll find the system works just as well for a dozen transplants as it does for a large planting.

In case you're working with rocky soils, Rose has one more turbo-planting technique. Before you plant, improve the soil by top-dressing the bed with 1 to 3 inches of compost or peat moss. That way, you won't have to dig as deeply into the bad soil, and you'll save time by not adding soil amendments to each individual hole. "Add peat moss or compost each time you plant, and you'll find that after a few years the soil is so soft you can almost dig it with your hands," she says.

JUST SAY "NO" TO FALL CLEANING

When frost puts your annual garden to bed, there are two good reasons to skip the fall cleanup. One is that you'll find that spring cleaning is easier and faster than fall cleanup, since annual roots break down in winter. Another good reason to wait until spring to clean up your annual bed is that you may get some free plants. "I clean up my annual beds in spring, partly from pure laziness and partly because many annuals will winter over in my Zone 6 climate," says Ellen Spector Platt, who grows 2 acres of flowers and herbs at her Meadow Lark Flower and Herb Farm in Orwigsburg, Pennsylvania.

Hardy annuals are real time-savers if you live in an area where the ground is too frozen or wet to plant in early spring. Among the hardy annuals that can survive winter at Meadow Lark Farm are dusty miller, pansies, 'Victoria' mealycup sage (*Salvia farinacea* 'Victoria'), and snapdragons. (See "10 Annuals That Never Need Replanting" on page 8 for more hardy annuals.) Ellen says about half of the annuals she sets out will survive the winter, but you can't tell which will be the lucky ones until spring comes.

For an even bigger jump on the season, Ellen recommends sowing cold-hardy annuals like larkspur (*Consolida ambigua*) and love-in-a-mist (*Nigella damascena*) in late summer. During fall, they grow into small seedlings that survive the winter nicely and start growing first thing in spring.

10 Annuals That Never Need Replanting

These sun-loving annuals reseed so reliably that you only need to plant them once to have them forever. To get self-sowing annuals started, plant open-pollinated (nonhybrid) cultivars; hybrids don't always come true from seed. Enjoy the flowers all summer, then delay your fall garden cleanup so the seeds have time to ripen and drop to the ground. Wait to mulch until seedlings are up—many seeds need bare soil to sprout. Thin out extra seedlings in early spring.

CHINESE FORGET-ME-NOT (*Cynoglossum amabile*)

The flowers of this old favorite are more sun- and drought-tolerant and they bloom longer than perennial forget-me-not (*Myosotis sylvatica*). The sprays of ¼-inch-wide brilliant sky blue, pink, or white flowers appear all summer long on 2-foot-tall plants with soft gray-green leaves. The flower sprays add an old-fashioned look to fresh bouquets—just make sure to leave some flowers uncut so they can go to seed.

CORNFLOWER (*Centaurea cyanus*)

Poke brushy branches in around the seedlings of this popular annual to help keep the 2-foot-tall plants upright. The 1½-inch-wide blue, pink, white, or bicolor flowers appear through midsummer (or longer if you cut off faded blooms). Stop cutting flowers in late summer and let the remaining flowers go to seed. These silvery green-leaved plants like dry soil.

COSMOS (*Cosmos bipinnatus*)

These deceptively delicate-looking plants pop up even in harsh, compacted soil—they seem to thrive on neglect. Pinch off the 2- to 4-inch-wide pink, magenta, white, or bi-color flowers after they fade to prolong their bloom. After midsummer, let the remaining blooms set seed. Stake the heavily branched 4-foot-tall plants, or let them flop and spread their lacy, lime green foliage across your garden.

GARDEN BALSAM (*Impatiens balsamina*)

Thin seedlings of this classic cottage flower to leave clumps of 3 to 5 plants for a lush display. Plants are covered with 1- to 2-inch-wide pink, white, purple, or red double flowers all summer long. Plants grow upright and reach 2 to 2½ feet tall. Garden balsam appreciates extra water or partial shade in hot, dry spells or in areas with hot, humid summers.

LOVE-IN-A-MIST (*Nigella damascena*)

These airy little plants don't like to be transplanted, so shake the ripe seedpods where you'd like flowers next summer. Blue, pink, or white flowers are set among lacy bracts. Blooms last all summer and are followed by balloonlike seedpods that are great for wreaths and crafts—but leave a few pods on the plants to reseed! The bushy 1- to 2-foot-tall plants have threadlike silver gray foliage and don't mind drought or poor soil.

MIGNONETTE (*Reseda odorata*)

Grow mignonette for its fragrance, not its flowers. The unassuming spikes of small coral, yellow, or green flowers appear on 1-foot-tall plants from late spring through mid-summer. Let mignonette self-sow in inconspicuous spots near benches or paths where you can enjoy its intensely sweet, citrusy perfume.

POPPIES (*Papaver* spp.)

Poppies, with their satiny petals, bloom in early summer and are especially effective in drifts. Blue-green leaves set off the colorful flowers. The red, pink, white, orange, yellow, and bicolor flowers come in single or semidouble forms that are 1 to 5 inches wide. Rake the soil lightly under the plants after the seedpods open to cover the dropped seeds.

POT MARIGOLD (*Calendula officinalis*)

Double 2- to 3-inch-wide cream, yellow, orange, or bicolor marigold-like flowers appear all summer in cool areas, and in spring and fall in hot-summer areas. Remove faded blooms until flowering slows down to prolong the display, then let the last flowers go to seed. The 1- to 2½-foot-tall plants have pleasantly fragrant leaves.

ROCKET LARKSPUR
(*Consolida ambigua*, formerly called *Delphinium ajacis*)

Grow this easy annual with its tall bloom spikes for the effect of delphiniums without the trouble. For full, healthy plants, thin seedlings to 8 to 12 inches apart. Look for royal blue, violet, light blue, pink, or white spurred flowers in early summer. The 3-foot-tall plants hold their blooms on branched spikes above dark green, feathery foliage. You'll get plenty of blooms for reseeding, and plenty more to use in bouquets or to air dry—larkspur flowers hold their color beautifully when dried.

SUNFLOWER (*Helianthus annuus*)

Birds love sunflower seeds and drop them in unexpected places—so you'll always have seedling surprises next year. In addition to the familiar large yellow and brown mammoth sunflower, there are smaller ornamental forms with single and double flowers in yellow, cream, russet, or brown. These robust plants bear 3- to 12-inch-wide flowers on single or multi-branched 2- to 8-foot-tall stems.

Mini-Mattock Makes Planting Easy

If your hands ache from planting and preparing annual beds with a trowel, get quick relief by switching to a mattock. "A hand trowel requires more power and force," says Leslie Scott, a garden designer in Cleveland Heights, Ohio. "I know a number of gardeners who get carpel tunnel disorders in their hands and wrists from using traditional tools; a mattock is much easier."

A mattock is an old-fashioned tool shaped like a long-headed hammer. Leslie uses a handheld version with a handle that's about 15 inches long. It's lighter and smaller than full-size mattocks. The metal head has a broad, flat surface like an anvil on one end and a long, pointed metal pick on the other. Use the anvil end to quickly pulverize and prepare your soil. This is also the end to use when you're digging holes. Once you put a plant in its hole, you can use the anvil to push the soil back around the roots. So what do you do with the pick end? "You can use the pick end to take out your aggressions on horrible soil—it's a great form of therapy!" Leslie adds.

Handle a mattock like a pick—use its weight to do the hard work so your hands and wrists don't have to.

Simple Seeding for Super Cut Flowers

Forget about the florist. It's a snap to grow your own long-stemmed annuals for cutting—if you choose tall cultivars and use a fuss-free seeding method. "Most garden centers carry short annuals that only make good bedding plants," says Ellen Spector Platt, owner of Meadow Lark Flower and Herb Farm in Orwigsburg, Pennsylvania. But for cut flowers you need tall annuals that can put on a show in a vase, bucket, or basket. To find flowers for cutting, you'll need to look through seed catalogs for species and cultivars with long stems. (See "Sources" on page 412 for seed companies that carry good flowers for cutting.)

Ellen recommends the following long-stemmed annuals,

which grow to 18 to 30 inches tall and are great for cutting.

- Bells-of-Ireland (*Moluccella laevis*)
- 'Blue Boy' cornflower (*Centaurea cyanus* 'Blue Boy')
- 'Blue Horizon' ageratum (*Ageratum* 'Blue Horizon')
- 'Century' cockscomb (*Celosia cristata* 'Century'); plume type
- Floradale Series and 'Chief' cockscomb; crested types
- 'Giant Imperial' rocket larkspur (*Consolida ambigua* 'Giant Imperial')
- Globe amaranth (*Gomphrena globosa*)
- Lion's-ear (*Leonotus nepetifolia*)
- Pompon dahlias (*Dahlia* hybrids)
- Strawflower (*Helichrysum bracteatum*)

FOR DO-IT-YOURSELF CUT FLOWERS, START WITH TALL PLANTS

Sow the bells-of-Ireland, cockscombs, cornflower, globe amaranth, and rocket larkspur in spring, planting them directly into your garden. Start the ageratum, lion's-ear, pompon dahlias, and strawflower indoors in late March or early April. It takes a little more effort to start flowers indoors, but it's worthwhile with these annuals because a head start gives you a much longer flowering and cutting season.

Ellen uses this super-simple technique for starting seeds indoors. Plant your flower seeds in a sterile, peat-based planting mix in individual six-pack trays, set the six-packs in plastic flats, and put them on your windowsills.

If your windows don't face south, your seedlings may get leggy (that is, long and lanky), but don't throw them out! When planting time comes, follow Ellen's advice: Bury seedlings deep and pinch off the top set of leaves. You'll be amazed at what great flowers can grow from awful-looking seedlings.

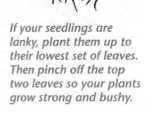

If your seedlings are lanky, plant them up to their lowest set of leaves. Then pinch off the top two leaves so your plants grow strong and bushy.

11

10 Annuals for All-Summer Bloom

Some annuals bloom all summer if you prune off faded blooms religiously, but others put on a show without any help from you. The care-free plants listed below don't need deadheading—they'll bloom and bloom until fall. Plant them in full sun where you normally use high-maintenance annuals like geraniums, marigolds, and petunias.

ANNUAL BABY'S-BREATH (*Gypsophila elegans*)

This airy plant sets off large, brightly colored flowers like cosmos (*Cosmos bipinnatus*)—use it to make your garden look like a bouquet. Baby's-breath is covered with delicate sprays of single white or pink ¼- to 1-inch-wide flowers. The bushy 18- to 24-inch-tall plants bloom heavily for eight weeks and lightly thereafter. They make a fabulous fresh or dried bouquet filler.

BRAZILIAN VERVAIN (*Verbena bonariensis*)

Try this tall annual behind smaller plants to add height to your garden, or plant it up front for a see-through floral screen. Tiny rosy lavender flowers are borne at the top of slender, well-branched 3- to 4-foot-tall stems. The leaves are small, toothed, and rough. Brazilian vervain is a perennial in Zones 7 to 10 but blooms well as an annual in colder zones. This butterfly favorite tolerates heat and drought, and it's great for cut flowers.

CLEOME (*Cleome hasslerana*)

Here's a big bold plant for the back of the garden. It looks particularly nice with 'Victoria' mealycup sage (*Salvia farinacea* 'Victoria') planted at its feet. The open, spidery heads of pink, magenta, or white flowers float over spiky 3- to 5-foot-tall stems. Cleome is heat- and drought-tolerant and often reseeds year after year. The flowers attract butterflies and bees and are lovely in bouquets.

FEVERFEW (*Chrysanthemum parthenium*, also called *Tanacetum parthenium*)

Plant these charming buttonlike flowers in front of sunflowers to hide the sunflowers' untidy lower stems. Sprays of ½- to 1-inch-wide white, yellow-centered daisies or cream-colored double flowers are borne on 1- to 3-foot-tall stems. The light green foliage is deeply cut and aromatic. Feverfew tolerates partial shade and self-sows generously. The flowers attract beneficial insects. They make an excellent fresh or dry bouquet filler.

'FLAMINGO FEATHER' WHEAT CELOSIA (*Celosia spicata* 'Flamingo Feather')

Plant a bold sweep of this flower for a dynamite display. The blooms resemble heads of wheat and are pale pink at the bottom and darker pink toward the top. The leaves are long and strap shaped. Each sturdy, well-branched, 3- to 4-foot-tall plant produces 40 to 60 flower heads that are excellent in fresh or dried arrangements.

FLOWERING TOBACCO (*Nicotiana alata*)

Place this plant near your bedroom window, since its blooms are only fragrant at night. Its white, pink, red, or lime green flowers open into 2-inch-wide five-petaled stars on 1½- to 4-foot-tall stems. The leaves are large and velvety. Old-fashioned white-flowered types are especially fragrant. Flowering tobacco makes an excellent cut flower that thrives in sun or partial shade and sometimes self-sows.

HELIOTROPE (*Heliotropium arborescens*)

Place this sweetly fragrant annual near a path or patio where you can enjoy it. The small, rich purple or white flowers are grouped in flat, 4- to 6-inch-wide heads on 8- to 24-inch-tall stems. The leaves are dark green and crinkled. Heliotrope flowers from spring until late summer.

MEALYCUP SAGE (*Salvia farinacea*)

Plant mealycup sage behind dwarf snapdragons for a wonderful display all season long. Spikes of violet blue, light blue, or white flowers stand above the leaves of this bushy, aromatic, 2- to 4-foot-tall plant. The flowers are excellent for cutting and drying. Mealycup sage is perennial in Zones 8 to 10 and makes a fine annual in colder zones.

SNAPDRAGON (*Antirrhinum majus*)

Snapdragons come in so many sizes that there's one for just about any part of your garden. They bear spires of red, pink, bronze, orange, yellow, or white tubular flowers that are sweetly scented. Plants range from bushy 7-inch-tall dwarfs to stately 3-foot-tall cutting types. Snapdragons prefer light shade in hot-summer areas and need extra water during droughts.

SWEET ALYSSUM (*Lobularia maritima*)

This dainty flower makes a pretty sight growing under rocket larkspur (*Consolida ambigua*). Domed clusters of tiny white, pink, or purple flowers appear all season long, often hiding the leaves of the 6-inch-tall plants. Alyssum tolerates drought, poor soil, and partial shade. It often self-sows. The honey-scented flowers are a butterfly favorite.

APPLES

Pollinate Apples with a Blossom Bouquet

BRING YOUR
APPLE TREE
FLOWERS AND
SHE'LL THANK
YOU WITH
APPLES

It takes two apple trees to make apples, since most apples need pollen from a different kind of apple cultivar to set fruit. But if you only want—or have room for—one tree, you can still get good fruit set with this old-time trick: Just substitute a bouquet of apple blossoms for the second tree.

Here's how it works: Ask a friend or neighbor if you can cut a few flowering branches from their apple tree. Place the bouquet in a small bucket of water, and hang the bucket from a branch in the center of your blooming apple tree or set it among the branches in a crotch of the tree. Bees will cross-pollinate the flowers, so you'll get apples without having to plant another tree. "A bunch of apple blossoms cut from a willing friend's tree will increase the rate of successful pollination," says gardener Valori Herrmann of Centerville, Utah. "And that means more apples."

Make a pollinating partner for a solitary apple tree. Tie a bucket of blooms from a friend's tree in your tree's branches. Bees will mix up the pollen and ensure a good harvest.

Stop Apple Maggots with Clean Sticky Balls

No more wormy apples—that's a promise if you keep your apple maggot traps clean. The apple maggot flies are lured to their doom by red sticky balls, which they mistake for early-ripening apples. But the fly-coated balls are as unappetizing-looking to the apple maggots as they are to us. To be effective, the sticky balls must be cleaned off regularly. But scraping off fly-encrusted gunk isn't most gardeners' idea of fun. Luckily, there's an alternative: "You can forget about scraping off dead bugs and goo if you wrap the balls in plastic instead," says Jean Nick, an enthusiastic home fruit gardener in Pennsylvania.

Start with new red balls or balls that you've already cleaned off and dried. Cover each ball with a plastic sandwich bag and seal it tightly around the ball with a twist tie. Then coat the plastic-covered balls with a gooey substance like Tanglefoot and hang them in your trees—one ball in each dwarf tree, and two or three in each semidwarf or full-size tree. When a ball gets covered with bugs or dust, simply slip off the plastic bag and throw it out. Place a new bag over the ball, add a fresh coat of goo, hang the ball in your apple tree, and you're back in business.

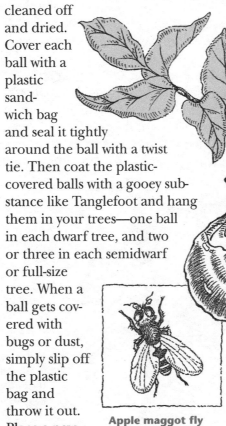

Apple maggot fly

Slip red balls into plastic bags before you apply the goo that traps apple maggot flies. The plastic cover makes trap cleanup as easy as removing a wrapper.

Small Trees Make Short Work of Pruning

You can get all the apples you need without spending lots of time pruning trees. How? By growing dwarf cultivars. These naturally small trees really don't need much pruning, says Murray Kereluk, Food Garden curator at the University of British Columbia Botanic Gardens in Vancouver. "If you just wanted to plunk one in the ground," Murray says, "after about three or four years it would require very little pruning, just a little bit to renew some of the old fruiting wood occasionally. But even if you just left it unpruned, it would still crop."

Dwarf trees make the whole pruning process much easier, says Murray, who tends more than 150 fruit trees in the Botanic Garden's ¾-acre Food Garden. Since all of his trees are 6 feet or shorter, Murray can do all his pruning with a pair of hand pruners and a pruning saw. "I can work my trees standing on the ground, and I don't have to lift my hands above my head," Murray says.

For super-productive dwarf apple trees, prune them the first three years after planting to train them into a strong, healthy shape. Start by cutting a dormant whip (un-branched sapling) back to 2½ feet tall to encourage side branches to sprout. In mid-June, prune off all but four

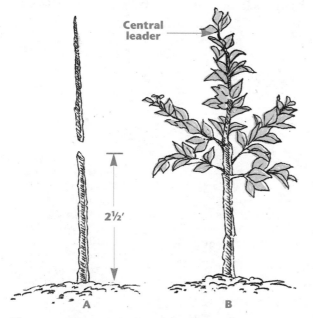

To get dwarf apple trees off to a good start—and avoid future pruning—start training trees when they're young. Plant a dormant whip in spring and cut it back to 2½ feet tall (A). In mid-June, choose four side branches that head in different directions and are spaced several inches apart. These branches and the uppermost shoot form the framework for your tree. Prune off all other branches (B).

Central leader

2½'

A

B

branches and the strongest uppermost shoot (central leader) as shown on the opposite page. These branches form the framework of your tree. The next spring, cut the central leader back to 2 feet above the previous year's side branches. In June, pick out another four side branches that are at least 1½ feet above the first set of branches, making sure they are spaced so they all get sun. Cut off all other side branches. Repeat the process of cutting back the top and selecting new framework branches for three years.

Once you've shaped your tree, you'll only need to prune now and then. Prune to keep the center of the tree open, so light and air reach all parts of the branches. Remove suckers (branches that sprout at the base of the tree) or water sprouts (branches that grow straight up from existing branches) in midsummer. Remove any crowded, crossing, or unproductive branches in late winter.

Bypass Problems with Scab-Resistant Apples

HERE'S THE EASIEST WAY TO HAVE SCAB-FREE APPLES

Save yourself a lot of headaches by selecting scab-resistant apple cultivars for your home garden. "I think that's the best thing people can do to reduce the time it takes to care for apple trees," says Sarah Wolfgang Heffner, orchard manager at the Rodale Institute Experimental Farm in Kutztown, Pennsylvania.

Apple scab is a fungal disease that makes apples develop olive to brown velvety spots on their leaves and fruits. The spotted leaves gradually turn yellow and drop, and the fruits crack and rot as they mature.

Plant scab-resistant apple cultivars like those listed below instead of highly susceptible trees such as 'Delicious', 'Empire', and 'McIntosh'. Your trees will get less apple scab. And you'll spend less time picking up infected leaves and fruits as they drop, and spraying the trees with copper, sulfur, or lime-sulfur.

Check your favorite nursery or mail-order source for these scab-resistant apples, originally listed in the Winter 1995 *Northeast SARE* (Sustainable Agriculture Research and Education Program) *Newsletter:* 'Enterprise', 'Goldrush', 'Jonafree', 'Liberty', 'Macfree', 'Prima', 'Priscilla', 'Pristine', 'Redfree', 'Sir Prize', and 'Trent'.

Try a Little Tenderness
for Longer-Lasting Apples

EASY-DOES-IT
HANDLING
MEANS HIGH-
QUALITY FRUIT

You'll keep fresh apples longer if you treat them gently when you pick them. These guidelines come from Galen Brown, formerly a fruit specialist at Michigan State University.

• Don't yank apples off your tree; you might pull the stems out of the fruit, leaving a hole where decay can get in and spoil your crop.

• When you harvest apples that are growing together in clusters, pick the first apple by cupping it in your hand, then gently pushing the apple in toward the stem and sideways to push it off the branch. Use this method with a few more apples, until you've got enough room to lift and rotate the remaining fruit.

• Once the apple is off the tree, don't squeeze or press it with your fingers or you'll bruise it. If possible, pick in the after-noon—bruising is most likely when the fruit is wet or cold, as it usually is early in the day.

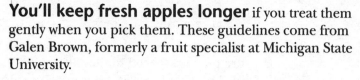

• Place the apple gently in the harvest bag or basket. Imagine that you're setting down an egg—except that an apple is more likely to bruise than an egg is to crack. (Galen's favorite method is to hold the apple cupped in his palm, rest the back of his hand on the apples already in the basket or bag, and then slide his hand out.) Never toss an apple into the basket; you'll bruise that apple and all the apples it hits.

For easy picking, cup your hand around a ripe apple, lift it slightly and rotate the fruit until it, and the stem, come off the branch.

ASPARAGUS

Asparagus Grows Best When You Dig Less

Now you can skip deep digging your asparagus beds with a good conscience. Asparagus plants grow best at the depth they're happiest, and that's just 4 inches. You'll get just as good results—or better—planting asparagus 4 inches deep as you'd get setting them at the recommended depth of 8 to 12 inches.

"You can plant deeper, but the crowns don't stay there," says extension vegetable specialist Jim Motes at Oklahoma State University. He measured the depth of asparagus crowns in a ten-year-old plot to see where they grew best. Although the crowns were originally planted at depths ranging from 4 to 12 inches, they all ended up at 4 inches after ten years.

Jim believes the crowns work themselves deeper into the soil or closer to the surface until they find the soil conditions they like best. He's found that in a sandy soil the crowns will grow a little deeper than 4 inches, while in a clay soil they'll be a little shallower.

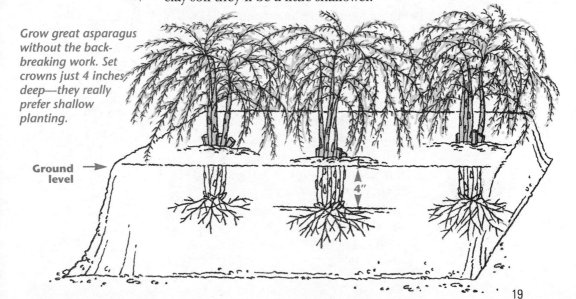

Grow great asparagus without the back-breaking work. Set crowns just 4 inches deep—they really prefer shallow planting.

Ground level

4"

Asparagus: Fat Is Where It's At

You'll get better flavor *and* better harvests from your asparagus patch if you grow fatter spears than those you see at the grocery store, says Roger Swain, host of PBS's *Victory Garden.* "I don't mean to sound like an asparagus snob," he says. "I just think that grocery stores make it seem like thinner asparagus spears are better, but that isn't true." According to Roger, thinner spears are just a sign that the plants are worn out. Any asparagus thinner than your thumb should be a no-keeper. In your garden, leave thin spears alone. They'll develop feathery foliage that produces food for the weak plants and replenishes their strength. "Asparagus—and the fatter the better—is one heck of a good food," says Roger. Here are his secrets for growing super-fat spears.

PAMPER YOUR ASPARAGUS FOR FAT, FLAVORFUL SPEARS

Control weeds with thick mulch. Roger puts 3 to 4 inches of sawdust on his asparagus bed in spring. The sawdust discourages many annual weeds and makes it easy to pull up perennial weeds that manage to push their way up through the mulch. You can use fresh or aged sawdust, but before you buy a load, make sure your sawdust comes from untreated wood.

Encourage growth with lots of fertilizer. Asparagus is a fairly heavy feeder. What nutrients you take away when you harvest, you have to give back for good growth. Roger recommends applying a complete, balanced fertilizer with the sawdust mulch or

Pick asparagus that's thumb-thick or fatter— it's tasty and tender.

spreading a layer of well-rotted horse or cow manure over the bed in fall.

Choose high-yielding cultivars. Roger recommends the all-male hybrids, like 'Jersey Giant'. Unlike female asparagus plants, male plants don't devote any energy to making seeds and can put all their resources into developing more and stronger spears. And without seeds, there are no asparagus seedlings, which can become pesky weeds themselves.

Mulch Means a Longer Asparagus Harvest

Stretch your asparagus season by doing less work in spring. Instead of removing the protective winter mulch from your entire asparagus planting, uncover only half of the bed when it's time for spears to start growing in early spring. The uncovered part of the bed will warm up more quickly and begin producing spears faster, says extension vegetable specialist Jim Motes at Oklahoma State University.

The area that's still under mulch stays cooler, delaying spear growth for a week or more. "That allows you to cut a little later into the late spring and early summer," says Jim. You don't have to pull the mulch off the covered portion of your asparagus bed—just leave it in place and wait for the spears to start popping through.

 ### JUST SAY "NO" TO WAITING FOR ASPARAGUS

Why wait to start harvesting your asparagus? Ignore the recommendations that say you have to wait until the second or third year after planting before you begin cutting spears, says extension vegetable specialist Jim Motes at Oklahoma State University. Research at Oklahoma State and at the University of California found that a light harvest the first year had no effect on second-year spear production or actually even increased the harvest. "It doesn't hurt to harvest for about a month the year following planting," Jim says. But he notes that the research took place where growing seasons are fairly long, and suggests that gardeners in more northern locations harvest for a shorter time in the first growing season.

BEANS

Top Crops with Bean Trellises

What's the secret to big bean harvests? Pole beans and trellises. You'll get more than twice as many beans from your trellised plants as from bush beans, because pole beans keep bearing while bush beans set one crop, then stop. Of course you can grow pole beans on prefabricated metal or mesh trellises, but you'll save money with this do-it-yourself version from Alan Kapuler, director of research for Seeds of Change, a national organic seed company in Santa Fe, New Mexico.

Alan recommends that you set wooden 2 × 2s, bamboo stakes, or similar narrow pieces of wood along the row where you want to plant pole beans. Use stakes that are 5 or 6 feet tall. Sink the base of the poles about a foot deep so they're set securely in the ground. Run a wire across the top of the posts to link them all together, and attach it with staples from a staple gun. Then weave a trellis of lightweight string or twine between the wire and posts, going up and down and back and forth between the poles until you create a webbing that beans can climb.

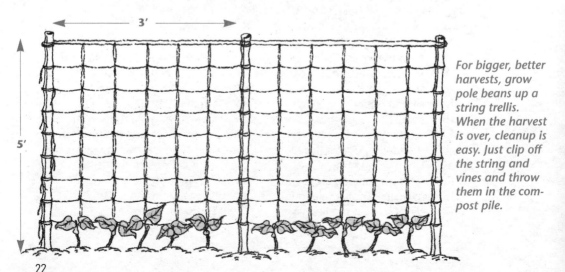

For bigger, better harvests, grow pole beans up a string trellis. When the harvest is over, cleanup is easy. Just clip off the string and vines and throw them in the compost pile.

Bean Tower Power

If you're not happy with the supports you've tried for pole beans, try bean towers. They're easy to work with and you'll get more beans. Before he discovered bean towers, community gardener Galen Bollinger of Austin, Texas, tried vertical poles, pole tepees, and various trellises for pole beans. Now he only uses the towers, which are available in garden seed catalogs. Galen gets more beans per square foot with towers than with other vertical support systems. And he says the towers are easier to put up, take down, and store than other supports he's tried. (He stores them in the boxes they came in.) The beans are easier to harvest too.

Galen describes a bean tower as a string trellis in a tepee shape. "The top of the tepee is cut off, so the beans don't grow out of human reach," he says. The top of the tepee is narrower than the bottom so the strings that form the support aren't vertical, but slanted. This slant allows bean pods to hang down inside the trellis, where they're easy to see and harvest.

The first time Galen assembled the tower, the process was slow and awkward because he wasn't familiar with the device. Now that he's used to it, he says the setup (and takedown) are quick and easy. Galen allows a 3-foot-square space for each tower of beans. He places them so they don't cast a shadow on nearby crops.

LEANING TOWER OF BEANS BEARS A BOUNTIFUL HARVEST

You'll probably only need one bean tower—but if you plant several, stagger the planting dates to spread out the harvest.

Beans by the Foot

Plant fewer beans more often and you'll get a steady supply of fresh green beans without all the work and waste of large, one-time plantings. "I sow about 1 foot of row per person every two weeks for both green and yellow beans," says Jean Nick, an enthusiastic home gardener in Pennsylvania. Try her system—when it's time to harvest, one picking will give you enough beans for a meal, without a lot of leftovers to deal with.

By making smaller sowings, Jean says she no longer spends hours picking and preserving beans. And fewer beans go to waste or get too big and tough because she doesn't have time to harvest them. For her family of four, Jean typically plants one 4-foot row each of green beans and yellow (wax) beans every two weeks throughout the growing season to keep just the right amount of beans coming to her table.

Scattering bean plantings around her garden is another key to Jean's success. If you put later plantings right next to earlier ones, she explains, any pest or disease problems can spread easily onto the new plants. When you separate your plantings, you leave disease and pest problems behind.

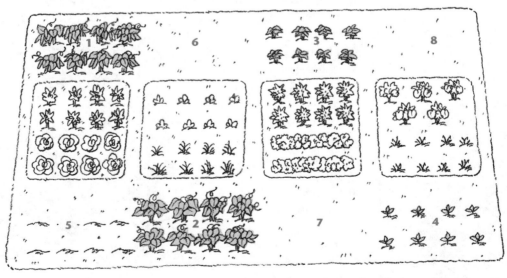

Make seven or eight small bean plantings a season for a steady supply of beans—when one planting ends, the next one is ready to harvest. Start plantings two weeks apart, in a different part of your garden each time, as shown above, to confuse pests and discourage diseases.

Fast French Beans

Speed beans to your table and extend your snap bean harvest by planting filet beans first. Also called haricots verts, these longtime French favorites are ready for picking about 45 to 55 days after planting—5 days to two weeks earlier than traditional green beans.

"The first time I grew filet beans was just for fun," says Fern Marshall Bradley, a Rodale garden book editor. Now, she grows them for their excellent flavor and the promise of an early harvest. By planting the filet beans first and sowing other snap beans later, Fern stretches her harvest of fresh green beans over a longer time period.

She warns that it's important to harvest filet beans when they're pencil thin—just as the catalogs recommend. They're delicious at that stage, she says. But if you let them get bigger, they get tough and develop strings that never soften up, no matter how long you cook them. Fern recommends that you pick the beans every day to get them when they're just the right size.

JUST SAY "NO" TO A BACKBREAKING HARVEST

When bush bean harvests start dwindling, stop stooping over to search for beans and just pick the entire plant. "After two or three pickings, bush green beans are pretty much through producing," says Jean Nick, an enthusiastic home gardener in Pennsylvania. "And your back is pretty much done in."

Jean recommends that you yank the plants out and carry them to a shady spot where you can sit in comfort and pull off the beans. If you're not sure if your beans are through producing, look for flowers. When you don't see any blooms on the plants, their productive time is over and you can yank them out without losing future bean harvests.

If you make successive plantings of bush beans every two weeks, you'll have a new crop coming on as you finish your current one. After another two weeks of picking, you and your back can look forward to another brief break.

BENEFICIAL INSECTS

Landscaping for Good Bugs and Friends

Add landscape features to attract beneficial insects, birds, and reptiles, and they'll eat the pests that damage your plants. Here are six simple steps you can take to encourage hardworking insect-eaters to thrive and raise hungry families in your yard.

Stretch your plant palette. "The more diverse your garden is, the more beneficial insects it will attract," says Nancy Bechtol, chief of the Horticultural Services Division at the Smithsonian Institution. Nancy suggests that you grow a wider variety of plants than usual to attract beneficials. As an example, she points out that the Smithsonian's butterfly garden has 550 different flower species planted in a 330-foot-long, 10-foot-wide border.

Make a reptile retreat. "If you take care of reptiles, they'll take care of bugs," says Inga MacGuire, a Master Gardener with the Washington State University Cooperative Extension Service. She leaves small stacks of wood or rocks in her garden to shelter garter snakes—she's seen them eat slugs wider than they are.

Give birds a place to perch. Insect-eating birds do the most good when they're actually in your garden—where the pests are. Paul Reinartz, a former president of the Men's Garden Club of Austin (Texas), gives birds a perch in the middle of his plantings where they can sit and scope out bugs. Paul finds that a piece of rebar bent in the shape of an upside-down U makes a good perch as long as it's tall enough to keep cats away from the sitting birds.

Welcome birds with water. Lure insect-eating birds to your yard with the sound of dripping water, suggests Diane Relf, extension specialist in consumer horticulture at Virginia Tech. Here's how she makes a delightful water

VARIETY IS THE SPICE OF LIFE FOR BENEFICIAL INSECTS TOO

feature with a plastic milk jug: Punch a tiny hole in the bottom of the jug with a sewing needle. Fill the jug with water and adjust the size of the hole so the water drips very slowly, approximately one drop every ten seconds. Hang the water jug from a tree and put a clay or plastic saucer or birdbath underneath. The jug will empty in about two days.

Leave some weeds alone. Let dandelions grow outside your garden to attract aphids, which in turn attract beneficial lacewings and ladybugs. Paul Reinartz, a former president of the Men's Garden Club of Austin (Texas), collects the beneficial insects from his dandelions and moves them to his vegetable garden, where they get to work right away.

GOOD BUGS
AND BIRDS
FLOCK TO FOOD,
WATER, AND
SHELTER

Plant good nectar sources. Adult beneficial insects need nectar, so gardener Phil Bunch of San Diego provides them with plants that produce plenty. Phil plants cilantro, fennel, and other members of the carrot family whose flowers attract caterpillar-killing wasps plus predatory syrphid flies. Phil finds that the insects bring more than pest control to the garden. "Insect watching can be as interesting as bird watching once you pay attention," he says.

The gentle drip, drip of a water-jug fountain says "You're welcome here" to visiting birds. They'll repay your kindness by munching pesky insect pests.

27

Plant a Beneficial Bug Border

Big gardens mean lots of bugs and weeds, unless you outcompete them with beneficial insects and plants. To get the upper hand in the pest battle, plant a 2-foot-wide strip of flowers and herbs around your garden. Use plants that attract beneficial insects, and they'll control the insect pests for you. Choose vigorous plants, and they'll spread so stray weeds can't move in.

Good choices for a beneficial border include plants in the umbel family such as dill, fennel, and parsley; plants in the composite family such as artemisias, asters, feverfew, marigolds, pot marigolds (calendulas), sunflowers, yarrows, and zinnias; plus herbs such as basil, sages, and thymes.

If you don't have much space, scatter beneficial insect-attracting plants throughout your garden and mow down the surrounding weed competition. Janet Britt, who operates a community-supported farm in the Hudson River Valley in New York, mows a 2-foot-wide border around her garden. Janet says the mowed strip prevents a lot of nearby weed seeds from blowing in. Without weeds, bad bugs don't have as many places to hide.

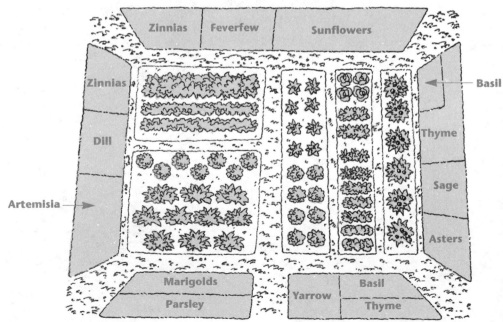

Protect your vegetables from pests with a beautiful border of flowers and herbs that attracts beneficial insects and crowds out weeds.

Shop Smart for Beneficial Insects

When you discover a pest problem in your garden, get the situation under control by ordering beneficial insects by mail. Shopping for insects is like shopping for anything else—you'll get the best value and the best results if you know what to look for. To make sure you get healthy, hardworking beneficials that stay in your garden, use these suggestions from Lee Anne Merrill, president of M & R Durango Insectary in Bayfield, Colorado.

Buy from a reputable source. Lee Anne suggests buying from a member of the Association of Natural Biocontrol Producers. For a list of members, contact the association at 10202 Cowan Heights Drive, Santa Ana, CA 92705, (714) 544-8295.

Ask questions—and make sure you get answers. When you contact a supplier, find out as much as you can about the insects you're buying and the service you can expect. Don't buy from anyone who won't give you straight answers. You can start with these questions:

ASK THE RIGHT
QUESTIONS TO
GET BETTER
BUGS

• Do you guarantee live delivery of the insects? (They should.)

• How will the insects arrive?

• If you're receiving eggs, how long will they take to hatch?

• How should I handle and release the insects?

• Is this the right insect to solve my problem and will it survive in my climate?

• Is this the right time of year to release the beneficial insects I'm ordering?

Once insects arrive, make sure they're alive. Insects may be shipped as live adults, eggs, or pupae. Adult insects that are packed in ice should start moving around within 30 minutes. If the beneficials arrive in the egg or pupal stage, you can hatch them out in a jar and release them as live insects. Hatching won't work for all beneficials—some are cannibalistic and will eat each other. Make sure you follow the directions of your supplier.

Treat Beneficials Right for Best Pest Control

Make sure mail-order insects stay alive when you release them into your garden—dead beneficials do you no good. Here are some pointers from Jeanne Houston of A-1 Unique Insect Control, a California supplier of beneficial insects.

Green lacewings. The tiny eggs of green lacewings are shipped mixed with rice or another grain for easier handling. Shake the container to make sure the eggs are mixed throughout the grain, then scatter them on the pest-infested parts of the plant, if possible. If you can't put eggs on the pest site, spread them at the base of the plant—the larvae will instinctively crawl upward when they hatch.

You can also hatch the eggs in a jar and release live insects on the plant—it's a good way to test the quality of the eggs you're buying.

Lacewing larvae eat aphids, mealybugs, red spider mites, and insect eggs and larvae. After feeding for a few weeks, they'll spin a fluffy cocoon—don't be alarmed when you see it. About a week later, the adults will hatch and begin laying eggs.

Ladybugs. Release ladybugs in the early spring, when plants have new leaves and pests (usually aphids) are out. Let your ladybugs loose in the late evening or early morning—never while the sun is shining. Since they usually arrive in the mail during the daytime, store ladybugs in the refrigerator

Green lacewing adult

Larva

Lacewing larvae look like tiny alligators. The adults are ¾ inch long, light green, and have transparent wings.

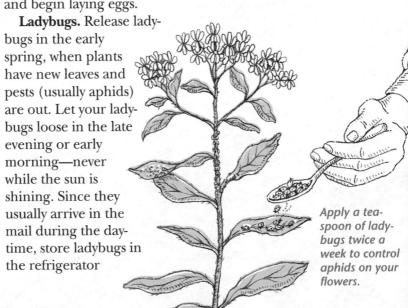

Apply a teaspoon of ladybugs twice a week to control aphids on your flowers.

while you wait for sunset. Sprinkle the release area with water beforehand so the ladybugs, which will be thirsty, can get a drink.

Because most of your ladybugs will fly away once sunlight warms the area, plan to release them in small doses—about a tablespoon on each infested shrub and a handful on each infested tree, less for smaller plants—twice a week for up to two weeks. Store extra ladybugs in the refrigerator until you need them.

Egg case

Praying mantid adult

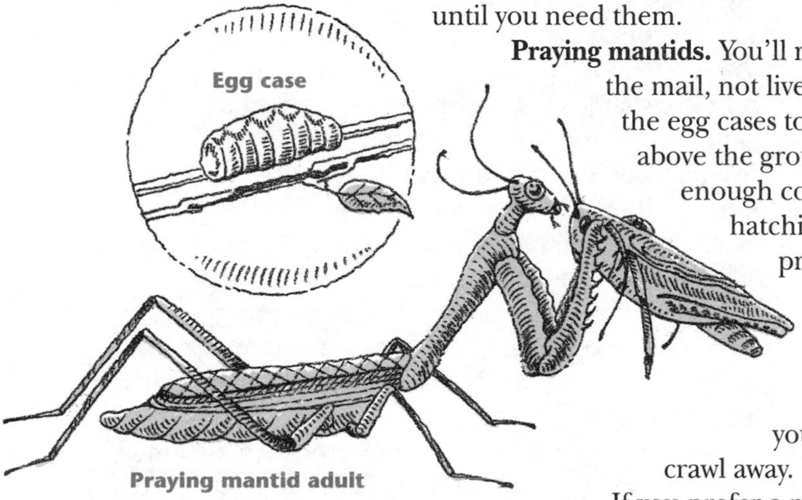

Adult praying mantids are 2 to 3 inches long. They'll feed on just about any insect they can over-power. You'll receive egg cases in the mail which you can place where you need insect control.

Praying mantids. You'll receive egg cases in the mail, not live insects. Attach the egg cases to a plant 1 to 2 feet above the ground where there's enough cover to hide hatching young from predators. With this technique, you probably won't be able to tell when the young hatch and crawl away.

If you prefer a more hands-on approach that lets you keep tabs on when man-tids hatch, you can incubate the egg cases in-doors. Place the cases in a paper bag and close the top with a paper clip. Keep the bag on a windowsill in direct sunlight. Carefully open the bag every few days to check for hatched young; as soon as they begin to hatch—and it can take two months—take them outside and release them in the same place you'd put egg cases.

BERRIES

Let Brambles Ramble Away from Disease

Reduce diseases in small fruits that spread by runners or layering by letting them roam where they will. "In nature, the wild relatives of blackberries, raspberries, and strawberries don't grow in the same spot each year," observes Sharon Conboy, a Master Gardener with the Washington State University Cooperative Extension Service. By sending out runners, these berries move to a new spot every two or three years, outwalking diseases and pests that attack plants that stay in one place.

You can mimic nature by letting berry plants spread. When new runners take root, dig out and dispose of the old plants that are left behind—you'll dispose of disease problems at the same time.

If you'd rather direct where your berries spread, pin strawberry runners to the ground where you want them to root. For brambles, bend flexible stems to the ground in late summer. Pin each branch tip firmly to the soil with a piece of wire. The tips will root in their new site by fall and you can cut them loose from the parent plant.

Tip layer brambles to move your plantings to a new site. Fasten stem tips to the ground with wire in late summer just as the top leaves start to curl.

Old Christmas Trees Keep Berries Weed-Free

RECYCLED
CHRISTMAS
TREES MAKE AN
UNTRADITIONAL
MULCH

Save those old Christmas trees if you're tired of crawling under your berry plants to pull weeds. You can mulch them with the Christmas tree branches. "I never have to weed my raspberries and blueberries," boasts Philadelphia gardener Libby J. Goldstein. After Christmas, Libby prunes all the branches off her neighbors' discarded Christmas trees and mulches her flower beds with them for extra winter protection. In spring, she throws the used branches on her berry beds.

The evergreen branches keep Libby's berries well mulched and absolutely weed-free, so she saves water in addition to weeding time. In fact, the tree branches keep so much moisture in the soil that Libby only has to water her berries once or twice in the hottest part of the summer. And, she adds, "all those green branches make the yard look alive all winter long."

Sunglasses Aren't Cool When Picking Berries

Hold on to your hat and leave your sunglasses behind when you pick berries: You won't have to sort out unripe fruit. "Polarized sunglasses tend to make colors, especially blues, look deeper and darker than they really are," says Rodale garden book editor Deb Martin. Use a hat, instead of shades, to keep the sun out of your eyes and you'll quickly be able to tell what's ripe and what's not.

A hat is definitely the way to go, agrees Ellen Phillips, editor of the Organic Gardening Book Club. "Bending to pick in the hot sun will give you a tension headache quicker than anything," she says. Ellen wears a straw hat and lets her knees do the work—instead of her back—for painless picking. Kneeling and squatting are great ways to zoom in on ripe fruit when you pick berries that are close to the ground. You can miss a lot of berries in the middle of bushes if you stand up and bend over to pick.

❧ **For more information on berries, see the Blueberries and Strawberries entries.**

BIRDS

Berry Bushes Make Bird Feeding a Breeze

You can forget about bird feeders but still have a yardful of delightful birds when you plant their favorite foods—fruit-bearing trees and shrubs. Instead of making a year-round chore of buying birdseed and filling and maintaining feeders, try growing the plants birds like best.

David E. Benner, president of Benner's Gardens in New Hope, Pennsylvania, has two favorite shrubs for bringing birds to his property: highbush blueberry (*Vaccinium corymbosum*) and American elderberry (*Sambucus canadensis*).

"Highbush blueberry is a must in sun or shade," David says. He adds that he has 15 of the plants in his yard and they attract all kinds of birds. David says that blueberries are easy to grow on sites with acid soil in Zones 3 to 8, and their brilliant red fall color makes them great landscape plants. More than 90 different birds eat blueberries, including bluebirds, chickadees, orioles, and robins.

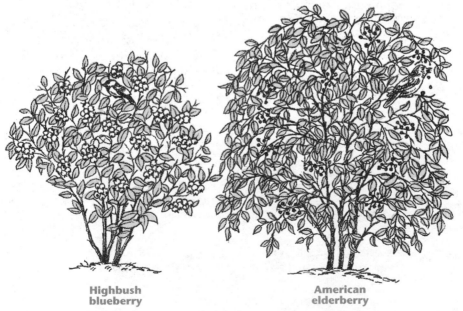

Blueberries make great bird feeders and stunning landscape plants. Elderberries attract lots of birds but look untidy— they're better for the back of your yard.

Highbush blueberry

American elderberry

Think that's impressive? Well, over 100 species of birds eat the purple-black fruits of the American elderberry, including doves, finches, grosbeaks, mockingbirds, waxwings, and woodpeckers. This shrub prefers damp soil in Zones 3 to 9, but David notes that it will tolerate dry conditions too. For more great bird-feeding plants, see "Proven Plants That Bring On the Birds" below.

PROVEN PLANTS THAT BRING ON THE BIRDS

Trees and shrubs make no-fuss bird feeders. So if you enjoy watching birds and having them dine on the pests in your garden, add fruiting plants to your landscape. Choose trees and shrubs with fruits that ripen at different times to keep birds coming to your yard all year long.

SUMMER- AND FALL-FRUITING TREES AND SHRUBS

Cherries (*Prunus* spp.)
Clusters of purple, red, or black fruit ripen in summer or fall.

Currants (*Ribes* spp.)
Clusters of small black, red, pink, green, yellow, or white fruit ripen from mid-June through September.

Honeysuckles (*Lonicera* spp.)
Black, blue, or showy red berries ripen in late summer or fall.

Serviceberries and juneberries (*Amelanchier* spp.)
Black, blue, or white berries ripen in June—you'll have to move fast if you want to eat them before the birds do.

Viburnums (*Viburnum* spp.)
Showy clusters of black, blue, or red fruit last from summer or fall through winter.

FALL- AND WINTER-FRUITING TREES AND SHRUBS

Bayberries and wax myrtles (*Myrica* spp.)
Fresh-scented gray, waxy fruit decorate plants from fall until spring.

Crabapples (*Malus* spp.)
Green, red, or yellow applelike fruit, up to 2 inches in diameter, ripen in fall (some cultivars ripen in summer) and last into winter.

Dogwoods (*Cornus* spp.)
Flowering dogwood (*C. florida*) has small clusters of red fruit in fall through winter; gray dogwood (*C. racemosa*) has white fruit in fall; Kousa dogwood (*C. kousa*) produces raspberry-like pink fruit in fall.

Grape hollies (*Mahonia* spp.)
Clusters of small blue-black berries look like grapes and ripen in fall.

Mountain ashes (*Sorbus* spp.)
Showy clusters of bright orange to red fruit ripen in fall, and birds quickly eat them.

Smooth and staghorn sumacs (*Rhus glabra* and *R. typhina*)
Bold horn-shaped clusters of red hairy fruit ripen in late fall and may stay on shrubs until spring.

JUST SAY "NO" TO FALL CLEANUP

Put off your garden cleanup chores this fall and you'll give visiting birds a great source of seeds through winter. Barbara Pleasant, *Organic Gardening* magazine contributing editor in Huntsville, Alabama, finds that leaving some of the seedstalks from summer-blooming perennials provides great food for birds. Daisy-family flowers like asters, black-eyed Susans, coneflowers, and sunflowers are some of the birds' favorites.

"A lot of times, fall debris is chock-full of tiny nutlets and seeds," says Barbara. "It's just what some of the smaller migratory birds need." When spring arrives, you'll find that plant stalks are easier to pull out, since winter's freezing and thawing cycles loosen their roots.

You'll get another bonus if you leave your flowers alone—many seedstalks have wonderful textures that give your garden interest in winter. "Besides," Barbara says, "you never know when you'll need arms for snowmen—flowerstalks work just great!"

Sunflowers: Big, Bold Bird Feeders

Sunflowers are #1 when it comes to attracting birds to your landscape. Sowing a few sunflowers at the edge of your garden is an easy way to produce some ready-made, no-fill feeders for your feathered friends.

You'll attract more kinds of birds if you grow the small, black oil–type seeds rather than the larger gray-and-white striped seeds that people snack on, says Bill Butts, a professor of biology at the State University of New York at Oneonta. But he adds that *any* type of sunflower seed will attract birds, so pick the one that suits your garden site and size best. New introductions let you choose from sunflowers with different flower colors and sizes, as well as dwarf plants that yield a full-size head of seeds.

Plant sunflower seeds in a sunny site after the soil has warmed up in late spring. You may need to protect your newly sown seeds from hungry birds—some birds are unwilling to wait until there's enough seed for everyone! Once your sunflowers bloom, you can enjoy the cottage-garden charm they bring to your garden. When the seeds have set, simply leave the plants in place as homegrown feeders, or remove the seed heads and attach them with string or wire wherever you want them.

Stop Bird Feeder Litter and Save Your Grass

SQUIRREL
BAFFLE SERVES
AS A SUN-
FLOWER
CATCHER

You'll save hours of raking if you catch sunflower seeds and hulls before they hit the ground—and you'll keep them from stunting or killing the grass below your bird feeder. Sunflowers contain a chemical that inhibits the growth of other plants, so it makes sense to keep them off the grass.

"The best thing I've used to keep sunflower seeds and hulls off the ground under my bird feeder is one of those Plexiglas dome squirrel baffles," reports gardener Gail Martin of Lawrenceville, Georgia. Gail mounts the dome upside down under her feeder. The seeds and hulls fall into the dome, and when the feeder is empty, birds, squirrels, and chipmunks hop down into the dome and eat what's been spilled.

To make a sunflower catcher, attach a screw eye to the bottom of a bird feeder. Use S-hooks and a piece of wire to attach an upside-down squirrel baffle to the feeder.

These Bird Feeders Are Wired!

Save seeds, money, and maybe even birds

when you keep birdseed in your feeder with a piece of chicken wire. When birds kick seeds out of your feeder, some get eaten but a lot are wasted. If the seeds get wet, they can mold and create a health hazard for birds. You can avoid these problems if you tack a piece of chicken wire over the tray of your bird feeder, says Bill Butts, a professor of biology at the State University of New York at Oneonta. The wire limits birds' ability to kick the seeds out, but they can still get to the seeds they want.

Bill also recommends laying a tarp, a piece of cardboard, sheets of newspaper, or other catchall on the ground beneath your feeder. You'll catch any seeds and hulls that fall and you won't have to rake or scrape up the debris. Use rocks or other weights to keep ground covers from blowing away, or "staple" them to the soil with pins cut from metal coat hangers.

Pick up the covering beneath your feeder every few weeks to quickly clean the area. This technique means less weeding too, since spilled seeds won't have a chance to sprout. If your catchall material is biodegradable, like paper or cardboard, you can simply roll it up, seeds and all, and put it in your compost pile. If your compost pile doesn't get hot enough to kill weed seeds, throw the left-overs in the trash instead.

Staple chicken wire over your bird feeder to keep birds from scattering seeds. To empty out wet seeds, turn the feeder upside down and give it a shake.

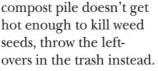

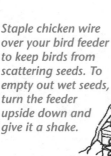

Clean Feeders Fast

HULL-LESS
SEEDS MAKE
FEEDING EASY
ON YOU AND
THE BIRDS

Say good-bye to dirty feeders with these two easy tricks. All you need are shelled seeds and a dishwasher to make short work of cleaning bird feeders—a chore we all dread. After all, the easier it is to keep feeders clean, the more likely you are to do it—and that means healthier birds. Here's what to do.

"The easiest, cleanest way to feed birds is to use seeds that have no shells," says Heidi Valega, education director of the Florida Audubon Society. Heidi uses hulled sunflower seeds and split peanuts without the shell. With these bird treats, there's no shell debris to fall to the ground, so you don't have to rake up a mess from under your feeder.

Rather than scrubbing her feeders by hand, Heidi finds it's much easier to run them through the dishwasher every two weeks. She soaks her feeders in a mix of 9 parts hot, soapy water—use laundry detergent, not dishwasher soap—and 1 part bleach for five minutes, then puts them in the dishwasher. She recommends Droll Yankee feeders because their durable polycarbonate plastic construction stands up to her cleaning regimen and discourages bacteria. Feeders made of soft plastics become brittle if you wash them and put them out in the sunlight, Heidi warns. It's worth it to buy a well-made feeder to begin with.

Thirsty Birds Need Winter Water

Put your wallet away and head for the potting shed when it's time to put out water for the birds. Experts have found that birds need a reliable source of water even more than bird food in winter. Many bird-watchers set up an elaborate freeze-proof water system for their thirsty friends, but if you don't want to buy a heating setup, try a large, heavy-duty plastic flowerpot saucer instead. A plant saucer will make winter watering a quick and painless process, says research editor Cheryl Long at *Organic Gardening* magazine.

Cheryl says the thick saucer is tough enough to withstand some battering, so you can knock ice out of it when the water freezes. Durability is important, since you'll have to refill the saucer at least once a day during freezing weather to keep birds supplied with fresh water.

BLUEBERRIES

High Yields in Tight Spaces

Get a bumper blueberry crop by spacing the plants close together. Usually, you plant blueberry bushes 4 feet apart. But when Dr. James Moore, Distinguished Professor of Horticulture at the University of Arkansas, compared the yield from a standard planting to the same number of plants spaced 2 feet apart, he found that the closer spacing yielded almost 50 percent more berries over a five-year period. Another benefit of the close spacing is fewer weed problems. Because the ground is shaded between the closely spaced blueberry bushes, weeds can't take hold.

As the blueberry bushes get bigger, they will get too crowded in the narrow rows, and your harvest will drop off. When that happens, Dr. Moore advises digging up every other bush and planting it elsewhere or giving it away. "Blueberry plants have shallow roots, so they're easy to move at any age," he says. "I've dug 10- and 12-year-old plants without any problem."

Yield Comparison

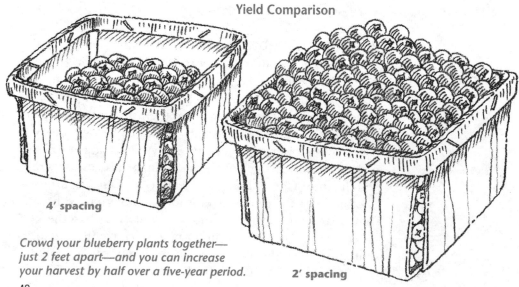

4' spacing

2' spacing

Crowd your blueberry plants together—just 2 feet apart—and you can increase your harvest by half over a five-year period.

An Early Cover-up Nets More Berries

Set nets out early—before blueberries are ripe—and you'll be able to leave the bushes uncovered once the harvest begins. Pulling nets off and on bushes every time you pick is an unnecessary chore, says David Chambers, manager of Mr. Cason's Vegetable Garden at Callaway Gardens in Pine Mountain, Georgia.

"The birds are more of a bother when the berries are in the red-to-blue stage—before they're ready to pick—than they are later in the season," David explains. If you keep the bushes covered during that early ripening stage, you can remove the net to pick berries and leave it off. The birds will get their share once the bushes are uncovered, David says. But they'll take a lot less than when the berries are turning red. You'll still have plenty.

Blueberries Won't Pine Away

GIVE YOUR
BLUEBERRIES
ACIDIC SOIL, THE
EASY WAY

Is your soil acid enough for blueberries? If you live in an area where the soil isn't naturally acidic, adding sulfur or peat moss to your soil to make it right for acid-loving blueberries can be a real trial. But planting blueberries near your pine trees saves you the time and effort of constantly amending the soil. That's because of the acidic pine-needle mulch they drop.

Blueberries thrive in the light shade of pine trees, says David Chambers, manager of Mr. Cason's Vegetable Garden at Callaway Gardens in Pine Mountain, Georgia. He explains that you'll get a fine crop of berries under the trees, but that's not all. A bed of blueberries can turn your simple pine planting into a beautiful landscape. Blueberry leaves turn gorgeous shades of yellow, orange, or red in the fall, and they look striking beneath the green of the pines.

If you can't plant under your pines, gather some of the pine needles and move them to your blueberry patch for mulch. But make sure you leave a light covering of needles in place for your trees—the needle mulch keeps pine roots from drying out and eventually breaks down into soil-improving humus.

BROCCOLI

Row Covers for Wormless Broccoli

Hide your broccoli under floating row covers and you'll never have to pick off little green cabbage looper worms again. "If you use floating row covers, you don't have to worry about worms or dusting or anything," says Sally Roth, coauthor of *Rodale's Successful Organic Gardening: Companion Planting*. With a cover, cabbage looper moths can't get to your broccoli to lay eggs, so no worms hatch to lurk among the broccoli heads.

Sally puts row covers over her broccoli when she transplants it into her garden. She leaves the cover on until she's finished harvesting. Even in the hottest summers, she's had no trouble with plants overheating under the lightweight fabric. (See "Sources" on page 412 for row-cover sources.)

Weed-Free Broccoli

Don't let weeds get your broccoli when you're using row covers. When you leave a row cover on all season, it's hard to get to weeds. Rather than pull the cover on and off each week to pull weeds out, head off weed problems

A living mulch of clover and a floating row cover keep weeds and pests away from your broccoli. For easy access to plants, staple the row cover to a 4 x 4 x 2-foot framework of lathe. At harvesttime, just lift the frame to reach your broccoli.

with mulch. Here's how: Mulch your broccoli with 2 inches of straw or another organic mulch right after you plant, then put on the row cover.

If organic mulch is hard to come by, plant a living mulch, suggests Sally Jean Cunningham of Cornell Cooperative Extension. Sally Jean crowds out weeds by sowing dwarf white clover around her broccoli transplants. (She uses the low-growing clover because it doesn't compete with the broccoli.) Then she puts on the floating row cover and forgets about weeds *and* broccoli worms.

When her spring broccoli harvest ends, Sally Jean takes off the row cover and sets warm-season transplants like eggplants, peppers, and tomatoes into the cover crop. She notes that crops like peppers and tomatoes get off to a faster start if you clear away a circle of clover around them to let the soil warm up. If Sally Jean doesn't need the space for warm-season crops, she just leaves the area in clover until it's time to plant broccoli, cabbage, kale, or other transplants for fall.

❧QUICK FIX MIX

Salty Broccoli Bug Bath

Use a saltwater bath to wash inchwormlike cabbage loopers out of your broccoli before they reach the dinner table. That's the advice of Rodale garden book editor Deb Martin, who got plenty of experience picking cabbage loopers off broccoli when she was growing up in Indiana.

"It's hard to see those little green worms clinging to the broccoli florets," notes Deb. "And it's gross to find them when the broccoli's cooked and on your plate." Deb's mother, Mary Ann Rusk, taught her to evict the unwanted pests quickly and easily by giving the broccoli a saltwater bath in the kitchen sink. Here's her recipe:

¼ cup salt
1 sinkful cool water

Pour salt in water and add broccoli. (Use a large bowl of water and less salt for smaller broccoli harvests.) Swish the broccoli around in the saltwater, making sure the water gets into the florets where the worms tend to hide. Let the broccoli soak in the water for about 10 minutes. "The little rascals float right to the top for easy removal," Deb says. Rinse the broccoli after its bath to remove the excess salt.

# BULBS

"Self-Cleaning" Bulbs Save Time

Don't plant daffodils and tulips and you won't have to tidy up dying foliage after they bloom. Some people braid, tie, or knot fading daffodil and tulip leaves together so they'll look neater—a time-consuming process that harms the plants, says Brent Heath, co-owner of The Daffodil Mart in Gloucester, Virginia. If these bulbs' faded foliage bothers you, avoid the problem by planting early-blooming crocuses (*Crocus* spp.), winter aconites (*Eranthis hyemalis*), and common snowdrops (*Galanthus nivalis*).

The leaves of these little bulbs are thin and unobtrusive, and they shrivel up shortly after the flowers stop blooming. These "self-cleaning" bulbs save you effort at planting time too since you plant them half as deep as large bulbs.

If you can't bear to give up your tulips and daffodils, learn to look the other way after they bloom and leave their foliage alone. "Wait until the leaves begin to turn yellow, and then you can cut them off," Brent says. If you bind the leaves up while they're green, they can't photosynthesize and strengthen the bulb for next year's bloom. You can also hide the fading foliage by planting the bulbs in vinca, English ivy, or another groundcover.

Extend your garden's bloom season by planting small bulbs around perennials like peonies (left), hardy geraniums, or hostas. You'll get an early splash of color without the mess of large bulb leaves.

Try Bulb Drills for Easy Planting

Why spend hours digging holes for bulbs with a shovel or bulb planter when you can do the job in minutes with a bulb drill? This gadget cuts holes in the ground fast and is simply a large metal drill bit attached to an electric drill.

If you have a drill, all you need are extra-large drill bits, which you can buy through garden supply catalogs. Use a 2½-inch-wide bit for small bulbs like crocuses, a 2¾-inch-wide bit for intermediate-size bulbs like gladiolus, and a 3-inch-wide bit for larger daffodil, lily, and tulip bulbs.

FASTER THAN A SPEEDING SHOVEL—IT'S A BULB DRILL

"Bulb drills cut bulb-planting time down to almost nothing," says Marianne Goodman, a gardener in Acton, Massachusetts. "When my family plants bulbs, we work as a team. My husband makes the hole, since the drill is hard to control, then I plant the bulb and our son fills the hole—it's a real assembly line." How fast is a bulb drill? The Goodmans can plant 100 gladiolus bulbs in 15 minutes.

If you've got sandy or loamy soil, a bulb drill works great, but don't try it on heavy clay or rocky soils. In lousy dirt, make holes with a mattock or a spear-shaped bulb planter (available through bulb catalogs) that you can stab into the ground to part the soil.

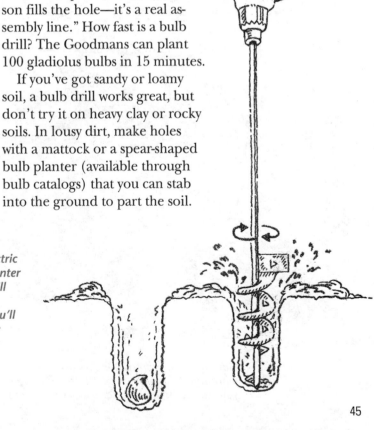

Transform your electric drill into a bulb planter with extra-large drill bits. It makes bulb planting so easy you'll want to plant more bulbs!

Stop Playing Hide-and-Seek with Bulbs

Where did you plant those bulbs? When bulb foliage fades away, it's hard to remember exactly where all those bulbs were growing. But if you mark the spot with bulb markers, you'll know where to fertilize and where *not* to dig new holes. If you rely on your memory to locate bulb plantings, you may put fertilizer on bare ground instead of your daffodils, or dig up your tulips by mistake.

Brent Heath, co-owner of The Daffodil Mart in Gloucester, Virginia, recommends using grape hyacinths as bulb markers. Surround your spring bulbs with a sweep of grape hyacinths and their foliage will come up in fall, just when it's time to fertilize. There's no more guessing where spring bulbs are hiding.

If you don't want to use plants as markers, you can put golf tees around the edge of bulb plantings in your lawn or garden beds. "Golf tees are low enough to avoid the lawn mower and remain unobtrusive. But they're also colorful enough to find when you're looking for them," Brent says.

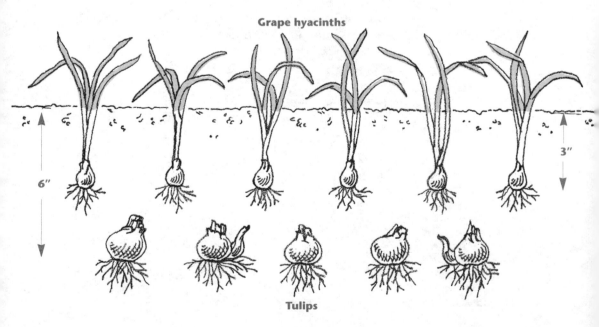

Grape hyacinths

6"

3"

Tulips

Plant grape hyacinths 3 inches deep around tulip and daffodil plantings. The grape hyacinth leaves come up in fall and outline your spring bulb plantings so they're easy to find and fertilize.

Another time to use markers is when you get the urge to dig up and take home blooming bulbs. Suppose you're on a plant rescue mission at an old homesite; bloom time may be the only time you know where bulbs are. But Ted Snazelle, past president of the American Daffodil Society, says it's best to wait awhile before digging them up.

"Disturbing bulbs while they're in flower usually won't kill them," Ted points out. "But it can cause them to skip a year of blooming." To make sure you'll have flowers in spring, wait a couple of months before you dig. Meanwhile, so you don't forget where they are, mark the bulbs before they go dormant.

Lay down some kind of marker (a piece of colored glass, a small stake) near the bulbs and make a note where it is in relation to a fence post, tree, or other easy-to-find object. Once the foliage fades away, you can dig the dormant bulbs without hunting all over for them.

JUST SAY "NO" TO REPLANTING TULIPS

Do your tulips stop blooming—or even disappear—after one or two seasons? Buy old-fashioned tulips and you'll get spectacular displays without replanting your bulbs every year. Many modern tulip cultivars use up all their energy the first time they flower, then fade away, never to be seen again. Luckily, older heirloom cultivars are more durable—they come back and flower beautifully year after year.

Scott Kunst, a Michigan-based landscape historian, says that these three old cultivars of single early tulips are particularly nice and long-lived.

• 'Couleur Cardinal', a deep crimson tulip bred in 1815

• 'Keizerskroon', a rich red tulip with a yellow edge, bred in 1750
• 'Prince of Austria', an orange-red, delightfully fragrant tulip bred in 1860

"I planted these heirloom cultivars in my yard five years ago," Scott says. "And they're still coming back as strong as ever." He adds that he makes sure to grow them in a good sandy loam soil and full sun—the kind of conditions tulips prefer.

Scott also recommends species tulips such as the lady tulip (*Tulipa clusiana*), *Tulipa schrenkii* (also known as *T. suaveolens*), and *Tulipa marjolettii* because they come back each year and multiply too.

P R O V E N   P L A N T S
F O R   M O R E   S P R I N G   B L O O M S

When you don't have time or money to plant lots of bulbs, buy daffodils that grow into big, beautiful clumps on their own. Bulbs that naturalize (multiply and spread) give you more for your money, as long as you choose the ones that thrive in your part of the country.

Heirloom daffodils naturalize particularly well, claims Michigan landscape historian Scott Kunst. He recommends the following old-fashioned daffodils for northern and southern gardens.

DAFFODILS FOR NORTHERN GARDENS

'Golden Spur'
This dark yellow flower was one of the most popular daffodils for naturalizing in 1885 and still grows well over a wide range of the United States. It's a great cut flower too.

'W. P. Milner'
A pale yellow trumpet and partly twisted petals make this miniature daffodil look like a wildflower. It was bred in 1869.

DAFFODILS FOR SOUTHERN GARDENS

April beauty (*Narcissus* × *medioluteus*, also known as *N. biflorus*)
In late spring, look for little white flowers with short yellow cups. Alias Twin Sisters, Cemetery Ladies, and Primrose Peerless narcissus, it originated in 1597.

Campernelle daffodil (*Narcissus* × *odorus*)
This fragrant yellow-flowered hybrid has a bell-shaped trumpet. It's been grown in gardens since 1601.

Trumpet narcissus (*Narcissus pseudonarcissus*)
This early-blooming yellow trumpet daffodil was grown as early as 1570. It's a very vigorous grower, even in northern areas.

Whom should you buy bulbs from? If you live in the North, Dutch bulbs are reliable. If you live in the South, buy from southern growers whenever you can. Southerners raise the best naturalizing daffodils for the South. (See "Sources" on page 412 for a list of southern bulb growers.)

Avoid Bulb Burnout

For fantastic blooms, feed your bulbs every fall. That's all it takes to keep your bulbs blooming beautifully. Many gardeners find that suddenly one spring, their bulbs refuse to bloom. Then they waste time and effort by digging up the bulbs, dividing them, improving the soil, and replanting. All they really need is organic fertilizer. Here's why:

"Most bulbs multiply by two each year. By the time they've multiplied to 16 bulbs where you once had only one, they've used up all the nutrients in the soil around them," says Brent Heath, co-owner of The Daffodil Mart in Gloucester, Virginia. Fertilizer is usually all it takes to get bulbs blooming again. Sprinkle a complete organic fertilizer over the surface of the soil—one that's custom-blended for bulbs. Fall's the best time to feed bulbs, since that's when they begin to grow new roots and pull in nutrients from the soil.

Bonemeal is often recommended for bulbs, but it isn't a great fertilizer by itself, Brent says. It's a good source of phosphate and calcium, but it doesn't have any of the nitrogen, potassium, or trace elements that bulbs need, and it can attract rodents and dogs. Brent recommends blood meal to give bulbs a nitrogen boost. Blood meal does double duty around tulips and crocuses, because it repels chipmunks, voles, and other animals that love to bite on bulbs. Use 2 pounds per 100 square feet of planting area.

Brent makes and sells his own favorite fertilizer blend called Bulb Mate. It's made out of granite sand, Kricket Krap (a fertilizer made from cricket droppings), compost, rock phosphate, dolomitic lime, and blood meal. You can make your own bulb fertilizer by mixing 1 part bonemeal, 1 part blood meal, 1 part New Jersey greensand, and 1 part compost. Use 2 pounds of each for a 100-square-foot planting area and sprinkle the mix on top of the ground.

If you don't get around to fertilizing in fall, apply some liquid kelp to your bulbs' leaves when they come up in spring. Kelp gives bulbs a pick-me-up when they're crowded and not blooming well. If your bulbs don't perk up after their first dose, keep giving them liquid kelp every two weeks for a month or two.

FADING FLOWER
BULBS NEED
FEEDING

For Early Blooms, Force Bulbs to Chill Out

Pot up bulbs in fall to get indoor bloom this winter. You don't have to spend big bucks at the florist's or through a catalog to get spring-flowering bulbs that will bloom early indoors. It's not hard to do it yourself if you know an easy way to chill them outdoors.

To force bulbs into bloom, all you have to do is hurry them through their winter dormant period. The trick is to keep the bulbs cold, but not to let them freeze and thaw over and over again. One way to protect bulbs from changing weather is to pot up the bulbs, then put the pots in cold frames and surround them with leaves or straw.

Burlap

Leaves

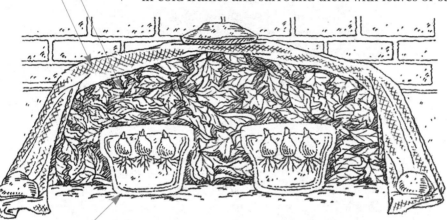

Use the great outdoors to chill bulbs for forcing. It's cheaper and more convenient than the alternatives: buying bulbs from a florist or keeping them cool in your fridge.

Flowerpot

If you don't have a cold frame, you can protect your bulbs with this quick and easy method from Steve Frowine, vice president of horticulture for White Flower Farm in Litchfield, Connecticut. In fall—about mid-October—plant the bulbs you want to force in wide, shallow pots with drainage holes. Group the pots outdoors in a place where they're easy to find in winter, maybe next to your back porch or garage. Water the pots thoroughly, then cover them with at least 2 feet of loose autumn leaves to insulate them against the cold. Throw a piece of burlap or plastic bird netting over the leaves so they won't blow away, and anchor the leaf cover with rocks.

After 10 to 12 weeks (once roots grow out the bottom of the pot and green shoots appear at the top), it's super simple to brush aside the leaves and bring the pots indoors. "This just works great!" Steve says.

Beat Back Bulb-Eating Voles

"Voles are the worst bulb problem of all," says Brent Heath, co-owner of The Daffodil Mart in Gloucester, Virginia. "You'll know they're around if your bulbs keep disappearing and you find quarter-size tunnels kind of like snake holes in your garden." You don't have to lose any sleep about voles roaming near your bulbs, though. Brent suggests that you try one or several of these easy vole-controlling ideas.

• Grow daffodils. They're poisonous, so voles won't bother them.

• Plant tulips 8 to 10 inches deep. Most voles only tunnel 4 inches deep.

• Put a handful of sharp crushed gravel around bulbs when you plant them. Voles don't like to dig through gravelly soil and will leave your bulbs alone.

• Put used cat box litter or composted sewage sludge on the surface of the soil around the bulb planting. Voles don't like cat litter and sewage odors (who does?) and will avoid them.

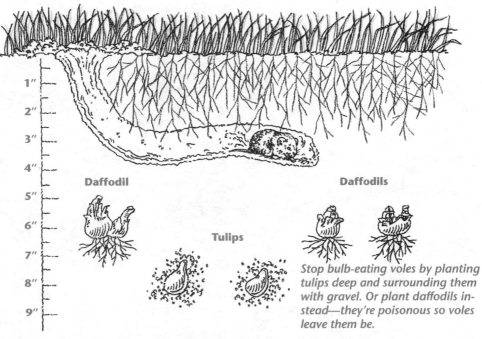

Stop bulb-eating voles by planting tulips deep and surrounding them with gravel. Or plant daffodils instead—they're poisonous so voles leave them be.

CABBAGE

Cabbage Companions Keep Worms Away

Plant herbs to keep cabbage butterflies and their voracious offspring, called imported cabbageworms, out of your cabbage patch. "Cabbage butterflies love hyssop (*Hyssopus officinalis*) and catmints (*Nepeta* spp.), both of which bloom about the time the butterflies lay their eggs," says Sally Roth, coauthor of *Rodale's Successful Organic Gardening: Companion Planting*. To take advantage of the butterflies' plant preferences, Sally grows a bedful of catmint and hyssop near her cabbage. The butterflies are either distracted by it or attracted to it—either way, she never has any trouble with imported cabbageworms.

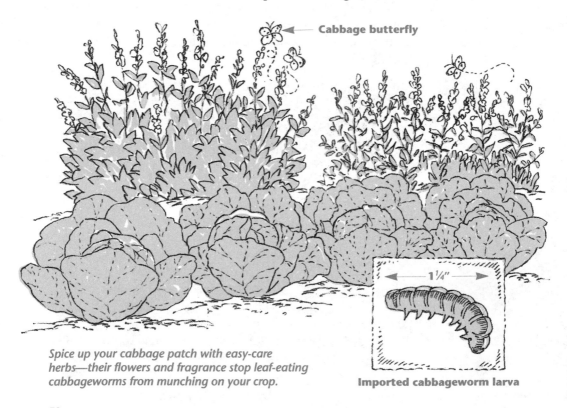

Cabbage butterfly

1¼"

Spice up your cabbage patch with easy-care herbs—their flowers and fragrance stop leaf-eating cabbageworms from munching on your crop.

Imported cabbageworm larva

Free Shade for Fall Transplants

COOL YOUR
CABBAGE
TRANSPLANTS
WITH SIMPLE
SHADES

Is the sun stir-frying your cabbage transplants? When it's time to set out your fall crop of cabbage, guarantee your plants a good start with a little shade from a wooden shingle. Felder Rushing, coauthor of *Passalong Plants,* got tired of reviving his cabbage, broccoli, and cauliflower transplants when they wilted in the blazing July sun. Then he noticed that a group of neighboring gardeners kept their transplants cool with easy-to-find materials from around the house.

Felder discovered that you don't need elaborate shade structures to protect young transplants from sunscald. Simply place a wooden shingle in the ground at a slant on the south side of each seedling to serve as a sunshade. No shingles? No problem. If you've done some summer pruning, use branches from your evergreen trees and shrubs for shade. As the needles wither and drop, the plants will gradually get used to the sun.

Raised Beds Prevent Cracked Heads

Say good-bye to spoiled cabbage crops by growing your cabbages in raised beds. A heavy rain can turn your cabbage crop into a mass of split heads unless your plants have perfect drainage. That's because thirsty cabbages take up so much water when a rain hits, they can't handle it all and they crack open. Cracking is particularly bad after a dry stretch.

"It's depressing to have cabbages spoiled by cracking when they're so close to harvest," says Sally Roth, coauthor of *Rodale's Successful Organic Gardening: Companion Planting.* So Sally plants her cabbages in raised beds. She adds lots of organic matter to the soil in the beds. The organic matter in the soil holds a steady supply of moisture to keep her cabbages growing well, even when she can't find time to water. And when a big rain comes along, the beds' improved drainage keeps water from lingering near the cabbages' roots. The cabbages don't take up too much water, so they keep their heads intact.

CARROTS

Grow Tiny Carrots for Timely Crops

Why wait for homegrown carrots? For a faster crop of sweet homegrown carrots, make your first planting of the season a short-rooted selection. "Carrots are not the quickest crop in the world," notes Sally Roth, coauthor of *Rodale's Successful Organic Gardening: Companion Planting*. "But if you grow short ones, they mature faster, and you'll have carrots to eat sooner."

In addition to shaving as much as 15 days off the time it takes to put carrots on your table, short-rooted carrots can produce a crop in heavy soil. If you've given up on long carrots because they get stunted in your clay soil, try the new shorter selections. These carrots are often dubbed "baby" or "mini" and may be rounded or ball shaped. Since they don't grow very deep, you'll get perfectly formed carrots despite lousy soil. Look for 'Thumbelina', a ball-shaped cultivar that's widely available. Other baby carrots to look for include 'Kinko' and 'Minicor' from Johnny's Selected Seeds, 'Little Finger' from Pinetree Garden Seeds, and 'Planet' from Shepherd's Garden Seeds. (See "Sources" on page 412 for the addresses of these seed companies.)

Baby carrots grow just one-fifth to one-half the size of standard carrots so they're ready to harvest in a hurry. Plant two to four times as many mini-carrots to get the same size harvest as from longer carrots.

2"   4"   6"   8"   10"

JUST SAY "NO" TO CARROT MAGGOTS

It pays to plant late when you're sowing your carrot crop. That's because early plantings often get carrot rust fly maggots. Wait to plant until early summer, and you'll avoid the time when these flies lay eggs that grow into root-riddling carrot maggots.

But if you must plant your carrots in the early spring, use this tip from Sally Jean Cunningham of Cornell Cooperative Extension. Cover the newly seeded area with floating row cover to protect your crop from carrot rust flies. You could use wire hoops or branches to hold the cover above the growing carrots. But floating row cover is so lightweight that it's easier to just lay the material down loosely over the planted area— the carrot leaves will push the cover up as they grow.

Make sure you bury the edges of the row cover with soil so carrot rust flies can't sneak in and lay their eggs. Keep the cover in place until you're ready to harvest and you'll get perfect carrots every time.

Little Hands Make Light Work of Thinning

Avoid carrot thinning and still get big carrots with this simple tip. Thinning carrots is a tedious chore—it takes time, patience, and a strong back. Sally Roth, coauthor of *Rodale's Successful Organic Gardening: Companion Planting*, recommends sowing carrots thinly to begin with (six seeds per inch), but notes that this crop usually needs even more thinning once it's up. That's where kids come in.

"Thinning carrots is a great task for kids," says Sally, because it's not a painstaking job. Kids don't mind doing it because they're fascinated by the little carrots they pull out, plus they get to eat them. "And it's easier for them," Sally adds, "since they're closer to the ground than you or I am."

Put your kids to work when the carrot tops reach 3 to 4 inches tall. Show them the kind of spacing you're looking for—3 to 4 inches apart—then turn them loose.

CAULIFLOWER

Broken Leaves Make Blanching a Breeze

Snow-white cauliflower is most gardeners' goal. But to get snowy heads instead of cauliflower tinged with green, you've got to keep the sun off the heads as they form. The simplest way to cover the heads is to buy self-blanching cultivars—their big leaves keep the sun off without any help from you. But if your favorite cauliflower isn't a self-blanching type, break a few leaves to get the same effect.

"Select two or three of the oldest leaves from the bottom of the plant and bend them over the bud just when it's starting to form," says Veet Deha, a horticulturist in Ithaca, New York. Snap the leaves just enough so they'll stay in place to protect the curds. The idea is to bend the midvein but not break the "skin" of the stem completely open. The broken leaves will brown off, Veet says, but by that time the cauliflower is ripe and beautifully white to boot.

Breaking a few leaves won't hurt your plants, and it's a lot faster than tying cauliflower leaves together or setting up boards to keep the sun off plants.

Bend a few leaves over your cauliflower heads to make simple sun shades. It's the fastest way to blanch your crop.

Rubber Bands Make Blanching a Snap

Stretch a rubber band around the leaves of your cauliflower to blanch developing heads. "It's much quicker than tying the leaves up with string," says Rodale garden book editor Fern Marshall Bradley, "and it makes it really easy to peek in and see if the cauliflower is blanched and ready to harvest." Rubber bands are not only fast, they're a great solution if you can't bring yourself to break healthy leaves to cover the heads.

Better Cauliflower Begins at Home

HOMEGROWN
TRANSPLANTS
OUTPERFORM
STORE-BOUGHT
TYPES

Start from seed to succeed with cauliflower. That's the advice of David Chambers, manager of Mr. Cason's Vegetable Garden at Callaway Gardens in Pine Mountain, Georgia. "Unless you have a really good nursery or plant source, you'll find that most cauliflower transplants are already potbound or woody by the time you're ready to plant them," David says. Once you put them in the ground, they bolt (go to seed) without producing much of a head.

You'll get better-quality transplants and bigger, better heads in the end if you start your seeds at home, says David. He sows cauliflower seeds indoors in January and puts transplants in the garden in late February to early March. His biggest challenge is the warm Georgia weather, which brings insect problems early and makes cauliflower unhappy. By starting his own transplants, David can set cauliflower out extra-early and beat insect invasions.

Start your fall cauliflower crop indoors as well if you want top-quality heads, David says. He shades fall transplants with lattice A-frames to keep the Georgia sun from wilting the young plants. He notes that direct-seeding into the garden is a fall-crop option, but shading transplants is easier. That's because it's hard to keep fall seedlings well watered unless you have drip irrigation or another good watering system.

COMPOSTING

Give Your Garden a Compost Trellis

BUILD A SIMPLE

COMPOST BIN

THAT'S HANDY

AND HIDDEN

Move your compost pile into your garden and composting becomes as easy as tossing an overripe tomato. In big gardens there's plenty of space for a bin, but in small ones, you'll need to use some ingenuity. Gardeners in the Chicago Botanic Garden's GROW (Gardening Resources On Wheels) program save space by making their compost bin do double duty as a trellis. According to GROW coordinator Paul Pfeifer, the gardeners surround their in-garden bin with snow fence, then use the fence to support a bumper crop of tomatoes or other vegetables.

The fence and tomatoes hide the pile from view—an important feature in this very visible garden—but don't get in the way of the composting process. Grow any tall or vining plant up an in-garden bin and you'll have compost close at hand and easy pickings at harvesttime too. When the growing season is over, pull the plants off the bin and add them to the compost. Don't bother turning the pile—the materials will continue to break down and you can dig finished compost from under the bin in spring.

Compost Pile Container Garden

No space for pumpkins? If you want to grow large vining plants like pumpkins but don't have the room, turn your compost bin into a tall container garden. Here's how Felder Rushing, coauthor of *Passalong Plants,* recommends that you build a compost container for vining plants.

In spring, make a simple compost bin by bending a 10-foot-long piece of 48-inch-tall welded-wire fencing into a circle. Tie the ends of the wire together to hold it closed, and put the bin in a sunny area.

Pack the bin with garden waste and top it with an inch or two of topsoil. Punch tiny holes in the sides and bottom of a

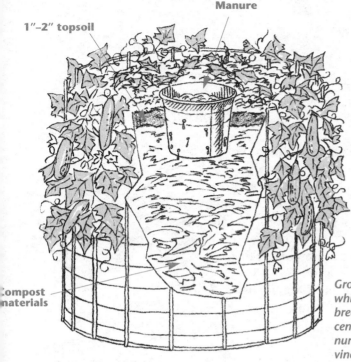

Manure

1"–2" topsoil

Compost materials

plastic bucket and sink it into the center of the pile. Around the bucket, sow cucumber, gourd, melon, pumpkin, or squash seeds.

Watering and feeding are easy. Add a shovelful of manure to the bucket, fill it as needed with water, then let the manure tea slowly "leak" into the pile. In fall, simply pull the wandering vine stems into the compost bin for a quick cleanup.

Grow vine crops in your compost while you wait for the materials to break down. Set a leaky bucket in the center of the bin, then fill it with manure and water to feed and water the vines as your compost cooks.

A Dog of a Compost Bin

You don't have to be handy to build a sturdy, long-lasting compost bin using wire dog-run panels. Gardener Eva Hoepfner of Oakville, Ontario, makes her compost bins out of four galvanized steel panels normally used to construct dog runs. They're fairly pricey, she says, but they do last a very long time.

Eva sets up the 4-foot sections in a square and slips in the thin steel rods that come with them to hold the corners together. She lines the bins with perforated black plastic and holds it in place with wooden clothespins. The plastic works great to keep the sides of the compost from drying out. Once the compost is done, Eva slips out the rods to remove a panel section and digs in.

It's easy to expand on Eva's design. Just get three more panels and attach them to one side of the first bin so they share a side. "I guess it just imitates compost containers I've seen advertised," Eva says. "But this one is bigger, easy to put up and take down, and I like how it looks."

Quick Pickled Compost

If you need compost and you need it now, buy a compost bin made out of a recycled plastic pickle barrel. The barrel sits upright and is supported on two legs—an axle through the center of the barrel lets you turn it end over end.

GIVE YOUR

COMPOST A

TURN WITHOUT

TOOLS

Of all the compost bins on display in the compost demonstration area at the University of British Columbia Botanic Gardens in Vancouver, this composter stands out for its speed and efficiency, says Food Garden curator Murray Kereluk. "I like it the best because it's really fast," Murray says. "You fill it up with garden refuse, throw a handful of soil in it, rotate it a couple of times a day, and within two weeks you've got fresh compost."

Murray claims the pickle-barrel composter is probably the best model for home gardeners because it's clean, compact, and rodent-proof. He notes that the composter's size also makes it easy for most people to use; it's not that big, so it's not that heavy. To get your own pickle-barrel composter, see "Sources" on page 412.

For quick compost in a small space, try an easy-to-turn bin made from a recycled plastic pickle barrel. Its compact shape even fits into tiny condominium and townhouse gardens.

Compost in the Trenches

For an easy way to fertilize your garden, and save trips to and from the compost pile, try trench composting. Community gardener Steve Coyle composts his garden waste in trenches that he digs in the footpaths between his garden beds. He keeps the trenches covered with straw most of the year so he can still use the footpaths.

MAKE YOUR
VEGETABLE
GARDEN PATHS
PRODUCTIVE

There's a lot of plant matter to compost in Steve's Austin, Texas, garden, so he digs deep trenches—2 to 3 feet down. If you've got less material to compost, or just don't want to dig that much, make a 6-inch-deep trench and it will work just fine.

Steve starts his compost in June, since that's when he harvests lots of vegetables and has the most material to compost. "I fill the trenches with the waste from my garden," he says. "Spent flowers, old plants, fallen vegetables, that sort of thing." Then he covers the trench with straw and lets the compost cook through the summer, fall, and winter.

In spring, when he needs fertilizer, Steve simply tosses the finished compost from the trenches onto his beds with a garden fork. Then he plants his beans, cucumbers, summer squash, and tomatoes in the freshly composted beds. Steve has plenty of compostables to refill his trenches right away, but if you don't, just fill the trenches with straw so you can walk on them until you can refill them with garden debris.

Tim Miller of Millberg Farms in Kyle, Texas, a strong advocate of trench composting, offers this tip for easy digging: "Dig out what you can with ease, then soak the trench with water and come back two days later—the water will have softened up the soil another 6 to 12 inches." Tim adds that the compost-filled trenches provide a cool, comfortable home for worms during hot weather and don't attract fire ants like aboveground composting can.

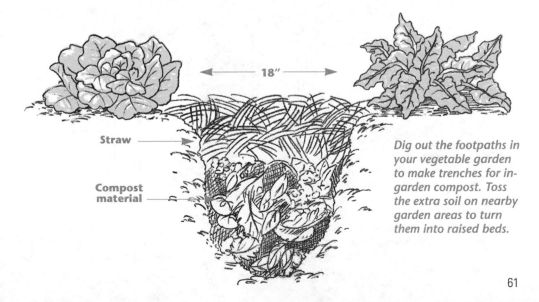

18″

Straw

Compost material

Dig out the footpaths in your vegetable garden to make trenches for in-garden compost. Toss the extra soil on nearby garden areas to turn them into raised beds.

Mice Can't Trash This Compost Bin

Are mice making a mess in your compost bin? You're not alone. "Mice smelled corncobs in my bin and climbed in—I caught eight of them," recalls gardener Bill McConnell of Boise, Idaho. Now Bill lets kitchen scraps decompose in a modified kitchen garbage can before he puts them in his compost bin. Mice aren't interested in the aged scraps and leave his bin alone.

Here's how Bill makes a simple mouse-proof composter.

• First, drill 20 breather holes, $\frac{1}{16}$ inch in diameter, on the bottom and on each side of a plastic kitchen garbage can—Bill prefers the kind that opens with a foot pedal.

• Next, line the bottom of the can with a 1- or 2-inch layer of folded $\frac{1}{8}$-inch-mesh plastic netting—it's available at hardware stores. The mesh keeps the composting materials from plugging the air holes on the bottom of the can. That's all there is to it!

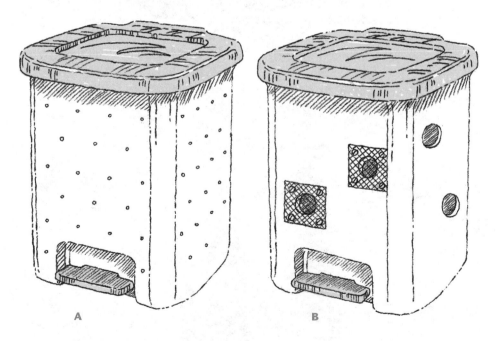

A   B

To build the rodent-proof compost bin that's right for you, start with a kitchen garbage can with a foot pedal. Try a low-tech multi-hole model (A), or the fancier version (B) with big, 2-inch-wide breather holes.

Put the compost can by your back door for easy access, and start adding scraps. When the can fills up, empty it into your compost bin and start the process over again.

If you'd like a fancier mouse-proof composter, one that also keeps the flies out, here's Bill's improved version. Drill two 2-inch holes on the bottom and on each side of a plastic kitchen garbage can, using the kind of drill bit used to make doorknob holes. Cover the holes from the outside with 3-inch squares of metal screen. Use sheet metal screws, #8 machine bolts, rivets, or a washer and covered nut (the nut goes on the inside) to fasten each corner of the screen to the container. Add a layer of mesh inside to keep scraps off the bottom air holes, and your composter is ready to go.

The Best Recipe for Kitchen Compost

USE NEWSPAPER
TO DEODORIZE
YOUR KITCHEN
COMPOST

Compost right in your kitchen without making a smelly mess. A compost bucket in your kitchen is a real time-saver if your compost bin is far away from your house. But the time-savings vanish if your kitchen waste smells so bad that you have to make frequent trips outside to dump it. An easy way to insure clean-smelling compost and cut out extra treks to the compost bin is to add carbon-rich materials like shredded newspaper to the mix.

"I start by adding a layer of high-carbon materials to the bottom of the bucket," explains community gardener John Schumacher of Albany, New York. That's all it takes to deodorize kitchen scraps in the 5-gallon bucket he keeps under his kitchen sink. John uses a 4- to 5-inch layer of newspaper strips, leaves, or straw for his carbon layer, then fills the bucket with kitchen scraps, which are high in nitrogen. This carbon/nitrogen mix makes the perfect environment for the microorganisms that make compost. If you only put food scraps in your compost bucket, microorganisms get nitrogen overload, and the excess nitrogen escapes as ammonia and stinks. Adding the carbon-rich layer cuts the odor in the bucket, which is John's main priority. But it also makes scraps turn into compost faster—your food scraps will start breaking down right in the bucket. Here's an added bonus: The scraps will shrink as they compost, so you won't need to make the trip to the compost pile as often.

Keep Your Compost Cooking

If you want fast compost, you have to find a way to get air into the center of the pile. That's because the beneficial microorganisms that help your compost materials heat up and decompose work best with plenty of oxygen.

The easiest way to add air is to build your compost bin on top of a foot-deep pile of coarse brush or a wooden pallet, says "Compost King" Joe Keyser, who teaches home composting techniques in Maryland. As the compost heats and steams, it uses up air, Joe says. But you won't have to worry about your pile running out of oxygen. The coarse materials on the bottom of your pile will keep spaces open, so the rising hot air will pull fresh air in right behind it. The oxygen-loving bacteria, fungi, and worms in your compost will get all the oxygen they need to work at high speed and give you a hot pile that turns into humus in a hurry. It's a pretty nice payback for a simple pile of sticks.

If you build your compost bin on a pallet, compost researcher Charles Rhyne at Jackson State University in Mississippi recommends a hardware cloth cover. Staple the hardware cloth to the pallet so fine compost won't fall out of your bin and mice won't climb in.

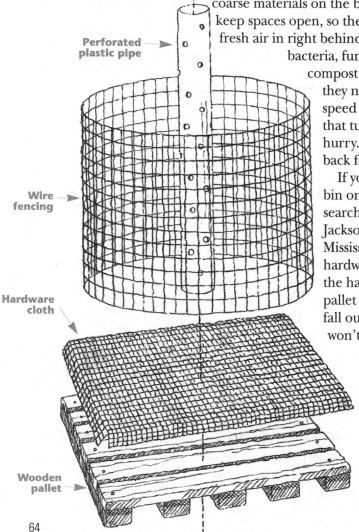

Perforated plastic pipe

Wire fencing

Hardware cloth

Wooden pallet

A perforated plastic pipe is another way to get air to the center of your compost pile. Place the pipe in the center of your pile when you start adding materials. Use PVC or corrugated plastic drainpipe.

No-Work Composting

No time to turn your compost? Make extra bins and forget about turning. You'll have compost at several different stages so you can deal with it when you're ready, not when you're face-to-face with a mountain of yard waste.

Ed Nichols, an herb grower near Canton, Mississippi, has four large circular wire bins out behind his shed. He throws all of his compostables into whichever bin is "freshest," then leaves it alone. His almost haphazard "slow-cook" approach is 100 percent maintenance-free—he doesn't turn the piles at all.

You'll start getting finished compost a year after you set up your multiple bins. Once all four bins are up and running, one or two bins will be ready to "harvest" while the others are working. Place the bins within 4 feet of one another, then fill the space in between with mulch and spilled compost so you don't have to weed or mow.

JUST SAY "NO" TO RAKING LEAVES

Does leaf raking get you down? Jeff Ball, the "garden guy" on the *Today Show,* estimates that ½ inch of leaves over 1,000 square feet of lawn would fill 30 bags. Luckily, there's no need for all that raking and bagging.

As soon as a light covering of leaves falls, start mowing them on your lawn. (Don't wait for leaves to pile up ankle deep on the lawn!) The chopped leaves will compost right where they sit—just as Mother Nature intended—and give your lawn a natural fertilizer boost.

When you use your mower to mulch your lawn with leaves, the worms pull right in, Jeff says. And quick as a wink, without a compost pile or bin, they turn your lawn mulch into lawn compost. He adds that the new "mulching mowers" with their specially designed blades are much more efficient at chopping leaves finely. In fact, they're so good at it, Jeff says "it's worth throwing away the old mower."

Compost More, Mow Less

If you've got a big yard and like the natural look, try this composting technique. Instead of hauling fallen limbs, weeds, spent flowers, and leaves from your yard to a small compost pile or the curb, build big piles. You can put any compostable material in a large pile without chipping it, and that includes everything from large limbs to entire trees. Arrange your compost piles so they take up lawn space, and you'll have less mowing to do too.

Neil Odenwald, professor of landscape architecture at Louisiana State University in Baton Rouge, throws nothing away from his 1-acre garden. He uses every scrap to make compost piles that eventually become planting areas.

Neil places limbs and other large debris in lines between trees and across open spaces. On top of the coarse materials, he piles leaves, weeds, vegetable scraps, and anything else he knows will decompose. In time, it all breaks down and sags into the soil, making a humusy mix that's perfect for planting azaleas, ferns, hostas, and impatiens.

"It used to take my whole weekend just to mow," Neil says. "Putting all my landscape waste to use in compost, I've turned a big lot into several smaller garden 'rooms'—and now it takes just over 50 minutes to mow what's left."

Build large compost piles wherever you want a planting area. Place limbs and compostables in straight or curved lines, depending on the shape of the planting bed you eventually want there.

CONTAINER GARDENING

This Soil Mix Means Less Repotting

BARK CHIPS
MAKE POTTING
MIXES LAST
AND LAST

Cut down on messy repotting sessions by whipping up a light soil mix containing bark chips for your large potted plants. Using a chunky-style potting mix in containers over 5 gallons helps keep the soil mix loose, says research editor Cheryl Long at *Organic Gardening* magazine. With better drainage and root penetration, your plants will thrive longer without a soil change, which can be a time-consuming task for large plants in big pots.

Harry Phillips, a North Carolina wildflower enthusiast and author, suggests this blend: 3 parts bark chips, 2 parts peat moss, and 1 part coarse-grade sand. He also recommends adding about a pound (roughly a pint) of ground limestone per wheelbarrow-load of mix. The bark helps this mix drain well and the peat moss holds enough moisture to keep your plants from sudden death in a dry spell. Sand adds weight to the potting mix so it's heavy enough to hold your flowerpot upright, even if you or a wandering pet happen to nudge it. The lime neutralizes organic acids that can form as materials in the mix decompose.

You can adapt the mix to match the way you water. If you want your mix to hold more moisture, use composted chips. If you need a drier mix, use uncomposted chips. To compost bark chips, pile them up like any other compost heap and let them weather for a year. Turn the pile and moisten it when it gets dry if you want to hurry the process.

Cheryl notes that some nurseries sell coarse potting mixes designed for large containers for gardeners who don't want to make their own mix. "The main thing," she says, "is to make the soil structure hold up for several years so you don't have to repot the plant."

Make-Ahead Potting Mix

If you grow lots of plants in pots, it pays to preblend your own potting mix in large quantities. You'll save time on making small batches of mix, and your plants will grow better too.

Donna Iarkowski, owner of Nature's Way Herbary in Muncy Valley, Pennsylvania, uses this custom blend.

1 part topsoil
1 part peat moss
1 part vermiculite

Donna adds another custom touch to her potting routine by adding a small handful of sand and compost to every pot as she fills it.

"We go through tons of soil here and have found the synthetic, peat-based blends are too expensive," says Donna.

"They also dry out very quickly. My custom-made soil keeps plants growing considerably longer. I also can adjust the blend of my home-made soil mixes: If a flower needs soil that's a little moister, I can make a heavier soil mix and get away with watering less."

Blend your potting mix ingredients on a plastic tarp, stirring them together with a hoe or rake. If you don't use all of the mix, wrap what's left in the tarp and put it in a dry place, like a garage or shed, until you need it.

Compost Mix Keeps Potted Plants Perky

ADD COMPOST
AND YOU CAN
FORGET ABOUT
FERTILIZING

Potted plants need less fertilizer when there's compost in the soil mix. "I always tell people to put some compost into their potting soil; that sort of reduces the pressure to fertilize," says Cheryl Long, research editor at *Organic Gardening* magazine.

Because most commercial potting mixes are made of peat moss, sand, and perlite—with no natural soil—container plants need regular fertilizing to stay attractive and healthy. Many mixes contain a small amount of fertilizer that gets plants by for six months or so, Cheryl says. After that, it's up to you to supply the nourishment. Adding some compost to the mix before you pot up your plants gives them a little something to snack on when your memory or schedule keeps you from your appointed fertilizing rounds. Cheryl recommends adding up to 20 percent compost to your mix (1 part compost to 4 parts potting mix).

Make sure you use compost that's completely finished decomposing or it could stunt your plants' growth a bit. If it's really chunky, you may want to pour your compost through a ¼-inch mesh screen so it's easier to mix in with the other ingredients. But don't worry about sterilizing the compost before you use it. Fresh compost contains disease-fighting microbes that are actually good for your plants.

Plants Love Coffee, Too

If you drink coffee, you've got a great source of fertilizer for potted plants. When you clean out your coffeemaker, sprinkle a thin layer of coffee grounds right on the surface of the mix around potted plants. Coffee grounds are high in nitrogen and other nutrients, and will slowly decompose into a slightly acid-forming source of nutrients. If you spread a thick layer, you won't harm the plants, but the grounds may not decompose as quickly.

"Compost King" Joe Keyser, who teaches home composting techniques in Maryland, offers one caution. If you plan to store the grounds before using them, let them air dry first. Otherwise, they'll ferment and turn into a smelly mess. Or as Joe says, "It'll ferment, but not into Kahlúa."

6-Pack Solution

SODA CANS

SAVE YOUR POTS

FROM GAINING

WEIGHT

Save potting mix—and your back muscles—by using soda cans to take up some of the space in supersize planters. Shallow-rooted annuals, and even some perennials, are unlikely to root deeply enough to reach the bottom of a very large container, so filling the entire pot with potting soil is a waste of time and money. But by filling the bottom of a large container with empty soda cans, you'll reduce the amount of soil mix you need. "You use less soil, which is a real factor sometimes," says *Organic Gardening* magazine's research editor Cheryl Long. "Filling those things can eat up your compost pile pretty fast." Plus, the planters will be much easier to move, Cheryl notes. So before your next potting session, take a break with your family and share some cold sodas.

You can use other lightweight fillers instead of the cans. Rita Hall, an English-American gardener in Brandon, Mississippi, lightens large pots by putting a layer of sweet gum balls or even recycled Styrofoam packing "peanuts" in the bottom. It's a good use for packing "peanuts" since you not only get a long-lasting pot filler but also keep the Styrofoam out of landfills. You can come up with other good filler materials, such as pinecones or broken twigs, if you look around your house and yard.

Add soda cans to the bottom of big containers to cut down on their weight and the amount of potting soil you need. Turn the cans upside down so they don't fill up with potting mix.

Plastic Pots Beat Clay

Potted plants can be water hogs that need daily attention in hot weather. To lessen watering woes, use only plastic pots for container plants, recommends Cheryl Long, *Organic Gardening* magazine's research editor. "If somebody wants to reduce their watering chores," says Cheryl, "they should keep all their plants in plastic pots. They definitely cut down on watering."

Many gardeners prefer the look and feel of traditional clay pots rather than their plastic counterparts. Cheryl satisfies herself with plastic pots molded to look like clay rather than give up the advantages plastic offers. If you aren't ready to give up your clay pots, use them as decorative containers. Pot your plants in plastic containers, then slip them inside clay pots—your plants will look good and stay upright too. Make sure you choose clay pots that are at least an inch wider than the plastic ones so it's easy to slip your potted containers in or out of the decorative ones as needed.

In addition to reducing the time spent watering, Cheryl also likes using plastic pots because it's easy for her to judge quickly when a plant needs to be watered. To test whether a container plant needs water, Cheryl lifts the pot to see how heavy it is. "Sometimes the soil surface will look dry, and it still really doesn't need water," she says. "You can tell by the weight." Clay pots have some heft even when empty, so a clay pot may feel heavy even when the soil is dry. But a plastic pot is practically weightless, so when the soil is dry, the pot is unmistakably light.

Newton's Law Makes Soil Mixing Quick

Let gravity do the work when you mix a large batch of potting soil. Elbert Taylor, a horticulturist in Indianola, Mississippi, taught this trick to Felder Rushing, coauthor of *Passalong Plants*. Spread the lightest materials—such as vermiculite—first when mixing potting soil. Spread heavier ingredients such as topsoil on top of the light materials, and use a shovel to blend it all together. As you mix, the heavier ingredients naturally gravitate downward, making the task go more quickly and easily.

Use Wicks to Save on Watering

TIE YOUR
PLANTS INTO
AN AUTOMATIC
WATERING
SYSTEM

Don't run yourself ragged watering thirsty pots of annual flowers on hot summer days. Instead, set up an inexpensive watering system that does the job for you. Sherry McHone, a home gardener in Illinois, has perfected a way to include a watering wick when she pots up annuals.

"We have about 30 pots of flowers on our decks and sidewalks," Sherry says. "It's really time-consuming to water them all without making a mess of everything. Besides, there are some hot days when the soil gets so dry you'd need to water flowers two or three times a day just to keep them alive."

Sherry solved all three problems with a watering wick—a length of cord that connects the soil in a pot to a reservoir of water. To prepare a wick, run a piece of cord through the hole in a pot before you add soil. Tie a big, loose knot in the cord to keep it from slipping out of the pot. Leave a short length of cord inside the pot (6 inches long for big pots, less for smaller pots) and a longer piece outside.

"You can use regular rope that you have around the house," Sherry explains.

When you pot up plants, put one water wick in every 6-inch-diameter pot and two or three wicks in larger pots. On hot summer days, they'll do the watering while you relax.

"Natural fiber rope will rot over time, but this isn't really a problem because you generally repot annual flowers every summer. I use parachute cord that's about ¼ inch thick." For pots larger than 12 inches in diameter, Sherry uses more than one wick to be sure the soil is evenly watered.

As you fill the pot with potting mix, make sure the wick is stretched through the soil, not bunched up in one spot. Feed the long end of the cord into a water reservoir.

Sherry recommends using a gallon milk jug or covered bucket for a water reservoir. (The cover keeps insects and other critters out of the water.) Hide the bucket or jug between the plant pots or in some leaves or mulch so it will be unobtrusive. A gallon of water will last from one to three weeks, Sherry says, depending on weather conditions and on how many plants it's supplying. To fertilize the plants, add fish emulsion to the water reservoir, at half the strength recommended on the label.

Use Gel and Wait a Spell between Waterings

You'll spend less time watering container plants if you stir a little gel into your potting mix. Long used by commercial nurseries, water-absorbent gels are now more widely available and packaged for home gardeners. You can buy water-absorbing polymer crystals (another term for the gels) by the pound from mail-order garden supply companies. One pound costs about $10.

Water-absorbing gel is easy to use. Simply mix a small amount of the dry powder or flakes into your potting soil as you pot up plants. Check the package directions for the correct amount to add.

If you don't get around to buying some gel, you can try this low-tech technique to make potting soil more absorbent. It's recommended by Felder Rushing, coauthor of *Passalong Plants*. Felder says to water your potted plants twice during each watering session. Water once and let the water soak in for a few minutes—that allows the potting mix to swell. Then water again, and this time the water will really soak into the expanded mix. Felder finds that this small effort saves him an extra day or two between waterings.

Water by the Drip

Save time and money on watering container plants by investing in a drip irrigation system. "The easiest way to water plants in pots is to buy a timer and put all the pots on a drip system," claims Paul Barina, who grows about 100 plants in containers in and around his patio in Santa Paula, California. Paul discovered that with a drip system, the plants looked better and were easier to water. Plus, he found that he was saving money on his water bill.

Paul says the system is almost invisible and took him less than a day to install from start to finish. (The parts are available by mail from garden supply catalogs or from your local garden center.) Here's how to do it.

MAKE YOUR

FAUCET DRIP

AND YOU'LL

SAVE WATER!

1 Put a ¾-inch black plastic irrigation tube around the perimeter of your patio. This is the main tube.

2 Use a tool called a hole punch to punch holes in the main tube. Make one hole for each pot, close to where the pot will sit.

3 Push a connection fitting into each hole along the main tube.

4 Attach a ¼-inch feeder tube to each fitting that's long enough to reach inside each pot.

5 Attach a drip fitting to the other end of each feeder tube, and place one drip fitting into each pot.

Paul finds that his feeders stay put in the pots, but for extra security you can buy special stakes to hold them in place, or make your own wire stakes from pieces of wire from coat hangers. You can operate the system manually, but Paul finds that using a timer is more effective. "You don't walk off and leave the system running, or forget to water on the hottest day of the year," he explains.

This same system works just fine to water hanging plants. Paul uses it to water plants hanging from wooden fences beside his patio. He ran the main hose behind the fence on the top 2 × 4 railing, then drilled ¼-inch holes in the fence just above the brackets that support the rods that hold the hanging plants. He ran the feeders through the holes and into the pots. The plants end up hiding the irrigation tubes

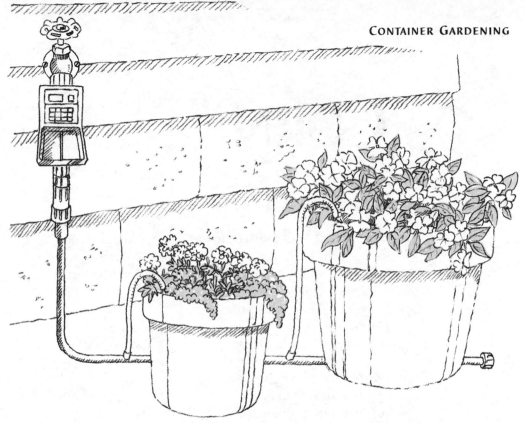

To get the most time-savings from a drip watering system, use a battery-operated timer. It will operate reliably despite the low water pressure drip systems run on—some flow-operated timers won't.

from view. "Both the hanging plants and those on the patio grow completely over and around the hoses," Paul says.

For information or help in planning your own drip irrigation system, check with a local garden center that carries drip irrigation equipment.

Stop That Soil!

Stop soil from escaping through the hole in the bottom of a pot by reusing an item from your laundry room. Brenda Pink, a gardener in Lethbridge, Alberta, lines pots with fabric softener sheets. She uses the sheets in her clothes dryer several times first, until they seem to be free of softener and perfume. They're easier to use than potsherds and better for the plants than a layer of gravel, which can actually interfere with drainage. "You can use used coffee filters in the same manner," Brenda says.

75

CORN

Clover Keeps Corn Weed-Free

Your corn will be in clover if you use this work-saving technique. Surround young corn plants with a cover crop and you'll get great weed control without the usual hassle of digging, pulling, or hoeing.

Sally Jean Cunningham of Cornell Cooperative Extension weeds her corn only once, then uses a cover crop of clover to fight weeds. "Since corn has so many surface roots, it's hard to weed without damaging the crop," she says. "That makes it one of the single best plants to use cover crops with."

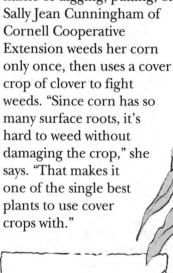

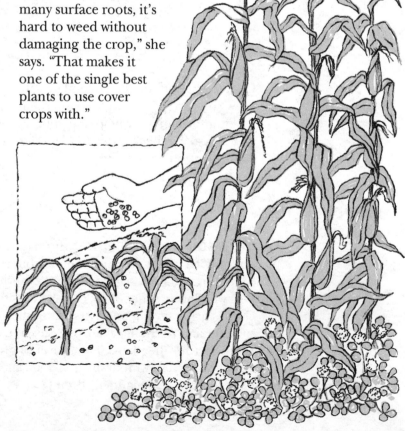

Scatter clover seeds around your corn seedlings when they're about a foot tall. The clover will form a thick carpet that keeps weeds out of your planting.

To prepare her site, Sally Jean weeds her young corn thoroughly one month after her usual June 1 planting date. Then she sows all around the corn with dwarf white clover at a rate of 1 ounce per 100 square feet. To insure a good stand, she scatters the seeds evenly and rakes soil on top to cover them. Sally Jean stresses that the timing is important—if you plant your cover crop too early, it will smother the corn seedlings. But, if you wait and give your corn a month's head start, you can sow your cover crop right up to the plants without worrying about competition.

The clover does more than keep weeds away; it's a great green manure crop too. If you till it into your soil after the corn harvest, it will add nitrogen to your garden soil. Since clover is a legume, it can absorb nitrogen from the air and convert it into a form your future crops can use. Sally Jean says she uses dwarf white clover (*Trifolium repens*) because it's what she usually has on hand at planting time, but notes that alsike clover (*T. hybridum*), red clover (*T. pratense*), and yellow clover (*T. agrarium*) work equally well.

Outfox Raccoons with a Repellent

A FOXY SCENT

MAKES CORN

THIEVES REPENT

The scent of a fox is all it takes to keep raccoons from feasting on your sweet corn. In Coolspring, Pennsylvania, gardener Victoria Burkett uses fox lure, a fox urine product sold by hunting supply stores, to protect her sweet corn from hungry raccoons.

When her corn begins to form kernels, Victoria sprinkles drops of lure on the ground throughout her corn planting and around its perimeter. It only takes 15 to 20 drops of lure to treat a half-acre plot—at that rate, one bottle will protect your garden for several years. You will have to reapply the fox scent occasionally, but one treatment lasts through three or four rains. "We used to lose almost all our corn to raccoons," Victoria says. "But we haven't lost any since we started using fox lure more than five years ago.

"My husband asked me if I thought there were still raccoons around here. Just the other day we were walking the dogs and they chased two raccoons—they just don't bother our corn anymore."

Plastic Perplexes Raccoons

Outsmart wily raccoons with a slick plastic-covered fence and they'll never bother your corn crop again. Years ago Alton Eliason, a veteran organic gardener in Northford, Connecticut, found that black plastic makes a simple, long-term raccoon solution. "If you already have a fence around your garden, you're almost home," Alton says. He recommends that you buy enough 36-inch-wide black plastic to stretch around the entire fence. Attach the plastic to the fence with plastic clothespins, clipping it in place so the plastic reaches up 30 inches, then spreads out on the ground about 6 inches. "Mr. Coon can't get a grip on the slippery plastic and he won't dig under," Alton insists. "Raccoons don't dig unless they're trapped."

This simple fence has kept raccoons out of Alton's garden for more than 10 years, and he's recommended it to hundreds of other gardeners with success. Be sure you use black plastic, since it lasts a lot longer than the clear kind. Alton's plastic is already 15 years old and still going strong.

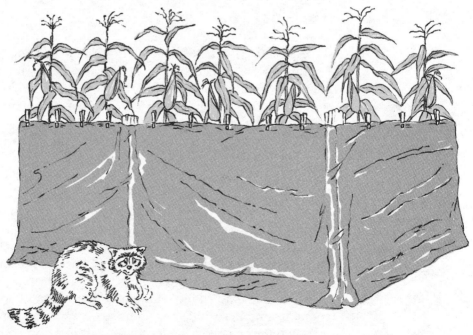

It's easy to keep raccoons from climbing in to eat your corn. Simply attach sheets of slippery black plastic to an existing garden fence with clothespins. If you don't have a fence, drive sturdy stakes into the ground about 3 feet apart, and stretch the plastic between them.

In the Trenches, Corn Withstands Wind and Crows

Solve corn problems at planting time by using a simple trenching technique that thwarts damaging winds and birds. Sally Jean Cunningham of Cornell Cooperative Extension sows her corn in trenches, then gradually hills soil around the seedlings as they grow.

To try Sally Jean's method, dig your rows 4 to 5 inches deep to form trenches, and plant corn seeds along the bottom. (You can use the trencher attachment on a tiller to dig deep rows in a hurry.) Cover the seeds with just an inch or so of soil. As the corn emerges, keep filling in the trench. When the seedlings

are small, the trench protects them from wind, and as they grow, the extra soil keeps them from lodging (blowing over).

For extra protection, cover the trenches with mesh gutter guard to keep crows from pulling up the shallow-rooted seedlings. "It's the perfect shape to cover the trench," Sally Jean notes. Remove the gutter guard when the corn reaches it—it will be big enough to fend for itself by then—and hill soil around the plants a final time. You won't have to hill again later.

On windy sites, grow corn in trenches to give the stems extra support. Place gutter guards over the trench tops after planting to keep pesky birds from stealing your seeds or pulling your plants.

CUCUMBERS

Cucumbers and Sunflowers— Perfect Companions

A winning combination—that's what you'll get when you plant cukes and sunflowers together. This time- and trouble-saving combination is a favorite of Donna Iarkowski, owner of Nature's Way Herbary in Muncy Valley, Pennsylvania.

"For the last three years, I've planted my cucumbers between two full rows of 'Mammoth' sunflowers," Donna says. The sunflowers provide morning and noon shade and the cucumbers love it! "They produce more cucumbers than ever before and have fewer fungal diseases," Donna says. "I won't plant them any other way now."

The sunflowers also get their fair share of benefits. The cucumber vines make a living mulch around the sunflower roots, keeping the soil moist in summer and discouraging weeds. And that means big, vigorous, productive plants.

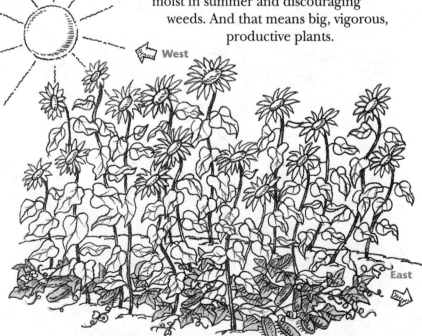

Plant big-leaved sunflowers to shade your cucumbers from the hot summer sun. Arrange your rows from east to west so your cukes get just the right amount of light.

West

East

A New Fungus-Fighter

KEEP CUKES

MILDEW-FREE

WITH A HUNGRY

FUNGUS

Punch out powdery mildew, that pesky disease that destroys cucumbers and disfigures roses and other flowers, with a new biocontrol. Instead of spraying your cucumbers and other plants with fungicides, coat them with a parasitic fungus to give mildew the old heave-ho.

Commercial growers are already fighting powdery mildew with this fungal parasite sold under the name AQ10—and now you can use it too. It eats mildew from the inside out and dies when the mildew is gone, says Bill Jarvis, plant pathologist for Agriculture Canada. He explains that AQ10 is a fungus that exists naturally wherever you find powdery mildew.

Entomologist Tim Johnson is director of product development at Ecogen, a biopesticide company that sells AQ10. He says AQ10 is registered for use on cucumbers, wine grapes, pome fruits like apples and pears, tomatoes, roses, and ornamentals, although it's currently labeled only for grapes. (Ecogen will add more uses to the label as their market expands and the product becomes more popular.)

To apply AQ10, mix the granules with water and AddQ, a surfactant that slows down the drying process and gives spores time to germinate. (AddQ is sold with the AQ10.) Do not apply it with fungicides—even organic ones—since they would kill the parasite as well as the mildew. AQ10 works best if you use it as a preventive, so apply it every ten days throughout the summer (powdery mildew season). Once you see powdery mildew, it's too late for AQ10—the fungus population is so high that the parasite will have trouble battling it.

You can get commercial-size packets of AQ10 at farm supply stores. A package only weighs an ounce but treats an entire acre. Use what you need and store the rest in the refrigerator; it will keep at least three years. Tim says they plan to make homeowner-size packages so keep checking your farm supply store for availability.

DEER

Cut Fence Expense While Deterring Deer

A 7-foot-tall fence around your property is a surefire way to keep deer from dining on your plants. But what if you don't have the time, energy, or money to install one?

David E. Benner, president of Benner's Gardens in New Hope, Pennsylvania, has found an inexpensive, easy-to-install fence that blocks out deer without blocking his view. David says he spent five years struggling with deer-control devices before he heard about people who were successfully using plastic fencing. After experimenting with a couple of different kinds, David enclosed his entire 2-acre woodland with black polypropylene netting. He found, to his delight, that the lightweight fencing kept the deer out as well as a more traditional fence would.

David's fence is 7½ feet tall and has a 2- by 3-inch mesh. He says you can stretch the netting quite a distance—up to 20 feet—so you don't need many fence posts to install it. Use wood or metal posts, and pin the fence to the ground every 12 feet with galvanized stakes to keep deer from pushing the fence up and crawling in under it.

Since David's fence is set against a woodland backdrop, visitors rarely notice it. "I really have to tell people that I have this fence up," he says. "They can't see it unless I point it out—that's how invisible it is." In fact, so many visitors were impressed by the effectiveness of the fencing and the fact that it didn't disrupt the appearance of the garden that David and his son began selling rolls of the plastic netting. (See "Sources" on page 412 for ordering information.)

EASY PLASTIC FENCE SAVES PLANTS FROM HUNGRY DEER

Deer Don't Go for Soapy Trees

Hang the right bar of soap in your tree or shrub and you'll have a speedy, safe deterrent to deer browsing. Soap is a simple solution if you've only got a few trees or shrubs to protect, says wildlife damage specialist Paul Curtis at Cornell University's Department of Natural Resources. But to make sure it's an effective solution, you've got to read the label. Paul explains that in order for soap to repel deer, it has to have a base of tallow (which is made from animal fat). Coconut-oil soaps or soaps made from other non-tallow products like pumice won't repel deer. Deodorant soaps work, but not because of the deodorant—it's because they're made from tallow.

GIVE DEER THE

HEAVE-HO WITH

SOAP MADE OF

TALLOW

Paul notes that a single bar of soap will reduce deer browsing by about 70 percent within a circle about 1 yard in diameter. "If you need to protect many plants, or you have large plants that are going to take several bars of soap, you're better off using the commercial spray repellent Hinder, because it has the same active ingredient," Paul says.

He also offers this warning about hanging bars of soap from your plants. "Soaps may not be the repellent of choice in areas that are prone to damage by meadow and pine voles." In orchard trials, Paul and other scientists noticed that voles girdled and damaged the bases of trees more when soap washed down the tree trunks. Maybe they liked the taste.

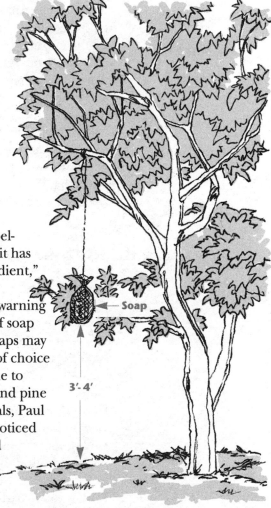

← Soap

3'- 4'

Protect small trees and shrubs from deer with bars of tallow-based soap. Place each soap bar in a mesh bag and hang it 3 or 4 feet off the ground.

Blood Repels Deer (But Watch Out for Dracula!)

Protect your plants with a blood meal drink

Deer can't stand the smell of blood. Sprinkling dry blood meal near plants is an old trick for repelling deer and other wild animals, but it has some drawbacks. The blood meal dissolves into the soil each time it rains and needs to be replaced, and all the washed-in blood meal can add too much nitrogen to the soil.

Rose Vincent of Vincent Landscapes in Austin, Texas, has a simple solution for both problems: Fill a 5-inch-tall plastic cup with 1 part blood meal to 2 parts water. Don't fill the cup all the way to the top—you want to leave room for water from rain or irrigation. Then dig a hole behind the plant and set the cup into the hole. "When the deer bend down to nibble the plant, they smell the blood and think something has died, and that they're next," Rose says.

This method makes the blood meal last through all kinds of weather and through many waterings. As the water evaporates, Rose adds more water or blood meal as needed. She notes that the mix is "really fragrant" at first, but after awhile, humans don't notice it while the deer still do!

2 Sprays Keep Deer Away

If you have a part-time deer problem, spraying your favorite plants with a commercial repellent is a quick way to save your landscape. According to wildlife damage specialist Paul Curtis at Cornell University's Department of Natural Resources, two products that gave good results in Cornell research trials are Big Game Repellent (BGR) and Hinder. BGR's active ingredient is rotted egg solids and Hinder's is ammonium soaps.

Although repellent sprays are a fast way to protect plants, Paul points out that they do have drawbacks. They must be reapplied monthly—more often if it rains; they're expensive; and none of them are 100 percent effective. So, says Paul, if you live where your plants are susceptible to deer damage for more than three months a year, fencing may be a more cost-effective way to go. But where damage from deer occurs occasionally—during extreme winter weather, for example—repellent sprays can deter deer in a hurry.

Deer Won't Dine on These

Deer don't eat everything, though it often seems that way. So, if you choose your landscape plants carefully, you can reduce deer damage—and the time, effort, and money you spend protecting plants with sprays, soaps, and fencing. No one can predict which foods deer will eat when the pickings get slim, but there are some plants that are less likely to become lunch for Bambi, says wildlife damage specialist Paul Curtis at Cornell University's Department of Natural Resources.

Paul explains that deer tend to avoid some plants and seek out others. To take advantage of deer preferences, he recommends that you look at lists of plants deer do and don't like, such as the ones in "Proven Plants for Dealing with Deer" on this page. Use the lists when you're designing your landscape. You can create an attractive landscape with deer-resistant plants. And by avoiding the plants deer seek out, you'll be able to enjoy your new landscape a lot longer.

PROVEN PLANTS FOR DEALING WITH DEER

Plant lists may change depending on where you live, but here's a basic list of plants that deer don't like—as well as ones they do. When you're considering plants that aren't listed, remember these guidelines. Deer especially like young fruit trees and lush, well- to over-fertilized plants with lots of new growth. They tend to avoid aromatic herbs like rosemary and leathery, fuzzy-leaved, or spiny plants.

10 PLANTS DEER AVOID
American holly (*Ilex opaca*)
Barberries (*Berberis* spp.)
Boxwoods (*Buxus* spp.)
Clematis (*Clematis* spp.)
Colorado blue spruce
  (*Picea pungens*)
Columbines (*Aquilegia* spp.)
Common lilac (*Syringa vulgaris*)
Delphiniums (*Delphinium* spp.)
Foxgloves (*Digitalis* spp.)
Iris (*Iris* spp.)

10 PLANTS DEER LOVE
Arborvitae (*Thuja* spp.)
Azaleas (*Rhododendron* spp.)
Cotoneasters (*Cotoneaster* spp.)
Crabapples (*Malus* spp.)
Euonymus (*Euonymus* spp.)
Hostas (*Hosta* spp.)
Impatiens (*Impatiens wallerana*)
Roses (*Rosa* spp.)
Yews (*Taxus* spp.)
Zonal geraniums
  (*Pelargonium* × *hortorum*)

DISEASES

A Quick Rinse for Plant Diseases

Wash disease problems away with a hydrogen peroxide spray. It's just what the doctor ordered for leaf and fruit diseases caused by bacteria or fungi. "I'm using it in a big way, with a lot of success," reports Ed Lidzbarski of E. R. & Son Farm near Jamesburg, New Jersey. Ed, who grows vegetables organically for market, sprays high-value crops like tomatoes to prevent disease attacks. Hydrogen peroxide cleans leaves and fruits and leaves no residue, Ed notes.

You can spray plants with the straight 3 percent hydrogen peroxide solution you buy at the pharmacy, or use a dilute solution of the stronger commercial mix. (See "Quick Fix Mix" on the opposite page for Ed's recipe.) Whether you mix your own or buy it ready to use, a little solution goes a long way. One gallon covers about 1,500 square feet if you use a sprayer that applies a fine mist—a sprayer with larger drops works too, but it uses more hydrogen peroxide. Wet the plants thoroughly, and be sure to spray both sides of the leaves. Don't worry about getting spray on the ground—the solution won't hurt the soil.

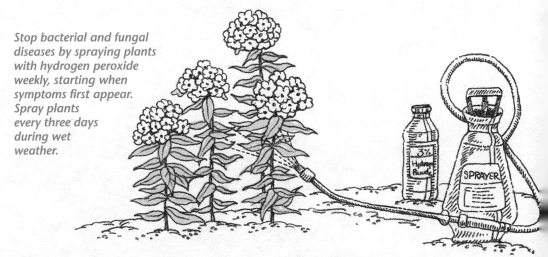

Stop bacterial and fungal diseases by spraying plants with hydrogen peroxide weekly, starting when symptoms first appear. Spray plants every three days during wet weather.

QUICK FIX MIX

Homemade Disease-Dousing Spray

Ed Lidzbarski of E. R. & Son Farm near Jamesburg, New Jersey, swears by hydrogen peroxide to prevent bacterial and fungal diseases on vegetables and fruits. Ed has lots of plants to spray, so he mixes his own spray from food-grade 35 percent hydrogen peroxide, which many health food stores sell. This concentration of hydrogen peroxide is caustic, so Ed wears protective gear, including rubber gloves and goggles. Here's what you'll need.

1 tablespoon 35% hydrogen peroxide
1 gallon water

Mix the hydrogen peroxide into the gallon of water. Ed suggests mixing up several gallons at once and storing the spray, so you deal with the concentrated material as little as possible.

Note: To prevent disease, spray once a week during dry weather and every few days when it's wet. Or, for a less intensive approach, wait until you see symptoms before you spray. Ed says not to spray transplants until they've settled in and started growing. For direct-seeded crops, spray after the first few true leaves appear.

2 Tricks for Stopping Powdery Mildew

Control is only a spray away. Safe and simple sprays can stop powdery mildew before it coats your plants with white fungus. That's the good news from Nancy Bechtol, chief of the Horticultural Services Division at the Smithsonian Institution, who offers these two simple methods for mildew control.

Mist daily. The spores that cause powdery mildew can't germinate on a wet surface, so you can prevent the disease by misting your plants each day. In the Northeast, you'll need to spray from late June until late September. For plants like roses that require almost daily care, a water spray is easier to fit into your routine than other treatments.

Give leaves a protective coating monthly. Using an anti-desiccant spray (like Wilt-Pruf) once a month also stops powdery mildew. These sprays are normally used to keep evergreen leaves from drying out in winter, but they give leaves a waxy coating that also keeps mildew from getting a foothold. Use one-third of the recommended summer rate on low-maintenance plants such as lilacs and garden phlox.

Disease Control Starts with a Positive ID

If your plants are dying and you suspect that a disease is the culprit, you'll save time and money by having the problem diagnosed by a laboratory.

"Many diseases are impossible to identify without a lab test," cautions Nancy Bechtol, chief of the Horticultural Services Division at the Smithsonian Institution. You can waste a lot of time treating a problem that isn't diagnosed correctly. She uses the disease phytophthora as an example; it's often blamed when junipers or rhododendrons suddenly turn brown and die, but it's the real cause in only about a fifth of the cases. Overwatering or underwatering is usually the problem.

To find out if a disease is killing your plant, contact your local Cooperative Extension Service. They'll tell you how to send a plant to the state's diagnostic laboratory. Some extension services will submit the specimen for you, others ask that you send it directly to the lab. Either way, you should send a fresh, living sample, not one that's dead or dried.

Once you know what the disease is, Nancy recommends that you contact the Cooperative Extension Service or a reputable nursery for a list of resistant plants and start over. That's because if a plant gets a serious disease, there's usually nothing you can do to save it. Pull the plant out and throw it in the trash before it infects others. Luckily, lethal diseases aren't all that common, and Nancy believes that most gardeners can take a casual attitude toward run-of-the-mill afflictions. "There's not a plant that's blotch-free, so don't worry about it," Nancy says. "Accept that it's natural."

TO REALLY KNOW IF DIS-EASE IS THE FOE, GET A LAB TEST

Manure Tea Spray Keeps Diseases Away

Protect your transplants from diseases by giving them a drink of manure tea. One foliar feeding is all it takes for Ken Muckenfuss, owner of Mill Creek Organic Farm in Medford, New Jersey, to keep his seedlings disease-free. After Ken sets his plants in the ground, he soaks the soil thoroughly with water to settle them in. Once the soil dries out, he sprays the transplants' leaves with manure tea. "Not only does it feed the plants, it also surrounds them with good bacteria, so the bad bacteria can't get them," Ken explains.

Any wounded plant is susceptible to diseases, Ken says. He points out that plants can be nicked or bruised during transplanting, so that's when they're especially vulnerable. If you need a lot of manure tea, try Ken's recipe in "Quick Fix Mix" on page 304. If you've only got a few plants, try the "Quick Fix Mix" recipe on this page.

❧QUICK FIX MIX

Seedling-Strength Manure Tea

When you set out new transplants, spray them with a weak solution of manure tea to get them off to a disease-free start. Here's a recipe from Nancy Ondra, owner of Pendragon Perennials, a nursery in Emmaus, Pennsylvania, that's just the right strength for tender seedlings.

1 shovelful horse, cow, or poultry manure (fresh or aged)

1 pillowcase or burlap bag

1 5-gallon plastic bucket

water

Put the manure in an old pillowcase or burlap bag. Tie the bag shut with a piece of twine and place it in the 5-gallon bucket. Fill the bucket with water but keep the top of the bag dry so you can pull it out when the tea has finished brewing. Let the tea sit for two or three days, then pull the "tea bag" out and dump the dregs in your compost heap—toss the bag in too, if it's an old one.

Before you use the tea, Nancy says it's really important to dilute it with water. If you don't, you can burn young plants. Mix 3 parts water to 1 part tea and see how it looks. What you want is a solution that looks like weak iced tea. Sprinkle the dilute mix over young plants until they're established.

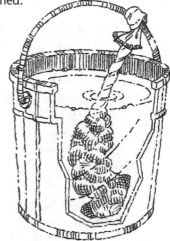

Make your own "tea bag" for manure tea by putting a shovelful of manure in a pillowcase or burlap sack. Or get creative and use other materials you've got on hand like old panty hose.

89

Use Marigolds to Fight Fungi

Marigolds are magic when it comes to pest and disease control. You've heard of using marigolds to control nematodes. Now, researchers have discovered that using marigolds as a green manure also protects crops from Verticillium wilt, an incurable fungal disease that can infect flowers, vegetables, fruits, and ornamentals. Diseased plants wilt and may turn yellow.

At Montana State University, associate professor of entomology Florence Dunkel and her coworkers inoculated a field with the fungi that cause Verticillium wilt. In late May, they broadcast seeds of African marigolds (*Tagetes erecta*) over the field and let them grow. In September, they plowed the marigolds into the soil, and the following spring, they planted a perennial mint in the field.

"The control was excellent the first year," Florence reports. "By the end of the second year, the mint wasn't doing as well. The problem was that we planted a perennial, so we couldn't repeat the marigold treatment. But still, the control lasted a long time."

CHOPPED
MARIGOLDS
KEEP WILT
FUNGUS AWAY

For areas where Verticillium wilt is definitely a problem, Florence suggests planting marigolds in April, then turning them under with a tiller or shovel in June. That way you can follow the marigolds with a late crop like tomatoes and you won't lose a season's harvest.

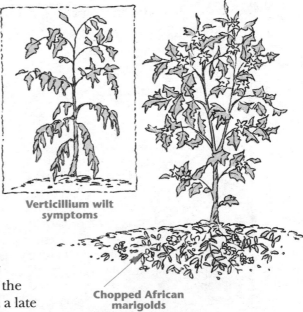

Verticillium wilt
symptoms

Chopped African
marigolds

Till African marigolds into your soil to protect tomatoes and other susceptible crops from Verticillium wilt.

Keep Roots High and Dry So They Won't Die

Soggy soil promotes a deadly disease called phytophthora. It's especially likely to strike plants in heavy clay soils where the drainage is poor. But you can reduce the chance of phytophthora by improving soil drainage.

"The best thing if you're planning to plant a new tree or shrub into heavy soil is to put in drain tiles," says Dr. E. Thomas Smiley, a researcher with Bartlett Tree Research Laboratories in Charlotte, North Carolina. But he admits that most people aren't willing to go to that expense, so he offers an alternative. "You can avoid a lot of phytophthora by planting in a mound or a raised bed," he says.

He notes that phytophthora can be hard to diagnose because it strikes the plant's roots: "Most people see a plant that all of a sudden dies, usually in the heat of summer." When it's dug up, the roots are black, especially the tips. Or the root system may be flat like a pancake and be brown or black on the inside. The discoloration may continue up into the stem as high as a foot above the soil level. Since those symptoms may be hard to see, the only accurate diagnosis comes from a test done at a diagnostic clinic. (To find out where to have a plant tested, call your local Cooperative Extension Service office.)

Improve your landscape's health by grouping trees and shrubs together and planting them on low berms. Raising your planting area 6 to 12 inches makes it drain better and that discourages the disease phytophthora.

91

DRYING

Try a Drying "Sandwich"

To dry your harvest without tying up the oven or buying an elaborate machine, all you need are some wire racks and cheesecloth. "Use two refrigerator or oven racks covered with cheesecloth to make a 'sandwich rack' for drying fruit, vegetables, or herbs," recommends Yvonne Savio, gardening education coordinator for the Los Angeles County Cooperative Extension Service.

"Place cheesecloth on one rack, then spread out the fruit or herbs on it," says Yvonne. "Cover the produce with another layer of cheesecloth, and place the second rack on top. Flip the 'sandwich' each time the fruit needs to be turned for even drying." (Turn the racks once a day until the produce is dry—most fruits and fleshy vegetables, like tomatoes, become leathery; herbs and nonfleshy vegetables, like carrots, become brittle.) Yvonne says that bread and cake cooling racks also work.

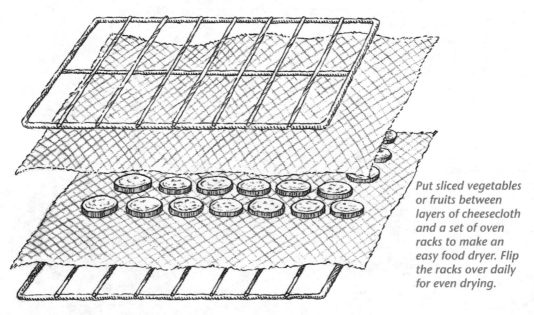

Put sliced vegetables or fruits between layers of cheesecloth and a set of oven racks to make an easy food dryer. Flip the racks over daily for even drying.

Make the Most of Heating Mats

Get twice as much from your heating mat.

That heating mat you bought to get seedlings to sprout faster doesn't have to gather dust after your seeds are up. Use it to dry herbs and seeds.

"I put a wooden box with shelves over my heating mat," explains Sharon Conboy, a Master Gardener with the Washington State University Cooperative Extension Service. "I have a large mat, so the box is 2 feet tall by 3 feet wide by 2 feet deep. It's made of plywood, with a two-piece sliding door." The shelves in Sharon's drying box don't extend all the way to the back of the box, leaving room for the heat to rise; a few small holes at the top of the door let excess heat and moisture escape.

Sharon's system is great, but a simpler setup works fine, too. If you have a smaller mat, try putting the herbs in a shallow box and setting it on the mat. If you can control the temperature of your mat, set it between 70° and 80°F. Preset mats are usually set at about 75°F.

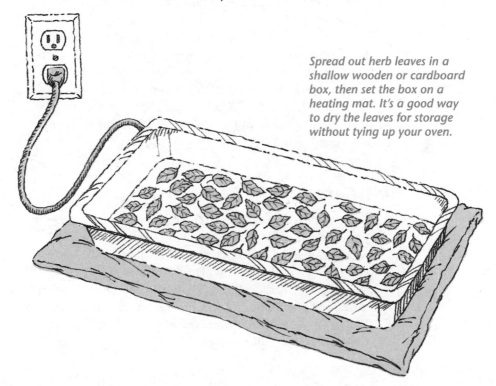

Spread out herb leaves in a shallow wooden or cardboard box, then set the box on a heating mat. It's a good way to dry the leaves for storage without tying up your oven.

EGGPLANT

Don't Jump the Gun on Eggplant

Take it easy next spring and put off planting eggplant transplants until warm weather arrives—you'll spread out your workload and your eggplant will thrive. Late-planted eggplant is more vigorous, so it has fewer pest problems and produces bigger crops than early transplants. "These are not cool-weather-loving plants," says David Chambers, manager of Mr. Cason's Vegetable Garden at Callaway Gardens in Pine Mountain, Georgia. "The later we plant them, the better the results."

A LATE START GUARANTEES SUCCESS WITH EGGPLANT

David says his success with eggplant at Callaway comes from starting the plants really late (around May 1 in central Georgia), so they never have to deal with cool weather. For great results in your area, plant eggplant a month after your frost-free date.

"The trick with eggplant is getting the plants to grow fast," David says. "Otherwise they get into problems with flea beetles and other insects." If you set eggplant out in cool weather, the plants struggle and grow slowly, even after warm weather arrives. The stunted, less-vigorous plants can't fight off pest and disease problems, and their small size means smaller yields.

Far East Eggplant Yields Faster Harvests

If you want early eggplant, don't try to rush the planting season—these heat-loving plants sulk in cool weather. Instead, plant when it's warm and grow early-yielding oriental eggplant. That's the secret technique of Roger Swain, host of PBS's *Victory Garden*. Oriental eggplant don't like cool temperatures any better than the classic or Italian types, says Roger, but once temperatures warm up, they are a whole lot more prolific than other eggplant.

Many oriental cultivars have long slim fruits, but cultivars with short or rounded fruits are available too. The only way to really tell them apart from the classic types is to check the color of the calyx (the leaflike structure that surrounds the eggplant stem). Oriental types have purple calyxes, while other types have green calyxes. Check the descriptions in seed catalogs to be sure you get an oriental type.

Calyx

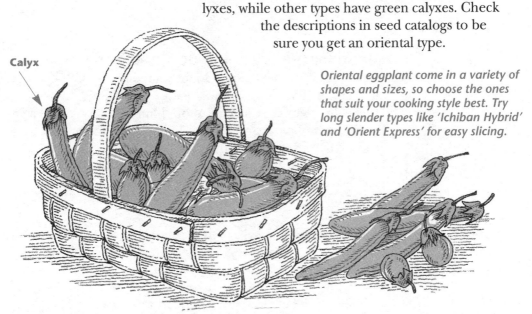

Oriental eggplant come in a variety of shapes and sizes, so choose the ones that suit your cooking style best. Try long slender types like 'Ichiban Hybrid' and 'Orient Express' for easy slicing.

Elbowroom Means Extra Eggplant

Let your eggplant stretch out and you'll enjoy a bigger harvest. "We space our eggplant a lot farther apart than most people," says David Chambers, manager of Mr. Cason's Vegetable Garden at Callaway Gardens in Pine Mountain, Georgia. "It looks like a lot of wasted space, but the plants use every bit of it." David leaves 4 feet between rows and sets plants 3 feet apart within the rows. Seed catalogs and books suggest planting eggplant in rows that are 3 feet apart with 1½ to 2 feet between plants.

David cultivates deeply around the transplants four weeks after setting them out, and then mulches to keep the soil moist and weed-free. "The plants are starting to touch by the time we start to harvest," David says, noting that the big, vigorous plants yield plenty of eggplant. "We've picked as much as a bushel of eggplant from one plant," he says.

95

FERTILIZING

All-Purpose Alfalfa

For an inexpensive high-powered fertilizer, try the kind of dried alfalfa used to feed large livestock. "I use alfalfa meal almost every time I plant," says Dennis Dubbelde, a gardener in East Alton, Illinois. "I just spread a liberal amount on the ground and till it in. I had record crops of beets, beans, and peas last year." Alfalfa is a great nitrogen source, although it needs time to break down before the nitrogen becomes available for plants. Dennis says he began to notice results during the second year he used dried alfalfa.

You can buy the meal at some feed stores; a 50-pound bag costs about $7. Some nurseries can also order it, but they may charge a higher price. Alfalfa meal is dusty, so it's a good idea to wear a dust mask when applying it.

Roses love alfalfa too, says Ciscoe Morris, director of grounds and landscaping at Seattle University. In the spring, Ciscoe scratches 1½ cups of alfalfa meal into the soil around each hybrid tea rose and waters it in. He also adds a quick-acting nitrogen source (such as blood meal) to cover the period while the meal breaks down. Every six weeks thereafter, he applies another 1½ cups of meal without the nitrogen source. "The roses go crazy," Ciscoe says. "They have good sustained growth and flowering." He's also had good results applying the meal to perennials—about half a handful per plant.

Compressed alfalfa cubes also do the trick, according to Jennifer Weaver, a gardener in Lancaster County, Pennsylvania. Jennifer dumps a 3-inch-deep layer of cubes in her wheelbarrow and adds a couple of buckets of hot water. After an hour, she breaks up the softened cubes and then works a ½-inch layer into her soil. "They improve my soil texture," Jennifer explains. "But be careful not to add too much or you'll turn your soil into a hot compost pile."

Soften Clay Soil with Pelleted Gypsum

You can improve your clay soil's structure and drainage by adding pelleted gypsum. Gypsum (calcium sulfate) is an effective soil conditioner. It also adds calcium and sulfur to the soil without making the soil more acidic or alkaline. To get the benefits fastest, use pelleted gypsum instead of the ground form.

"Straight ground gypsum can have small chunks that are hard to dissolve—they can lay in the soil for three, four, five years," explains Floyd Crary of Ampel Corporation in Des Moines, which sells gypsum and other farm products. But pelleted gypsum dissolves to a fine powder as soon as it gets wet, so it goes to work rapidly, says Floyd.

Gypsum can also boost potato production (because it gives potatoes the calcium they need). Floyd says potato growers often apply pelleted gypsum to the hill around the plants when the tubers begin to enlarge.

Use a fertilizer spreader to apply pelleted gypsum. Floyd recommends using 20 to 30 pounds of pelleted gypsum per 1,000 square feet of garden. Pelleted gypsum is available at garden centers, nurseries, and hardware stores.

❧ QUICK FIX MIX

Fast-Cooking Fowl Fertilizer

To make a rich fertilizer fast, try composting poultry manure with leaves. Ken Muckenfuss, owner of Mill Creek Organic Farm in Medford, New Jersey, uses a manure spreader to mix leaves and manure in bulk. His recipe is simple.

1 part leaves

1 part fresh chicken manure

"The manure is high in nitrogen, so the composting process is fast," Ken says. "And it's high in water, so there's no need to water the pile."

As it composts, the mix will cook down to nearly half its original volume. If you don't have a manure spreader handy, you can mix the ingredients with a pitchfork. Ken recommends turning the pile often so it won't develop an unpleasant odor.

Local farms that produce eggs and chickens are the most likely source of chicken manure. Avoid sources that treat the manure with an insecticide to kill flies, because you don't want to introduce those pesticides into your garden.

Make Fertilizing Squeeze-Easy

Fertilize houseplants quickly and easily by keeping a squeeze bottle of fish emulsion at the ready. Cheryl Long, research editor at *Organic Gardening* magazine, buys fish emulsion in large jugs because they're the most economical choice. But the larger-than-life jugs are cumbersome, so Cheryl repackages her fish emulsion in smaller squeezable bottles with pop-up or flip-top lids. (She's found that empty ketchup or soap bottles work great.)

Cheryl says she found herself reluctant to get out the big jug of fish emulsion and pour from it into her watering can when she wanted to fertilize. Now, because her recycled containers make using fish emulsion so effortless, she fertilizes her plants more consistently. Cheryl likes the ease with which she can squeeze a small amount into her watering can and then close the top. She stores one dispenser with each of her watering cans. The smaller bottles save her steps too. "I don't have to run downstairs and get the jug when I'm thinking of fertilizing; it's all right there," says Cheryl.

Whenever you put fertilizers or garden sprays into containers like ketchup bottles that formerly held food, label the contents clearly. Transfer the mixing instructions from the big jug to your handmade labels so you don't have to read the instructions each time.

Hunt and Fish for Free Fertilizers

Eggshells and tropical fish are the source of two great free fertilizers. Give them a try instead of making a trip to the store.

Turn eggshells into treasure instead of trash. Crush the shells and add water to make a free nutrient brew, suggests Rose Vincent of Vincent Landscapes in Austin, Texas. Add smashed eggshells to a gallon jug filled three-quarters full with water. After several days, shake the solution, then use it on blooming perennials to give them a calcium boost.

Get goldfish to keep plants growing. "Whenever I change the water in my aquarium, I water the plants with the old water," says Roger Hagley, a gardener in Ashland, Kentucky. "This has cut my use of purchased fertilizer down to almost nothing."

Send Fertilizer down the Pipe

Inexpensive PVC pipe can serve double duty in your garden. Use the pipe both to stake your plants and to send liquid fertilizer to their roots.

"Use 2-inch-diameter PVC pipe as a support for vine crops such as beans and cucumbers," says Lyn Belisle, a gardener in San Antonio. Lyn drills ¼-inch holes in a 5-foot length of PVC pipe, starting 6 inches from the base and drilling holes in the next 6 inches of pipe. She sinks the pipe a foot into the ground beside the plant at planting time. To fertilize, she pours a diluted fertilizer solution into the pipe support—it goes straight to the roots.

A piece of PVC pipe makes a great combination plant stake and liquid-fertilizer delivery system for tomatoes and other plants that need support.

FLOWERS

Add Care-Free Color with Quick Tile Trick

TURN WEEDY
LANDSCAPES
INTO FLOWERING
ISLANDS

Adding flowers to your landscape doesn't have to add hours of weeding time to your busy schedule. By planting flowers in sections of concrete field tile (which look like pieces of pipe made from concrete), you can create landscape areas that feature all-season color with virtually no weeding. Wayne Tholen and his son, Steve, co-owners of Tholens' Landscape & Garden Center in Kankakee, Illinois, hit on this technique of using 1-foot-long sections of concrete tile to turn landscape sites into weed-free flowering islands. (For another weed-free gardening technique, see "Sheet Compost for Weed-Free Flowers" on page 400.)

Wayne sinks the tiles into the ground upright and surrounds them with landscape fabric. He uses a layer of stone mulch to disguise the landscape fabric, but wood chips work too. He fills the tiles with potting soil and plants them with bulbs, annuals, or perennials. "The flowers quickly cover over the cement tile, and you can't even see it. And you don't have any trouble with weeds because there's landscape fabric under the mulch around the tiles," Wayne says. He notes that it's easy to tuck in some annuals for a summer display once spring bulbs begin to fade.

Folks who like more frequent color changes can use empty tiles as holders for pots of flowering plants. It's a simple task to remove a pot and replace it with another. Wayne explains: "It makes it very easy to change your landscape color. If you want to set a pot of annuals in there, you can; if you want to change them and put tulips in there, it's easy. Just slip one pot out and put another one in there." The tiles are available in inside diameters of 8, 10, 12, and 15 inches, so you can accommodate different sizes of containers. The Tholens find that the concrete tiles freeze with the soil, so there's little of the cracking and heaving that can happen if you try to use plastic pots as planters.

Buy 1-foot-long sections of concrete field tile to use as weed-free flower planters. Leave just 1 inch of the tile above ground so plants can hide your planters.

"I like annuals and perennials in the landscape," Wayne says, "but many people do not want the maintenance of weeding. The stone with the landscape fabric underneath it works well, unless you want to plant flowers in it. Because if you start cutting the landscape fabric, you ruin its effectiveness as a weed barrier, and then you get dirt mixed up into the gravel, and pretty soon you've got a mess. Well, the flower tile eliminates all of that."

One caution regarding the concrete tiles: Lifting them is no picnic. If you have back problems, get someone else to heft the tile into place. And even if you're in good physical condition, you may appreciate having a helper if you plan to dig several holes and install several concrete tile planters.

Plastic tiles have largely replaced concrete field tiles in their original use as drains for agricultural fields, but there are still manufacturers of the concrete tiles. Tholens' Landscape & Garden Center buys tiles from a local concrete company. To order flower tiles, write to Tholens' at 31 E. 2500 S. Road, Kankakee, IL 60901.

PROVEN PLANTS
FOR BEAUTIFUL SCREENS

Are you tired of looking at your garbage cans, compost pile, or tool-shed? If so, change the scene with a flowering screen. Mix big, bold annuals and perennials with grasses to hide ugly views fast. The flowers and grasses grow, spread, and fill in faster than most woody shrubs and are more interesting to look at than a wooden fence. Gradually add a few shrubs to the screen as you have time—they'll extend the seasonal interest of your planting. If money is a concern, plant small, inexpensive shrubs. "The flowers will fill in until the shrubs are big enough to make a permanent screen," says C. Colston Burrell, owner of the Minnesota-based design firm, Native Landscapes. He recommends the following flowers and grasses for screens.

ANNUALS

Canna (*Canna* spp.)
These tender bulbs have long, lush, banana-like foliage and brilliant long spikes of brightly colored flowers. They reach 3 to 6 feet tall. Treat cannas as annuals unless you live in the Deep South.

Castor bean (*Ricinus communis*)
This tropical plant grows 6 to 12 feet tall and bears huge star-shaped leaves, which are purple on some cultivars. All parts of this plant are extremely poisonous.

PERENNIALS

Joe-Pye weed (*Eupatorium purpureum*)
Coarse whorls of lance-shaped leaves and large plumes of lavender-pink flowers make an impressive display on 4- to 6-foot-tall plants. Zones 3 to 8.

Plume poppy (*Macleaya cordata*)
These plants grow to 10 feet high, with huge lobed leaves up to 10 inches long and billowy clusters of tiny, soft pink flowers. Zones 3 to 8.

Queen-of-the-prairie (*Filipendula rubra*)
Large pink or white flower plumes appear above bold leaves in summer on 4- to 7-foot-tall plants. Zones 3 to 9.

ORNAMENTAL GRASSES

Frost grass (*Spodiopogon sibericus*)
Thick tufts of bamboolike leaves and silvery seed spikes grow 3 to 6 feet tall. Zones 5 to 9.

Maiden grass (*Miscanthus* spp.)
Choose from an assortment of handsome arching grasses—adored for their beautiful nodding seed plumes in fall. They grow 4 to 6 feet tall. Most species hardy in Zones 5 to 9.

Pampas grass (*Cortaderia selloana*)
Wiry leaves and huge grass plumes grow up to 8 feet high. Zones 8 to 10.

Ravenna grass (*Erianthus ravennae*)
Long, slender leaves and grass plumes can reach 14 feet high. Zones 6 to 10.

Wipe Out Watering Worries with a Water Garden

Are you fed up with watering potted plants?

Instead of growing container plants and wondering if they've got too much or too little water, try an easy alternative that never requires watering! Grow aquatic plants. "Keeping water plants in containers is the simplest thing you can do," said Steve Frowine, vice president of horticulture for White Flower Farm in Litchfield, Connecticut. "You never have to worry about overwatering or underwatering them."

To set up a container with water plants, start by planting one water plant or small water lily in a pot about 12 inches in diameter, and two plants in pots that are 24 inches in diameter or wider. Be sure to use heavy clay soil, and top it with gravel to stabilize the soil. Set the potted water lilies or lotus plants on the bottom of a large decorative container filled with water. Steve uses glazed ceramic Chinese pots to hold his water plants. But you can substitute a plastic-lined half whiskey barrel or a large, thick plastic pot.

If you want to grow bog plants such as dwarf variegated sweet flag (*Acorus gramineus* var. *variegatus*) and spike rush (*Eleocharis montevidensis*), plant them in shallow pots and position them with the pots just below the water surface.

For more information on growing plants in water, see the Water Gardens entry.

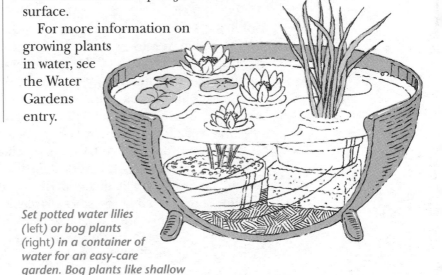

Set potted water lilies (left) or bog plants (right) in a container of water for an easy-care garden. Bog plants like shallow water, so prop them up on bricks.

103

FRUIT TREES

Dwarf Fruit Trees Save Time

SMALL TREES
YIELD FULL-SIZE
FRUIT CROPS
FAST

If you want lots of fruit but don't have much time for tree care, grow dwarf trees. You'll get the yield of a standard-size fruit tree and spend a fraction of the time on pruning and picking, says Murray Kereluk, Food Garden curator at the University of British Columbia Botanic Gardens in Vancouver. All parts of dwarf trees are easy to reach, so you won't have to struggle with heavy ladders or juggle long-handled tools. Pruning branches and picking fruits have never been easier.

Murray points out that smaller-than-standard fruit trees grow on dwarfing rootstocks. To come up with a dwarf tree, nursery workers graft a section of topgrowth from a large tree onto a root system that reduces its size. "Depending on what rootstock you use, you can grow a tree that's 6 feet tall at maturity," Murray says.

Check the catalogs of reputable mail-order nurseries to find out which rootstocks they offer and what size tree you'll get from each one. In apples, for example, two popular dwarfing rootstocks are MARK and EMLA 26—both produce trees that are 30 to 40 percent of full size. Small apple trees for containers are usually grown on EMLA 27 rootstock, which keeps plants at roughly 15 percent of full size. (See "Sources" on page 412 for nurseries that offer dwarf and superdwarf [also called miniature or minidwarf] fruit trees.) If you'd like to try growing fruit trees in containers, choose the smallest trees available and plant them in containers that are 20 inches in diameter or larger.

Most of the dwarfing rootstocks available do not form strong root systems, Murray says, so you'll need to stake your trees. (See "Stop Staking Trees" on page 359 for the proper staking method.) He feels that the heavy crops you'll get from dwarfs and the small amount of space and care they require more than make up for this extra chore.

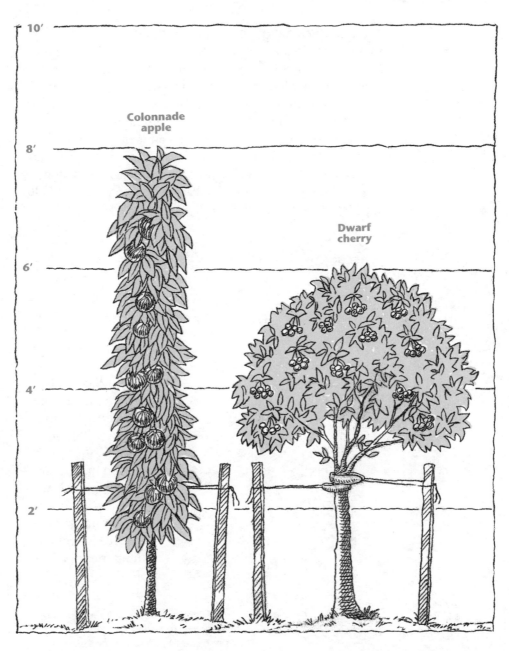

10'

8'

Colonnade
apple

Dwarf
cherry

6'

4'

2'

When you're short on time and space, dwarf fruit trees are the answer. For easy picking and pruning, choose trees that grow only 6 to 10 feet tall. For really small spaces, look for narrow trees like Stark Bro's Colonnade series of apples that grow only 2 feet wide. (See "Sources" on page 412 for ordering information.)

No More Mower Burn

Sick of scraping your tree trunks with the lawn mower? Take a look at what recycled tires can do for your fruit trees. Arnold and Ruth Gorneau, gardeners in West Chester, Pennsylvania, find that tires make easy, inexpensive, and super-effective tree guards that keep mulch in place and protect fruit tree trunks from mowers.

According to the Gorneaus, you can make two tree guards from one old car tire using the simple steps pictured on this page. If looks are important, turn each tire half inside out to hide the worn tread and make an attractive bell shape. Or leave the tire "as is," and place it upside down like a funnel. Fill the guard with mulch, but keep the 2 or 3 inches closest to the tree bare so insects won't have a place to hide. For easy fertilizing, you can fill the tire guard with composted manure instead of mulch and let rainwater do the work of making manure tea for your young trees.

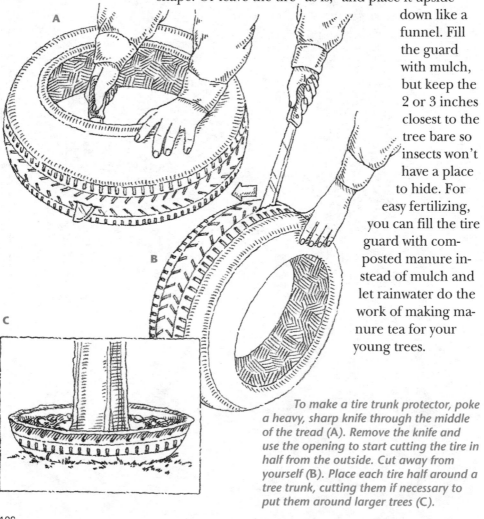

To make a tire trunk protector, poke a heavy, sharp knife through the middle of the tread (A). Remove the knife and use the opening to start cutting the tire in half from the outside. Cut away from yourself (B). Place each tire half around a tree trunk, cutting them if necessary to put them around larger trees (C).

Hungry Birds Help Fruit Trees

There's no need to mulch your fruit trees when you can get birds to do the job for you. Philadelphia gardener Libby J. Goldstein uses this trick so she can avoid weeding and watering. "I keep two bird feeders in the apple tree, which I fill just about daily with sunflower seeds," says Libby. "The finches, sparrows, and other birds are really sloppy eaters and just cover the ground with hulls and uneaten seeds."

Not only does the seed mulch keep water in the soil, but because sunflowers contain a chemical that's toxic to other young plants, the hulls and dropped seeds also keep weeds down. You'll find that trees are immune to the sunflowers' effect and so are earthworms. "Worms love life under the sunflower seed mulch—they're under there by the hundreds or maybe even thousands," says Libby.

Stop Pests and Sunscald with Drainpipe

Protect the tender bark of your newly planted fruit trees from gnawing rodents with inexpensive plastic drainpipe collars. "Mouse and vole damage is a real threat during the winter," says Jim Lindemann, who has more than a hundred apple trees in his McFarland, Wisconsin, home orchard. He keeps mice, voles, and rabbits at bay with homemade tree guards. Here's how Jim does it.

Buy 10-foot lengths of 4-inch-diameter plastic drainpipe. Cut the pipe in 1- to 1½-foot sections. Slit each section so you can slip it around the tree base, taking care not to damage the delicate new bark. The guards protect tree trunks from sunscald damage too.

Remove plastic tree guards in spring so they won't interfere with new growth and so you won't give insects a place to hide. The plastic is long-lasting so you can use the guards over and over again.

107

Fowl Play Takes Care of Orchard Weeds and Insects

Feed a flock of hungry fowl on the weeds and insects that attack your orchard. If you've got geese and chickens on hand, fence them in with your fruit trees. Use metal posts and chicken wire, and remember to pen your birds up at night so they won't become dinner for predators. (If you don't have birds, see the Insects and the Weeds and Weeding entries for other pest control ideas.)

DOMESTIC BIRDS ENJOY DOING YOUR DIRTY WORK

At Michigan State University, researchers are using African geese and White Rock and Barred Rock chickens to control weeds and insects in apple orchards. Researcher Sean Clark says, "Foraging geese consume large amounts of grasses and some broadleaf plants." Dandelions and broadleaf plantain are particular favorites. If nothing better is available, they also eat ragweed, lamb's-quarters, and seedling Canada thistles.

Sean estimates that you'd need 50 geese per acre to keep weeds down if there are no crops planted between your tree rows. If you grow vegetables between your fruit trees to save space and suppress weeds, you'll only need half as many birds. But remember, some vegetables work better with geese than others. Sean's found that geese leave green beans, broccoli, cauliflower, peppers, and tomatoes alone, but they will eat young squash, cucumber, and watermelon plants. To protect crops from geese, set out older transplants or train plants up trellises.

Chickens also eat some weeds but are much better at gobbling up insects that spend at least part of their lives on or below the soil surface. They devour Japanese beetles, may eat Colorado potato beetles, and may help control plum curculio if you put the chickens in the orchard in late spring or early summer. The chickens do a better job if the insects don't have a lot of weeds to hide in.

New Fruit from Old Trees

Is your fruit tree a loser? If you decide you don't like the kind of fruit tree in your yard, don't just change your mind, change your tree by grafting. "It's real frustrating to coddle a fruit tree for three or four years, then find out it's a cultivar that doesn't do very well," says Felder Rushing, coauthor of *Passalong Plants*. Rather than start over, Felder finds a cultivar that grows and fruits well in his area. Then he takes cuttings in the winter and grafts them to the old tree in spring.

Grafting is an age-old skill, but it takes practice. Often, you'll be able to find a local rose, camellia, or fruit expert who delights in grafting and is willing to help you. There are several different methods of grafting you can try, but Robert Seip, owner of Lennilea Nursery in Huffs Church, Pennsylvania, prefers bark grafts for starting a new cultivar on an existing fruit tree. (See the illustration on this page.) It's easy, he says, and the only tool you need is a sharp pocketknife. Here's what to do.

In late winter, cut 6-inch-long, ¼-inch-diameter dormant stems (called scions) from the new tree, making a long sloping cut on one side. Store the scion pieces in plastic bags in a refrigerator. In spring, when the sap begins to rise, cut off part of a 1-inch-diameter limb on the old tree (the rootstock plant). Place the side of the scion with the sloping cut against the cut limb and trace the outline with a sharp knife, cutting just into the bark. Pry out the cut bark and insert the scion into the slot where the bark was removed. Match the green growing parts (cambium) between the rootstock tree and the scion. Secure the scions with vinyl tape and coat cut surfaces with white latex paint.

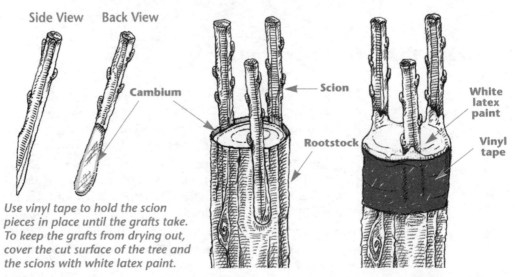

Side View   Back View

Cambium

Scion

Rootstock

White latex paint

Vinyl tape

Use vinyl tape to hold the scion pieces in place until the grafts take. To keep the grafts from drying out, cover the cut surface of the tree and the scions with white latex paint.

GARLIC

Oats Keep Garlic Weed-Free

There's no need to weed your garlic in spring, if you top it with a cover crop of oats in fall. The oats crowd out early spring weeds and improve your soil when they break down into organic matter, says Frank Pollock, a garlic grower in northeastern Pennsylvania.

On his Saylorsburg farm, Frank plants top-size garlic cloves in early October. (He believes that the largest cloves give the largest bulbs.) Once the garlic is in the ground, he sows a cover crop of oats over the area at a rate of 2 to 3 pounds per 1,000 square feet. "Garlic is not a great weed competitor," Frank notes, adding that it's important to use some method of weed prevention to keep your planting from being overrun.

You could use other cover crops, but Frank prefers oats because they get some growth in the fall and then get winter-killed. That creates a nice mulch for the garlic. The garlic will emerge through the mulch in late winter, but the dead oats will keep out the weeds for quite some time, Frank says.

Great Taste from Green Garlic

For garlic flavor fast, grow "green garlic." You'll be able to get several tasty harvests in one season. "It's a lot like growing green onions," explains Larry Butler, owner of certified-organic Boggy Creek Farm in Austin, Texas. He plants his garlic 1 inch deep and harvests it early—just 40 to 45 days after planting. By then the plants have four true leaves or are at least pencil-size. Pull the whole plant, Larry says. It will only have a little bit of a bulb, but you can use the whole thing in cooking. Is it tasty? "You bet!" says Larry, who recommends that you use green garlic the same way as you use green onions.

In central Texas, Larry plants green garlic—also called spring garlic—from October to March for a nearly endless supply. The soil is too warm for garlic to grow the rest of the year. In northern states, you can make the first planting of garlic after the ground thaws, and the last one about eight weeks before the ground usually freezes.

❧ QUICK FIX MIX

Great Green Garlic Shanks

What's an easy way to use green garlic? Fry up a batch of tempura-dipped garlic shanks. "They're to die for," says Larry Butler, owner of certified-organic Boggy Creek Farm in Austin, Texas. Garlic shanks are a favorite with chefs, and they'll be a favorite with you, too, if you try this simple recipe.

1 egg
water
1 cup flour
20 to 25 green garlic plants
vegetable oil for deep frying

To make tempura batter, beat the egg and mix in water until you have ⅔ cup of liquid. Stir in the flour and set aside.

Cut off the roots and tops of the green garlic plants so you're left with the shanks—the 3- to 5-inch-long section that starts at the garlic bulb and ends where the leaves start to branch. Split large shanks lengthwise (leave smaller pieces whole). Dip the shanks in the tempura batter and deep-fry them. Drain and serve hot.

Use the leftover garlic tops for garlic toast or bread. Finely chop the tops and saute them in butter. Spread the flavored butter over bread. No matter how you use garlic greens, Larry says "It's fabulous stuff!"

Once you taste garlic shanks, you'll be tempted to eat all of your garlic green. But leave a few plants alone to mature into bulb garlic next year.

Shank

Garlic Greens Are Tops

No garlic heads to dig, no cloves to peel. You can enjoy fresh garlic flavor earlier in the growing season and with much less effort by harvesting the leaves of your garlic instead of the heads, says Frank Pollock, a garlic grower in northeastern Pennsylvania.

Frank says he begins harvesting the garlic greens on his Saylorsburg farm in late April, when the foliage is about 8 inches tall. He cuts it back nearly to the ground. Frank makes from three to five cuttings each spring before letting the plants rest and rejuvenate until the next year, much as you'd do with asparagus or rhubarb.

To grow garlic greens, plant individual garlic cloves or entire small heads in the fall. Frank says he spaces his garlic greens plantings much closer together than the 5 inches he leaves between the cloves he plants for producing heads. The closer spacing makes it easy for him to harvest quickly, since he can cut along a solid row of greens. Frank recommends against harvesting greens from the garlic you're growing for heads: "It's self-defeating," he says. That's because cutting the foliage forces the plant to use up energy to replace the greens instead of putting it into producing a nice big head.

Set garlic cloves or small heads close together—just 2 inches apart—for quick and easy garlic green harvests. You'll get several cuttings each spring.

2"

The garlic you grow for greens does best with two doses of fertilizer per year, Frank says. He feeds his crop once at planting time, with bonemeal or a good organic bulb fertilizer. Then he feeds the crop again in spring with compost or another organic fertilizer.

Frank describes his garlic greens as a semiperennial crop, since they don't compete well with weeds. He says if you don't keep your garlic patch well mulched and weeded, you'll probably need to dig it up every three years or so to clean out the weeds.

Extra-Early (Garlic) Pesto

Garlic greens make a quick solution when you get a craving for pesto in early spring. Your basil harvest is still months away, but you can dine on delicious pesto if you substitute garlic greens for basil, using this recipe from Frank Pollock, a garlic grower in northeastern Pennsylvania.

2 to 3 cups chopped garlic greens

¼ cup grated Parmesan or ¼ cup ricotta cheese

olive oil

salt

pepper

Chop the garlic greens in a blender and mix in the cheese. Blend in olive oil until the mixture becomes a smooth paste. Add salt and pepper to taste and serve over pasta.

The amount of ingredients given here is just an estimate to get you started. Frank doesn't recommend any specific amounts, so feel free to experiment. "The proportions of all these things are to taste," he says.

Frank adds that there are lots of other ways to cook with garlic greens; he recommends adding them to soups and stir-fries.

Cheap Grocery Garlic Can Be Costly

You can buy grocery-store garlic and plant it—it's less expensive than garlic starts from a seed catalog—but the cents you save might not be worth the disease problems you can get. "You only need to buy garlic once, so why not spend a little more to be sure of what you're getting?" asks garlic grower John Mertus of Rumford, Rhode Island. You'll save all kinds of time and trouble in the long run.

Garlic can be infested with a variety of diseases, including basal rot, pink root, white rot, and John's personal bane, penicillium mold. The problems can be long-lasting. White rot can live in your soil for ten years even if you stop growing garlic or onion relatives there, John says. That's why states and countries that produce lots of garlic require inspections for imported garlic stock.

The problem with grocery-store garlic, John explains, is that no one inspects it. That's because they expect you to eat it, not plant it. But if you buy garlic from a seed catalog, they have to inspect it or buy certified disease-free garlic.

GERANIUMS

Brown-Bag Geraniums

Overwintering geraniums is easy. All you need are a few brown paper bags. And with this technique, you won't have to buy new geraniums each spring. It's a simple solution if you don't have room indoors to overwinter the plants in pots. "I don't have a sunny window to keep many plants in," says gardener David Alleman of Harrisonburg, Virginia. "That's why bagging geraniums in the fall and re-potting in the spring makes sense."

Here's David's technique: In the fall, dig out the plants and shake off most of the soil. Put the plants in one bag, and put another paper grocery bag over the top of the first bag. David keeps his bagged geraniums in the basement where it's cool but not too moist. The following spring, shake off the remaining dirt and cut the tops back to stubs. Cut back some of the roots, too, and you can repot fairly large plants into 4- or 6-inch pots.

Paula Schenone, a gardener in Henryville, Pennsylvania, has a slightly different method. She bags just the roots of

Dig and bag your geraniums before the first frost to keep them over winter. Try either of these two easy methods for great results: Bag the entire plant (A) or just the roots (B), and keep them cool.

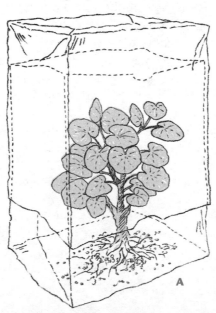

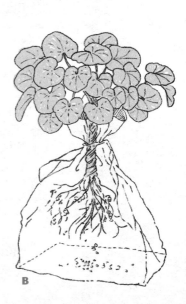

A   B

114

the geranium plants. She ties the bag loosely, leaving the plants exposed to the air. She warns, "Don't wash the soil off the roots! You'll never get it dry enough and you'll get rot." Paula lets the leaves stay on her plants; they eventually dry up and fall off.

She keeps her bagged geraniums in the ideal climate in her basement, which stays at around 40° to 45°F and about 30 to 50 percent relative humidity. In late winter, the plants sprout leaves even though you don't water them. Then it's time to pot them and bring them into light and warmth, Paula says, adding that she pulls off any remaining dead leaves and stems first.

More Plants with No Money Down

SAVE FAVORITE
GERANIUMS
WITH PLASTIC
OR MOTHERING

Free geraniums for your flower beds are a quick snip away. Just take cuttings from your favorite zonal and scented geraniums (*Pelargonium* spp.) in late summer and root them indoors over winter. It's simple—stick several 4- to 5-inch cuttings in a flat filled with a half-and-half mix of sand and sphagnum moss. Place the flat in a window that gets bright but indirect light, and keep the growing medium moist. You'll save money on new plants and use up a lot less space than overwintering grown plants. For maximum cutting success, try the techniques below, recommended by Philadelphia gardener Libby J. Goldstein.

Pack 'em in plastic. As soon as you take geranium cuttings, put them into a plastic bag with the leafy end in the bag and the stem sticking out. After a few days, the end of the stem will have developed a callus, which makes it root better and keeps it from rotting. The plastic holds in enough moisture so the leafy end won't wilt, Libby says. Once they're calloused, remove the plastic from the cuttings and put them in a growing medium.

Take finicky cuttings to Mother. Stick cuttings of scented geraniums that are hard to root into the pot with the mother plant. "I don't know if the mother plant produces special hormones or what," Libby says, "but it does work." Libby had a hard time rooting 'Mabel Grey' scented geraniums, but when she put the cuttings in with the mother plant, they rooted right away.

GRAPES

Stick It to Grape Pests

You can grow pest-free grapes. Set up yellow sticky traps so sucking insects won't have a chance to ruin your grapes. A California company markets a sticky yellow tape that's easy to set up in the garden.

The tape, called Hopperfinder Monitoring Tape, is a 6-inch-wide UV-resistant yellow band of plastic that's covered with a thin coating of a nondrying adhesive. "It was originally intended to trap grape and variegated leafhoppers in vineyards," explains Paul Wulf, owner of Entosphere, which sells the tape. "But then I started getting calls from vegetable growers and greenhouses, because it can be used to control aphids, whiteflies, thrips, and cucumber beetles—any pest that's attracted to yellow." It's very good in a garden setting, Paul says, if it's set up correctly.

It works by trapping insects before they can lay eggs, so their populations get smaller and smaller with each generation. To be effective, Paul says, the tape should be placed a foot or two above the ground, and it should be attached to supports that are no more than 8 to 10 feet apart. Paul

Protect your grapes from leafhoppers with strips of sticky yellow tape. The yellow-colored tape attracts the insects but won't let them go.

suggests stapling the tape to wooden stakes (using the stapling strips that come with the tape) or wrapping it around metal poles. With either method, the tape needs to be attached so it stays open; otherwise, it will fold onto itself and form a skinny band that's too narrow to trap anything.

Paul warns that the glue that covers the tape isn't the most pleasant thing to have on your hands. He recommends wearing thin surgical gloves (available in drugstores) to install the tape. If you get the glue on you, wash it off with a waterless hand cleaner, since the glue doesn't dissolve in water—a good thing during rainy weather.

Grape Growing Is Easy

LET GRAPES GO
—THEY'RE
BOUND TO
GROW

Plant grapevines and you'll have grapes—that's all there is to it, says Sally Roth, coauthor of *Rodale's Successful Organic Gardening: Companion Planting*. Sally says she thinks people worry too much about grapes and deny themselves a truly easy-to-grow fruit. Here are her simple tips for growing bumper crops of homegrown grapes.

Choose disease-resistant cultivars. Check nursery and seed catalogs and your local cooperative extension office for grapes that resist anthracnose, black rot, botrytis, and mildew. "If you choose a resistant grape, you don't even have to think about disease problems," Sally says.

Don't sweat the pruning. It doesn't really matter how you prune, you're going to get more grapes than you need anyway, assures Sally. "If you need to do some kind of pruning to satisfy your soul, you can cut the vines back by a third of their length in late winter," she says. Sally notes that pruning is really only necessary to confine the grapes to the structure you want them to grow on and to let light into the vines to stimulate fruiting.

Leave the extras for the birds. When you've had your fill of grapes, just leave the rest on the vine, says Sally. Grapes ripen right around the time of the fall migration. The grapes you don't want will attract brown thrashers, cedar waxwings, grosbeaks, mockingbirds, rose-breasted tanagers, thrushes, and many others.

GREEN MANURE

Mix Green Manures for Maximum Results

More is better when it comes to planting green manure crops to improve your soil. "Sowing two or three kinds of green manure crops at the same time gives the soil more balanced nutrition," says community gardener Galen Bollinger of Austin, Texas. It doesn't take any more time than sowing one type of green manure, and if one type doesn't germinate well, you still end up with a crop.

Robert Kourik, author of *Designing and Maintaining Your Edible Landscape—Naturally,* says the key to green manure mixes is using annual grasses *and* legumes (plants that can gather and use nitrogen from the air). He says most people get all excited and plant only legume crops for the nitrogen, but the grasses and grains have lots to offer too. They produce more growth in a shorter amount of time than the legumes, and that means you're putting more fiber and organic matter into your soil.

You can blend your own green manure mix (see "Quick Fix Mix" on the opposite page for a good combination), or buy a preblended mix (see "Sources" on page 412 for mail-order suppliers of green manure seeds).

Once you've got the seed, planting is simple, Robert says. You can plant green manures in spring, summer, or fall—whenever you have the time or a gap between crops. To get green manures off to a good start, prepare the soil well, as you would if you were planting a root crop like carrots. Till or dig the planting area to loosen the soil, then rake the ground smooth to create a good seedbed, and broadcast the seed. You can pull the back of the rake over the seeds to cover them with soil or bury them with a light layer of compost or straw mulch.

GIVE YOUR SOIL
A BOOST WITH
GRASSES AND
LEGUMES

If you plant your green manure mix in spring, let the plants grow until just before the legumes bloom. Then turn or till the plants into the soil and wait two to four weeks to give the plant material time to break down and release nitrogen. Next, you can plant tomatoes or other hot-weather crops. Or wait until fall and plant a cool-weather green manure crop like winter rye (*Secale cereale*), which will protect your soil from drying winds during the winter and add more organic matter to your soil when you turn it under in spring.

❧ QUICK FIX MIX

Four-Green Blend

These four plants make a perfect green manure mix—one that works better than any single green manure crop for improving soil. This recipe makes a good spring-planting mix for most parts of the country. It's from Mark Fenton, co-owner of Peaceful Valley Farm Supply Company (a mail-order firm in Grass Valley, California).

20% Austrian peas (*Pisum sativum*)
40% broad beans, also known as
    fava or bell beans (*Vicia faba*)
30% hairy vetch (*Vicia villosa*)
10% oats (*Avena sativa*)

Mix the seeds together according to the proportions listed above. For example, if you need 10 pounds of mix, combine 2 pounds of Austrian peas, 4 pounds of broad beans, 3 pounds of hairy vetch, and 1 pound of oat seeds. Sow your green manure mix in spring, using 3 to 5 pounds of seed per 1,000 square feet of garden space. (Treat legume seed with an inoculant—a powder that contains bacteria that help the plants "fix" or store nitrogen—before planting.)

Mark says green manure blends are great for attracting beneficial insects, if you let the plants flower. Because the plants flower at different times, they provide food for beneficials for a longer period of time than a single crop.

Once the plants are in full bloom, but before they set seed, till them into the soil to take advantage of the nitrogen in the leaves and roots.

Great Soil in 1 Growing Season

What builds soil faster than compost? Green manures! According to Robert Kourik, author of *Designing and Maintaining Your Edible Landscape—Naturally,* "You'll get more rapid soil development from planting green manure crops than from adding compost." Most people don't have enough compost to build up their soil quickly, and that's where a green manure crop like buckwheat (*Fagopyrum esculentum*) comes in. The seeds are available at any farm supply store and they're cheap—especially compared to buying loads of topsoil!

Whether you're preparing a new garden site or trying to improve an old site fast, here's what to do.

GROW BETTER

SOIL IN A HURRY

WITH BUCK-

WHEAT

1 In spring, plant a crop of buckwheat (use 2 pounds of seed per 1,000 square feet of garden).

2 Let the buckwheat grow 6 to 8 inches high. You could let the plants get as tall as 1 foot, but it's easier to work with them when they're shorter.

3 Use a shovel to turn the buckwheat into your soil, but don't make lots of work out of it. Just get the green matter into the ground—you don't have to do lots of digging or chopping.

As soon as the green manure is turned under, you can repeat the process, planting buckwheat, letting it grow, and turning it into your soil when it gets 6 inches tall. The more times you plant and turn under buckwheat, the better your soil will be, so keep planting and turning the buckwheat into the ground until frost. You'll be able to plant a new buckwheat crop once a month or so. By the next growing season, your garden soil will be in fantastic shape.

Here's how it works. Soil microorganisms break the plant matter down into humus which adds nutrients and fiber to your garden. Plus, while the plants are growing, their roots help break up clay soils and create air spaces for better drainage. In sandy soils, humus helps hold the crumbly grains of sand together so your soil retains moisture better. So, no matter what kind of soil you have, you can improve it with repeated plantings of buckwheat.

To improve your garden soil fast, (1) sow buckwheat in spring, (2) let the plants grow 6 to 8 inches tall, and (3) turn them into the soil with a spade, shovel, or tiller. Replant more buckwheat immediately and start the process over again. Keep at it, planting and tilling in buckwheat crops until frost.

GROUNDCOVERS

Shortcuts for Shady Places

CREATE A CARE-
FREE SHADE
GARDEN WITH
GROUNDCOVERS

If your flowers are fading and your lawn is losing ground to weeds, turn your shady yard into a trouble-free shade garden. "Many people complain about shady yards," says Martha Oliver, owner of The Primrose Path mail-order nursery in Scottdale, Pennsylvania. "But they're easier to maintain than sunny ones, if you choose adaptable plants." Martha offers this creative design idea to give your shady spot a low-maintenance makeover.

First, imagine the trail of a deer as it meanders through your yard. It twists from side to side as the deer explores and moves around obstacles like trees. Mark the trail with stakes and install it before you do any planting—it's the starting point for your garden.

Next, Martha suggests planting clusters of groundcovers at intervals along the path and letting them spread. What you're after is a billowing effect with different types of groundcovers growing into each other. Once the plants have grown, you can forget about mowing and dead-heading flowers. Hardy groundcovers can take care of themselves. And since everything grows more slowly in the shade, you won't have to fight to keep control.

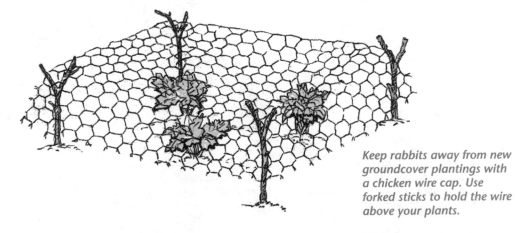

Keep rabbits away from new groundcover plantings with a chicken wire cap. Use forked sticks to hold the wire above your plants.

Turn your shady yard into a garden by planting masses of groundcovers beside a meandering path. The twisting path draws you into the landscape to see what's around the next bend.

Dual-Duty Groundcovers

*P*lanting groundcovers is a great way to cut down on mowing chores. Choose flowering perennials as groundcovers and you can add color to your landscape at the same time. It's like getting a blooming garden without the maintenance of a mixed perennial border or the yearly planting chores of an annual bed. Use a string trimmer or mower if you get the urge to tidy up tall plantings in early spring.

ALLEGHENY FOAMFLOWER (*Tiarella cordifolia*)

This maintenance-free woodland wildflower is perfect under trees and shrubs. It's especially nice mixed with medium-size green-and-white hostas. Low mats of heart-shaped to triangular apple green leaves choke out weeds; 6- to 10-inch spikes of fluffy, white, sweetly fragrant flowers appear in spring. Plant 18 to 24 inches apart. Zones 3 to 8.

ASTILBES (*Astilbe* spp. and hybrids)

Astilbes will thrive almost anywhere—sun to full shade—as long as the soil stays moist. The feathery white, red, or pink flower plumes appear in early to late summer on 6-inch- to 4-foot-tall stems—height and bloom time depend on the species or cultivar you choose. The dark, glossy, fernlike foliage is handsome all season. Plant 18 to 24 inches apart. Zones 3 to 9.

'BIOKOVO' CRANESBILL
(*Geranium* × *cantabrigiense* 'Biokovo')

Masses of pale pink to white 1-inch-wide flowers cover these 4- to 6-inch-tall mounded plants in late spring and early summer. The deeply cut, apple-scented foliage turns red in winter. Like most cranesbills, this plant thrives in full sun to light shade and isn't picky about soil. Plant 18 inches apart. Zones 4 to 8.

CREEPING JACOB'S LADDER (*Polemonium reptans*)

Use your imagination and you'll see how this plant got its name—the divided leaves do look like small ladders. They grow on 8- to 16-inch-tall mounded plants that are topped with ½-inch-wide sky blue flowers in spring and summer. These spreading plants grow in full sun or partial shade and like evenly moist, humusy soil. Space plants 9 to 12 inches apart. Zones 2 to 8.

CRESTED IRIS (*Iris cristata*)

This native woodland iris is perfect for partial shade but will grow in full sun if the soil is moist. The fragrant blue, violet, or white 1½- to 2-inch-wide flowers appear in spring on short stalks. Handsome bladelike 4- to 8-inch-long leaves stay green all summer and turn yellow in fall. Plant 12 inches apart. Zones 3 to 9.

GREEN AND GOLD (*Chrysogonum virginianum*)

This cheerful wildflower blooms happily in partial or full shade. You can plant it in full sun, but only if it's in a spot that stays constantly moist. The 1- to 1½-inch-wide starry yellow flowers cover the 6- to 10-inch-tall plants in spring and appear sporadically throughout the summer. Green and gold is evergreen in the South. Plant 12 to 18 inches apart. Zones 5 to 9.

HARDY ICE PLANT (*Delosperma cooperi*)

If you need an easy plant for a sunny, dry site, try this tropical-looking succulent. It's extremely drought-, wind-, and salt-tolerant. Deep rose-pink 2- to 3-inch-wide flowers blanket the low (6 to 8 inches tall) blue-green foliage all summer long. Plant 12 to 18 inches apart. Zones 5 to 9.

HEARTLEAF BERGENIA (*Bergenia cordifolia*)

Big bold 10-inch-tall evergreen leaves are the main attraction for this plant, but 5- to 6-inch-long sprays of pink, rose, or white flowers are showy in spring. The glossy leaves make a nice groundcover in partial shade or sun and take on an attractive reddish tinge in winter. Protect leaves with hay or straw mulch in cold no-snow areas. Remove weather-worn foliage in very early spring. Plant 18 inches apart. Zones 3 to 9.

PERENNIAL SWEET PEA (*Lathyrus latifolius*)

This vigorous sprawler happily climbs dry sunny slopes where even gardeners fear to tread—or push a lawn mower. Sprays of pink, white, or red pealike flowers cover the blue-green 18-inch-tall tangle of 10-foot vines all summer long. If you want a tidy planting, rake off old vines in winter, but if you don't mind the natural look, leave old vines be and let next year's growth clamber over them. Plant seeds 2 feet apart. Zones 3 to 9.

PLUMBAGO OR LEADWORT (*Ceratostigma plumbaginoides*)

You'll get a solid 6- to 12-inch-tall mat if you plant this tough perennial in full sun or partial shade. Clusters of 1-inch-wide intensely blue flowers start in early summer and often continue until frost. The glossy leaves turn bright red in fall. Prune out winter-damaged stems in spring before the new growth sprouts. Plant 18 inches apart. Zones 5 to 9.

SHOWY EVENING PRIMROSE (*Oenothera speciosa*)

A large sunny area is all it takes to make this plant happy—sometimes too happy. It spreads so well it can become a nuisance, so keep it far from garden beds or use it in areas surrounded by concrete or paving. Also, look for new cultivars that are less invasive. The 1- to 2-foot-tall plants have a sprawling habit. They're crowned with pink or white 2- to 4-inch-wide cup-shaped flowers throughout the summer. Space plants 2 to 3 feet apart. Zones 4 to 9.

PROVEN PLANTS
FOR TOUGH CLIMATES

Finicky ornamentals may wither and die when severe weather hits, but native plants usually survive tough times. According to James Kraemer, owner of Silver Springs Nursery in Moyie Springs, Idaho, once a native plant gets established, it can handle conditions like drought and extreme cold better than an exotic plant (one that's introduced from another country). Natives have built-in adaptations to their habitats that make them particularly maintenance-free. For example, when water is scarce, a native plant like bearberry goes dormant, but an exotic like Japanese pachysandra will try to keep growing and will die without irrigation.

"Compared to common perennials, native plants are a dream come true," says James. "There's no need for pruning or deadheading, and you don't have to divide them every five years." Try some of James's favorites.

Bearberry (*Arctostaphylos uva-ursi*)
This drought-resistant shrub grows 1 foot tall but its stems may stretch as wide as 5 or 6 feet. It has light pink flowers in spring that are followed by persistent red berries, plus the evergreen foliage turns red in fall. Plant in sun to partial shade in any type of soil. Zones 2 to 7.

Bunchberry (*Cornus canadensis*)
This carpet-forming groundcover grows only 6 inches tall. It has white dog-woodlike flowers that are followed by red berries. Plant it in partial to full shade in moist acid soil. Zones 2 to 6.

Cascades mahonia (*Mahonia nervosa*)
The leathery evergreen leaves that cover this plant have spiny edges. They look attractive year-round if you plant this low-growing (1- to 2-foot-tall) shrub in partial shade in a spot out of the wind. Bright yellow fragrant flowers bloom in 8-inch-long clusters in spring and are followed by small dark blue fruits. Zones 5 to 9.

Creeping mahonia (*Mahonia repens*)
This low-growing (6 to 12 inches tall) shrub has yellow spring flowers and blue berries. The evergreen leaves have spiny teeth along the edges and turn an attractive purple color in winter. Plant it in sun or partial shade in any soil type. Zones 5 to 9.

Paxistima (*Paxistima canbyi*)
Try this groundcover where you need a low-growing (8 to 12 inches tall) evergreen. The yewlike foliage turns bronze in fall. It grows in shade or sun— as long as it gets plenty of water—in a wide range of soils. Zones 3 to 7.

Twinflower (*Linnaea borealis*)
Trailing branches form an evergreen mat just 4 to 6 inches tall in cool, partially shady areas. The leaves are small (1 inch long) and the flowers are tiny but fragrant. The pink blooms appear in summer and are followed by yellow fruits. This plant likes well-drained peaty soil. Zones 2 to 3.

Wintergreen (*Gaultheria procumbens*)
It's hard to resist breaking off dark green leaves from this 4- to 8-inch-tall groundcover for a wiff of their fresh scent. Pinkish white flowers bloom in spring and are followed by scarlet berries. Set plants in partial to full shade in an acidic soil. Zones 3 to 8.

Prepare the Site and Then Sit Back

There's only one shortcut to preparing a site for groundcovers and that's do your homework first. "You'll be home free once the groundcovers take off," says Bob Gutmann, a wholesale grower in Cornelius, Oregon. "It's so much easier to prepare the site when it's open than to weed around growing plants." He recommends that you clear the site of weeds, amend the soil for the type of groundcover you've selected, and use an organic mulch like chopped leaves to keep weeds away and help the soil hold moisture.

Bob offers this additional solution for particularly weedy sites. Try spacing the groundcover plants twice as close as recommended. The spacing charts in books and mail-order catalogs generally aim for complete coverage within three years. Obviously, if you can fill the area in faster, there won't be as much opportunity for weeds. "Groundcovers are communal plants, so they won't suffer from dense planting," Bob says. "The only drawback is cost."

Bring Home Groundcover Bargains

Large-scale groundcover plantings can set you back big bucks, so it pays to find ways to squeeze your groundcover dollars. Try these tips from Gene Dickson, owner of Prentiss Court Ground Covers in Greenville, South Carolina.

• Dig your own groundcovers from a friend's overgrown garden. Offer to remulch the bed in return.

• Buy plants in flats instead of individual pots.

• Buy large (gallon-size) plants and divide them into smaller sections.

• Watch for end-of-the-season bargains.

• Buy from companies that sell bareroot groundcovers, which are much cheaper to produce and ship than potted plants. You may have to search a little for bareroot plants—most nurseries carry potted groundcovers. (See "Sources" on page 412 for suggestions.)

Cover the Ground with Clematis

When you've got lots of ground to cover, forget about slow-growing perennials and let a clematis vine do the job. "Most people think you have to trellis clematis vines," says Bob Gutmann, a wholesale grower in Cornelius, Oregon. "But many are happy to crawl through a perennial border or spread out as an unusual groundcover."

Bob recommends planting summer-blooming types, since they ramble the best. Good candidates include those in the Viticella group—they have smaller blossoms than the ever-popular Jackman clematis (*Clematis* × *jackmanii*) but bloom profusely and come in a wider color range. Some to choose from include 'Alba Luxurians' (white), 'Etoile Violette' (violet-purple with yellow anthers), 'Madame Julia Correvon' (red), 'Polish Spirit' (rich purple-blue), 'Purpurea Plena Elegans' (double violet-purple), and 'Venosa Violacea' (white with purple veins).

Clematis are healthy plants, so you'll probably never have to worry about diseases, adds Bob. But if clematis wilt is a problem for you, avoid the large-flowered early-spring bloomers. Susceptible cultivars include 'Henryi', 'Nelly Moser', and 'Ramona'. Instead, choose a clematis that blooms later in the summer—Jackman and other late-bloomers are resistant. Or pick a cultivar or variety of the small-flowered spring-bloomers (April through June), like anemone clematis (*C. montana*), which are also wilt-

Clematis vines mix well with other groundcovers like creeping juniper. They won't over-power established plants and the blooms make a nice surprise when they appear in the foliage.

resistant. Try 'Grandiflora' (white), 'Marjorie' (pink-yellow), 'Pink Perfection' (deep pink), the variety rubens (pink), 'Rubens Superba' (rich pink), 'Tetrarose' (rose), and the variety wilsonii (white).

Free Groundcovers from Houseplants

TURN YOUR

FAVORITE

HOUSEPLANTS

INTO GARDEN

PLANTS

Need a low-cost groundcover for a shady spot, or a quick way to fill gaps in a new perennial garden? Tina James, a landscape consultant in Reisterstown, Maryland, has discovered that houseplants are ideal. Vining plants like ivies (*Hedera* spp.), philodendrons (*Philodendron* spp.), Swedish ivy (*Plectranthus australis*), and wandering Jews (*Zebrina* spp.) love damp shady corners, Tina explains.

Use 2- to 6-inch-long cuttings and don't even bother to root them before planting them outdoors. Spread an inch of moist growing mix (leaf mold or potting soil enhanced with compost) over the planting area—just enough to cover the rooting ends of the cuttings an inch or so. "Remember to keep the area moist for several weeks," Tina says, "and by midsummer, that bare spot will look like a tropical jungle!"

Spider plants are one of Tina's favorite houseplant groundcovers since the plantlets—those curly appendages hanging from the mother plant—already have roots. She clips the babies from their streamers and plants them in moist soil in sun or shade. As with any plant moved from indoor growing conditions, protect them from sun and temperature extremes for a few days until they harden off.

Other popular shady groundcover recruits include begonias, coleus, crotons, flame violet (*Episcia cupreata*), oxalis, and polka-dot plant. Most tropical houseplants are jungle natives and will thrive in moist shady locations, so have fun experimenting. True, unless you live in a frost-free climate, tropical plants won't survive the winter. But the price is right, and they're ready for planting at a moment's notice.

Speedily Spreading Groundcover Shrubs

*M*any shrubs that spread by creeping underground stems make splendid large-scale groundcovers. And because you need fewer plants to start with, they're less work to install and often less expensive than more traditional groundcovers.

Use groundcover shrubs whenever you have to cover large difficult areas of your landscape, like areas too steep or wet to mow. Keep these spreading shrubs in place by mowing along their boundaries every few weeks. If suckers get established where you don't want them, cut or dig them out.

AMERICAN ELDERBERRY (*Sambucus canadensis*)

If you want to cover a moist spot, this multistemmed shrub will do the trick in a hurry. Its white flat-topped flower clusters open in summer and completely cover the plant. Birds love the purple-black fruits that appear in fall—you'll love them too if you like making elder wine, preserves, or jellies. Coarse compound leaves and 6- to 12-foot-tall sprawling branches give this shrub an informal look. Plant 8 to 10 feet apart. Zones 3 to 9.

FRAGRANT SUMAC (*Rhus aromatica* 'Gro-Low')

Here's an incredibly tough, drought-tolerant, problem-free shrub that makes a great groundcover for dry, sandy, or rocky slopes. Small flower spikes open in early spring, before the leaves emerge—they're followed by clusters of fuzzy red fruits. Glossy fragrant leaves cover the 1½- to 2-foot-tall bushes and turn fiery orange in autumn. Plant 6 to 8 feet apart. Zones 3 to 9.

JAPANESE KERRIA (*Kerria japonica* 'Pleniflora')

This spring-flowering shrub looks nice interplanted with white bridalwreath spirea (*Spiraea prunifolia*). Its golden yellow double 1- to 2-inch-wide flowers last until early summer. The slender, arching 4- to 6-foot-long lime green stems are lovely in winter, and the dainty lime green leaves look fresh all season. Remove dead stems in early spring. Plant 8 feet apart in a shaded, well-drained spot. Zones 4 to 9.

RED-OSIER DOGWOOD
(*Cornus sericea*, also known as *C. stolonifera*)

This multistemmed native shrub tolerates a wide range of soil and moisture conditions—including moist sites. Flat clusters of creamy flowers bloom in early summer. White fruits appear in late summer and are set off by medium green leaves (some cultivars have variegated leaves) that turn purplish in fall. The 4- to 9-foot-tall stems are brilliant red, coral, or yellow in winter. For the best color (but no flowers or fruit), cut the stems to the ground in early spring. Space 8 to 10 feet apart. Zones 2 to 8.

RUGOSA ROSE (*Rosa rugosa*)

The upright prickly branches of this shrub grow 4 to 6 feet tall and make a good barrier where foot traffic is a problem. Choose a sunny spot and you'll get good growth results, since rugosa roses are disease-resistant and drought-, wind-, and salt-tolerant. The single or double pink, red, yellow, or white flowers are fragrant and bloom all summer. Crinkled apple green foliage turns yellow, bright orange, and purple in fall and sets off the large orange-red hips. Plant 6 to 10 feet apart. Zones 2 to 7.

ST.-JOHN'S-WORT (*Hypericum calycinum*)

Stems of this low shrub grow just 1 foot tall and are covered with semievergreen leaves that turn reddish purple in fall. Plant in sandy or well-drained soil in sun or shade. Bright yellow flowers bloom all summer and look like 2-inch-wide puff balls. The stems may die back in severe winters, but they'll resprout quickly from the roots. Mow the plants to the ground in early spring if you want to encourage fresh new growth. Plant 1½ feet apart. Zones 5 to 8.

SUMMERSWEET (*Clethra alnifolia*)

This shrub is a good bet if you've got a moist acid soil in sun or partial shade. It grows 3 to 8 feet tall, depending on the cultivar you choose and the amount of moisture it gets. Long spikes of honey-scented pink or white flowers bloom in summer into fall and are followed by dark brown peppercorn-like seedpods. Leathery green leaves turn gold in fall. Plant 6 to 8 feet apart. Zones 3 to 9.

SWEET FERN (*Comptonia peregrina*)

Here's a perfect choice for extremely dry and poor soils—this native shrub is one of the few nonleguminous plants that can fix its own nitrogen. The flowers are barely noticeable, but you'll enjoy the fernlike dark green delightfully fragrant leaves set on slender, erect 2- to 5-foot-long stems. Plant 4 feet apart. Zones 2 to 6.

URAL FALSE SPIREA (*Sorbaria sorbifolia*)

Cover meadows or banks with this quick-growing multistemmed shrub. It does best in moist but well-drained soils in sun or partial shade. The 5- to 10-foot-tall plants are covered with showy 6- to 8-inch-long plumes of small white flowers in early summer. New leaves are tinged red, then turn apple green. Plant 8 to 10 feet apart. Zones 2 to 8.

WINTER JASMINE (*Jasminum nudiflorum*)

Try this trailing shrub on sunny or partly shaded slopes—it makes a nice combination with rockspray cotoneaster (*Cotoneaster horizontalis*). The waxy yellow ¾- to 1-inch-wide starlike flowers open in early spring before leaves appear on the slender 2- to 5-foot-long stems. Lustrous, deep green leaves are beautiful all summer long. Plant 3 to 4 feet apart. Zones 6 to 10.

Lift Leaves Off Groundcovers

When leaves fall on your groundcovers, it can be a real mess. And it's frustrating trying to rake leaves out of your groundcovers and woodland plants without damaging them. David E. Benner, president of Benner's Gardens in New Hope, Pennsylvania, has come up with a way to avoid raking altogether. He discovered, and now sells, a special plastic mesh that keeps plants clean. (See "Sources" on page 412 for ordering information.)

David says he used to spend nearly 1,000 hours each fall clearing fallen leaves from the groundcovers that blanket his 2-acre woodland property. Not anymore. Now, when leaves start to fall, he covers his gardens and moss paths with a piece of lightweight long-lasting plastic mesh. He ignores the mesh until November, then just rolls it up and dumps it out on his compost pile. Even when filled with leaves, the plastic mesh is very light, David says, and his one-time fall cleanup is a breeze.

The mesh makes a wonderful solution for moss-covered areas, David explains, because you don't risk tearing up your plantings with a rake. He lays ¼-inch mesh over the moss pathways in his garden and walks over it all the time. "It just lays flat on the moss, and it's no problem," he says. In addition to collecting leaves, this mesh captures a healthy harvest of acorns that would otherwise sprout in the moss. And, David adds, the mesh works just as well for cleaning fallen

Cover hard-to-rake plants with 5- to 6-foot-long sections of plastic netting to make fall cleanup easy. Simply roll up the mesh after leaves fall. Pick a dry day when the leaves weigh the least.

leaves off of groundcovers such as pachysandra and peri-winkle (*Vinca* spp.).

Over his rock garden, azaleas, and other shrubs, he lays green 1- by 2-inch netting. It also traps the falling leaves and is virtually invisible when plants are viewed from a short distance away.

Control Groundcovers with Clay Flue Tiles

INVASIVE
GROUNDCOVERS
CAN'T ESCAPE
THESE "POTS"

Overenthusiastic groundcovers like mint don't understand boundaries. But you won't have to spend time wacking them back if you plant them in clay or heavy-duty plastic pots and set them in your garden, container and all. Or try this control method from Cynthia McKenney, a horticulture teacher at Texas Tech University in Lubbock. "I plant unruly plants inside clay flue tiles that act like bottomless containers," she says. They come in different lengths and widths, so you can choose whichever tiles suit your site.

Cynthia prefers flue tiles because they look attractive, but any handy sturdy container will do, even an old washtub. (See "Keep Ornamental Grasses in Bounds" on page 240.) Sink your container into the ground so only an inch or two shows and set the plant inside. The roots will stay put instead of wandering all over the garden and other plants.

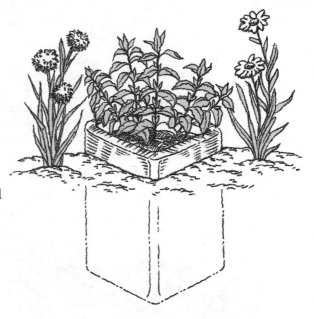

Clay flue tiles are great for keeping invasive plants in bounds. Since the tiles have no bottoms, you never have to worry about drainage—even during heavy rains.

133

HARVESTING

Mail Your Tools to the Garden

There's no postage due with this neat tool storage trick. You can save yourself dozens of trips between the garden and kitchen this summer by installing a mailbox near your flowers and vegetables. "A mailbox makes a great storage place for harvest tools and containers," says Diane Relf, extension specialist in consumer horticulture at Virginia Tech.

Mailboxes are attractive, inexpensive, and easy to install, so you can put one or several in your garden to keep all of your harvest supplies dry and handy. The other nice feature of a mailbox is that you can decorate it to match your garden style. But if a mailbox doesn't suit you, or you'd rather not add any new structures to your garden, look for existing outdoor storage places. A gazebo, toolshed, playhouse, garage, or even a plastic trash barrel can serve as a supply station.

At harvesttime, stock your storage place with plastic bags and containers, berry baskets, paper towels to dampen and wrap around the stems of cut flowers, gloves, scissors, and pruners. Add whatever harvest supplies you think are essential: a favorite knife, a scrub brush for washing vegetables, newspaper to wrap flowers in. One thing that doesn't belong in the mailbox are seeds. "They can cook in there since it gets hot fast," Diane says.

A mailbox makes a great storage place for harvest tools. Add a notebook and pen to your stash to keep track of harvesting dates and the names of your favorite plants.

A Potpourri of Harvesting Tips

Make it easy on yourself at harvesttime by using quick-pick techniques and the right containers. Next season, try planting easy-to-pick plants too, and you'll finish harvesting faster and with even less effort. Try these fast and easy ideas from speedy harvesters.

Susan McClure, author of *The Harvest Gardener,* uses these four techniques to reduce her harvest workload.

Plant pole beans instead of bush beans. It's easier to stand and pick pole beans than stoop to reach bush types. Your back muscles will thank you.

Grow colorful crops. Try pole beans with purple or yellow pods, for example. You won't waste time hunting through the foliage for ripe beans.

HARVESTING IS EASY WHEN YOU KNOW THESE QUICK TRICKS

Take a cooler to the garden. Add ice or refreezable ice packs and cold sodas to the cooler when you're ready to harvest lettuce, spinach, or other delicate leafy crops. Store your greens on ice to keep them from wilting while you work, and use the sodas to keep yourself from wilting. Use a large cooler and you can haul your entire harvest inside in one trip.

Treat leafy herbs like cut flowers. Place herbs like basil and parsley in a glass of water after you cut them—they'll hold their texture and flavor longer. Use just enough water to keep stems wet and leaves dry. There's no need to refrigerate your herb "bouquet."

Here are two more harvest tips from Hal and Suzanne Taylor, who grow and pick large quantities of crops at their River Side Homestead Farm in Cinnaminson, New Jersey.

Leave stems in the garden. Pinch off beans and snow peas with your fingers, right where the pod meets the stem. Destemming in the garden saves a step when it's time to cook your vegetables.

Fit your container to your crop. For small berries, choose a shallow container so the weight of the top berries won't bruise those below. Use a peach basket for large vegetables such as eggplant, peppers, and tomatoes. The basket's flat bottom makes it stand firmly without tipping, and it's easy to carry, even when full. Most farm supply stores carry peach baskets and they'll only cost you a couple of dollars.

Hands-On Harvesting

Pick twice as fast when you use both hands. Whether you're picking fruits or vegetables, a harvesting container that leaves both your hands free is like having an extra helper along. Sam Benowitz, owner of Raintree Nursery in Morton, Washington, recommends a canvas apple-picking bag for quick harvesting. Since the bag hangs from your shoulders, it lets you use both hands for picking and saves you "all kinds of time," Sam says.

Picking bags offer features that speed up the harvest and make it more comfortable. Look for wide or padded shoulder straps that are easy to put on and take off. Bags with bottom openings let you empty your harvest into another container without removing the shoulder straps, so you can get back to your harvest fast.

If the fruits and vegetables you're harvesting are smaller and lighter than apples, try picking into a lightweight bag or bucket tied to a cord around your waist. You'll be able to strip berries off bushes, or pluck cherry tomatoes off of tomato plants in a two-handed hurry. The bucket will tug at your waist as you fill it—a good reminder that it's time to empty the container to keep fragile fruits like raspberries from getting smashed.

For quick-pick harvests, choose containers that let you use both hands to pick. Try an apple-picking bag (left) for large produce, or a berry basket (below) for small fruits.

Quick Veggie Cleanup Keeps Soil Outside

You can cut out kitchen cleanup chores if you wash and air dry your produce in the garden instead of the sink. Bobbi A. McRae, author of *The Frugal Gardener*, uses an old plastic dish drainer as a "rinse station" to quickly clean and dry produce in her Austin, Texas, garden. She says the dish drainer makes it easy to rinse her vegetables with the hose while letting the excess water drain away. Her soil stays in the garden where it belongs and off her floors, sink, and countertops.

Bobbi notes that a dish drainer isn't the only container you can reuse as a rinse station—any waterproof, perforated container works well. Look for containers you have on hand: An old laundry basket makes a great rinse container for big vegetables, while a plastic colander is perfect for small crops.

Put your picked produce into a laundry basket, then wash and dry it outside—instead of dirtying the kitchen sink.

MOVE YOUR CLEANUP CHORES OUTDOORS

Harvest Hose-Off

Cut down on harvesting chores. It's easy! Just pick your produce and clean it in one handy container—a mesh bag. It's a lot less trouble than using a basket or bucket, says Lyn Belisle, a gardener in San Antonio. She used to haul vegetables inside in an unwieldly basket, unload the produce, wash it, set it out to dry, and clean up the kitchen. Not anymore.

"Now I use a plastic mesh bag, the kind onions from the store come in," Lyn says. The bags are especially handy for harvesting crops like snap beans, green onions, and peas. Just hose the vegetables off outside, right in the bag, then hang the bag on a nail or clothesline to drain. Once it's dry, bring your clean produce into the house to eat or store.

Poolside Produce

Here's a great way to clean produce fast. All you need is a wading pool, a screen door, and the great outdoors. "I harvest armloads of herbs and vegetables in the summer, and believe me, they can really make a mess indoors," says Donna Iarkowski, owner of Nature's Way Herbary in Muncy Valley, Pennsylvania. She came up with this outdoor system to save time and trouble.

Fill a wading pool with fresh water and swish your produce around just like you would in the kitchen sink. (When you have small harvests, use a plastic dishpan instead.) If necessary, use your fingers or a nylon brush to scrub off the dirt that hides underneath thyme sprigs or clings to carrot roots.

When you're done, let the produce dry off outdoors on a drying rack, and save yourself the expense and trouble of using paper or cloth towels. Donna made a drying table out of the legs and frame of a 6-foot-long table covered with wire screening instead of a tabletop. For an even easier drying rack, set an old screen door on two sawhorses. The screen lets air circulate up, over, and around the damp plants to allow the excess water to evaporate quickly.

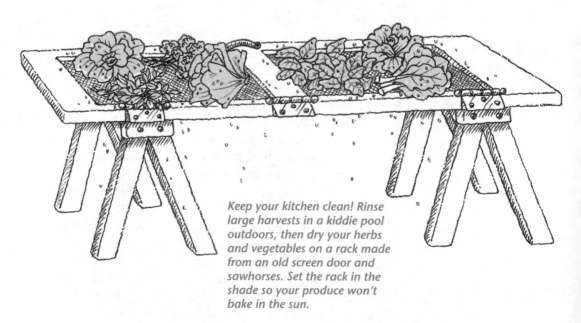

Keep your kitchen clean! Rinse large harvests in a kiddie pool outdoors, then dry your herbs and vegetables on a rack made from an old screen door and sawhorses. Set the rack in the shade so your produce won't bake in the sun.

Put More Life in Your Produce

SIMPLE

CLEANING STEPS

MAKE PRODUCE

LAST LONGER

You can improve the storage life of your fruit and vegetables by using two cleaning techniques from Ken Muckenfuss, who owns Mill Creek Organic Farm in Medford, New Jersey. These washing tips won't add any time to your cleaning chores, and they'll help you do a better job.

Wash in warm water. Clean your harvest with water that's at least as warm as the produce or even warmer, advises Ken. "When you wash sun-warmed produce with cold water, some water is absorbed into the fruit as pores close, carrying bacteria from the surface in with it."

Use hydrogen peroxide as bathwater. You'll extend the storage life of your produce a few more days since the hydrogen peroxide kills bacteria and fungi on the surface of your crops. Use the straight 3 percent hydrogen peroxide solution found at pharmacies. This treatment can add up to a bit of money, so save it for your most perishable crops.

Keep Produce Fresh in High-Tech Bags

Extend the life of your refrigerated produce by using breathable plastic bags. One choice is Evert-Fresh bags, which are lined with a greenish coating of powdered oya stone. (See "Sources" on page 412 for ordering information.) The stone absorbs the ethylene gas that is given off by the fruit and veggies and releases it outside the bag. Ethylene gas causes ripening—removing it puts produce into a sort of suspended animation that keeps it fresh.

Melanie Arabsky, who gardens in Vancouver, British Columbia, says the bags are great. "I've had vegetables last quite literally for months and still be edible," she says.

Another choice is Ziploc Vegetable Bags, which are covered with tiny holes that let excess moisture escape. The bags, available in grocery stores, are a good alternative to regular plastic bags, which can make produce slimy, or no bag, which makes produce dry out, says garden writer Erin Hynes of Austin, Texas. "I've always been pretty bad about forgetting lettuce at the back of the vegetable drawer," Erin admits. "These bags give me a few extra days for remembering."

HEDGES, FENCES, AND SCREENS

Hedgerows Minimize Mowing

PLANT A

COLORFUL

LIVING

SCREEN

Do you really need so much lawn? If not, cut down on mowing the quick way by replacing some of your grass with thickly planted evergreen trees and shrubs. That's the advice of Russell Studebaker, horticulturist for the Tulsa Zoo. He says your tree-and-shrub planting will not only reduce mowing chores, it will also make your landscape more colorful, block strong winds, and give you privacy from neighbors. Here's what to do.

Choose a lawn area that you don't need for picnics or yard games, or an area that's tough to mow, and get rid of the grass. In early spring or fall, smother the sod with cardboard boxes that have been cut open and flattened out. Make sure to overlap the cardboard so *no* light reaches the grass. The grass will die out in a month, and you can plant the area with low-maintenance trees and shrubs.

For year-round color, start by planting three or more different species of evergreens in a double or triple row. (See the list of easy-care evergreen trees and shrubs in "Proven Plants for Evergreen Hedgerows" on the opposite page.) Fill in around the evergreens with flowering shrubs for even more color. Space the plants close together—3 to 4 feet apart for shrubs, 5 to 6 feet apart for trees—and they'll grow into an almost impenetrable hedgerow.

Mulch the trees and shrubs heavily right after you plant them and you won't have to worry about weeds. Once the hedgerow is established, it will almost never need watering, even in arid climates.

Let Birds Do Your Planting

Hedgerows are for the birds. Of course hedgerows reduce the amount of mowing and maintenance in your yard by taking up lawn space. But they make great wildlife habitat too, if you let birds give you a hand with the planting. Here's how. Just plant a double or triple row of three different types of evergreens across the back of your yard and sit back.

Russell Studebaker, horticulturist for the Tulsa Zoo, says it won't take long for birds to find nesting spots in the evergreens, and soon they'll drop seeds of the kinds of plants they eat. "It'll quickly become a real slice of the natural world out there, right in your own side yard," says Russell.

PROVEN PLANTS FOR EVERGREEN HEDGEROWS

A mixed planting of evergreen shrubs and trees can transform a section of your lawn from a mowing headache into a wildlife sanctuary. The tough evergreens listed below make great nesting sites for songbirds and were recommended by Russell Studebaker, horticulturist for the Tulsa Zoo.

American holly (*Ilex opaca*), Zones 5 to 9.
Canada hemlock (*Tsuga canadensis*), Zones 3 to 7.
Carolina cherry-laurel (*Prunus caroliniana*), Zones 7 to 10.
Chinese holly (*Ilex cornuta*), Zones 7 to 9.
Chinese privet (*Ligustrum sinense*), Zones 7 to 10.
Dwarf mugo pine (*Pinus mugo* var. *mugo*), Zones 3 to 7.
Eastern red cedar (*Juniperus virginiana*), Zones 2 to 9.
Glossy abelia (*Abelia* × *grandiflora*), Zones 6 to 9.
Inkberry (*Ilex glabra*), Zones 5 to 9.
Japanese holly (*Ilex crenata*), Zones 6 to 9.
Korean boxwood (*Buxus microphylla* var. *koreana*), Zones 5 to 8.
Mountain pieris (*Pieris floribunda*), Zones 5 to 8.
Northern bayberry (*Myrica pensylvanica*), Zones 4 to 9.
Norway spruce (*Picea abies*), Zones 2 to 7.
Possum haw (*Ilex decidua*), Zones 5 to 9.
Pyracantha (*Pyracantha coccinea*), Zones 5 to 9.
Rugosa rose (*Rosa rugosa*), Zones 2 to 8.
Thorny elaeagnus (*Elaeagnus pungens*), Zones 6 to 9.
Wax myrtle or southern bayberry (*Myrica cerifera*), Zones 6 to 9.
Yews (*Taxus* spp.), Zones 3 to 9.

Shrubs for (Almost) Instant Screening

Whether it's for hiding an unsightly area or providing privacy, almost everyone needs screening somewhere around the yard. With the fast-growing shrubs listed here, you can have a screen in a short time.

AMUR MAPLE (*Acer ginnala*)

This fantastically tough and hardy multistemmed shrub or small tree grows 10 to 20 feet tall. It tolerates partial shade but has better fall color in full sun. Tiny fragrant flowers appear in spring followed by red winged seeds; glossy dark green summer foliage turns brilliant red and orange in fall; brown seeds add winter interest. Space plants 5 to 6 feet apart. Zones 2 to 8.

BORDER PRIVET (*Ligustrum obtusifolium*)

Spreading or arching branches make this 10- to 12-foot-tall shrub wider on top than on the bottom. It thrives in a wide range of soil and moisture conditions. Look for small white flowers in early summer and blue-black berries all winter; 1- to 2-inch-long medium green leaves may turn russet in fall. Plant 3 to 5 feet apart. Zones 3 to 10.

BOTTLEBRUSH BUCKEYE (*Aesculus parviflora*)

Large five-leaflet leaves cover this multistemmed shrub and give it an almost tropical look. It grows 8 to 12 feet tall in sun or partial shade and spreads by suckers. Long thin white and red flower clusters look like bottle brushes and make the plant extra attractive in summer. The leaves turn yellow or yellow-green in fall. Space plants 5 to 6 feet apart. Zones 4 to 8.

FLOWERING QUINCE (*Chaenomeles speciosa*)

The rounded form of this 6- to 10-foot-tall shrub is made up of a twiggy tangle of branches. Showy single or double flowers open 1 to 2 inches wide in spring in shades of orange, pink, scarlet, or white. You'll get more flowers in full sun, but the plant does tolerate partial shade. Glossy leaves emerge after flowering; edible fruits (for preserves) ripen in fall. Plant 3 to 5 feet apart. Zones 4 to 9.

HEAVENLY BAMBOO (*Nandina domestica*)

This trouble-free evergreen shrub grows gracefully upright and reaches 6 to 8 feet tall. Feathery fine-textured leaves are reddish when they're new, blue-green when they mature, and red in autumn. In spring 8- to 15-inch-long clusters of pink buds open into white flowers. Bright red or white berries last from fall through winter. Dwarf cultivars are too short for screening so use the species and set plants 4 feet apart. Zones 6 to 9.

JETBEAD (*Rhodotypos scandens*)

The arching branches of this multistemmed shrub grow 4 to 6 feet tall. Jetbead tolerates almost all soil, moisture, pollution, and light conditions—it even flowers in deep shade. The 1- to 2-inch-wide single white flowers appear in late spring through early summer and are followed by clusters of shiny black seeds that last into winter. Crisp green toothed leaves may turn light gold in autumn. Plant 2 to 3 feet apart. Zones 4 to 8.

PINEAPPLE GUAVA (*Feijoa sellowiana*)

Gardeners in the South and the Pacific Northwest can grow this beautiful 10- to 20-foot-tall evergreen shrub. In early summer, 1½-inch-wide crimson flowers, with edible petals, open. They're followed by yellow 2- to 3-inch-wide white-fleshed edible fruits in early fall. The leaves are dark green above and silvery beneath, giving a two-tone effect. Plant 5 to 10 feet apart. Zones 8 to 10.

REDLEAF ROSE (*Rosa glauca*, also known as *R. rubrifolia*)

Brownish purple leaves make this 6- to 8-foot-tall fountain-shaped rose a real knockout in full sun. The disease-resistant leaves are only slightly less showy in partial shade. Dainty single 2- to 3-inch-wide pink flowers appear in early summer and are followed by masses of red fruits called hips. Plant 4 to 6 feet apart. Zones 2 to 7.

SPREADING COTONEASTER (*Cotoneaster divaricatus*)

This rounded 3- to 7-foot-tall shrub has drooping outer stems and is the most trouble-free of the cotoneasters. Pinkish ¼-inch-wide flowers bloom in spring and are followed by many bright red berries. Dark glossy green fine-textured leaves turn fluorescent yellow to wine red in fall. Plant 5 to 8 feet apart. Zones 4 to 7.

WINTER HONEYSUCKLE (*Lonicera fragrantissima*)

The graceful wide-spreading branches of this 5- to 10-foot-tall shrub provide dense screening. Small cream to yellow intensely fragrant flowers appear in late winter to early spring. They're followed by red fruits that birds love. Stiff leathery dark green leaves don't fall until early winter, making winter honeysuckle semievergreen in mild climates. Plant 8 to 10 feet apart. Zones 4 to 8.

YAUPON (*Ilex vomitoria*)

This 15- to 20-foot-tall Southeastern native is the most adaptable evergreen holly for the South. Female plants bear tiny flowers in spring, followed by many small translucent scarlet fruits that persist until the following spring. (Plant at least one male yaupon to pollinate the female's flowers so you'll get fruit.) Small lustrous dark green leaves are attractive year-round. Yaupon tolerates many soil types, dry to wet conditions, and even salt spray. Plant 10 to 20 feet apart. Zones 7 to 10.

Grow an Instant Hedge

No time for a hedge? If you think planting a flowering hedge takes too much time and effort, think again. Wilma Gene Rushing, a harried gardener living in the Mississippi Delta south of Memphis, accidentally found a way to create an instant flowering hedge without moving heavy shrubs or trying to match plant sizes and shapes.

One year, Wilma Gene stuck some cuttings of forsythia, quince, rose-of-Sharon, and spirea into several spots around a flower border and forgot to move them when the time was right. The next spring, Wilma Gene had an instant "mixed" hedge of color, which she describes as looking like a "kaleidoscope having a stroke."

CREATE A QUICK AND COLORFUL HEDGE WITH CUTTINGS

Plant your own dramatic color-splash hedge the same simple way using a mixture of plants or a single species. Prepare your planting site in spring. If you have heavy clay soil, dig in an inch or two of coarse sand; sandy or light soils are fine as is. Then take 6- to 8-inch cuttings of the deciduous flowering shrubs you want in your hedge. Roses, weigela, and the shrubs Wilma Gene grew will all root easily. In the South, you can take cuttings anytime from November through March. In the North, take cuttings in late winter to early spring.

You can snip off pieces of your own shrubs, or ask friends and neighbors for cuttings of their plants. Insert the cuttings two-thirds of the way into the prepared soil, and surround them with 4 inches of mulch. Water the cuttings through the first summer and jump back. Before you know it, you'll have a row of small shrubs that should begin flowering the following spring.

Simple Ways to Screen Utilities

You can hide utility poles and other modern necessities from sight if you know a few landscaping tricks with trees. C. Colston Burrell, owner of the Minnesota-based design firm, Native Landscapes, shares these easy and effective ways to camouflage tall eyesores. Keep trees at least 10 feet away from the objects you're hiding so utility workers have easy access.

Hide tall poles with a single tree. Plant a basswood (*Tilia americana*), oak, pine, or other tall, spreading tree between the pole and your main viewing point. The upright line of the trunk will block the pole. "The farther you are from the utility pole, the wider the tree should be, so the pole won't show no matter where you are in the yard," Cole says.

Block eyesores with narrow trees. In a tiny yard, there's no space for large spreading trees. Instead, plant narrow upright trees or shrubs such as American arborvitae (*Thuja occidentalis*). Cultivars like 'Nigra' and 'Wintergreen' grow 20 to 30 feet tall but only 5 to 10 feet wide. They're so narrow that they won't take up all your yard space, even if you set them 10 feet away from power poles.

Screen utilities with a grove. Hide wide eyesores with a cluster of trees like hemlocks (*Tsuga* spp.) or poplars (*Populus* spp.). If you don't have room for a large grove, group two or three multistemmed trees like birches (*Betula* spp.) together to make a minigrove.

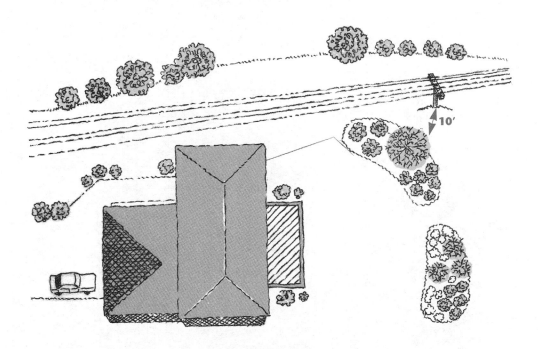

Take a utility pole out of the picture by hiding it behind a tall, spreading tree. Then use island plantings of shrubs to draw your eye toward more attractive sights.

Lattice Hides Eyesores in a Hurry

There's nothing faster than a lattice arbor, fence, or trellis for hiding an unsightly spot in your yard. "Lattice is miraculous," says Bill Mulligan, author of *The Lattice Gardener.* "It solves so many problems at once." A lattice screen gives you instant relief from eyesores. It also creates shade and privacy, and is a perfect place to show off vining plants.

Here are some of Bill's suggestions for using lattice.

• Hide the pipes and utility meters on building walls with a simple lattice panel covered with climbing vines.

• Make a lattice gazebo and plant vines on the sides that face your neighbor's yards to give you some privacy.

• Divide the yard into separate working, utility, and entertaining areas with a lattice fence. Add "moongate" panels with framed oval openings to provide an enticing peek-through from one area to another.

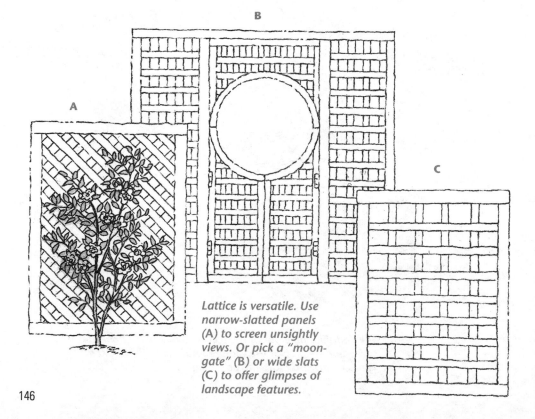

Lattice is versatile. Use narrow-slatted panels (A) to screen unsightly views. Or pick a "moongate" (B) or wide slats (C) to offer glimpses of landscape features.

To build your own lattice project, visit a lumberyard or building supply store and choose from a wide variety of styles of lattice. It comes in different sizes (2 × 8-foot and 4 × 8-foot sheets are common) and materials.

You can find or make lattice with narrow or wide slats. Use raw or painted wood, bamboo, split timbers, or other materials. Match the wood to the architecture of your home, gazebo, fence, or another feature in your yard so it fits into your landscape.

The spacing of the lattice pieces and whether or not you grow vines on the screen determine how much you can or can't see through it. To hide an unpleasant view, buy or make a tightly woven lattice fence that only provides a peek through it. For a partial screen, use a lattice with 2½-inch openings and plant it with clematis (*Clematis* spp.) or trumpet vine (*Campsis radicans*).

If you'd rather decorate your screen with stout plants like climbing roses, use lattice made out of sturdy timbers with 6-inch openings. For most other vines, store-bought lattice nailed to 4 × 4 support posts will do.

Wall Off Ugly Sights with Fabric

Nothing beats fabric walls when you're in a hurry for a screen—they're easier to install than shrubs and cheaper than fences. As Barbara Pleasant, *Organic Gardening* magazine contributing editor in Huntsville, Alabama, points out, "Most shrubs are slow by nature. There's not much we can do to speed them up for an instant effect." Fabric walls, on the other hand, are ready at a moment's notice. For an instant screen, nail or tie canvas or other heavy-duty fabric to 4 × 4s or fence posts.

To add even more interest to your garden, take a hint from the landscapers who developed the gardens for Ameriflora, a giant garden show in Columbus, Ohio. They needed a quick fix to hide an unsightly view from visitors, so they stretched oilcloth between posts placed 4 feet apart. A local artist painted garden scenes on the oilcloth, and the fabric quickly became an attraction for visitors.

Need a Screen Fast? Plant a Fence

If you need instant privacy or want to get your neighbor's trash cans out of sight *now*, don't hesitate. Install a mix of quick-growing plants and fences or walls and you'll get an attractive screen in a fraction of the time it takes to grow a hedge.

Garden designer Rosalind Creasy of Los Altos, California, found that a simple trellis of reinforcing material—the heavy wire mesh used in concrete—can make an inexpensive screen. Ros sprays it black or brown, suspends it between posts, and covers it with vines. "It creates just the right amount of privacy without that 'walled-in' feeling," she says. "And it still permits air circulation."

You don't have to have a solid fence or wall—a partial screen is all it takes to block an objectionable sight. For example, if all you need is privacy between your deck and a neighbor's kitchen, a piece of siding or lattice raised on posts can do the trick. An innovative paint job, wall sculpture, or flowering vine will make your screen a landscape feature. Or you can plant evergreen shrubs on either side of the lattice to help your screen blend into the landscape.

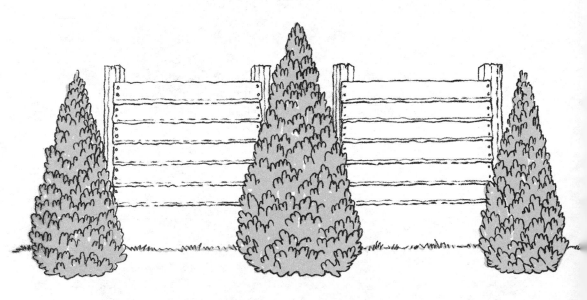

Mix shrubs with fencing when you want a privacy screen but don't have time to grow a hedge. Mount siding or lattice between fence posts to make quick fence sections, and plant shrubs on either end.

Unchain Your Yard

MAKE CHAIN-
LINK FENCES
DISAPPEAR WITH
LATTICE

Chain-link fences are ugly. Let's face it, a chain-link fence works great for keeping your dog in the yard, but it can make your gorgeous garden look bleak. If you're saddled with an ugly yard or garden fence, decorate it using "Green Guerilla" techniques and turn it into an asset.

When the Green Guerillas (a nonprofit New York City group that converts abandoned building sites into community gardens) take over a rubble-strewn lot, the first thing they do is put up a chain-link fence, mostly for security but also to create a sense of enclosure and ownership.

They tone down the harsh look of the fence with paint or hang it with coverings. In keeping with their low-input style of gardening, they use covering materials, like used reed mats and old window blinds, scrounged from a variety of sources. Some of the materials make the fence blend in with the garden but others are downright ugly.

If pretty covers aren't available, Green Guerillas like Kim Mulcahy resort to vines. Kim, who tends one of the oldest reclaimed gardens on the Lower East Side of Manhattan, grows easy annual vines such as cypress vine (*Ipomoea quamoclit*), hyacinth bean (*Dolichos lablab*), moonflower (*Ipomoea alba*), and morning glory. "They not only give fast coverage," he says, "but they also grow in some of the poorest soils we have." The seeds are easy to scrounge from friends and neighbors too.

*Beautify an ugly chain-
link fence by tying lattice to it with
plastic-coated wire. Add vines for color.*

149

HELP

Tap Into Dependable Garden Resources

FIND GARDEN
ANSWERS WITH
YOUR COMPUTER

Where do you turn for garden advice? Not all garden books have the right answers for your part of the country, much less your soil type and climate. Even the library may not have the best references.

If you're computer-literate, Diane Relf, extension specialist in consumer horticulture at Virginia Tech, recommends that you cruise the Internet. Or tap into the computer services at local universities or colleges and find their Gopher server—a big computer filled with all sorts of information. Access it, scroll down to the home horticulture entry, find what you want, and dump it on a disk. You'll find all the information you need, plus sympathetic fellow gardeners who can help you out.

"The best source of gardening information," Diane says, "is having a network of garden friends—a lot of people who have similar interests." What better way to find them than through a worldwide computer bank of gardeners.

If computers aren't your style, check with your local extension service, especially if it has Master Gardener programs. The extension agents can direct you to experienced gardeners and provide you with quite an array of publications. Although extension agents are not all going to be organic enthusiasts, you can usually persuade them to come up with alternatives to chemicals.

You can also check your local garden centers and see if they have a trained, experienced horticulturist who can help you. "One of the ways the better ones stay in business is by helping their customers," Diane explains. Employees at local botanic gardens may be available to help you too, so don't hesitate to give them a call.

And don't overlook horticulture programs at local universities, community colleges, and high schools. They're close by and will have your garden conditions in mind.

Quick-Pick Reference System

ORGANIZE YOUR GARDEN INFOR-MATION THE SMART WAY

Remember the last time you had to stop what you were doing to look something up in a garden book? Either you couldn't put your finger on it or you got distracted reading other stuff.

To get around this pleasant time waster, gardener Norman Kent Johnson of Birmingham, Alabama, came up with what he calls his "least stupid" system for organizing his 3,000-plus references. "Place your books together based loosely on general topics, such as design, plant selection, how-to, floral design, biographies, and so on. Then work out subsections within each group," he says.

Norman arranges each title in each group according to its depth of information or how often he uses it—the more specialized, the farther down the shelf it goes. That way, if he needs a quick refresher, he can grab the first book he comes to. If it doesn't have enough information, Norman just keeps going down the shelf until he finds what he needs.

It sounds well organized, but Norman calls it his "Dewey Doughnut" system—"There are holes in it," he chuckles. Still, it's a simple, easy way to retrieve or replace anything he needs, saving him time to browse leisurely whenever he feels like it.

Put your library in order by arranging garden books from general to specific topics. You won't have to hunt when you want garden answers fast.

Little Hands Make Light Work

So many things to do, so little time! Whenever you can get help, go for it. Family members, both older and younger, can lend a hand with tasks such as rooting cuttings or starting plants from seed.

John Cretti, the "Rocky Mountain Horticulturist" in Golden, Colorado, finds that his small children (elementary-school age) can save him time in the garden and have fun in the process. John never has time to plant all the seeds he orders or take all the rose cuttings he wants, so he and his wife show their boys a few simple tricks, and let them go.

"They love rooting cuttings in clear plastic bottles, so they can see the roots grow. They even take their new plants to school for show-and-tell," John says.

Children are especially helpful when it comes to saving seed. You get the seeds you need and they get to spend quality time with nature, coaxing next year's crop from seedpods. Little hands are especially good with the larger seeds like those found on flowering vines such as hyacinth bean and moonflower and with prolific producers such as celosia, cleome, and four-o'clocks. These collections can lead to a lifelong love of gardening and may even yield enough seeds for gaily-wrapped garden gift packages.

Other things children can help with include:

- Staking or tying tomatoes and other vines

- Pruning roses (watch those fingers!)

- Mulching

- Saving recyclables (egg cartons and plastic bottles for seed starting)

- Composting (especially carrying kitchen materials outside)

- Hand-collecting beetles and caterpillars

- Picking peas and beans

- Pinching faded flowers

- Watering potted plants

- Picking up sticks and toys before you mow the lawn

KIDS ARE WHIZZES WHEN IT COMES TO GARDEN CHORES

When you've got lots of yard and garden chores but no time, ask kids to help. They're great at handpicking pests (A), picking up the yard before you mow (B), watering plants (C), and saving seeds (D).

HERBS

Take Your Herbs to the Beach

All it takes is sand to make your herb garden thrive and look great for months—a 1-inch layer of large-grained sand, to be precise. "Light-colored sand reflects sunlight and gives Mediterranean herbs such as lavender and rosemary the intense sunlight they need," explains Brian Holley, director of Cleveland Botanical Garden. "It also helps prevent weeds from coming up. If any weeds do emerge, they're easy to pull out of the loose sand."

SAND MULCH MAKES HERBS FEEL AT HOME

Brian says the sand mulch gives the garden a tidy look and helps moderate temperature swings, just like an organic mulch. But unlike organic mulches, it doesn't hold moisture so it won't encourage the root and crown rots that can cause a quick end to herbs. Beach sand is too fine to give your plants the drainage they crave, so look for a coarse version like mason's sand at building supply centers.

Put a ½-inch layer of sand on top of the potting soil if you grow herbs in containers, Brian adds. On the ground, or in containers, a sand mulch helps reduce the amount of soil that splashes back up on herbs when it rains or when you water. Your herbs stay clean so you can harvest without having to wash them—and that saves time and essential oils.

Ornamental Herbs Add Garden Spice

If you have a small garden, try double-duty herbs to get good looks and taste in the same space. You could develop elaborate planting schemes to squeeze in both ornamental plants and culinary herbs, but why struggle with growing plants up or over each other? "You'll get twice the results for half the effort with ornamental herbs," says Jim Nau, variety manager for Ball Seed Company in Illinois.

Jim recommends the following hardy and reliable herbs for small gardens.

• Apple mint (*Mentha suaveolens*): The woolly leaves of this mint add texture to your garden and pizzazz to your desserts. "Put a sprig of apple mint on a plate of cookies and it really makes them special," Jim says.

• Common chives (*Allium schoenoprasum*): In spring, use the attractive lavender flowers in salads or vinegar.

• Garden sage (*Salvia officinalis*): Colorful cultivars like 'Purpurea' and 'Tricolor' complement your planting scheme as well as the flavor of stuffings and breads.

• Golden lemon thyme (*Thymus* ✕ *citriodorus* 'Aureus'): The gold-variegated leaves brighten your garden and give any dish a wonderful citrus flavor.

• Greek oregano (*Origanum heracleoticum*): Slightly furry leaves and light pink flowers add charm to your garden and a rich aroma and flavor to your cooking.

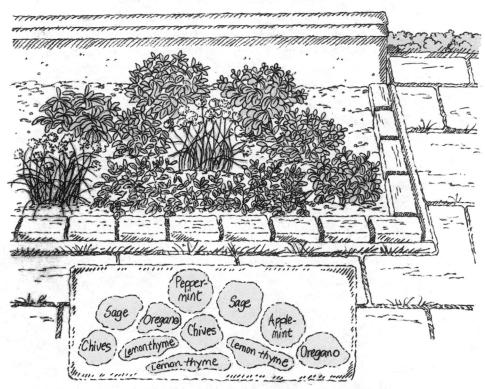

You don't need separate herb and flower gardens. Grow edible herbs with ornamental features for a planting that's as beautiful as it is tasty.

Herbs That Self-Seed Save Time

THESE HERBS
DO THEIR OWN
PLANTING

You can save hours of planting and soil preparation time by letting herbs such as borage, calendula, chervil, dill, and summer savory self-sow. The first time around, buy seeds or transplants and plant them outside where you want them to grow. Let a few flowers of each herb go to seed and sow themselves in the garden. Avoid rotary tilling or heavy cultivating, and next growing season you'll have a new generation of seedlings emerging trouble-free.

"I rarely clean up everything in the herb garden in fall," says Brian Holley, director of Cleveland Botanical Garden. "Letting plants go gives the seeds time to scatter." In the spring, Brian pulls a few weeds, renews his mulch (he uses a layer of sand, 1 inch deep), and presto, he has a nice seedbed. The seedlings pop up here and there, making pleasant, effortless surprises.

A few herbs can get out of hand if you let them self-sow, so Brian suggests that you use caution with garlic chives, fennel, and bronze fennel. "Garlic chive seeds seem predisposed to falling into cracks or the middle of clumps of thyme where they're hard to get out," Brian explains. "What's worse is that they turn to green slime in your hand when you try to yank them out." Keep ahead of invasive herbs by removing all the flowering heads as soon as they open. Use the flower heads in herbal vinegars or toss them in the compost pile.

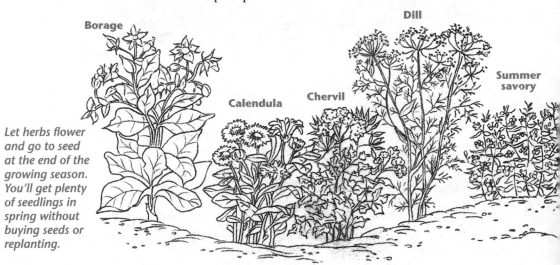

Borage

Dill

Summer savory

Calendula

Chervil

Let herbs flower and go to seed at the end of the growing season. You'll get plenty of seedlings in spring without buying seeds or replanting.

156

Prune Herbs Early for Longer Life

For better health and vigor, give your perennial herbs one hard pruning in early spring, just when they begin growing. (For one exception, see "Just Say 'No' to Pruning Sage" on this page.) Pruning rejuvenates herbs and saves you from having to replace them, says Holly Shimizu, chief horticulturist of the United States Botanic Garden in Washington, D.C.

"Lavandin, which is my favorite form of lavender, needs pruning as soon as you see new growth begin to develop in spring," Holly says. "Cut it back to one-third of its original size and it will resprout compact and bushy." If you cut lavandin (*Lavandula × intermedia*) and other herbs back heavily later on, she explains, they'll usually die. Holly also prunes English lavender (*L. angustifolia*), rue, French tarragon, thyme, and winter savory heavily early to reap similar benefits.

You'll find that French tarragon responds to pruning particularly well. It resprouts with lots of new stems so there's more to harvest—an important benefit for any herb lover.

JUST SAY "NO" TO PRUNING SAGE

Slack off on pruning your sage plants next spring and you'll get bigger plants and a blue flower bonus. "Leaving sage plants alone is one thing that makes life easier," says Brian Holley, director of Cleveland Botanical Garden. "You don't have to find extra time for pruning when you're busy, and best of all, you don't cut off the sage flower buds. You can look forward to the most glorious blue flowers in June."

Once the sage flowers begin to fade, cut the plants back lightly as you harvest the foliage for cuisine or crafts. Harvest several times until late summer arrives. Then stop harvesting so your plants can produce flower buds for the following year.

Garden sage

Super-Sage Saves the Day

When sage plants go bad, year after year, you may think they're not worth the trouble. But don't give up yet! A new hybrid, silver leaf sage, offers hope for healthy plants. "Sometimes sage just wilts away at the end of the summer," laments Holly Shimizu, chief horticulturist of the United States Botanic Garden in Washington, D.C. "It's especially disappointing if you're looking forward to some sage in your Thanksgiving stuffing." She explains that sage plants get in trouble when the humidity is high, particularly if they're overcrowded so the air circulation is low.

Luckily, Madalene Hill, coauthor of *Southern Herb Growing,* found a hybrid sage that can beat heat, humidity, and fungal diseases even in her home state of Texas. (It's still being tested for cold-hardiness.) Madalene's discovery, silver leaf sage, is a cross between garden sage (*Salvia officinalis*) and *Salvia fruticosa.* Watch for it in plant catalogs.

❧QUICK FIX MIX

Easy-Does-It Rose Hip Tea

You could buy rose hips for tea, but it's easy and less expensive to grow and use your own. Start by planting rugosa roses (*Rosa rugosa*) and dog roses (*R. canina*)—they're both disease-free and have great hips, so you're guaranteed great results. "Roses like these that don't need sprays make handsome and easy-care additions to the herb garden," says Holly Shimizu, chief horticulturist of the United States Botanic Garden in Washington, D.C.

When she wants a quick sip of citrus flavor, Holly adds a few hips to a pot of regular tea. For a super vitamin C boost, try this tea recipe.

1½ teaspoons rose hips
1 cup water

Harvest rose hips after a light frost and wash them. Bring the water to a boil in a stainless steel or enamel saucepan—copper and aluminum pans destroy vitamin C. Add the rose hips to the water, cover, and continue boiling for 5 minutes. Strain and serve with a slice of lemon.

Use rose hips as soon as possible after picking since they lose vitamin C quickly. If you can't use them right away, store them in plastic bags or containers and freeze.

A Simple Basil-Starting Secret

FOR QUICK BASIL
HARVESTS,
START PLANTS
FROM CUTTINGS

Get harvest-size basil faster by growing plants from cuttings instead of seeds. Brian Holley, director of Cleveland Botanical Garden, reveals that basil cuttings are super-simple to root in a bottle of water.

For best results, take cuttings from a thriving plant in the morning. Cut a 6-inch piece of stem from a large plant like sweet basil or a 4-inch piece from a dwarf or bush basil plant. Remove the leaves from the lower half of the stem, leaving about three sets of leaves on top.

Fill a narrow-necked bottle with lukewarm water, and put the lower half of the stem into the water. The upper leaves will hold the cutting in place. Keep the water fresh and the water level high and in a couple of weeks the cutting will grow roots. Once it's rooted, slip the cutting out of the bottle and put it in a 4-inch pot of peat-based growing mix.

"I've grown flats of new basil plants this way from a handful of mother plants," Brian says. He adds that cinnamon and camphor basils are especially vigorous and easy. Sweet basil has about a 90 percent success rate. Lemon basil tends to be a little weaker than the others but still works about 70 percent of the time.

You won't have long to wait for a basil harvest if you start new plants from rooted cuttings. Strip the leaves off the bottom half of a 6-inch-long cutting and place the stem in a bottle of water. It will root in about two weeks.

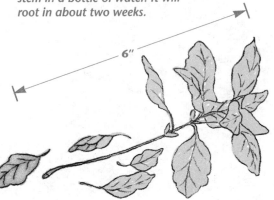

6"

159

Container Herbs Are Easy

LIVEN UP A
DOORWAY AND
YOUR COOKING
WITH HERBS

Keep herbs close at hand where they're easy to harvest, and you'll improve both your cooking and your landscaping. The easiest way to plant herbs near your kitchen door is to cluster plants together in containers. "I have a kitchen garden on the patio outside my back door where my daughter and I grow many different kinds of herbs," says Holly Shimizu, chief horticulturist of the United States Botanic Garden in Washington, D.C. "You can't beat the convenience of back-door herbs at harvesttime." And by planting in containers, you can get an early start on the season, filling containers with herbs in March and April, before the ground is ready to work.

Holly puts her herbs in redwood planters, but you can use any type of wood or plastic box, homemade or store-bought, depending on your budget and available time. According to Holly, almost any herb will grow in a container. She especially enjoys these:

• Common thyme (*Thymus vulgaris*): This wonderful edging plant combines well with most foods, so feel free to experiment, adding it to breads, eggs, and vegetables.

• Garden sage (*Salvia officinalis*): Use fresh or dried leaves for a balsamlike fragrance and sage flavor.

• Golden lemon thyme (*Thymus* × *citriodorus* 'Aureus'): The strong lemon scent adds a touch of citrus to fish, chicken, or tea.

Group herbs together in large containers near your kitchen door. Big containers don't need watering as often as individual pots, so plants are easy to care for. Plus, you'll get hooked on having herbs handy when you're cooking.

• Greek oregano (*Origanum heracleoticum*): Grow this bushy herb to add spice to any tomato dish.

• Nasturtium (*Tropaeolum majus*): Use the peppery-flavored leaves and colorful flowers to spice up salads and sandwiches.

• Pot marigold (*Calendula officinalis*): Use yellow or orange flowers to color and flavor rice or soups.

• Scented geraniums (*Pelargonium* spp.): These plants are available in every scent from coconut to peppermint. Holly prefers lemon-scented 'Prince Rupert' and fragrant rose geranium (*P. graveolens*).

• Summer savory (*Satureja hortensis*): The peppery-thyme flavor perks up beans and most other vegetables.

Winter Herbs Keep Their Cool

SUNSHINE KEEPS HERBS GOING UNTIL CHRISTMAS

If you love to use fresh herbs in winter, don't bother setting up lights—all you need is a sunny window. With a little sun, you can keep hardy herbs such as chives, parsley, and thyme growing deep into winter in an unheated but protected outbuilding or porch.

"I put chives in a deep pot in late summer and then shear the plant back close to the ground," says Jim Nau, variety manager for Ball Seed Company in Illinois. (The sheared chives grow back fast, and Jim snips the new foliage whenever he needs it for cooking.) Jim lets the chives sit outdoors, where they adjust to being potted, until night temperatures stay in the 40s. Then he moves the pot into a south-facing window in his garage, where the chives continue to grow. Jim gets fresh chives until Christmas, when the garage temperature usually drops below 40°F and the plants quit growing. At that point, Jim moves the chives out of the light and lets them go dormant. This technique also works with parsley and thyme.

Jim recommends using pots that are 12 to 20 inches deep. Shallower pots dry out too fast and hurt the plants' chances for winter survival. If you use clay pots, make sure they have thick walls so they'll be less likely to break.

INSECTS

Panty Hose Keeps Bugs Off Produce

QUICK COVER
MAKES PEST
ATTACKS A
THING OF THE
PAST

Pest-free produce is a cinch with this easy trick. It works the same way as floating row covers without the cost. Just use old panty hose to cover individual fruits and vegetables when they first start forming.

"To protect corn, cucumbers, grapes, melons, peaches, small pumpkins, and squash from birds, earwigs, slugs, snails, and other munchers, slip a length of panty hose over them," suggests Yvonne Savio, gardening education coordinator for the Los Angeles County Cooperative Extension Service. Tie knots at the top and the bottom of the hose so there are no openings where pests can get in. Panty hose work great because they dry quickly after a rain and don't hold heat.

Use panty hose to protect fruits and vegetables from pests. The hose should fit closely but have enough give for the produce to grow.

Hot Pepper Spray Drives Bugs Away

Chase pests from your plants with the same culinary hot pepper that brings tears to your eyes and fire to your throat. You can save money by mixing your own pest-repellent spray using the "Quick Fix Mix" recipe on this page, or save time by using a long-lasting commercial spray like Hot Pepper Wax, which combines peppers with an anti-desiccant (a waxy coating that keeps plants from drying out).

"Hot Pepper Wax controls soft-bodied insects such as aphids, whiteflies, mites, thrips, leafminers, leafhoppers, and scale," says Jim Akers, director of marketing for Hot Pepper Wax in Tacoma, Washington. The wax base means that the spray won't wash off leaves as quickly as a home-mixed spray when it dries. Jim recommends applying pepper spray once every three weeks to crops that have a history of insect infestations. One or two applications are usually enough for minor insect outbreaks.

Jim says that the waxy coating does more than keep the pepper spray from washing away. Some growers have told him it's cut back the amount of water plants need by 20 percent.

Apply Hot Pepper Wax in the morning or evening when temperatures are cooler to get the best coverage. In really hot temperatures the wax may dry in less than 15 minutes—too fast for it to spread out and evenly coat the leaves.

❧ QUICK FIX MIX

Pest-Away Pepper Spray

Make your own pest-repellent spray with homegrown or store-bought hot peppers and this simple recipe.

½ cup hot peppers
2 cups water

Blend the peppers and water in a food processor. Strain the mix and spray on insect-prone plants. Reapply the spray after heavy rains. Wear goggles and gloves for protection—hot pepper spray not only bothers insects, it will bother you too if you get it on your skin or in your eyes.

Give Small Insects the Brush Off

A brush of your hand is all it takes to reduce the number of small insects on young vegetable plants. Associate professor of horticulture Joyce Latimer and entomology professor Ronald Oetting at the University of Georgia found that just brushing the vegetable transplants they were growing in a greenhouse seemed to reduce the populations of aphids and thrips on the plants.

Because they were working with a large number of transplants, the researchers brushed the plants twice a day by stroking across them with a wooden pole 40 times. If you have a few plants, you can accomplish the same thing by brushing them with your hand gently during your visits to the greenhouse. Ron says that brushing the plants is a mechanical way of getting pests off plants, like handpicking or using a high pressure water spray (which may injure tender plants), but only brushing reduces the population of small insects like thrips on vegetable transplants.

Bugs Don't Like a Hot Shower

A few seconds and a spray of hot water are all it takes to wash small pests like aphids, mites, scales, thrips, and whiteflies out of your garden. In Thousand Oaks, California, gardener Jim Nichols has experimented for several years with using hot hot water—about 150°F—for controlling small insects and he's been successful. But though insects hate it, a quick hot-water shower won't hurt your plants. "I've treated a wide variety of woody and herbaceous plants," Jim says, "and I haven't found anything the hot water damages."

Jim, who is developing equipment for applying hot water to plants on a commercial scale, gives these instructions for a simple system that homeowners can rig up.

1 Set your water heater so the water is a little too hot for home use—Jim recommends about 160°F, figuring that the water will cool about ten degrees on its way to the plant. (Remember to turn down the hot water thermostat when you finish treating your plants.)

2 Attach a fitting to the hot water spigot for your washing machine or laundry sink so you can hook up a ¾-inch insulated automotive heater hose to it.

3 Attach the insulated hose to the fitting. The length of the hose depends on how far you have to go to reach insect-infested plants—it comes in 50-foot rolls.

4 Feed the hose out a window or your dryer vent. If you're dealing with a lot of hose, feed it in from outside.

5 On the "plant end" of the hose, attach a nozzle that can apply the water in a soft spray of big drops.

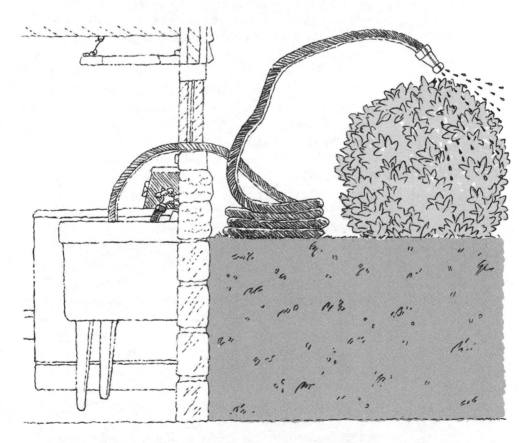

Run an insulated auto heater hose from your hot water spigot to pest-infested plants outside. Spray the stems or trunks and tops and undersides of the leaves of your plants with hot water for 1 to 3 seconds to control pest insects. And spray the surrounding ground to kill insects that might have been knocked off the plants.

Figure Out Pest Problems Fast

STICKY TRAPS
SHOW YOU
WHOM YOU'RE
DEALING WITH

You've got to know what's bugging you before you can take action against insect pests. The fastest way to identify bugs on your indoor or greenhouse plants is to stop them in their tracks with a yellow sticky trap. You can buy traps through garden supply catalogs—they're bright yellow cardboard or plastic sheets covered with a gooey substance. A quick look at the pests stuck to the traps will alert you to problems before damage shows up on your plants.

Hang the traps vertically so they are just 2 to 3 inches above plants—try using wire, a paper clip, or a clothespin. Use one trap for every 250 square feet. For houseplants, put one trap above each group of plants. Check the traps weekly and learn to recognize common pests. Once you know pests are there, you can wash them away with a hard blast of water or soap spray before they get out of hand.

When insects get glued to sticky sheets, they aren't so easy to identify, so here are some drawings and tips to help you figure out who's who. The descriptions come from Mike Cherim, president of The Green Spot, a mail-order source of biological controls. Mike says you should use sticky traps only in greenhouses, atriums, houses, or other structures—in the garden, they'll become loaded with all sorts of insects, including beneficials.

Aphids have small pear-shaped bodies and may or may not have wings. Only winged aphids will find the traps—once they're caught, the wings usually settle to the sides of the abdomen. Their legs and antennae are long and thin. The aphids may lay eggs or hatch live young while trapped.

Fungus gnats are black or gray and look like mosquitoes with long, segmented beadlike antennae. They struggle when trapped, so you'll find them in a variety of positions.

Leafminers are small flies with short antennae. Look for a yellow spot on the side of the thorax (the middle section). Like fungus gnats, they'll struggle once they're trapped, so they'll look pretty messy.

Thrips are so small that they're almost invisible. Use a hand lens to see their long thin bodies topped by short V-shaped antennae. Most insects are attracted to the color yellow, but thrips prefer blue. Use specially colored bright blue sticky traps where thrips are a particular problem.

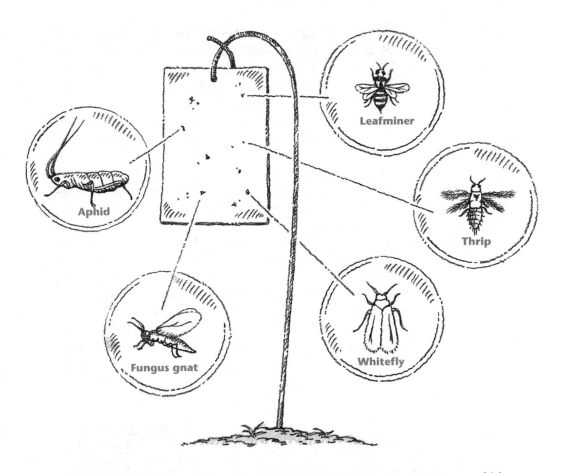

It's easier to treat plant problems when you know what you're up against. Learn which pests are bugging you by setting up sticky traps near houseplants or in your greenhouse. Check photos or descriptions to identify the pests glued to your sticky sheets.

Whiteflies may lose their white powdery covering when they're trapped, revealing their orange bodies.

If you see insects that don't fit these descriptions, look them up in a reference book like *The Organic Gardener's Handbook of Natural Insect and Disease Control*. Or get a copy of Mike Cherim's *Green Methods Manual*—it includes line drawings and descriptions of many insects and is available from The Green Spot Ltd., 93 Priest Road, Nottingham, NH 03825. If you're still stumped, ask your Cooperative Extension Service for help identifying the pest.

2 Tricks for Cutworm Control

Keep cutworms from chomping your young plants off at the soil line by shielding tender stems with newspaper or nails. "The newspaper method is fast and cheap," says Pamela Settle Jackson, a gardener in Braintree, Massachusetts. Before you set the plants in the ground, wrap the base of the stems with 2-inch-wide strips of newspaper. Half of the strip should be above the soil surface and half below it. Wrap the paper around loosely six times.

Pamela says the newspaper is too tough for the cutworms to chew through, and by the time the newspaper disintegrates (saving you from having to remove the collar), the stems are too wide for cutworms to get a toothless grip on.

Gardener Mary Lou Marchand of Bemidji, Minnesota, has a trick that's quicker at the start, but does require some cleanup later. "The best thing I've found for thwarting cutworms is a 10-penny finishing nail," she says. Put it in the ground alongside the plant so about 1 to 1½ inches of nail sticks out of the soil. The added width from the nail interferes when the worm tries to curl around the stem to feed. Later in the season when the plants are too large for cutworms, you can pick up the nails and reuse them.

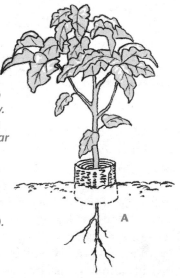
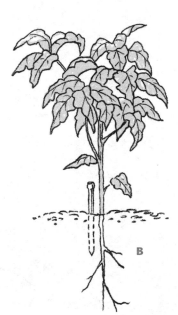

Simple household items keep cutworms away. Try wrapping a newspaper collar around young plants (A), or set a 10-penny finishing nail beside each plant's stem (B).

A

B

Surefire Ways to Fight Fire Ants

DESTROY FIRE
ANT MOUNDS
WITH DUSTS
AND SUN

If you live in the South, you need the sun and lots of other options to keep stinging fire ants out of your garden and compost. (If you're a Northern gardener, you don't have to worry about this pest...yet.) So, here are several great organic methods for controlling these stinging pests from John Dromgoole, owner of John Dromgoole's The Natural Gardener, a mail-order garden supply company in Austin, Texas.

John's favorite long-term control for fire ants in his compost, garden, and lawn is a mix of 1 part pyrethrum powder to 7 parts diatomaceous earth (DE). (See "Sources" on page 412 for ordering information for these products.) The blend is easy to use. Simply mix 4 tablespoons of the pyrethrum and DE combination with 1 gallon of water in a pump-type sprayer. Put the wand of the sprayer in the fire ant mound opening and spray the entire gallon into the mound.

John says beneficial nematodes are another really effective way to get rid of fire ants. Look for the nematodes labeled for ants at garden centers or in mail-order catalogs. Pour these microscopic beneficials into fire ant mounds and they'll parasitize the ant larvae.

Nematodes are also a good solution when fire ants invade your compost. To every foot of compost, simply stir in a cup or so of the nematodes. Or, when you're turning your compost anyway, zap fire ants with a light dusting of DE or a combination of DE and pyrethrum. (John says pyrethrum works the fastest, but nematodes and DE give longer-lasting results.) A little of these products goes a long way, so sprinkle any ants you see—don't bury them. Whichever dust you choose, John cautions you to play it smart and wear a dust mask and goggles. Even though products like DE are organic, they can irritate your lungs and eyes.

If your finished compost is infested with fire ants, you can use solar power to clean it up for free. John suggests that you spread the compost on your driveway, then cover it with clear plastic until the sun kills the ants. Then you can use the compost in your garden or screen it and use it in your potting soil.

Quick Ways to Keep Yellow Jackets at Bay

Leave yellow jackets alone when you can—they're good for your garden since they prey on insect pests. But, if they're nesting too close for comfort, try these quick ways to get rid of them from Mike Cherim, president of The Green Spot, a mail-order source of biological controls.

• Spray yellow jackets with cold water from a hose. It won't kill them, but will knock them out for a couple of hours so it's easy for you to get them while they're down.

• In the evening, when the wasps are calm, pour honey next to their in-ground nests. Raccoons, skunks, and other nocturnal animals may dig up and destroy yellow jacket nests while trying to find more honey.

• Lace canned dog food with parasitic nematodes—sold as entomogenous nematodes by companies that sell beneficial insects—and place it where foraging wasps can find it. They'll take the food back to the nest and feed it to their larvae, which will die.

• Trap yellow jackets in a commercially available bag, like the Rescue-Disposable Yellowjacket Control Trap made by Sterling International, that contains an attractant.

Keep pets from eating bait meant for yellow jackets by placing it in a margarine tub with quarter-size holes cut in the lid. The nematode-laced dog food won't harm animals, but if they eat the bait, you'll have to replace it.

❧ **For more information on controlling insects, look up the plant that pests are bothering.**

INTENSIVE GARDENING

Save Space with Soda Bottles

Accurate spacing is crucial when you're planting at close quarters in an intensive garden. At the organic community garden in Austin, Texas, gardener Steve Coyle noticed a fellow gardener's ingenious bottle-spacing technique. "He has a bunch of bottles with bases of different diameters," Steve explains. "During bed preparation, instead of fooling with strings or eyeballing the distance between plants, he uses the bottles to stamp a pattern in the loose soil—a bigger bottle for widely spaced plants, a smaller bottle for closely spaced plants."

Steve says the bottle-toting gardener plants beds quickly and accurately with this technique. Another benefit of the bottle-stamping method is that it eliminates the need for thinning once the seedlings come up. Thinning not only takes time, but it can also disturb the roots of remaining seedlings if you're thinning a shallow-rooted crop like peas.

Stamp a planting pattern in the soil with the base of a bottle, then drop a seed or two in each circle for quick and even spacing.

2 Simple Planting Shortcuts

An easy-to-make dowel spacer is the perfect tool for measuring seed spacing in intensive gardens. "I find that wooden dowel spacers are easy to use, carry, and store, and are cheap to make," says community gardener Galen Bollinger of Austin, Texas.

Galen makes his spacer from two 1-foot-long sections of ¾-inch-diameter dowel. (Look for wooden dowels at hardware or hobby stores.) He connects the two pieces in the center with a bolt to form a cross. Then he lays the spacer on the soil and uses it to quickly mark where seeds or transplants should be planted. Galen uses each of the four arms of the cross to measure 6-inch spacings. He makes a notch in the center of each arm so he can also measure 3-inch spacings. If he needs to set plants or seeds at other spacings, Galen uses dowels of different lengths to make spacers that are big or small enough to fit his planting plan.

Build a variety of spacers in winter when you place your seed orders. It's easy to figure out what size spacers you need when you have your catalogs out and the spacing information at your fingertips. In spring you can whip through plantings in a hurry and still get the accurate spacing necessary for successful intensive gardening.

His inexpensive homemade spacer isn't the only ace in Galen's hand. He has also discovered a handy tool for making planting holes that is literally at this fingertips. To make a seed hole, Galen just sticks his index finger into the soil. "I've tried three kinds of dibbles, but I find I have better control over planting, and can plant more quickly, by using my index finger to make the planting holes," he claims. "I know how long my finger is from the tip to the knuckle, and from the tip to the bottom of my fingernail." So measure your finger, and use it to get right to the point next time you plant.

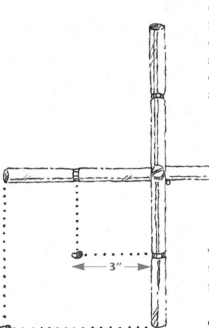

3"

6"

A spacer built from two 1-foot-long wooden dowels makes it easy to space plants and seeds accurately.

Comb-Shaped Beds Save Space

GIVE YOUR
PLANTING PLAN
SOME TEETH

For maximum efficiency, your intensive garden should look like a comb, says Steve Coyle, a community gardener in Austin, Texas.

Steve tried growing a classic intensive garden in small square beds but found that the checkerboard pattern wasted space. He also had trouble setting up a drip irrigation system efficiently in a garden of separate small beds. So he devised a layout that makes better use of his space and easily accommodates soaker hoses or drip irrigation tubes.

"I now use the shape of a comb, with 4-foot-wide beds for the 'teeth,'" Steve says. This arrangement gives the highest ratio of planting area to footpath space. It also allows Steve to run drip irrigation tubing down the beds without having to make the lines cross a footpath. "That saves wear and tear on the system and lessens the danger of tripping yourself up," Steve explains.

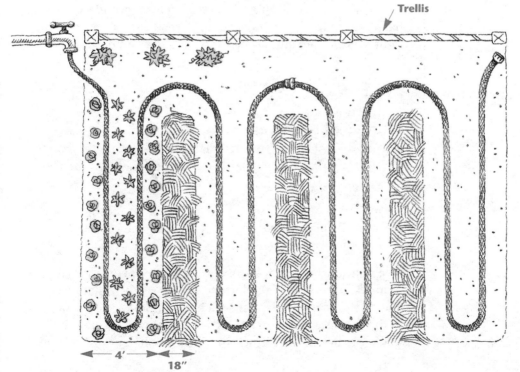

Get the most out of your planting area with a comb-shaped planting plan. Make beds ("teeth") 4 feet wide and straw-covered pathways ("spaces") 18 inches wide.

Less Work for High Yields

EAT YOUR WAY

TO BIGGER ROOT

CROP HARVESTS

Stop thinning root crop seedlings and you'll boost your harvest. Many gardeners sow root crops in rows, then thin the seedlings to standard spacings of 2 to 6 inches apart. But that takes time, and all those seedlings just go to waste. Steve Edmondson, a Master Gardener with the Washington State University Cooperative Extension Service, has found a better way.

Instead of sowing root crops like beets, carrots, radishes, and turnips in rows, Steve broadcasts the seed thickly across a bed in his intensive garden. He then covers the seed with soil, following the directions on the seed packet.

Steve doesn't bother thinning the young seedlings to precise spacings. Instead, he says, "I thin out the largest ones when they're big enough to eat and leave the small ones to get bigger. I get higher yields than the seed packets or garden books say to expect."

He offers a second shortcut based on his method: As you harvest and open up your planting, broadcast more seed right over the remaining plants to keep the bed producing.

Fast Ways to Full Beds

High-yield gardeners hate bare soil. Gardener Beverly Erlebacher of Toronto shares these easy methods for ensuring that every inch of your garden stays productive all season.

• Keep a bag of onion sets in the refrigerator all summer. Periodically plant some here and there in the garden for a constant supply of scallions.

• Plant a solid patch of lettuce early in the spring. Two months later, most of the lettuce will be ready to harvest. Plant heat-loving transplants such as peppers or tomatoes in the spaces where you cut lettuce. The transplants will shade the last of the lettuce so it won't bolt (go to seed) as quickly.

• Always have a flat of lettuce seedlings on hand to pop into bare spots.

Skinny Bed Yields 7 Crops

Harvest seven crops from 30 square feet using a high-yield method perfected by Philadelphia gardener Libby J. Goldstein. She uses trellising and succession cropping to get the most from a long, narrow garden bed.

"I have a 20-foot row that's only 18 inches wide," Libby explains. "A 5-foot-high trellis runs down the middle of it. The supports for the trellis are made from iron pipe that I bought and had threaded at a plumbing supply store." Libby strings the trellis with plastic bird mesh. She leaves 12 to 18 inches of loose netting at the bottom of the trellis to cover seedlings, because one of her worst pest problems is pesky birds that like to feed on young pea plants.

Libby explains how she optimizes yield from her small plot. "Last fall, I planted garlic on one side in the strip nearest the edge of the bed. Then this spring, I planted peas along the trellis on both sides. On the side that didn't have garlic, I planted radishes near the edge of the bed.

"After picking the garlic, peas, and radishes, I planted cucumbers and tomatoes along the trellis, and marigolds and nasturtiums in the strips near the edge. In other years, in the outer strip, I've planted lettuce, arugula, and cilantro in the spring and basil in the summer."

GROW PLANTS UP FOR BIG YIELDS IN A SMALL SPACE

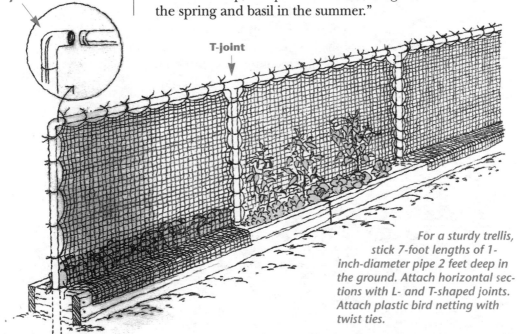

L-joint

T-joint

For a sturdy trellis, stick 7-foot lengths of 1-inch-diameter pipe 2 feet deep in the ground. Attach horizontal sections with L- and T-shaped joints. Attach plastic bird netting with twist ties.

175

Quick Supports for Higher Yields

Grow up! It's the best way to cram more plants into your intensive plot without taking up ground space. Here are three nifty suggestions for going vertical from community gardener Galen Bollinger of Austin, Texas.

Stack cages to support tall crops. Collapsible tomato cages made of galvanized wire are easy to store and set up. They can support heavy crops like tomatoes and can be stacked on top of each other for taller crops like vining cucumbers. "When I stack them, I use wire twist ties to fasten the stacked cages, two ties on each of the four sides," Galen explains. "When I expect the tomato crop to be heavy, I lash bamboo poles across the top to connect nearby cages." Galen stacks cages three high for cucumbers. He stabilizes the tall cages by fastening guy wires on either side. He attaches the guy wires to hooks screwed into the wooden boards that frame his raised beds. If you don't have framed beds, you can attach the guy wires to stakes driven into the soil 2 to 3 feet away from the tower of cages.

Corral wayward peas. For blockbuster pea yields, plant seeds thickly and give the crop plenty of supports to climb. Galen plants a bed of peas at a 3-inch spacing (he likes 'Sugar Ann'). Then he installs tomato cages over the planting and puts collapsible pea fencing down the long edges of the bed. By using these supports and making sure the germinating seedlings get enough water, Galen says he

Collapsible pea fence

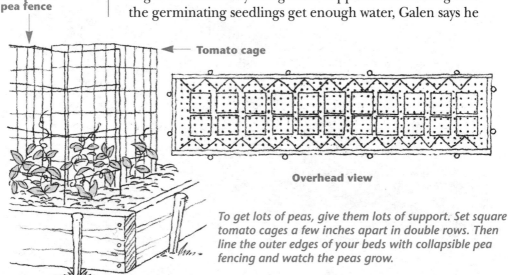

Tomato cage

Overhead view

To get lots of peas, give them lots of support. Set square tomato cages a few inches apart in double rows. Then line the outer edges of your beds with collapsible pea fencing and watch the peas grow.

gets "peas by the bowlful instead of the handful." He adds that for taller cultivars of peas, the tomato cages can be stacked two high.

Hold crops higher with heavy fishing line. To string a tall trellis for pole beans, Galen relies on 300-pound-test fishing line—the kind used for ocean fishing. The line is easy to work with, supports the heaviest crop without breaking, and is reusable. After bean season, Galen stores the fishing line by wrapping it around a piece of corrugated cardboard with notches in the edges to hold the line in place.

JUST SAY "NO" TO WASTED TRELLIS SPACE

Make the work you invest in building a trellis pay double dividends by using it to support two crops with different maturity times.

"In the middle of my raised bed, I have a trellis with horizontal wire supports," says Sharon Herth, a Master Gardener with the Washington State University Cooperative Extension Service. "I plant peas on one side and green beans on the other. When the peas are done, the beans are just getting going." This saves her the effort of building a second trellis for her bean crop. It's important to choose crops that won't compete with one another to make this system work well.

A wire trellis is strong enough to support two crops. Start an early crop like peas on one side, and a later crop like beans, cucumbers, or squash on the other.

KIWI

Grow Your Own Kiwis

What's the fastest, cheapest way to get kiwifruit to your table? Grow your own fuzzy kiwis (*Actinidia deliciosa*) if you live in warm areas like northern Florida or western Washington State (Zone 8). If you live farther north, grow hardy kiwis. (See "No Time to Trellis? Try Kiwis in a Pot" on page 180 for tips on growing hardy kiwis.)

"Kiwis are easy to grow, but they do take some attention," says Mary Gruver, a Master Gardener with the Washington State University Cooperative Extension Service. "They love sun, a lot of water, a well-drained soil, and shelter from the wind." Fuzzy kiwi vines are vigorous, so they also need a tall sturdy trellis. (See the sketch of Mary's trellis on the opposite page.)

You can plant fuzzy kiwis anytime, Mary says, but early spring is best. Grow one male and one female plant, and you'll have all the kiwifruit you can eat. Because kiwis grow fast, Mary cuts hers back three times a year to keep them manageable. If you don't want to prune them, you can grow the plants on an arbor for shade. You won't get as much fruit, but Mary says the leaves are just beautiful.

For the most fruit production, follow Mary's lead and prune your plants hard right after they flower, leaving some new growth and all the fruit-bearing growth. Mary cuts the branches just above where the fruits are forming. She prunes the plants again when the vines start to sprawl and curl to keep the plants from twining over themselves. In winter, prune the branches once more and leave about six buds on each vine.

Mary fertilizes her plants three times a year using this quick and easy method: Set a bucket filled with aged chicken manure at the base of each plant. Rainwater and irrigation water will dilute the manure and make the solution flow over the side of the bucket and around the base of the plants—it's the easiest manure tea ever.

PRUNING GETS YOU ALL THE FUZZY KIWIFRUIT YOU CAN EAT

Fuzzy kiwis take three to four years to bear fruit, but then bear prolifically. One year, Mary harvested over 1,700 kiwis from her pair of plants! The fruit is ready to pick in the fall, when it turns dark brown but is still hard. It will ripen gradually in the refrigerator, and it keeps well.

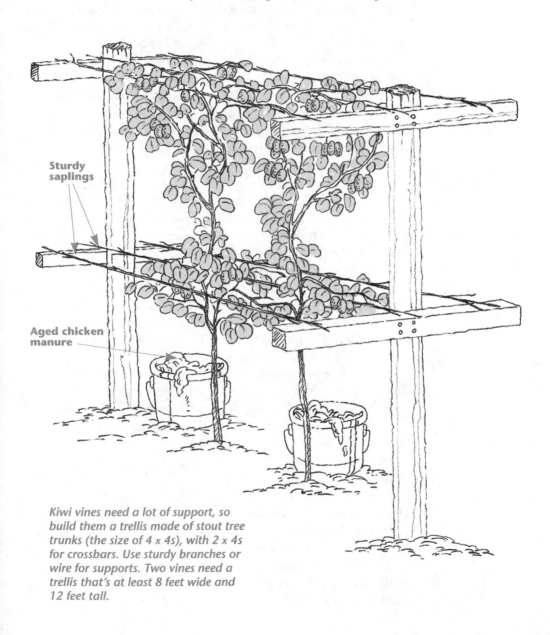

Sturdy saplings

Aged chicken manure

Kiwi vines need a lot of support, so build them a trellis made of stout tree trunks (the size of 4 x 4s), with 2 x 4s for crossbars. Use sturdy branches or wire for supports. Two vines need a trellis that's at least 8 feet wide and 12 feet tall.

No Time to Trellis? Try Kiwis in a Pot

GRAPE-SIZE
HARDY KIWIS
THRIVE IN
CONTAINERS

Try a container crop of hardy kiwis (*Actinidia arguta*) for tasty fruit without time-consuming trellising or waiting years for fruit. Hardy kiwifruits are only the size of large grapes, but their skins are smooth instead of fuzzy so you don't have to peel them.

David Kuchta, a hardy kiwi grower in Nesquehoning, Pennsylvania, recommends a Japanese cultivar called 'Issai' for container growing. 'Issai' is self-fertile, so you only need one plant. (Most kiwis need both male and female plants to produce fruit.) According to David, 'Issai' can bloom and produce fruit the first year after planting. By growing the plants in pots, you'll restrict their roots and topgrowth so they won't grow out of bounds.

If you have room for two plants and want to brighten your patio *and* please your palate, David recommends cultivars of the Russian species of hardy kiwi (*Actinidia kolomikta*), which bears fruit two to three years after planting. He says their slow growth and bushy habit make them good patio plants, plus they have other worthy features. Of all the kiwis, the kolomiktas have the most fragrant flowers, says David. They give off a beautiful lily-of-the-valley scent. Plus, the hardy kiwi leaves are showy—they're variegated with red, yellow, and white. Their fruits ripen around Labor Day, a week or two before other kiwis.

For the first two to three years, David keeps his young kiwis in gallon containers, then moves them into bigger pots as they grow. Although they don't need trellises, he provides a sturdy stake for support. He uses soilless potting mix to keep the pots light enough to move and to prevent soggy or compacted root zones—these plants need good drainage and evenly moist soil.

To prevent alternate freezing and thawing in winter, David recommends moving the pots into a sheltered site. "Don't let the soil dry out completely in the winter months, especially if it's not frozen solid," he warns. "And don't forget to provide some nutrients after plants begin growing in the spring. But go easy on the nitrogen; you don't want them to get too big."

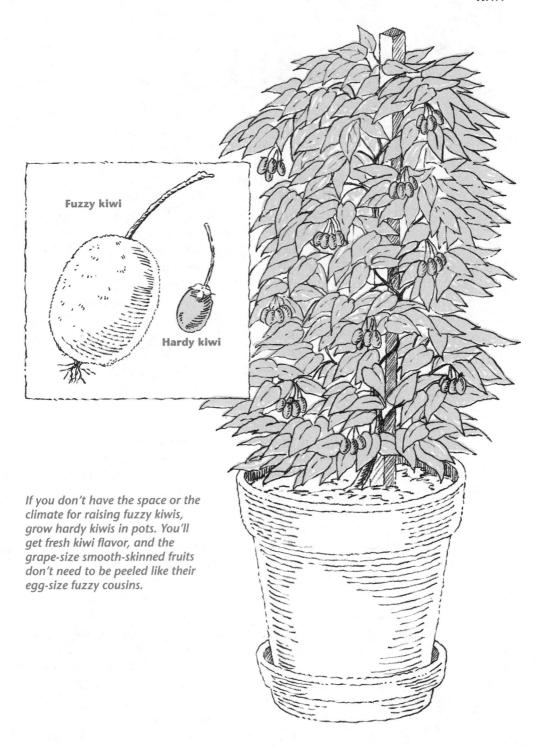

Fuzzy kiwi

Hardy kiwi

If you don't have the space or the climate for raising fuzzy kiwis, grow hardy kiwis in pots. You'll get fresh kiwi flavor, and the grape-size smooth-skinned fruits don't need to be peeled like their egg-size fuzzy cousins.

LABELS

2 Terrific Homemade Labels

SCROUNGE
PLANT LABELS
FROM HOUSE-
HOLD ITEMS

Don't leave off the labels when you plant. If you do, you're bound to forget what all of your plants are—or even *where* they are. You may mistakenly dig into dormant perennials and bulbs that you had forgotten about. So *do* label your plants—but save on the cost of purchased plant labels by making labels out of materials you have on hand.

Pieces of broken clay pots make wonderful plant labels, according to Master Gardener Les Manns of Lehigh County, Pennsylvania. Les says he prefers the appearance of his potsherd markers to typical plastic plant labels. He uses indelible pencil to write on each potsherd label, then sticks it in the ground next to the plant it names. The pottery has a nice smooth surface to write on, and its color looks nice among his plants, Les says.

Nancy Ondra, owner of Pendragon Perennials, a nursery in Emmaus, Pennsylvania, first saw her favorite homemade labels in pots at a plant sale. The pots sported names written on labels cut from vinyl miniblind slats! Nancy points out, "When you buy miniblinds you usually need to shorten them to fit your windows by removing some extra slats." Nancy uses a pair of scissors to cut the spare slats into label-size pieces. She finds that they're easy to write on and are long-lasting both in the greenhouse and in the garden. For labels for outdoor plants, Nancy makes an angled cut across the blind. That leaves a pointed end that penetrates the soil easily.

"I use a pencil to write on my plant labels, and I have some labels that are still clear and easy to read after six years in the garden," Nancy says. An advantage of using a pencil, she adds, is that you can erase it and reuse the label as often as you want.

Look around your house and yard for other innovative labels you can use. You can paint labels on stones or pieces of wood for a natural look, or come up with your own ideas.

Bury Your Labels to Make Them Last

Lost labels and mystery plants can leave you rummaging through your flower beds, searching in vain for plant tags that have mysteriously disappeared. And if you do find some evidence of a label, it's usually the half without the writing. If this scenario is all too familiar, change your tactics and "bury" your labels for safekeeping, recommends Nancy McDonald, managing editor of *The American Cottage Gardener* magazine.

"I can't afford to lose track of my plants," says Nancy, whose Michigan garden houses the American Dianthus Society's Northern Test Garden. "Plus, I can't spend a lot of time and money on labels."

Nancy buys the better-grade 4-inch plastic labels—they're ⅝ inch wide and come in strips of eight (80 for $3.25)—and a permanent marking pen. She likes pens with extra-fine points and black ink because they fade the least. Nancy writes on the labels starting ¼ inch from the top of the blunt end.

When she sets labels in the garden, Nancy pushes them in deeply, leaving only the top ¼ inch exposed. This solves two problems. The labels can't get broken off or knocked out of place, and the ink lasts much longer because it's protected from the sun and weather. "My labels are still in perfect shape after five years. And not only that," Nancy laughs, "you avoid that gruesome graveyard look."

Plastic plant labels last longer when you bury them in the ground. If you place them in the same position in relation to your plants, they're always easy to find too. Try putting labels at the northwest corner of each plant, or use your favorite direction.

LANDSCAPING

Get a Bird's-Eye View of Your Garden

CLIMB THE ROOF
FOR A QUICK
GARDEN
OVERVIEW

Seeing your garden in a new light may be all you need to improve its design. But how do you get a new view? A movie scene inspired landscape architect Rick Griffin of Jackson, Mississippi, to climb on his roof to see his garden from a new perspective. It was such a dramatic experience that he's been urging clients to do it ever since.

If you decide to give this a try, be careful. And expect to experience a completely new garden view. You'll see how plants or structures that seem important from the ground may not make sense in the overall picture. For example, you may notice that a huge shrub you thought was a garden focal point may actually be blocking a gorgeous view. You'll be able to note subtle changes in soil types by how similar plants are growing differently—better in one area than another. You may find ways to improve your mowing patterns, see opportunities for new paths, or identify where problem areas are or where there's wasted space. This bird's-eye view may or may not change your garden style, but it's the fastest way to evaluate your garden layout.

What was the movie that inspired Rick? *Dead Poets Society*. And the scene was when a teacher had his students climb atop their desks for a new perspective on life.

Zone In on Your Garden

Take a look at your landscape and decide which areas you use the most and which you use the least. You can save lots of running around if you arrange your yard so gardens or plants you visit a lot are close to the house, and those you don't go to very often are farther away.

Dividing areas up into "use zones" is something we all do anyway, consciously or not. Think of how your kitchen is arranged—you keep your most-used pots and cooking utensils within easy reach, and arrange food in the fridge so the items you need most are in front or easy to get to.

John Cretti, the "Rocky Mountain Horticulturist" in Golden, Colorado, urges his radio listeners to keep things simple and close in the garden as well. John says you should arrange garden areas, and plants within those areas, closer to or farther from the house, shed, or wherever, depending on how much you use them. "For example, the kitchen garden should naturally be as close to the kitchen door as possible," he says, "and certainly within easy reach of a garden hose." John adds that firewood should be stacked close to the door—but not so close that it touches the house, or insects may move from the wood to your home. And consider carefully where you place the garbage, the compost, and old flowerpots—they need to be convenient, but not in a place where you have to always step over them.

■ High-Use Area　　　■ Medium-Use Area　　　■ Low-Use Area

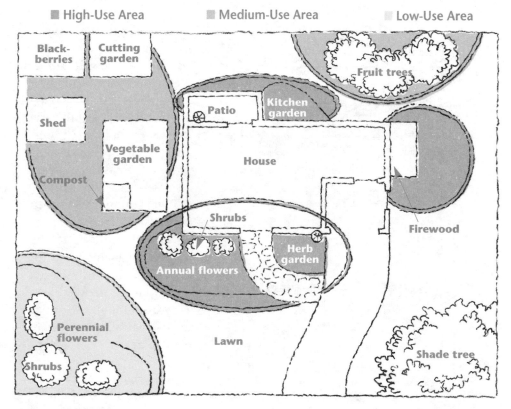

Identify your landscape's "use zones" before you add or change features. Put gardens and structures you visit often close to the house, and move less-used features farther away.

Kick-Start Your Landscape Design

What if you're ready to landscape your yard but don't know what to do first? Try this one-step starter system from Felder Rushing, coauthor of *Passalong Plants.* Felder says it's great for giving first-time gardeners direction, and it even helps experienced gardeners who are stumped by a new or old yard.

Here's what to do. First, stand at an entrance to your yard, or look out a window or door, and focus on a spot far from where you're standing. Then decide on a "hard" feature such as a rock, a bench, or a piece of fence that you'd like to put in the faraway spot. This serves as a starting point or "footprint" from which everything else can evolve.

Pick a route for a path that leads to the new feature. Sometimes it ends up being a formal, straight walk, sometimes a bold curve, sometimes a meandering path—it just depends on your taste and house style. Imagine the path in your head, draw it on paper, or use flags to mark it out and get it just the way you want. The path divides the yard area in two, so you have two small areas to landscape instead of one big one.

What you make the path out of isn't as important as just putting something out there and making a way to get to it. The path and new feature create a "people place" away from the house and are the official start of your landscape plan.

Create a focal point in your garden, then build a path to bring people to it. That's all it takes to start a landscape design.

Once you have a path, either on paper or in reality, draw or place mulch and shrubs and flowers on one side of the path and lawn on the other. The plants and inviting path create a visual strong point that guides your eye to that new feature out in the garden. On one side of the path you'll have lots of opportunity to plant shrubs, flowers, trees, and other plants. The grass on the other side unifies the area and gives an illusion of roominess. The footprint plan works, even in the smallest garden space.

Don't Be Afraid to Ask for Help

Sometimes it's hard to get started on a landscape project. Taking that first step can be scary or confusing. That's when it helps to have professional prodding. Mississippi landscape architect Clifton Egger gets his clients off to a good start by asking what they do and don't like in a garden. This review may be just what you need to make decisions about your garden.

If you can't decide on a garden style or layout, talking with a professional is a good way to sort things out. "Finding out what colors the gardener likes, if he likes to cook out or mow grass, or if her lifestyle is too busy to do much gardening is crucial to giving good advice," Clifton says. He feels it's more important to spend an hour talking with a gardener than to draw up a detailed plan of what he thinks they want.

FOR A GREAT LANDSCAPE, ALL YOU NEED MAY BE ADVICE

You can get a quicker start and avoid costly mistakes by asking for advice before you get in too deep. For the best and least expensive results, find a licensed landscape architect who's willing to work on a consulting basis. All you need is a pro who will take a paid walk through your garden, a walk with no strings—like guaranteed plant sales or an expensive plan—attached. Check your phone book for listings of members of the American Society of Landscape Architects (ASLA) so you'll get someone who follows professional standards. Ask if you can visit gardens of former clients. Develop a rapport before agreeing to spend a lot of money on a plan. If all you need is someone to help you figure out what you want, that's what you should pay for, not a high-priced plan or maintenance contract.

Snow Makes a Cool Garden Design Tool

Use the materials you've got on hand to help you visualize your landscape, and you'll get the design you want without a lot of expense or bother. Jeff Lowenfels, garden writer for the *Anchorage (Alaska) Daily News,* urges his readers to use snow to figure out how they want to plant their yards come summertime.

"Snow helps me plan my garden design," Jeff says. "Whenever it snows—which, of course, is a *lot*—I take the snowplow or shovel and pile the white stuff into hedges and walls, and even reshape my normally straight walk into a curve or semicurve."

Winter is a great time to experiment with garden ideas. You can try out different plant sizes and planting styles. Build dwarf- and standard-size shrubs to see which fit best, then keep adding snow to find out what they'll look like as they grow. Or see what your yard will look like with an informal planting like an island bed, or a formal garden with neatly clipped plants of snow.

If you want a more realistic look, spray your "snowplants" with a bottle filled with water and several drops of green food dye. Spray a snow

Sculpt a landscape out of snow to see how your plan looks before you buy a single plant. You can "install" a few snow-shrubs, a snow-hedge, or even a snow-path.

pathway with other food colorings, and you can decide if you want your future walkway to be red brick, brown wood chips, or gray slate.

Jeff says you can also use Christmas trees, either your own, ones your neighbors have discarded, or ones you pick up from your local recycling center, to experiment with plantings. Try them out for an instant effect in the winter—if you like the way they look, replace them with growing trees in the spring. Before your creations melt away, draw them on paper or photograph them, so by the time spring arrives you've got a landscape plan and are ready to go.

Jeff has discovered that snow makes a particularly good way to plan paths. He says that in the winter you can see where your *real* paths are—not the ones that pave their way to your front door, but the ones you and visitors use for shortcuts, and where your dogs normally walk. You can use this information to your advantage when you plan the location for new garden paths. If you've already got paths, you can see where you'll need to set up barriers or other means to retrain the dogs (or visitors).

Easy Landscaping with Paper "Plants"

If you have trouble picturing how your landscape design will look once it's installed, make a "mock landscape" out of brown paper, newspaper, or similar material. It's a favorite technique of Ann Milovsoroff, landscape architect at the Royal Botanical Gardens in Hamilton, Ontario. Ann says to start with a wide roll of brown paper—the kind used in florist shops. Wad large pieces of the paper into globes, cones, rectangles, or other shapes to match the plants on your plan. Make trees by putting the brown paper shapes on broom handles or sticks.

Set the paper shapes around your yard in the positions they're shown on your plan and see what you think. "Look at them from the front yard, backyard, and from inside the house so you can get a good idea of how the space will look and feel," Ann says. You can easily move your plant replicas around to adjust the design; it's much simpler than moving around heavy shrubs and trees.

Convenient Computerized Landscape Design

DOUBLE-CLICK
YOUR WAY TO A
NEW GARDEN
DESIGN

Whether you're starting from scratch at a new home, improving your current landscape, or helping friends with their yard designs, a computer design program can help you do the job faster and easier. Maybe. Bobbie Schwartz, a garden designer in Cleveland, tested two software design programs and found remarkable differences in how convenient they were to use.

The best program that she tested was Land Designer for Windows. Within an hour, she had the program up and working while she designed a bed and put plants in it. She was able to work fast because the tutorial was helpful and was backed up with a good instruction book. Bobbie says the graphics were colorful and useful—although they didn't print out well on her black-and-white printer.

Bobbie says the printout gives you a good feel for the way plant groups are positioned and for the outline of the bed. But pink, green, blue-green, and some other colors print out in similar shades of gray, so you can't see how they'll work together. And Bobbie adds that even if you had a color printer, there aren't enough gradations in color to give you an accurate picture of the landscape.

She says she was less impressed with the second program she tried. "The whole program was aggravating!" she fumes. It was difficult to start, the directions were poorly written, and the tutorial didn't give information for basic tasks like saving a program. In four hours, Bobbie was unable to get the program up and working. The moral of this story is: Make sure you find out what a design program is like before you buy it.

If you have a good program, you'll find that it's easier to make changes on a computer screen than to have to do a lot of erasing and tracing on paper. Computer programs are a great way to start designing—they can give you the confidence to experiment, and they're especially handy if you're trying out lots of plans. But the best programs can't match the convenience of drawing while you're actually standing in the landscape. For the best of both worlds, use a computer program to narrow down your design choices, and finalize your design with a hand drawing.

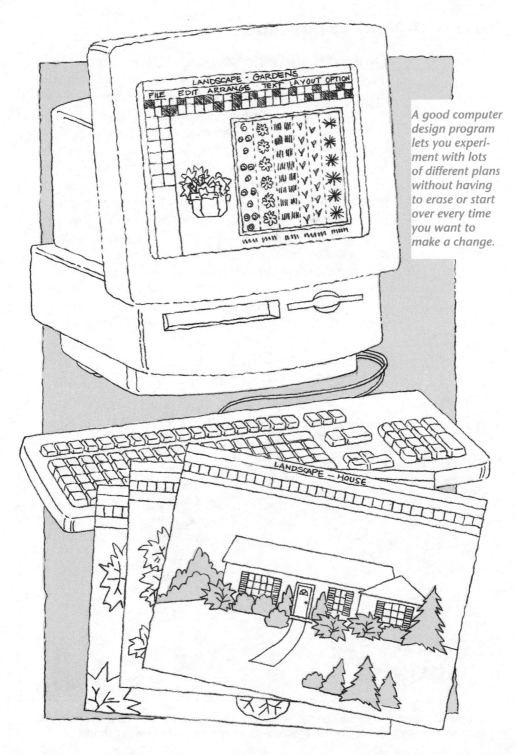

A good computer design program lets you experiment with lots of different plans without having to erase or start over every time you want to make a change.

191

Grow with Your Landscape

Times change, and so do gardens. You can put off some changes, fight others, or simply go gracefully with the flow. When it comes to maturing landscapes, it's often easiest and least expensive to go with the changes.

Andy Hull, senior vice president of Post Landscape Services, an affiliate of Post Properties in Atlanta, has to be as efficient as possible, so he's found ways to let landscapes age gracefully with simple design changes. There's less maintenance, which makes him, his clients, and his employees happy. "As our property matures, we change with it," Andy says. You can use this same plan for easy success with your own maturing landscape.

Getting started: Quickly cover your yard with a variety of plants—trees, groundcovers, annual and perennial flowers, and shrubs that will fit your property, even when they're mature. Reduce the time and money you spend on

Annuals add color to a landscape but increase the maintenance. Use them to brighten a young garden, but replace them over time with perennials and flowering shrubs.

Turf areas shrink as the landscape matures, and easy-care groundcovers and shrubs fill in spaces that once required regular mowing.

pruning, pest control, watering, and other chores by choosing healthy plants that thrive in your climate. A plant that's the right size for your house or yard and that likes your growing conditions will stay healthy for years and won't need much care.

First and second years: New gardens need plenty of water to get established and lots of seasonal color to make them attractive. Use annual flowers to add instant color and a variety of perennials for seasonal interest. Use lawn grass in areas that erode rather than as an overall groundcover. Turf is the cheapest material to put out, but the most expensive to maintain unless it's easy to get to with a really big mower.

Third or fourth year: Start replacing annuals with perennials or colorful shrubs. Let groundcovers take over some of the lawn areas, so they'll need less mowing and edging.

Later years: Bring in more shrubs and groundcovers to fill in areas that have become shaded. Add natural leaf litter as a mulch.

Enjoy Your Garden Longer with Lighting

HERE'S A
BRIGHT IDEA FOR
GETTING MORE
GARDEN TIME

Does dusk come before you get home from work, leaving you with only weekends to enjoy your garden? Add inexpensive lights to your landscape and get out of the house and into an evening wonderland. And you don't have to know beans about electricity to do it.

Complete kits, available at garden centers and building supply outlets, are inexpensive, easy to install, and, being low voltage, completely safe even around wet soils and water. And low voltage isn't dim—car headlights are low voltage! For super-easy lighting, look for solar-powered units. Lee Runnels, greens coordinator—he sets up outdoor movie scenes for a Hollywood studio—says he just sticks the solar units wherever he needs some interesting mood lighting. "It's great for me because there aren't even any wires involved," he says.

Well-placed lights let you enjoy your garden after dark. You can use lights to illuminate steps and paths, highlight special plants or garden features, or create a dramatic mood.

When you install the lights, don't string them out like airport runway lights—move them around until you find the most dramatic effect. Place them under shrubs, behind trees, beside steps, anywhere except where their glare will shine directly in your eyes. (There's nothing worse than having guests stumbling around outside with spotlights shining in their eyes.) Backlight steps and other potential night hazards so you can see them clearly. Make use of shadows created by the lights too—they can give your garden a more dramatic look.

Personalize your lights by replacing standard-issue light covers with homemade ones. Try covering lights with clay pots, metal cans, copper sheets shaped like seashells, or wooden boxes. It's an easy way to make functional night lighting fixtures look "garden-friendly" by day.

Rock (and Roll) Gardening

There's nothing more relaxing than sitting in your garden in the evening listening to the natural sounds of crickets chirping and grasses sighing in the breeze. But if instead of nature, you hear clanking dishes from a neighbor's kitchen or the muted roar of a nearby interstate, relief is within earshot.

John Cretti, the "Rocky Mountain Horticulturist" in Golden, Colorado, solved his noise-pollution problem with a set of easy-to-install outdoor speakers. John connected the speakers to a radio/CD player, and now he pipes his own version of night sounds right out into the garden.

While few outdoor speakers are truly weatherproof, most will resist temperature extremes, humidity, wind, and all but the most constant dousing of rain. Instead of paper cones, outdoor speakers have high-grade plastic (polypropylene) ones, and they're encased in steel. Mount them under an eave or on a protected wall and they'll last longer. Some speakers are freestanding and can give 360 degrees of sound. John even found some that are encased in a surprisingly realistic artificial rock material, so they're perfect for nestling in a flower bed or rock garden.

LAWNS

Ecolawns Need Less Care

GROW A LESS-
HUNGRY, LESS-
THIRSTY LAWN

Cut back on mowing and give up fertilizing your lawn. Impossible, you say? Not at all, if you learn to love a new kind of lawn—the ecolawn.

An ecolawn combines grasses that aren't aggressive with legumes and flowering broadleaf plants that can tolerate mowing. Tom Cook, an associate professor of horticulture at Oregon State University in Corvallis, finds that ecolawns require less work but still look and act like real lawns. They're comfortable to sit and walk on, and they tolerate heavy use. While an ecolawn doesn't offer the manicured perfection of a solid stand of grass, it gives the appearance of lawn with scattered small flowers in it.

After years of striving for a lawn with identical blades of grass, a flowering lawn may take a little getting used to. But the flowers will grow on you, and the time and effort you save with an ecolawn will make it more attractive right away.

The ecolawns Tom has tested last two weeks between mowings during the spring and three weeks when growth is less vigorous. They require no fertilizer other than clippings left on the lawn after mowing.

To start an ecolawn, plant in the spring on graded bare soil or into a dethatched lawn. Sow seed at a rate of 2 pounds per 1,000 square feet. Don't fertilize before planting unless the soil is poor. In that case, Tom recommends a fertilizer that's low in nitrogen and high in phosphorus and potassium (one possibility is a mix of bonemeal and greensand). If you mulch the seeded area, apply only a light covering to keep from smothering the seedlings of the broadleaf plants.

Once your ecolawn is established, water it once a month during the summer. Tom applies about 1½ inches of water during each watering. "This amounts to about one-third to one-quarter as much water as a regular lawn," Tom says.

PROVEN PLANTS FOR ECOLAWNS

Ecolawns contain a mix of typical lawn grasses and some broadleaf plants, including legumes. According to Tom Cook, an associate professor of horticulture at Oregon State University in Corvallis, the best ecolawn mixes include nonaggressive grasses that won't choke out the other plants. The ratio of grass seed to broadleaf seed can vary, but Tom has gotten the best results by blending 80 percent grass seed to 20 percent broadleaf seed (by weight). Here are some grasses and other plants that Tom recommends for ecolawns in northern regions.

FLOWERING BROADLEAF PLANTS

Common yarrow (*Achillea millefolium*)
Perennial with feathery leaves. Grows well in poor, dry soil. Will not bloom if kept mowed short. Hardy to Zone 2.

English daisy (*Bellis perennis*)
Rosette of long broad leaves and daisylike white or pink flowers in spring. Grows to 6 inches tall. Hardy to Zone 3.

GRASSES

Kentucky bluegrass (*Poa pratensis*)
A fine-textured deep green lawn grass. Withstands a wide range of climate conditions. Disease-resistant hybrids are available. Hardy to Zone 3.

Perennial ryegrass (*Lolium perenne*)
A fine-textured lawn grass that establishes rapidly. Insect-resistant cultivars are available. Hardy to Zone 5.

Red fescue (*Festuca rubra*)
A fine-textured lawn grass with moderate heat tolerance. Good for humid, cool regions. Hardy to Zone 2.

Tall fescue (*Festuca arundinacea*)
A coarse lawn grass with a bunching habit. Good heat and drought tolerance; tolerates acid soils. Hardy to Zone 2.

LEGUMES

Strawberry clover (*Trifolium fragiferum*)
This legume resembles white clover but is less vigorous. Flowers throughout summer. Flowers are pink or white. Hardy to Zone 4.

White clover (*Trifolium repens*)
Legume with well-known three-part leaves and small white flowers throughout summer. Low-growing, spreading stems up to 1 foot long. Hardy to Zone 3.

Get Your New Lawn Off to a Great Start

Here's a trio of tricks for making a new lawn look attractive faster, from Rose Vincent of Vincent Landscapes in Austin, Texas.

Mix a special soil blend. When you plan to sow grass seed, top-dress the area with 2 to 3 inches of weed-free sandy loam. (If you're not sure the soil is free of weed seeds, solarize it before planting; see "Easy Ways to Handle Prickly Plants" on page 255.) Cover the sandy loam with a thin layer of peat moss, and rake gently to mix the peat moss and soil. Then spread seed according to package directions. The new grass will root quickly in the soft surface soil.

Stagger sod for a finished look fast. When laying sod pieces, stagger them as you would when laying bricks. The rows of sod pieces will be less noticeable.

Get a grip on edgings. Use corrugated black plastic edging rather than smooth edging to separate grass and flower beds. The corrugated plastic grips the soil better, so it's less likely to pop out—meaning you won't waste time reinstalling it.

Place sod in staggered rows—instead of lining all the seams up directly under each other—and your new lawn will look grown-in faster.

Sod Solves Runoff Woes

Start with sod, not seed, for success in maintaining your lawn in spots where runoff is a problem. When they're first planted, lawns established with turfgrass sod are 15 times more effective in controlling runoff than seed-established lawns, according to research by Dr. Thomas Watschke, professor of turfgrass science at the Pennsylvania State University. The difference in the amount of runoff is greatest when the plantings are just getting established, Dr. Watschke says. As seeded lawns grow, their ability to control runoff improves, but in test plots, sodded slopes had less runoff than seeded ones even after three years.

While starting a lawn from sod is more expensive than using seed, there's no savings if surface water runoff keeps washing out your seedling lawn. To protect your investment in sod, be sure you choose a sod grown from grass cultivars that thrive in your area. Check with your state's land grant university before you buy. Most conduct evaluation programs on sod and will recommend specific cultivars for you.

Mulch Makes Grass Seed Stay Put

End the frustration of watching your newly seeded lawn wash away in a sudden rain. You can save yourself from losing seed (and from the hassle of reseeding) by shaking a very thin layer of pine needles, straw, or hay over freshly sown seeds. Use just enough mulch to catch seed before it washes away, but not enough to shade seedlings.

SAVE NEW LAWNS FROM WASHING AWAY

Individual pieces of straw or hay may seem too small to have any beneficial effects, but even the thinnest layer shields the soil and prevents it from forming a hard crust. Friable soil is easier for seeds to poke through, so they'll sprout faster and anchor themselves in place.

If you don't have pine needles or straw, you may want to try a commercial product called Pennmulch, made of pelleted recycled paper. Pennmulch may have advantages over straw, according to its developer, turfgrass instructor George Hamilton at the Pennsylvania State University. "Straw often contains weed seeds, tends to blow away, and is difficult to store and handle," George says.

Pest-Proof Grasses

Plant insect-resistant lawn grasses to get a head start on a healthy lawn. These grasses, called endophytic grasses, have a built-in pest control. "Endophytic grasses have a naturally occurring fungus that deters insects," explains Michael Merner, who owns The Organic Landscape Company at Earth Care Farm in Charleston, Rhode Island. "By planting endophytic grasses, you have a long-term solution to insect pests."

The most common lawn-damaging insects you're likely to encounter are sod webworms, chinch bugs, and white grubs. Endophytic grasses repel the sod webworms and chinch bugs, "so that's 66 percent of the problem gone," Michael notes. The grasses also deter armyworms, bluegrass billbugs, and harmful nematodes.

Fescues and perennial ryegrass are the most endophytic types of grasses. There's also variability in resistance from cultivar to cultivar. Michael advises buying a mix of

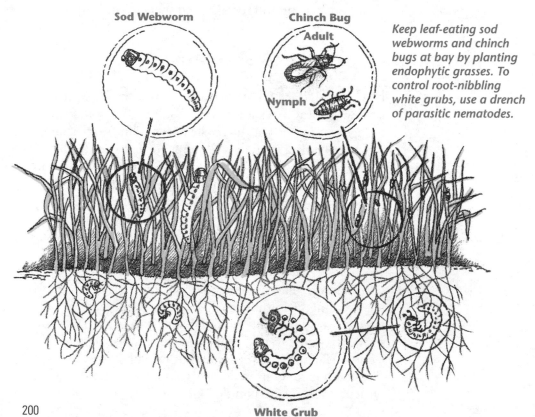

Sod Webworm

Chinch Bug
Adult
Nymph

White Grub

Keep leaf-eating sod webworms and chinch bugs at bay by planting endophytic grasses. To control root-nibbling white grubs, use a drench of parasitic nematodes.

endophytic grass seed from a company that changes its blend in response to annual variations. Endophytic grass mixes are available at most garden centers and are usually labeled as endophytic.

Michael does have one warning about endophytic grasses: They are for lawns, not for pastures. The same fungus that repels insects can cause health problems in grazing animals.

JUST SAY "NO" TO MOWING AND WATERING

Your lawn can get through a dry summer with less water than you might think, if you manage it right. These summer lawn-care tips are for northern cool-season grasses, such as Kentucky bluegrass and fescues, says turf specialist Bill Pound of the Ohio Cooperative Extension Service.

Mow less. Grass grows more slowly when water is in short supply. Keep an eye on how fast the grass is growing; once you see a slowdown, cut the mowing frequency from every five days to every eight or more days.

Keep cool. Mow in the morning or evening hours, Bill suggests. That way both you and your lawn will suffer less heat stress.

Cut sharp. "Make certain the mower blades are properly sharpened to avoid tearing the ends of the grass blades," Bill advises. A bad cut stresses the grass; it also makes the ends turn brown.

Go slow with fertilizer. When grass is suffering from drought, adding fertilizer makes matters

worse. Reduce the stress on your grass by letting it rest instead of pushing it to grow more. Use a slow-release form of nitrogen, like those found in most organic fertilizers, in the late spring or early summer.

Put off dethatching and aerating. While removing thatch and aerating can help your lawn in cooler weather, "they can significantly damage turfgrass under stress," Bill says. Wait until wetter weather for best results.

By following these suggestions, you can water less often. A light watering every two weeks is enough to keep a lawn alive without greening it up. If you want a green lawn, you'll need to water more often—applying ½ to ¾ inch every four or five days. "Irrigate early in the morning," Bill says. "The grass is already wet from dew, temperatures are cooler, humidity is high, and it's usually calm." The grass roots have a better chance of absorbing and using the water under these conditions.

Let Grass Clippings Fall Where They May

Stop raking your lawn clippings! You'll save time and the money that you used to spend on fertilizer. *And* your lawn will be healthier and more beautiful.

Collecting lawn clippings has been part of the dogma of American lawn care for decades. But whether you bag them or rake them, gathering up clippings eats up gardening time. In an extension service demonstration in Texas, home gardeners who did not rake found that they had to mow one extra time per month, but saved an average of 35 minutes per mowing. Overall savings averaged 12 hours of yard work per year per gardener!

Leaving clippings on the lawn feeds your grass. Commercial lawn care companies leave clippings on lawns because it saves on fertilizer costs. As the clippings break down, they supply some nitrogen, phosphorus, and potassium to the soil. Because the clippings break down, they do not create thatch—a matted layer of grass stems and roots at the soil surface. Horticulturist Wayne McLaurin at the University of Georgia says, "Letting the clips fall where they may does not cause thatch," noting that this is a long-held but mistaken myth about grass clippings.

The most important tips for success with this time-saving technique are:

• Keep your mower blades sharp. This ensures that they will make a clean cut and minimizes stress on the mower's engine.

• Use a mulching mower. You can choose from several brands of mulching mowers. Their specially designed blades cut grass leaves twice, leaving a fine layer of clippings that quickly fall into the lawn without a trace.

• Mow a little more often. Tall grass is hard to cut with a mulching mower. If the layer of clippings left behind is too heavy, it won't break down readily, leaving behind an unsightly mess. A good rule of thumb is to remove only about a third of the grass blade at a time. (For example, if your lawn is 3 inches tall when you mow, you shouldn't cut it to less than 2 inches tall.)

FEED YOUR LAWN EFFORT-LESSLY WHEN YOU MOW

• Mow the grass when your lawn is dry, not wet, to keep clippings from sticking and clumping together, which also slows their breakdown.

Lawn Vac to the Rescue!

Your yard's a mess and company's coming. Don't panic, get out the vacuum! Gardener Vicki Milam of Denver relies on this trick for picking up fallen crabapples in a jiffy. "I use a shop-type vacuum to pick them up. I don't have to stoop, and it gives the neighbors a good laugh," Vicki says. You can also use the vacuum to extract other types of fruit tree drops, as well as seeds of Norway maples and goldenrain trees that work their way into your grass. It's also handy for a final cleanup of leaves and small twigs that can get left behind after you haul away prunings from trees or shrubs.

Vicki says that occasionally a crabapple gets stuck against the end of the wand, "at which time I pick the culprit off the wand and drop it in a pocket" for disposal later. You can empty the vacuum into the compost pile, or pick through the crabapples for the good ones and make them into jam or preserves—just be sure to wash them first in case the inside of the vacuum was less than spotless.

A shop vacuum makes short work of cleaning up fallen crabapples and other messy garden debris. Get one for your yard at your local home center or hardware store.

203

Quick Lawn Fix

COMPOST AND
SEAWEED SPEED
LAWN REPAIRS

Now you can skip seeding small bare patches in your lawn. Depending on the size of the bare spot, you can do a fast repair with compost and liquid seaweed, according to Nancy Browne Coleman, owner of Organic Lawns in Parsippany, New Jersey.

To fill in small bare patches in spring, Nancy applies a thin layer of compost over the bare area. "The grass around it roots into the compost and covers the area faster and thicker than reseeding would," she reports. That's because grass seedlings have to compete with weeds in spring and often lose the fight. In fall, reseeding works fine since weeds aren't sprouting. Nancy says her method works for spots 1 foot or less in diameter, in lawns with spreading grasses like bluegrass. It won't work for clump-forming grasses.

For larger areas, Nancy's quick fix does involve reseeding, but with a pretreatment that speeds germination. First soak the grass seed in liquid seaweed for 24 hours. Then drain the liquid and mix the seed with good soil and compost (2 tablespoons of seed in 1 gallon of soil and compost). Rake the bare area and spread the seed-and-soil mix over it. Keep the area moist while the seedlings get established.

Why Buy a Mulching Mower?

Keep your savings by keeping your old lawn mower. Before you give up on your conventional lawn mower and buy a new mulching type, consider a shortcut that can save you the purchase. (Mulching mowers save you time and make your lawn healthier, but you may not have money set aside for a new mower.) If you have a side-discharge mower, a change in your mowing pattern can make it act like a mulching mower, says gardener Beverly Erlebacher of Toronto. "I always discharge onto the unmowed part, which means the clippings get picked up and cut up several times, like with a mulching mower," Beverly explains.

If you have a rear-bagging mower, check with your dealer about a kit to retrofit the mower as a mulching mower. Generally, the kits cost about $50. Kits usually aren't available for mowers that are more than five years old.

Double-Seed to Double-Cross Weeds

Warm-season grasses can take the heat of southern summers, but they don't green up until temperatures are above 80°F. Their late start gives weeds that love cool weather plenty of time to take hold. But you can get a jump on the weeds and the growing season by overseeding your lawn with annual ryegrass in the fall. It stays green all winter, competes with fall and spring weeds, then dies out by summer. To get the best results, double-seed the rye, says Rose Vincent of Vincent Landscapes in Austin, Texas.

"Use 20 pounds of seed per 1,000 square feet, instead of the usual 10 pounds," Rose advises. "That allows for loss due to birds, washing away in heavy rains, and seeds that don't germinate. And it saves you from having to go back and re-seed bare areas two weeks later."

Rose also offers these tips for efficient seeding and care of winter lawns.

Seed small jobs by hand. Rotary fertilizer spreaders work for seeding large lawns but may overshoot small areas, which means wasted seed and extra weeding. Sow by hand or use a drop spreader instead.

Don't let grass go hungry. Fertilize every eight weeks with a blended organic fertilizer, because annual grasses like rye are voracious feeders. Otherwise, they'll steal nutrients from the soil that your perennial grass needs.

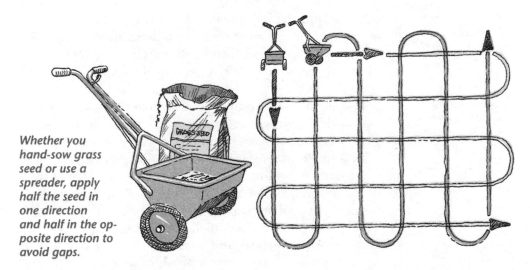

Whether you hand-sow grass seed or use a spreader, apply half the seed in one direction and half in the op-posite direction to avoid gaps.

Drop Your Drop Spreader

"I used to HATE fertilizing my lawn," says gardener Cindy Amack, who has a hilly yard outside of Denver. "It seemed like it took me as long to fertilize as it did to mow." For Cindy, the answer was to switch from a drop spreader to a handheld spreader. "Now I can get a big bag of fertilizer down in 15 minutes," she reports. "And I think the control is better—I can get extra in starved areas. And I never get stripes where the fertilizer has been applied unevenly."

Cindy attributes the faster application time to the design of the handheld spreader, which makes a broader sweep than the drop spreader. Plus, it's easier to tote up and down hill than a heavy drop spreader. Reloading a handheld spreader is simpler too. "It's much easier to reach

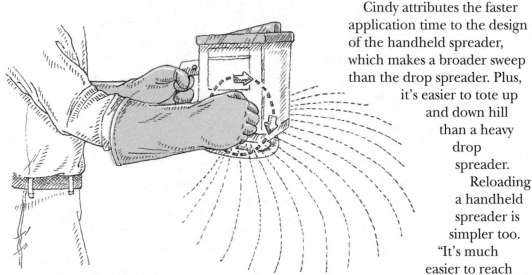

Crank out lawn fertilizer far (in 8-foot bands) and fast with a handheld spreader. Its small size makes it easy to fill and a breeze to use, even on rough terrain.

the little spreader into the bag than to lift a heavy bag and dump it into the big reservoir of a standard spreader," Cindy says. "I can't even rest the bag on the edge of my drop spreader when filling it, because if I do, the spreader scoots!"

Handheld spreaders are easy to find in hardware stores and garden centers. You can also find bagged blended organic fertilizers for lawns at most garden centers and nurseries, and they're available from mail-order garden supply companies. A fertilizer with an NPK (nitrogen-phosphorus-potassium) ratio of 3-1-2 or 4-1-2 is fine for most lawns and will give you good even growth. If you prefer, you can make your own organic fertilizer blend by mixing 3 parts blood meal, 3 parts bonemeal, and 1 part kelp meal. This and similar mixes will provide a steady supply of nutrients.

Get Greener Grass Fast

Give your lawn a green-up with these quick and easy fertilizing secrets from Nancy Browne Coleman, owner of Organic Lawns in Parsippany, New Jersey.

Soothe sunburned grass with seaweed. To green up a lawn that's suffering from heat stress, spray liquid seaweed on the grass. It may take several applications and you must keep the lawn watered once it greens up again. Nancy recommends that you use a hose-end sprayer to apply the seaweed and that you use a double dose along the edges of the lawn that border sidewalks and driveways, where reflected heat increases the stress on the grass.

Give hungry lawns a special mix. Some organic fertilizers last longer than others. "Fertilizers that are high in compost tend to get used up and have to be applied more often," Nancy says. To meet your lawn's nutrient needs in two annual applications instead of three or four, Nancy recommends using fertilizers that include mineral ingredients such as granite meal, greensand, seaweed, natural rock phosphate, and trace minerals.

A broadcast spreader (bottom) lets you feed your lawn in fewer trips than with a drop spreader (top). Overlap each pass slightly to get even coverage.

Wait for the rainy season. If your region has predictable rainy and dry seasons, make the spring fertilizer application during or after the rainy season, not before. "You don't want a fertilized lush grass going into the rainy season, because it will be more prone to disease," Nancy says. And by applying fertilizer during the rainy season, you can count on the rains to water it into the soil.

LEEKS

Give Leeks a Longer Lease on Life

Get a crop of leeks in half the time by replanting the roots. Leeks grown from seedlings typically take at least three months to mature. But William Allen, a home gardener in Jonesboro, Arkansas, has found a way to cut that time in half *and* get two crops from the same plant! Here's his secret: Before using homegrown or store-bought leeks in a recipe, "I always cut off their roots, leaving about ¼ inch of the stalk attached," William explains. He puts the root pieces in a bowl of water until he's ready to plant.

William's replanting technique is simple: Dig a hole a couple of inches deep (deep enough to accommodate the roots), pop the leek in, barely cover it with soil, and heap some leaves on top. In about a week, green shoots will start to appear. "When I plant them in spring, the new leeks are ready to harvest in five to nine weeks," William says. He uses the same method with green onions, but only has a 60 percent success rate, compared to about 90 percent with the leeks.

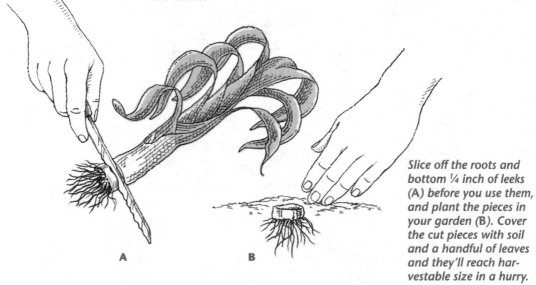

A   B

Slice off the roots and bottom ¼ inch of leeks (A) before you use them, and plant the pieces in your garden (B). Cover the cut pieces with soil and a handful of leaves and they'll reach harvestable size in a hurry.

JUST SAY "NO" TO EXTRA WORK WITH LEEKS

When fall and its chores are closing in—you still have to harvest the last tomatoes, rake leaves, and give the lawn a final mowing—things can get as hectic as spring planting. But you'll be happy to know that there's one chore you can skip—harvesting winter leeks. Just leave them in the garden and harvest as needed in late fall and winter, says Roger Swain, host of PBS's *Victory Garden*. That way, you don't even have to find space for them in your refrigerator.

"Leeks are a wonderful winter vegetable," says Roger. "But you have to start with winter leeks, such as 'Alaska' or 'Nebraska'; they'll survive the winter even in my Zone 4 garden."

Winter leeks may not be as long, succulent, and fast-growing as summer leeks such as 'King Richard', but they have a good flavor and extra hardiness. When the weather gets cold, Roger piles dry leaves around the stalks to protect them from severe cold and make it easier to harvest in mid-winter. (He likes to use leeks in a creamy leek and potato soup.)

Roger has one more trick to make sure *he* gets his winter leek harvest. "Deer love leeks and will eat them down to the roots, no matter how you bury them," Roger says, "so I lay down chicken wire over the leaves because they can't paw through it." You can make sure the chicken wire stays in place by using large wire "staples" to pin it to the ground.

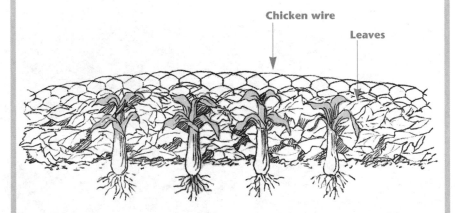

Chicken wire

Leaves

A blanket of dry leaves protects your winter leeks from freezing and makes it easy for you to continue harvesting your crop. Cover the leaves with chicken wire to hold the leaves in place and keep hungry deer away.

LETTUCE

Mulch Your Crops with...Lettuce?!

Plant lettuce in bands 18 to 24 inches wide instead of in skinny rows, and the plants will form their own mulch. The lettuce leaves form a canopy that shades out weeds.

Lettuce also makes a great living mulch under larger plants that need wide spacing. Tuck a few lettuce transplants underneath your broccoli or cauliflower for great weed control, plus a double crop in one space. Tina James, a landscape consultant in Reisterstown, Maryland, says this technique mimics nature's successful growing techniques. "Just look at the variety of life in one square foot of earth," Tina exclaims. "You'll find lots of plants growing together and covering every inch of ground." Take a cue and experiment with your own plant combinations to save weeding time and space. Try growing lettuce (or chard or spinach) under pole bean trellises, for instance.

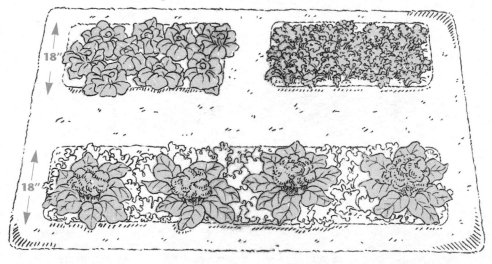

Try a living lettuce mulch to keep weeds away. Plant in thick bands (top) or plant lettuce around other veggies, like broccoli (bottom). Mixing lettuce with other crops has an added benefit—it confuses insects who come looking for a meal.

Add Kelp for Extra-Early Lettuce

HURRY YOUR
LETTUCE
HARVEST WITH
KELP EXTRACT

Harvest three weeks early when you feed your lettuce crop with kelp extract. "You can apply it to leaf lettuce that's not nearly big enough to harvest, and it doubles in size in one to two weeks," says Arpad Masley, a Master Gardener in Belfair, Washington.

For an experiment, Arpad grew 'Summertime', a head lettuce, with and without kelp extract, and found that the heads fertilized with the extract grew twice as big as those that weren't given kelp. With leaf lettuce, he's seen a dramatic growth spurt in treated plants—they're ready for harvest about three weeks early.

He has seen other benefits too. "Kelp seems to protect against frost," he says, noting that after two days of temperatures below freezing, untreated plants were killed or injured, while treated plants survived. He also finds that seed soaked in diluted kelp extract germinates two to three days earlier than normal.

Arpad dilutes 1 tablespoon of kelp extract in a gallon of water and applies it as a liquid fertilizer to the soil near the base of his plants. You can use the kelp in addition to your regular fertilization program.

Grow 3 Crops in ⅓ the Space

Triple your harvest when you grow three crops in the space it used to take just to grow lettuce with the "LRB" method. "LRB" stands for leaf lettuce, radishes, and broccoli, and is the brainchild of Alan Kapuler, director of research for Seeds of Change, a national organic seed company in Santa Fe, New Mexico.

Alan plants all three crops sparsely in the same row. The radishes emerge quickly and are the first crop he harvests. Removing the radishes leaves extra room for the lettuce, which Alan harvests soon afterward. Then the slower-growing broccoli has the run of the row, and it will produce main heads and later sideshoots for the rest of the growing season if you let it.

LOW-MAINTENANCE GARDENING

Free Your Foundation

Why plant anything up against the house?

Rosalind Creasy, a garden designer in Los Altos, California, thinks that most foundation plantings, which she calls the "mustache" across a home's face, can be ripped out. You'll cut way down on maintenance time. And since most houses don't have ugly concrete foundations anymore, there's nothing to hide anyway.

"And get rid of the soccer field, too," Ros continues, recognizing that the almost uniquely American phenomenon of wall-to-wall grass is finally going out of style—all the better for low maintenance. "No designer I know puts in a large lawn," she emphasizes.

Ros thinks you can have an interesting garden by simply forming a room with airy "walls" of flowering shrubs to create a feeling of enclosure. "Keep the interest in the garden, unless there's a mountain or church spire or other interesting feature nearby. Use entryways and try to create a sense of mystery—never reveal the whole picture; make the visitor seek more.

"When you create a front garden room full of interesting herbs and edible plants, for instance, you can see visitors sigh when they come in," Ros says. "Believe it or not, it won't take long for the neighbors to start doing the same. And the beauty is, shrubs and perennials take less time for routine care than do the lawn and a whole lot of tightly pruned shrubbery."

YOU CAN
FORGET ABOUT
FOUNDATION
PLANTINGS

If you've got existing trees or plants in your yard, you can use them as a starting point and build a garden room around them. Then add more garden rooms when you have the time and the money—it's the same simple approach you use when you're adding on to your house.

There's no need to hide your house behind a green "mustache" since most houses today have attractive fronts that don't need covering. Instead of a high-maintenance foundation planting, try a specimen plant near the house and an eye-catching garden feature in the front yard. Keep expanding the garden area over time to reduce lawn maintenance.

Try Laid-Back Gardening

No time to mow? Does it get dark before you get a chance to do yard and garden chores? Maybe you need a new approach. Take a tip from Ken Moore and let your lawn and gardens go natural—you can cut maintenance down to a few minutes of creative mowing.

When Ken finally finishes up after long hours at his job as assistant director at the North Carolina Botanical Garden in Chapel Hill, he barely has time to walk his garden paths and relax a few minutes by his pond before dark. "I know I ought to do this and do that, but first of all I don't want to. Second, I don't have the time," Ken says. Instead of scrambling to clean up his yard and gardens on the weekends, all Ken does is mow paths through the yard that are wide enough so nobody trips over anything in the dark. Mowed

PROVEN PLANTS FOR WET SPOTS

Make the most of damp sites instead of fighting them and you'll spend less time hauling water hoses and sprinklers around. "We were planning to put bulbs in a certain spot until we noticed how moist the soil there was when the air conditioner was running," recalls Roger Hagley, a gardener in Ashland, Kentucky. "We decided to turn the liability into an asset and plant something there that likes a lot of water. In this case, we chose four-o'clocks (*Mirabilis jalapa*). They really run amok!" Plant reseeding annuals like four-o'clocks or any of the perennial flowers listed below in your ugly wet site and turn it into a beautiful garden spot.

Fingerleaf rodgersia (*Rodgersia aesculifolia*)
Big bold leaves grow 2 feet wide and make a great camouflage for wet shady spots. The plant grows 4 to 6 feet tall and has long clusters of creamy white flowers in late spring or early summer. Zones 4 to 7.

Siberian bugloss (*Brunnera macrophylla*)
Look for blue forget-me-not–like flowers in early spring on this 1- to 1½-foot-tall plant. Leaves are heart shaped. Plant in a shady spot and let self-sown seedlings spread. Zones 3 to 8.

Turtlehead (*Chelone lyonii*)
Put them in full sun or partial shade and vigorous turtleheads will beautify your wet site for years to come. These 1- to 3-foot-tall plants have rosy pink flowers in late summer and fall on upright stems. Zones 3 to 8.

Yellow flag (*Iris pseudacorus*)
This 3- to 4-foot-tall iris thrives in full sun or partial shade. It has bright yellow flowers in spring and strap-shaped leaves that are great for hiding ugly wet spots. Zones 4 to 9.

paths aren't permanent, so you can change them with the seasons, Ken says. If it's too wet part of the year to get into one area, move your path over into a higher, drier area.

Ken uses his mowing patterns to highlight trees and shrubs, and even clumps of grasses that appear one year and are gone the next. Along his paths he sprinkles "yard art" such as a long row of concrete flamingos. Ken has fun with his lawn sculptures—he sites the flamingos so they crane their necks to peek shyly from a jumble of wildflowers and grasses along his path.

This laid-back version of gardening leaves you plenty of time to be creative, so let go and have fun. "It's my garden, my muse," Ken says of his yard. "My visitors seem to like it, and it certainly takes little effort to keep it going."

TRY LAND-
SCAPING WITH A
MOWER AND
LAWN ART

Don't Fool with Mother Nature

Don't let disasters get you down. There's not much you can do to head off natural disasters like severe winds, ice storms, heavy rains, and lightning. But when disasters happen, take the advice of Claire Sawyers, director of the Scott Arboretum of Swarthmore College in Swarthmore, Pennsylvania. "Mother Nature doesn't read the same garden books we do," she says. "Storms can provide us with incredible garden opportunities—before you grab the chain saw, at least explore the possibilities of leaving a dead tree for its sculptural potential."

That's exactly how Pete Hanlon, a retired North Carolina forester known locally as "the best gardener in Fairview," turned a lemon into lemonade. He planted fast-growing gourd vines around a storm-broken tree trunk and let them climb. He saved the time and effort of removing the tree and kept an important vertical element in his garden.

Storms are good at dumping too much water on your garden at the same time they're tearing up trees. Here's how Pat Stone, editor of *GreenPrints* magazine, deals with North Carolina's downpours. "I let nature help design my garden. When heavy rains and runoff from my hillside kept cutting my raised beds in half, I turned it into a natural waterway for drainage. There was nothing heavy or philosophical about it, just a practical way to 'go with the flow'."

215

Pickax Saves Backs

Have you ever tried to install edging in rocky soil? Before you start this backbreaking chore, learn from the aching back and experience of Erin Hynes, author of *Rodale's Successful Organic Gardening: Improving the Soil.* Erin says she struggled over two weekends to install the first two-thirds of 60 feet of black plastic edging, using a spade and a trowel, before a neighbor mentioned that a pickax was often handy for such work.

"So I got a pickax, and I finished the last 20 feet in under an hour," says Erin. "I think pickaxes are underrated as a garden tool." Her new tool, actually a pick mattock (see the illustration on page 10), features a head with a pointed pick on one end and a broad hoe-type blade on the other end. The head is mounted on a sturdy wooden handle. This combination allows her to pulverize small rocks and soil clods and grub out larger stones. It cuts her work time to a fraction of what it was with the spade and trowel.

Get an Edge on Weeding

The easiest way to keep grass out of your garden beds—and say good-bye to hours of weeding—is to install a physical barrier or garden edging. One choice is to surround your gardens with the inexpensive plastic or rubber edgings available in many garden centers. These will do the job—at least for a short while—until they slip out of place. You could also use homemade edgings made of boards, timbers, rocks, and bricks—they're more likely to stay in place, but take more time to build.

So what's the solution? A semipermanent aluminum strip edging that's held in place with metal stakes. The type you use should link together with flexible joints, so it will stay in place when the ground freezes, thaws, and shifts during winter. Rigid edgings may pop out of the ground, and that means more work to put them back in.

"I've used jointed aluminum landscape edgings for about 15 years now," says Doug Cole, nursery foreman for Katerberg Verhage Landscape Services in Grand Rapids.

"They are easy to install and will give you a good straight or curved line. And they stay put once you have them installed." Doug isn't so fond of plastic edgings that he says won't make a true straight line—they're wavy. And he adds that after a cold winter they pop up, then your lawn mower hits them and rips them apart.

Aluminum landscape edging keeps lawn and garden plants where they belong. Here's an easy installation tip from Dan Zwier, president of PermaLoc Corporation, makers of a jointed aluminum edging in Holland, Michigan. Dig trenches slightly deeper than the width of the edging. "It's easier to pull the edging up a little than to try to push it down into a trench that's too shallow," Dan says.

Squeeze Weeds Out

TRY PACKED
PLANTINGS TO
PREVENT WEED
PROBLEMS

Weeds won't wait for young plants to grow and cover bare spaces in your gardens. They'll jump right in and take the area over unless you fill gaps with plants of your own. Stan Beikmann, a garden designer in Niles, Michigan, says you'll have to spend more at first to fill your beds with plants, but you'll really save later on maintenance costs. "In my borders and beds I use lots of small shrubs and ornamental grasses, and plant as full as I can," Stan says. He leaves barely enough room for each plant's mature size and ends up with a lush cottage-garden look. The plants almost have to compete with one another for space, so weeds don't even have a chance to move in.

Planting close is good, but there are limits. Set plants so they'll just touch when they're mature—any closer and they'll be stressed and their health may suffer.

If you don't have the money to squeeze all of your plantings, use heavy mulches between plants. (A mulch layer 4 inches deep will keep most weeds out.) Whichever way you go—close plantings, thick mulches, or a combination of both—you can say good-bye to constant weeding.

Simpler Is Better

Simplicity is the key to low maintenance, according to Texas gardening guru Neil Sperry of Dallas. "Too many people overlook it by wanting their gardens to be involved and cute," he says, but "elegant and simple don't mean boring."

Neil recommends setting out "significant quantities" of one plant, wherever you have a lawn or garden spot that's hard to care for. Create a massed effect by covering the area with groundcovers, spreading shrubs like honeysuckles and junipers, or large plantings of daylilies or other spreading perennials. (See "Proven Plants for Low Maintenance" on the opposite page for good groundcover choices.)

Reduce maintenance around your home by planting groups of low-growing shrubs instead of a single accent shrub near your door or the corner of your house. Use three, five, or more shrubs in a group. You can also cut maintenance by planting groups of small trees in your yard. Try planting several evergreens together, or plant a group of three or five small deciduous trees with interesting trunk forms, like paperbark maple (*Acer griseum*). Cover a really big problem site naturally by massing several large shade trees, like red maples or sugar maples, together. Their leaves make a great natural mulch, so you won't even have the bother of raking.

Where shade, dogs, children, or foot traffic are heavy, Neil recommends that you go for cover. Use a bark mulch (shredded mulch stays put better than chipped) or interlocking concrete pavers. (Buy these small preformed stepping-stones or blocks at garden centers and building supply outlets.)

PROVEN PLANTS FOR LOW MAINTENANCE

It's easy to lower your yard maintenance if you plant large quantities of easy-care groundcovers. Try massing these proven performers in areas that are too steep or wet to garden in or mow. Or use them to replace grass or gardens in areas that are just too shady.

Ajuga (*Ajuga reptans*)
This low spreader has colorful oval leaves (look for cultivars with green, bronze, green and white, or green, pink, and white foliage). Blue or white flowers bloom on 6- to 10-inch-tall spikes in spring or early summer. Ajuga likes well-drained soil in sun or shade. Zones 3 to 9.

Cranesbills or hardy geraniums (*Geranium* spp.)
These mounded plants grow 6 to 24 inches tall in sun or partial shade—make sure they get shade in hot climates. Rounded pink, purple, or white flowers appear in spring and early summer above rounded lobed leaves. Zones 3 to 8.

Creeping Jenny (*Lysimachia nummularia*)
You can replace a wet lawn area in a hurry with this 2- to 4-inch-tall plant. The creeping stems thrive and spread where it's moist. Small rounded leaves are decorated with yellow flowers in summer. Zones 3 to 8.

Lily-of-the-valley (*Convallaria majalis*)
Give this groundcover extra shade if you live in the South—in cooler areas it thrives in sun or shade. Set plants in dry or moist soil and you'll be rewarded with fragrant bell-shaped flowers that bloom in spring. Zones 2 to 8.

MANURE

Don't Have a Cow If You Don't Have a Cow

To avoid sowing weed seeds in your garden when you add manure, choose that manure wisely. If you spread *cow* manure, you may end up hoeing tons of sprouting weed seedlings, says Ray Wheeler, a gardener in Dickinson, North Dakota.

Cow manure can contain weed seeds "in quantities you wouldn't believe," Ray says. And those weed seeds are hard to kill, unless the manure has been thoroughly composted at high temperatures. "Trust me, most amateur composters can't kill the weed seeds in cow manure," Ray says. "You can wreck a garden with cow manure."

Ray suggests sheep, horse, goat, and mule manure as alternatives to cow manure because they contain fewer weed seeds. But what if your only free source of manure happens to be from a dairy or beef farm? Then you better learn to make hot compost. Here's how to do it.

To get really hot weed-killing compost, you'll need to turn it a lot so decomposer organisms get enough air to work efficiently. It helps to have a thermometer too, since the inside of the pile should stay between 113° and 158°F until the manure is decomposed. Build your pile all at once, mixing the manure with whatever organic matter you have on hand—grass clippings, leaves, kitchen garbage, etc. Make your pile at least 3 feet high by 3 feet wide by 3 feet deep so there's enough material to really heat up. Turn the pile every few days.

While cow manure is a great source of nutrients and organic matter, it can also cause problems in the garden. Some cow manure contains large numbers of weed seeds.

Manure under Wraps Stops Weeds

COVER MANURE

WITH MULCH TO

MINIMIZE

WEEDS

Tuck manure under mulch to avoid spreading weeds around your garden along with the nutrients. "The main problem with manure is weeds," says Sally Jean Cunningham of Cornell Cooperative Extension. "It's the best way to add nutrients, but the weeds come with it."

To keep weeds at bay while still putting manure to work in her garden, Sally tops manure applications with a light-excluding mulch such as black plastic or newspaper. She says this works especially well if you haven't had time to completely compost the manure. "To age manure and control weeds at the same time, use manure anytime you're going to use black plastic or other solid cover. Under the hot plastic, in particular, it processes much faster, and it kills off the weeds."

She adds that a manure and black plastic combination is great for crops like pumpkins and squash that thrive on the heat and the nutrient boost. Sally also advocates topping manure with the pages of your daily paper: "The earthworms are in the manure and they love the newspaper."

Manure for the Taking

Why pay for bagged manure when you can usually find manure free for the taking? English-American gardener Rita Hall of Brandon, Mississippi, remembers the street where she was raised in London: "Ladies all but fought over manure droppings from the horses that passed through the neighborhood."

Fortunately, you won't have to fight for free manure, but you may have to do some sleuthing to find it. Potential sources include horse stables, livestock auction lots, rodeos, fairgrounds, and zoos, which generally have mountains of manure mixed with bedding straw for the taking. All you need is permission and a pickup truck (and a friend to help or just for company). Check out these sources by searching through the yellow pages in your phone book, or call your local extension office and inquire about nearby locations.

MELONS

"Bee" Sure of a Pest-Free Crop

COVER UP AND
POLLINATE FOR
PERFECT
MELONS

Growing melons under floating row covers is a surefire technique for preventing pest problems, but it leaves you with a dilemma—bees and other pollinators can't reach your melon flowers. So do the pollination yourself, and you can keep your crop covered for season-long protection, says extension educator Vernon Bryant at the University of Illinois Cooperative Extension Service in Chicago.

Here are a few tips and techniques from Vernon to help you make like a bee amid your melons. "Some people pick off the male flower and smush it onto the female flower," he says. "Or you can use a soft brush to take pollen from the male flowers and sort of paint it onto the female flowers. I've also seen people pick the anthers (the pollen-bearing parts) from the male flowers and brush those inside the female flowers."

Vernon recommends tackling this beelike behavior early in the morning when the flowers are fresh. "As the flowers age, they may not be as receptive to the pollen as they are when they first open," he notes.

Once you've completed your pollination project, carefully put the row covers back in place to protect your melons from insect pests. Check your plants occasionally to "bee" sure your pollination efforts paid off in producing a crop of young melons. If you're not satisfied with the number of fruits you see growing, make another round of pollen deliveries.

"After a certain point in the season," Vernon adds, "it doesn't make any sense to let your plants produce more fruit, because they won't have time to reach maturity before frost." For example, Vernon advises Chicago-area gardeners to pick off any new flowers that form as the end of August approaches, so that the plants can put all their energy into fruits already on the vines.

Melons, squash, and cucumbers bear separate male and female flowers. Male flowers appear first (A); females appear a week later and have a swelling at the base (B). To hand-pollinate, use a paintbrush to transfer pollen from male flowers to female flowers (C).

Early Crops Are Flops

Don't jump the gun and plant your melons too early. Save your spring gardening time for crops that need your attention early in the season, and let heat-loving melons wait until the soil is nice and warm. There doesn't seem to be much of an advantage to rushing to get your melons in the ground, says Rodale garden book editor Fern Marshall Bradley. "Those times when I've really worked to get my melons planted early, it seems like the plants have suffered more pest and disease problems and not set much fruit. I've gotten better crops from transplants or seeds that I've planted sometime in June," Fern says.

223

Better Melons from Seed

Don't transplant melons if you want strong, healthy plants. That's the advice of David Chambers, manager of Mr. Cason's Vegetable Garden at Callaway Gardens in Pine Mountain, Georgia. "We direct-seed all of our melons, because they have such tender stems," he says. David says he finds it easier to sow melon seeds directly in the garden than to risk injuring their soft, fleshy stems while setting out transplants started indoors.

Dry Soil Means Sweeter Melons

TIME MELON HARVESTS WITH CARE AFTER HEAVY RAINS

Waterlogged soil dilutes melon flavor. "Commercial melon growers stop watering anywhere from eight to ten days prior to harvest," says Gene Lester, a plant physiologist with the United States Department of Agriculture-Agricultural Research Service (USDA-ARS) in Weslaco, Texas. He explains that this allows the fruits to develop the sugars that give them their characteristic sweet flavor.

But when heavy rains interrupt the period between the last irrigation and harvest, growers complain that their melons look ripe but taste bland. Gene and fellow researcher Steven Huber, a USDA-ARS plant physiologist in Raleigh, North Carolina, investigated this phenomenon and discovered that cloudy weather and soggy soil combine to short-circuit sugar production in the fruit.

"A couple of days of rain reduces photosynthesis. And the ground often becomes saturated, reducing oxygen transfer to the roots," says Steven. The result is that the melon doesn't produce the sugars that make it sweet, and it may even lose some sugar that's there already.

An extended period of rain has the worst effect, Gene says. To avoid losing flavor after a real soaker, harvest right away—within one or two days. If you wait three or four days, you'll get a tremendous loss of quality. If you can't harvest right away, Gene suggests you wait a week before harvesting to let your melons resume the sweetening process.

MOSS

Moss-Starting Milk Shake

Moss may not grow on a rolling stone, but you can easily get it to grow on a stone wall, on a brick walk, on damp ground, or anywhere else you want its woodsy beauty. And to speed up its spread, try this simple recipe from gardener Nancy Swell of Richmond.

In a blender, mix moss, buttermilk, and water. "Proportions don't seem to matter at all," Nancy says. "If the mixture is thick, I add some water. Then pour it where you want moss to grow. I think this method would grow moss on a billiard ball."

If you don't have any moss growing in your yard, you can actually order moss by mail from companies that specialize in native woodland plants. (See "Sources" on page 412 for ordering information.)

Pour a slurry of moss and buttermilk over a shaded walkway to "seed" it with moss. It's easy to whip up the mixture in an old blender.

5 Quick Tricks for Growing Moss

For a low-maintenance groundcover on a moist, shady site, consider moss. Lucinda Mays, curator of Callaway Gardens in Pine Mountain, Georgia, gets lots of questions from visitors about moss. Usually they want to know how to get rid of it. But Lucinda has created moss gardens in Callaway's Home Demonstration Garden, and she recommends mosses as attractive, easy-care groundcovers for sites where it's almost impossible to grow grass. Lucinda offers the following tips for successful moss gardening.

Choose a site that's right. The best place to establish a moss garden is a site where moss is already growing naturally. In Georgia, moss grows readily wherever shade falls on the moist, acid clay soil, Lucinda says. "Poke around under trees and on the shady sides of buildings and see if moss is already growing. Choose a spot that's ideal for moss and not for other plants," Lucinda advises. Clear away any unwanted plants growing in the area.

Collect with care. After you've prepared your site, you need moss to "plant." Lucinda is quick to discourage gardeners from collecting *any* plants—mosses included—from the wild. But she offers this hint for gathering moss from a neighbor's garden or for moving it from one spot in your yard to another. "The best way to collect moss is to take some from the middle of the patch," she says. "It grows back more quickly. If you take a chunk the size of a 50-cent piece from the edge, it may never grow back." To plant, simply put your collected moss pieces on the soil.

Maintain moisture. When mosses dry out, they go dormant. "If you don't want to look at dormant moss, you need a source of water," says Lucinda. Try putting a birdbath in your moss garden. As the birds bathe, they'll splash water out of the bath and onto your moss. Or you can use a water mister like those sold for birdbaths to provide a light spray of water over the moss. Lucinda warns that some birds will gather bits of moss to add to their nests, but says the moss grows back quickly. "I like that interaction," she adds. "It's a way to create bird habitat by enhancing moss habitat."

Mound your mosses. Because moss is flat, notes Lucinda, a moss garden isn't terribly exciting to look at. She added

MOSS GARDENS
MAKE THE
GRADE IN SHADE

interest to one of her moss gardens by building small mounds of red Georgia clay and planting the moss over them. Look at how mosses grow in the wild for inspiration.

Give plants a second chance. Some species of moss go dormant seasonally, others respond to weather patterns. If your moss turns brown, don't give up on it, says Lucinda. "Water it, then wait 48 hours," she suggests. If it doesn't respond after a couple of days, perhaps the site wasn't right for moss after all.

Moss makes a great groundcover in shaded areas with wet or infertile soil. Let splashing birds keep your moss garden moist by giving them a birdbath to play in.

MULCHING

"Lite" Mulch Saves Trees and Shrubs

More is not better when it comes to mulch.

Sure, it seems like you'll save time if you pile mulch high around plants—you won't have to remulch for months, maybe years. But this "neck-deep" approach can seriously damage your shrubs and even cause rot to set in on your tree trunks.

While you may have never noticed what's going on under mulch, Thomas Perry, an urban forestry researcher for North Carolina State University, has. He's found that "excessively thick organic mulches can induce fermentation, immobilize nutrients, cut off the oxygen supply, and even kill trees." Sounds scary, and it's unnecessary.

Drip line →   ← Drip line

Spread mulch around your trees and shrubs to form islands you don't have to mow. Keep mulch 4 to 6 inches away from the base of plants and only spread it 2 to 3 inches deep and out as far as the drip line.

A simple solution is to mulch thin—2 to 3 inches deep is plenty. Spread the mulch out to the drip line of trees and 2 feet or more beyond the boundaries of shrubs. You may have to add mulch once or twice a year to keep weeds away, but that's a simple task compared to replacing dying plants.

Thomas says to leave a 4- to 6-inch-wide mulch-free area around the base of your trees and shrubs. The clear space discourages mice from nesting beside plants and chewing their bark. He also recommends that you fertilize plants before you mulch. That's because microbes that break down mulch take nitrogen away from your trees. Fertilizing before you mulch takes care of the problem by giving both trees and microbes the nitrogen they need.

Weed-Free Mulch—Get It Delivered!

HERE'S HOW TO BRING GREAT FREE MULCH TO YOUR DOOR

Mulch is great for keeping weeds out of your soil and keeping moisture in. The trick is to find weed-free mulch—and then move it with the least amount of effort.

"I get my mulch delivered," says George Van Patten, a garden writer and teacher in Portland, Oregon. He suggests that you call landscaping companies and ask if they have leaves or grass clippings to get rid of. You can probably find someone who's willing to drop these materials off at your door, since it saves them a trip and fee at the landfill. "Leaves and grass clippings are my favorite mulches," George says. "They're freebies and they're usually pretty free of weed seeds. Not only that, they add a tremendous amount of organic matter."

Gene Dickson, owner of Prentiss Court Ground Covers in Greenville, South Carolina, suggests you call your power company and ask if they have wood chips to give away. (Most utilities contract out tree-trimming operations, so you may need to deal directly with the tree service.) Call in the winter—you'll get more wood and less leaves when crews are pruning bare trees—and you can stockpile the chips you get so you'll have a ready supply for spring. Once spring arrives, spread them right away to avoid weed problems later. "I've found that fresh wood chips have far fewer weeds than those that have sat around for awhile," says Gene.

Make Holiday Decorations into Mulch

TURN HOLIDAY
GREENS INTO A
MERRY XMAS
MULCH

Don't throw out your old Christmas tree and wreath—recycle them as beautiful gifts to your favorite plants. Just remove the lights and ornaments, then cut off the individual branches and limbs and strew them beneath your roses and other shrubs, says Felder Rushing, coauthor of *Passalong Plants.* Their fluffiness will help insulate your plants through winter, and by spring their needles will begin to shed and break down into a finer, slug-repelling mulch. "No self-respecting slug wants to crawl over sticky, clingy needles," says Felder.

If you'd like a more decorative mulch, see if your municipality has a recycling program—most do to save landfill space. Often they'll shred your tree while you wait.

"By the way," adds Felder, "it's okay to leave a little tinsel in the mulch—sometimes it can draw wry smiles from visitors, as it's resurrected from the earth, atop emerging bulbs or perennial flower buds. It's a confession that here gardens a recycler!"

Mulch Free-for-All

Why bag leaves in fall when you can turn them into instant mulch with a rake and a shovel. That's what Sarah Dunn, a gardener in Fountain Hill, Pennsylvania, does.

In the fall, Sarah removes the low fence that surrounds her vegetable garden and rakes her yard leaves into the garden. She ends up with a 3- to 4-inch-deep layer of leaves. Sarah uses a shovel to turn the leaves under—there's no need to dig deep; just put enough soil on the leaves to keep them from blowing away in winter. If you don't have time to turn the leaves, sprinkle compost over the top or lay fencing down over the leaves to hold them in place.

"The leaves decompose over the winter, and I have a nicely mulched garden in the spring," Sarah says. "That way, I don't have to bag the leaves, and I don't have to buy mulch." Sarah finds that the leaves make a good soil amendment too. In spring, her garden is ready for planting *without* tilling. For early crops like peas, Sarah simply stirs the soil with a garden fork, and rakes it smooth before sowing seed.

Leaf Eater Munches Leaves into Mulch

LEAF EATER
SHREDS LEAVES
LIKE A STRING
TRIMMER

Turn fallen leaves into instant mulch with an Electric Leaf Mulcher—the process takes only seconds—and you'll save hours of weeding and watering.

"I have this neat, neat leaf eater, made by Flowtron," says Loretta O'Connor, a lifelong gardener in Columbus, Ohio. "It's shaped like a huge kettle and contains nylon strings like a string trimmer that grind the leaves up into wonderful mulch." (See "Sources" on page 412 for ordering information.)

The leaves from Loretta's two large shade trees and several small ornamental trees provide enough mulch for her small but productive gardens. When the leaves fall in autumn, Loretta moves her Electric Leaf Mulcher along with her as she rakes, dumping the leaves in the kettle and pulverizing them as she goes. The lines spin around, chopping the leaves in a minute or so, reducing them to a much smaller-size pile.

When the leaves are chopped, Loretta spreads a 6- to 8-inch-deep layer around her perennial flowers. She piles the rest of the leaf mulch by the vegetable garden and lets it decompose during winter. In spring and summer, she mulches her vegetables with the partly decayed leaves.

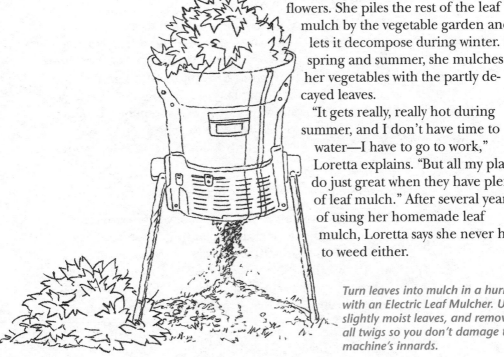

"It gets really, really hot during summer, and I don't have time to water—I have to go to work," Loretta explains. "But all my plants do just great when they have plenty of leaf mulch." After several years of using her homemade leaf mulch, Loretta says she never has to weed either.

Turn leaves into mulch in a hurry with an Electric Leaf Mulcher. Use slightly moist leaves, and remove all twigs so you don't damage the machine's innards.

231

JUST SAY "NO" TO BUYING MULCH

Put away your money. You've probably got plenty of great mulch materials around your house. In addition to shredded newspaper, you can find plenty of substitutes for expensive bark mulch for paths. Line your garden paths with handy leftovers like these, and you can get out in the garden in any kind of weather.

• Boards
• Cardboard
• Wool or cotton carpet
• Magazines
• Wood or slate roofing shingles
• Old clothes

Look in your garage and attic to find more unusual mulches.

More Mulch Means Less Digging

Stop digging, weeding, and watering! If your garden soil is too hard or rocky to work, cover it with a thick sheet of mulch. Within a single year, you'll have rich soil that's nice and moist, absolutely stuffed with worms, and free of weeds.

All you have to do is decide where you want your plants to grow and lay a thick layer of mulch and other basic ingredients over the area. Gardener Colleen Belk of Austin, Texas, explains: "I just cover the ground with lots of stuff, and before too long I can plant right through it." Colleen says this system really works for her—even in her normally hard soil, lots of worms just seem to appear.

The gist of sheet mulching is simple. Here's what to do.

1 Chop down large weeds with a hoe, mower, or whatever—no need to pull or till—and let them lie.

2 Cover the ground (and chopped weeds) with chicken, cow, goat, horse, or rabbit manure; kitchen wastes; composted gin trash (the leftovers from processing cotton); or other "soft" food for worms. A natural source of nitrogen such as cottonseed meal or blood meal—1 pound to 100 square feet—helps the process along.

3 Cover the manure and compostables with overlapping layers of newspaper and plain brown cardboard,

2 or 3 inches thick. You can even use nonsynthetic carpet scraps and cotton or wool clothes. Wet the pile well.

4 Apply another 2 or 3 inches of strawy manure (stable or poultry), leaves, and grass clippings. Water well.

5 Top the pile with several more inches of weed-free straw, leaves, wood chips, shredded bark, sawdust, or other "dry" materials.

Once you've mulched and moistened your growing area, plant it by moving aside some of the top layer and adding a handful of garden soil for each transplant or group of seeds. Plants may not grow as big the first year since their root space is limited, but your mulch garden will be in full swing by its second season. After it's up and running, your sheet-mulch garden frees you of weekly weeding and watering chores. If any weeds do blow in, you can handpick them in a moment from the heavy mulch, and rainwater alone will keep your garden moist except in extreme drought. Add new mulch ingredients to the garden whenever you have plant or food scraps to dispose of, then sit back, relax, and watch your vegetables thrive.

MULTI-LAYERED
MULCH GARDEN
PERKS UP
POOR SOIL

Sheet Mulch

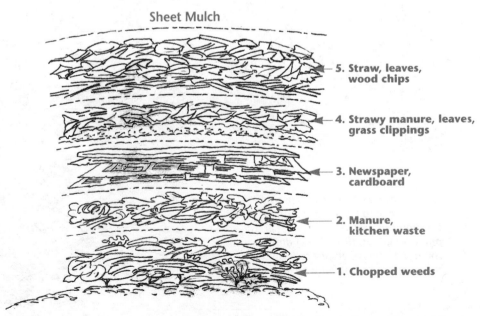

5. Straw, leaves, wood chips

4. Strawy manure, leaves, grass clippings

3. Newspaper, cardboard

2. Manure, kitchen waste

1. Chopped weeds

Turn poor soil into a fertile, weed-free garden with sheet mulch. Simply layer compostable materials on top of the soil, moisten, and let worms work their soil-building magic.

Sow Mulch, Save Fertilizer

Living mulches give you more. They smother out weeds just as well as standard mulches like straw, plus they build up your soil when they decompose. Ken Grymala, an innovative gardener in Nokesville, Virginia, uses winter rye as a living mulch in his vegetable garden.

For tomatoes, Ken sows winter rye in mid- to late October in the area where he wants to grow the plants. The rye survives the winter and really starts growing in spring. When it's time to plant tomatoes, Ken chops through a 2-foot swath of ryegrass with a bush hog to make a tomato row. "That grass can be 3 feet tall, so you need a tough machine," he says. (He uses a weed whacker or weed whip when he doesn't feel like firing up the bush hog.) Then Ken tills the mowed area and puts in his transplants.

The rye has still another benefit. Ken discovered that he can plant tomatoes two weeks earlier than normal, because the tall grass surrounding the planted rows acts as a

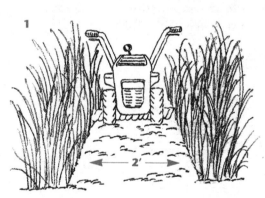

For a weed-free tomato patch, sow winter rye in fall. (1) Make a path through the rye crop in spring, (2) plant tomatoes, then (3) cut down the rest of the rye in June to form a dense mulch that stifles weeds.

windbreak for the young plants and holds in some heat too.

By June, the standing rye is about 4 feet high, with ripening seed heads that attract hundreds of ladybugs. At this point, Ken harvests the grain and cuts down the straw with his weed whacker. He lets the straw fall to the side as a mulch for the tomatoes. Even if you don't harvest the grain, the seed isn't much of a problem, Ken says. Consider it a self-sown cover crop and till it in at the end of the season.

Weeds Can Work for You

PUT PESKY
WEEDS TO
WORK AS
MULCH

"Use it or lose it" takes on new meaning when you're talking about a weedy garden. Do you spend backbreaking hours pulling weeds, or use them as a living mulch? If your weeds are tall, pull them. But if you've got a thick patch of low-growing weeds, use them as a cover crop.

"I try to work with the givens," says Veet Deha, a horticulturist in Ithaca, New York. "You can see common purslane as a curse, or you can try to work with it." If there's an area of your garden where purslane flourishes, choose a crop that can coexist happily with it. Salad greens aren't a good choice, because they're also low-growing; the purslane is too much competition, Veet explains. But it's not a problem for corn. In fact, the purslane holds in moisture, and it definitely smothers out other weeds. Veet keeps her corn rows weeded with a hoe until the corn seedlings are at least 6 inches tall, but after that she lets the purslane take over.

"Now I'm not suggesting you plant purslane in your garden," says Veet. "But if it's there already, it's easier to take advantage of the situation."

Nino Ridgway, owner of Squeaky Green Organic Produce in Mequon, Wisconsin, also uses benign weeds to crowd out pesky ones. "Prostrate spurge is a common weed here and it's very tedious to pull," Nino says. Luckily, she found that spurge grows in her onions with no loss in production. In fact, the spurge makes a living mulch for onions since it shades the soil and keeps out other weeds. "Since onions are a root crop, any low-growing leafy plant with shallow roots could make a natural companion," Nino says.

ONIONS

Row Covers Grow Giant Onions

A little extra heat in early spring means the difference between scrawny onions and nice big fat ones. If you're tired of puny onions, start your onion seedlings or sets inside a floating row cover tunnel. They'll get fatter than you ever imagined possible. Here's how Roger Swain, host of PBS's *Victory Garden*, gets giant onions and cuts down on weeding and watering chores.

Plant your onion sets or seedlings as soon as you can work the ground in spring. Put the onions in fertile, loose soil and mulch around them with 2 inches of grass clippings. "Grass mulches help hold in soil moisture and keep down weeds, which caters to the needs of shallow-rooted onions," Roger says. The mulch caters to your needs, too, by cutting down on chores.

When you've planted your onions, hold the heat around them by covering them with a protective tunnel. Set wire or plastic wickets over the plants. (They should be at least 18 inches tall to allow the onion greens room to grow.) Cover

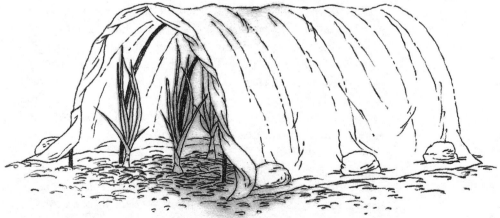

Cover your onion crop with a row cover tunnel in early spring. This can raise temperatures by 5° to 7°F, which means faster-growing plants and a bigger harvest come summer.

the wickets with floating row cover and secure the row cover edges under soil or rocks to keep it in place.

This setup will provide extra warmth, which will make the onion plants larger and stronger. You'll see how much more energy they've stored when they begin to produce bulbs in midsummer.

Fast, Easy Onion Planting

POUR ONION
SETS STRAIGHT
FROM THE BAG
TO THE BED

Let onion sets tumble into your garden, straight from the bag you brought them home in. "Don't bother setting them right side up," says Sally Roth, coauthor of *Rodale's Successful Organic Gardening: Companion Planting*. "It's an unnecessary waste of time, and you either have to bend over or get down on your knees to do it."

Instead of carefully spacing her onion sets and setting each one upright in the furrow, Sally advocates a much more casual, and much quicker, approach. "Just scrape out a furrow with the tip of a hoe and pour the sets in. Cover them with soil, walk on the furrow, and they'll come up just fine," she says.

These Onions Plant Themselves

Keep green onions coming year after year from a single planting of top-setting onions (*Allium* × *proliferum*). "There's no need to buy and plant onion sets every spring. Just plant these onions once and they'll keep coming back," says Rodale garden book editor Joan Benjamin.

Also called Egyptian or tree onions, top-setting onions produce stalks with clusters of small bulbs at the tips. The weight of the bulb cluster eventually bends the stalk to the ground, and the small bulbs root and form new plants. You can harvest them first thing in the spring for fresh onion flavor before any other plants are up.

Joan says she got her onions from a Vietnamese gardener about ten years ago and they're still going strong. They thrive without any winter protection in her Pennsylvania garden. She adds that it's easy to stop top-setting onions from spreading too far—"just cut off their heads."

ORCHIDS

Orchids on the Internet

It takes only minutes in this electronic age to get your orchid questions answered by experts from all over the world. In one morning, Bruce Ide, manager of information services for the American Orchid Society, used the Internet to visit the Royal Botanic Gardens at Kew, England, and botanical gardens in Alaska, New Zealand, and Denmark.

There are a number of general gardening discussion forums and specialty gardening groups that meet on the Internet too. These are great places to get your questions answered by experts and home growers—thousands log on every day and can reply within minutes. Or go explore new ideas using databases, libraries, and articles you can tap into via your computer. (It's more extensive and easier than going to the local library.) Bruce recommends these Internet stops especially for orchid-lovers:

• Internet orchid discussion group found at rec.gardens.orchids.

• Internet Orchid Digest, a compilation of information you can join by subscription. Send an e-mail message saying "subscribe orchids" to mailserv@scuacc.scu.edu.

• Compuserve Garden Forum has a subsection devoted to orchids. ("I hang out there," Bruce says.)

• On the Worldwide Web, Time Inc. operates a virtual garden that includes orchids and other flowers.

Look for user-friendly software to get you started. Netscape—Bruce's favorite software at publication—lets you choose where you want to go from a menu, then automatically connects you with your choice. When you're done, use another menu of related topics to move on. "When you find something you'd like to return to, you can set a bookmark so it's extra-easy to find again," says Bruce.

Cinnamon and Alcohol Cure Orchid Ills

It's not as hard as it looks to grow beautiful orchids—their few problems are easy to treat with simple home remedies. Orchids are surprisingly durable and healthy plants, if you plant them in coarse potting soil for good drainage. When a problem does appear, use rubbing alcohol to deal with pests and cinnamon to handle diseases, recommends Bruce Ide, manager of information services for the American Orchid Society.

Bruce recommends wiping pests off of orchid leaves with a cotton swab dipped in rubbing alcohol. Or you can buy a cheap quart-size hand sprayer to spray alcohol on pest-infested areas.

Cinnamon powder acts as a fungicide and works well to prevent or cure rots, spots, and other fungal diseases. Bruce explains how it might come in handy: Sometimes if you're not careful when you're watering a plant like a moth orchid (*Phalaenopsis* spp.), the water will sit in the center of the stems and the stems will begin to rot. To avoid the problem, change your habits and water the potting mix instead of the orchid. To cure the rot, sprinkle cinnamon on the soft and discolored areas.

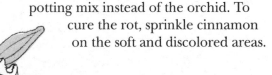
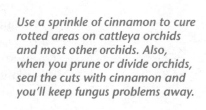

Use a sprinkle of cinnamon to cure rotted areas on cattleya orchids and most other orchids. Also, when you prune or divide orchids, seal the cuts with cinnamon and you'll keep fungus problems away.

ORNAMENTAL GRASSES

Keep Ornamental Grasses in Bounds

Head off headaches with invasive grasses like many bamboos, maiden grasses (*Miscanthus* spp.), and giant reed (*Arundo donax*) by planting them inside a bottomless washtub, garbage can, or tire planter.

Edith Eddleman, curator of a 400-foot perennial border at the North Carolina State University Arboretum in Raleigh, loves ornamental grasses. But she recognizes the need to keep them from romping over other plants. For a quick fix, she's heard you can dig ditches around grasses to slow their spread. But she recommends you set plants in containers when you divide them for long-term control.

At home, Edith sticks to clump-forming grasses like Japanese silver grass (*Miscanthus sinensis*) and switch grass (*Panicum virgatum*) that don't send out runners and don't need control barriers. At work, it's another story. "It's nice to be able to plant these invasive grasses on university grounds and have 20-year-olds do all the digging and dividing," she says.

CONTAINERS CAN CONTROL SPREADING GRASSES

A spacious metal washtub can contain the roots of large grasses like maiden grass. Leave 2 inches of the tub above the soil so roots and stolons can't sneak out.

Divide Your Grasses 1 Piece at a Time

There has to be an easier way to pull or dig a piece of an established clump of ornamental grass out of the ground. If that was your thought after spending a morning or afternoon trying, you're right.

Experienced grass growers take it in stages. Tony Avent, owner of Plant Delights Nursery in Raleigh, North Carolina, uses a technique that saves time and his back. Tony says of dividing grasses: "It's so easy anyone can do it; but it'll half kill you if you don't know this tip." First cut the grass nearly to the ground—it's only a temporary setback to the plant, but vastly helpful to the gardener. Then, using a sharp spade or even an ax, chop the clump in half, top to bottom, then quarter it. Then just pry out as much as you need, and fill in the hole with topsoil. The grass you leave will regrow and fill the space.

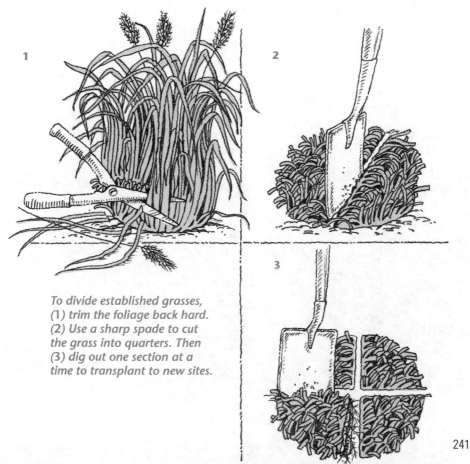

To divide established grasses, (1) trim the foliage back hard. (2) Use a sharp spade to cut the grass into quarters. Then (3) dig out one section at a time to transplant to new sites.

241

Easy Angle for Pruning Ornamental Grasses

Save wear and tear on yourself, your shears, and your grasses by giving a new slant to your pruning techniques. You'll wear out before you get ornamental grasses sheared if you attack weathered clumps of leaves head-on with pruning shears. But if you slant your pruners and cut at a 45-degree angle, you'll get the job done quickly and easily. Start cutting on the outside of the plant and circle around it, working your way toward the center of the clump. Be sure to cut grasses back early enough in the winter—certainly by early spring—to avoid damaging the emerging new green growth, or your plant will look ragged the rest of the season.

Why prune at all? Because there's a ratty-looking transition period before new growth covers the old, and over the years unpruned grasses can build up thatch above the crown that can cause rot.

Another reason for pruning is to keep ornamental grasses from flopping in midsummer. In warm, humid climates, grasses may grow too lush from spring rains. Felder Rushing, coauthor of *Passalong Plants,* solves that problem by cutting his plants back to the ground in June or July. The grasses resprout immediately, stay erect the rest of the season, and still have time to flower. "But let me warn you," Felder says. "One summer I was up to my armpits pruning a

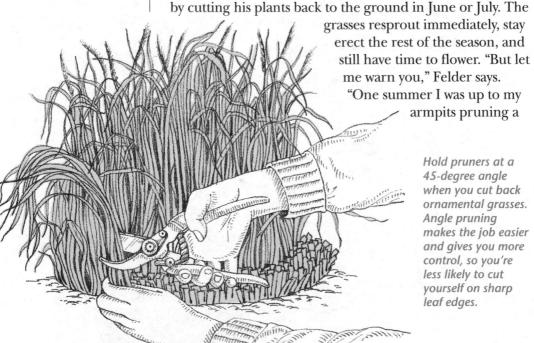

Hold pruners at a 45-degree angle when you cut back ornamental grasses. Angle pruning makes the job easier and gives you more control, so you're less likely to cut yourself on sharp leaf edges.

clump of zebra grass, and got a guinea wasp sting right on my nose! Check for wasp nests when pruning summer grasses!"

Fast Grasses from Seed

*G*et a quick start on an ornamental grass display with these four grasses that grow easily from seed. They're favorites of Barbara Kaczorowski, co-owner of Accent Gardens in Cicero, Indiana, because they all have attractive seed heads that look terrific in dried arrangements. These easy growers make a great alternative to buying plants when you need to fill a large space, and they're ideal for adding texture and substance to a meadow planting while slower-growing perennials are filling in. Barbara says she's never had a problem with any of these grasses becoming overly invasive, but notes that "any plant that's easy to start from seed has the potential to self-sow." Keeping them in check is relatively easy, she adds. Just cut the seed heads before they shatter and use them for indoor decoration.

CANARY GRASS (*Phalaris canariensis*)

Green and white seed heads add pizzazz to dried arrangements but wait to harvest them until the seeds mature so hungry birds get their fill. This annual grows 36 inches tall. It prefers a moist spot in full sun but does well on drier ground too.

HARE'S TAIL GRASS (*Lagarus ovatus*)

This annual has soft furry white seed heads that are as pretty in arrangements as they are in the garden. The plants grow 18 to 20 inches tall and are easy to grow in well-drained soil in sun or light shade. If you need an accent plant for your patio, try this one—it even thrives in containers.

LARGE QUAKING GRASS (*Briza maxima*)

A planting of this annual will delight your ears as well as your eyes, with pendulous seed heads that rustle softly in the breeze. Plants grow 18 to 22 inches tall and thrive in poor soil. It's fun to use in dried arrangements since the seed heads look like small fish on top of delicate-but-wiry stems.

RED SWITCH GRASS (*Panicum virgatum* 'Rubrum')

This perennial has graceful, deep red to violet seed heads that arch downward from strong stems. It makes an excellent landscape plant, especially in fall when the 3- to 3½-foot-tall leaves turn glowing red. It tolerates most soils, even wet ones, and is a good choice for controlling erosion. Zones 5 to 9.

PEAS

Planting Peas? Let 'em Pour

Ignore the usual spacing recommendations for your peas, suggests Sally Roth, coauthor of *Rodale's Successful Organic Gardening: Companion Planting*. Your pea planting will be done in seconds, and you'll get more peas from the same amount of garden space. "When it comes to peas, plant them extra thick," says Sally. "I just pour them into the row and give them wire mesh to climb."

By defying the traditional spacing rule—one pea every 2 inches—Sally saves lots of time when planting her crop, and she skips thinning altogether. Yet her more crowded peas don't disappoint her at harvesttime. "I get about five or six times the yield, in the same amount of space," Sally says. "I'll never plant them one at a time again."

Pea Brush Saves Time

Sticks and twigs make short work of trellising early peas. When Fountain Hill gardener Sarah Dunn plants her peas on St. Patrick's Day in southeastern Pennsylvania, she uses "pea brush" to make the task of getting supports in the ground as fast and easy as possible.

"Mid-March is always cold and rainy here," laments Sarah, a transplanted Virginian. "The last thing I want to do is freeze my fingers untangling last year's net trellis or stretching strings between stakes." Instead of fighting with newfangled pea-trellising contraptions, Sarah supports her peas the old-fashioned way, using pea brush made of fallen branches and prunings from trees and shrubs in her yard.

Sarah simply sticks the branches into the ground along her row of peas. "Big, twiggy branches are the best," Sarah says, "because they give the pea vines plenty to cling to." When her pea harvest winds down, cleanup is easy: "When I pull out the branches, the vines come out with them."

All Peas on Deck!

PLANT IN
CONTAINERS FOR
EXTRA-EARLY
PEAS

Well-drained soil is the secret to getting early peas off to a quick start, says Sally Jean Cunningham of Cornell Cooperative Extension. While it's warm enough to plant peas at Easter time in western New York, the soil is almost always too cold and wet, Sally Jean says. As a result, early pea plantings tend to germinate poorly until the soil dries out later in the spring, and seeds sometimes rot.

To get an early crop and avoid the hazards of overly cold and wet soil, Sally Jean plants her peas in containers. She sows her peas in a round container and installs a tube of chicken wire in the center of the pot for the peas to climb. "I can plant even earlier—as much as two weeks before Easter," she notes, adding that the same container can do double duty as the growing season progresses. "You can even use the tub where you will later have flowers growing on your deck," says Sally Jean. "But why not grow peas in it during the early spring when nobody's sitting on the deck?"

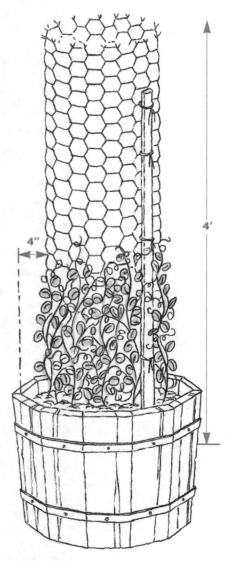

Give early peas the soil conditions they need by planting in a half-barrel or patio container. Make a 4-foot-long tube of chicken wire for a trellis, and sink it in the soil several inches deep. Sow peas all around the trellis.

4"

4'

PEPPERS

Early Picking Means More Peppers

PLUCK OFF
EARLY PEPPERS
FOR BIGGER
HARVESTS

You'll get bigger, more bountiful harvests if you pluck off any pepper fruits that form before you get your pepper transplants in the ground. "It's important to be hard-hearted about this," says Sally Roth, coauthor of *Rodale's Successful Organic Gardening: Companion Planting.* "Pick off the baby ones. Otherwise, your plants will put their energy into producing the fruit rather than establishing strong roots and stems." You might get a few small, early peppers from those first little fruits, but they'll come at the expense of a later, bigger harvest from healthier plants.

Once your peppers do start producing, Sally adds, keep them picked to keep them bearing. Leaving fruits on the plants tells them they've reached their goal of producing seeds, so they'll stop forming flowers and fruits. Waiting for peppers to color up (turn red, purple, yellow, or orange) on the plant has the same slowdown effect, Sally says. "Pick them green until late in the season, then let the last few ripen," she says. "Or you'll only get about four peppers per bush."

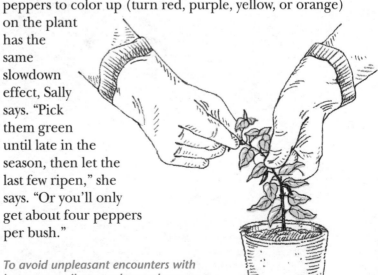

To avoid unpleasant encounters with hot pepper oil, wear gloves when you pinch hot peppers off plants. Better still, snip them off with scissors to keep from injuring your plants.

Brown-Bag Your Peppers

If you have problems drying peppers, here's a surefire way to get them to dry without rotting. Sally Roth, coauthor of *Rodale's Successful Organic Gardening: Companion Planting,* discovered this easy method by accident when she forgot some hot peppers in a bag on her kitchen counter. When she found them again they were nicely dried—a remarkable feat at Sally's southern Indiana home, where the humidity climbs with the temperature in the summer.

So instead of hanging her peppers or stringing them in the decorative pepper braids called ristras, Sally tosses them into a brown paper grocery bag. She puts enough peppers in the bag to just cover the bottom, and loosely pulls the bag closed with a piece of string or a clothespin. "Throw it on the counter and forget about it for a week or two," Sally says. "The peppers get nice and dry, and they don't rot."

QUICK FIX MIX

Hot Pickled Peppers

The quickest way to preserve your hot pepper harvest is with alcohol. Booze-pickled peppers just happen to be the easiest way to spice up your cooking too. Here's what you'll need.

1 quart hot peppers

1 quart brandy, rum, or sherry

2 1-pint canning jars with screw-top lids

Fill the canning jars to within an inch of their tops with peppers. Add enough alcohol to completely cover the peppers. Place a piece of wax paper or plastic wrap over the top of the jar and screw on the lid. When-ever you need peppers for cooking, take as many as you want out of the jar and tightly recap the jar. There's no need to refrigerate your pepper preserves.

"I keep a lot of hot peppers in booze," says Philadelphia gardener Libby J. Goldstein. She explains that the alcohol keeps the chiles from getting moldy, it's lots easier than drying your harvest, and the spiced-up booze can be used in any dish that needs a bit of heat. "Sherry is great for soups and gravies, rum is terrific for basting meats, and brandy makes a great cold remedy," Libby says.

PERENNIALS

Super-Simple Perennials from Seed

SAVE $$$ BY
STARTING
PERENNIALS
FROM SEED

If you can grow tomatoes from seed, you can grow perennials. It's a myth that only annuals are easy to start from seed—many perennials are just as simple. "I was astounded by how easy it is to grow my own perennials," says Ellen Spector Platt, owner of Meadow Lark Flower and Herb Farm in Orwigsburg, Pennsylvania. You don't have to wait long for results, since many perennials bloom the same year they're sown, and it's cheaper to start your own plants.

Ellen starts perennials such as baby's-breath (*Gypsophila paniculata*), delphinium, globe centaurea (*Centaurea macrocephala*), globe thistles (*Echinops* spp.), and lavender (*Lavandula angustifolia*) in February or March. She treats them just like tomato seeds, starting them in a sterile, peat-based planting mix in six-packs. She puts the six-packs in plastic flats and sets them on her windowsills where, depending on the light, some grow lush and some grow leggy.

When she moves them outside, Ellen sets the leggy seedlings extra-deep—up to their lowest set of leaves—and pinches off the top set of leaves. They respond the same way tomatoes do, growing healthy and bushy. Try it next season, and for no more effort than it takes to plant tomatoes, you'll have beautiful flowering perennials.

Prestart Seeds for Best Success

Presprouting perennials pays off, particularly with high-priced seeds, since you're sure to get good germination. You'll also cut out thinning chores, which is a big bonus, whether you start thousands of perennials a year like Kristl Walek, owner of Gardens North in Ontario, or just one or two kinds of plants.

To presprout the Walek way, you'll need unbleached coffee filters and plastic containers with tight-fitting lids.

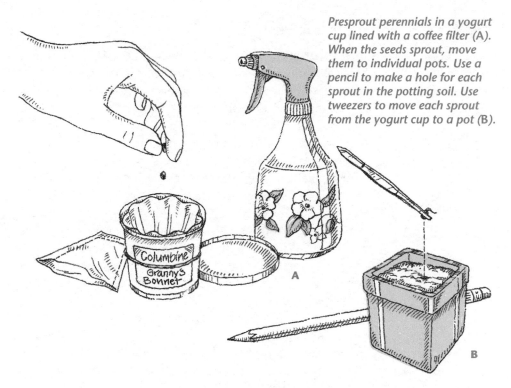

Presprout perennials in a yogurt cup lined with a coffee filter (A). When the seeds sprout, move them to individual pots. Use a pencil to make a hole for each sprout in the potting soil. Use tweezers to move each sprout from the yogurt cup to a pot (B).

Columbine
Granny's
Bonnet

A

B

Most seeds need light to germinate, so make sure you use clear lids—they make it easier for you to check for sprouts too. Use yogurt cups, deli containers, or whatever's handy.

Line each plastic container with a coffee filter. Then moisten the filter with a plant mister, being careful not to get the filter too wet—you don't want puddles!

Use seeds the size of columbine seed (about $\frac{1}{32}$ inch) or bigger, since they're easiest to handle, says Kristl. Place your seeds in the bottom of the plastic container, put the lid on, and attach a label with a rubber band. Put the planted containers on top of the refrigerator or somewhere else where it's warm. (Of course, if your seeds need a cold treatment, put them *in* the refrigerator. Check the seed packet to see what treatment they need.)

Start peeking through the lids for sprouts after three or four days. Some perennials are pokey, but you shouldn't need to add water as long as you don't open the lid. When the seeds do sprout, transplant them into cell packs or seed flats pronto. "You'll get no 'duds' and you can plant each seed individually, which saves hours of thinning," Kristl says.

Give These Plants a Close Shave

Give evergreen perennials a face-lift by cutting old leaves off plants like ferns and hellebores in early spring, before the new growth emerges. "You'll have to trim for a long time if you wait and try to cut out old fronds and leaves once they've mixed with the new ones," says Bob McCartney, vice president of Woodlanders, a native plant nursery in Aiken, South Carolina.

TRY A TIMELY

SPRING TIDY-UP

FOR PERENNIAL

FOLIAGE

For a quick cleanup, Bob suggests you cut the old stems back close to the crown before you see any new growth. Don't cut into the crown or you'll injure the buds that will open into new fronds or leaves. With most evergreen perennials, you can snip off all the old leaves at once with a pair of hedge shears. With Lenten roses (*Helleborus orientalis*), keep any good leaves and cut off tattered ones with a pair of pruning shears.

Try early pruning on evergreen ferns such as autumn fern (*Dryopteris erythrosora*) and Christmas fern (*Polystichum acrostichoides*), and perennials such as butcher's-broom (*Ruscus aculeatus*), cast-iron plant (*Aspidistra elatior*), and liriope (*Liriope* spp.). You'll breeze through spring cleanup.

Naturally Neat Perennials

You can avoid lots of summer cleanup if you select perennials with naturally neat leaves. Use these suggestions from John Elsley, horticultural director of Wayside Gardens in Hodges, South Carolina, to choose tidy plants.

Look for leaves that don't fade. Some perennials have leaves that look great through the entire growing season. Good options for a sunny border are gold-and-silver chrysanthemum (*Chrysanthemum pacificum*), hardy geraniums (*Geranium* spp.), and ornamental grasses. Northern gardeners can also grow peonies (*Paeonia officinalis*) for gorgeous foliage—but if you're a Southern gardener, peony foliage will fade in extreme heat.

Grow plants that disappear. Short-season perennials die back midway through the growing season, leaving a clean space in the garden instead of scraggly leaves. Common bleeding heart (*Dicentra spectabilis*) and primroses like

Siebold's primrose (*Primula sieboldii*) will completely vanish by midsummer. Plant late-emerging perennials like plumbago (*Ceratostigma plumbaginoides*) nearby and they'll fill in the opening and look great right up to frost.

Try the early-pruning plan. If you have plants that flop or look ragged part of the year, but can't bear to part with them, try John's early-pruning plan for a quick fix. When your plants finish their first flush of growth in late spring, cut them back by one-half to two-thirds of their total length. They'll resprout with bushy, healthy foliage.

Perennials that benefit from early pruning include 'Autumn Joy' sedum (*Sedum* 'Autumn Joy'), basket-of-gold (*Aurinia saxatilis*), Frikart's aster (*Aster* × *frikartii*), rock cresses (*Arabis* spp.), and scabious or pincushion flowers (*Scabiosa* spp.). To make pruning extra-easy, use your hedge shears and cut back plants in one snip.

Cut back fall-blooming and reblooming perennials in late spring—you'll get stockier plants that don't need staking and neater edging plants at the front of your beds.

251

Perennials That Don't Need Deadheading

*M*any perennials will only rebloom if you deadhead them—that is, cut off all their dead blossoms before they go to seed. But the perennials listed below keep blooming and blooming for months, and you don't have to lift a finger.

COMMON YARROW (*Achillea millefolium*)

These pink or red flat-topped flowers bloom all summer on 2-foot-tall stems. Their ferny foliage looks dainty but the plants are heat- and drought-resistant and spread quickly. The cultivar 'Summer Pastels' has soft "antique" pastel-colored flowers. Zones 3 to 8.

FRINGED BLEEDING HEART (*Dicentra eximia*)

Soft pink heart-shaped flowers bloom all summer on 18-inch-tall stems. The ferny blue-green foliage forms a mound and looks lush all season. These plants self-sow in moist shady areas. Look for cultivars like 'Alba' or 'Snowdrift' if you prefer white flowers. Try 'Boothman's Variety' for soft pink flowers on plants with blue-gray leaves. Zones 3 to 9.

GAURA (*Gaura lindheimeri*)

Spikes of delicate butterfly-like flowers open white and age to pink. They bloom on wiry 2- to 3-foot-tall stems from early summer until frost. The plants are shrubby with small dark green leaves. They are drought-tolerant once they're established, but do best in moist, well-drained soil. Gaura also handles heat and humidity well. Zones 5 to 9.

GRAYLEAF CRANESBILL (*Geranium cinereum*)

The pink cup-shaped flowers have darker veins and bloom from spring through fall. Deeply lobed leaves form a tidy mound only 6 to 12 inches tall in sun or partial shade. Plant them in moist, well-drained soil. Like most shorter cranesbills, this one tends to push its crown upward, so reset it more deeply every 2 to 3 years. Zones 5 to 8.

KALIMERIS
(*Kalimeris pinnatifida*, also known as *Asteromoea mongolica*)

This care-free aster look-alike has branched 2-foot-tall stems that are covered with small semidouble yellow-centered white daisies from midsummer to early fall. The almost leaf-less stems rise from a rosette of lance-shaped leaves, giving the plant a very airy effect. It thrives in moist soil in sun or partial shade. Zones 6 to 8.

KNAUTIA (*Knautia macedonica*)

Wine red fluffy pincushion-like flowers nod above this plant on long leafless stems from early summer until a hard frost. It grows in a loose clump that reaches 24 to 30 inches tall and is very drought-tolerant. The leaves are gray-green. Plant knautia in full sun and well-drained soil. Zones 5 to 10.

PINCUSHION FLOWER (*Scabiosa caucasica*)

You'll get masses of round flat lavender-blue flowers from May until a hard frost on this 18-inch-tall plant. The gray-green leaves are lance shaped. Give this plant a well-drained site in sun or light shade. It's excellent for the front of borders or blanketing the ground around roses, and it makes a good cut flower. Zones 3 to 7.

PURPLE CONEFLOWER (*Echinacea purpurea*)

Rose pink petals surround the mounded bristly orange center on each large daisylike flower. The blooms continue from June through September and even look attractive in fall and winter—leave the dried seed heads to feed the birds or use them in arrangements. This stiff plant thrives in full sun and is drought-tolerant. It grows 2 to 4 feet tall and has coarse leaves. Zones 3 to 8.

RED VALERIAN (*Centranthus ruber*)

Dome-shaped heads of small, intense raspberry pink, mauve pink, or white flowers bloom from June to November. Put these plants at the front of your flower border or behind a wall where they can cascade gracefully. They prefer sun and a well-drained site. The blue-green almost succulent leaves grow on 2- to 3-foot-tall plants that tend to sprawl. Zones 4 to 8.

RUSSIAN SAGE (*Perovskia atriplicifolia*)

Branched spires of tiny amethyst flowers cover this shrubby plant and create a cloud of color from July to frost. The toothed pale gray-green leaves are aromatic and grow on 3-foot-tall stems. Russian sage needs well-drained soil in full sun. It's drought-tolerant and makes a good cut flower. Zones 4 to 9.

THREADLEAF COREOPSIS (*Coreopsis verticillata* 'Moonbeam')

These pale yellow daisies are beautiful from June through frost—take a look at them at twilight and the flowers look luminous. Their threadlike leaves emerge very late, but once they do you'll have a 1-foot-tall mound that spreads slowly by runners. Give plants a sunny site and average soil and they'll thrive. Zones 3 to 9.

Choose Bamboo for Super Stakes

GIVE

PERENNIALS

A LIFT WITH

CUSTOM-

DESIGNED GRIDS

Sick of flopping flowers? If the weight of your perennials pitches them face-first into the mud, you can save yourself from the heartache of flopping flowers by staking your plants. "If you start early and build a support around a young plant, the plant can grow toward the light and be straight and natural looking," says John Elsley, horticultural director of Wayside Gardens in Hodges, South Carolina. In spring, when they're just coming up, it's simple to stake tall heavy-flowered perennials such as delphiniums, peonies, phlox, and Shasta daisy (*Chrysanthemum* × *superbum*). Later, once they've fallen over, they'll look awkward if you try to prop them up.

Garden supply catalogs and garden centers carry a huge variety of ready-made supports and cages that you can put around or over plants. You can use round wire rings, linking stakes that form a zigzag pattern, and wire grids on legs—all of which are easy to set over young plants.

But John prefers more natural-looking supports that you can make yourself in minutes, for just pennies. Use green bamboo stakes, which are available at most garden centers. Cut the stakes in pieces that match the width of the perennial you're supporting. Lay the pieces across each other in a crisscross pattern to form a support grid as wide as your plant. Tie the pieces together with black weather-resistant

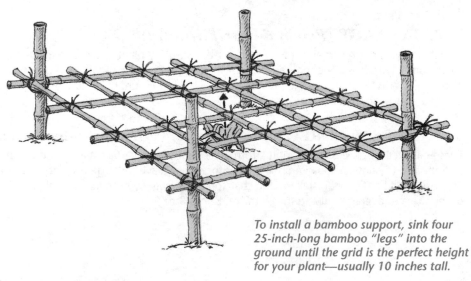

To install a bamboo support, sink four 25-inch-long bamboo "legs" into the ground until the grid is the perfect height for your plant—usually 10 inches tall.

cord and support the grid on four bamboo legs. "You can custom-design your supports to do whatever that plant needs," John says. You can surround the foliage or hold up individual stems.

Easy Ways to Handle Prickly Plants

MAINTENANCE
TRICKS SAVE
YOU FROM
PRICKS

Don't get stuck by plants with sharp thorns, irritating prickles, or spines. Perennials such as agaves (*Agave* spp.) and yuccas (*Yucca* spp.) have sharp spines on the ends of their swordlike leaves. Plants such as cacti, roses, thistles, and trifoliate orange (*Poncirus trifoliata*) are covered with spines that can catch leaves or your skin, especially when you're weeding. When you're faced with a thorny cleanup job, Bob McCartney, vice president of Woodlanders, a native plant nursery in Aiken, South Carolina, recommends blowing leaves away instead of raking them and mulching to control weeds instead of pulling them.

You can avoid raking fallen leaves out of the prickly patch—which could damage the plants or you—by using a backpack blower or handheld blower to blow leaves away.

With weeds, it's smart to tackle potential problems before they get started. Before you plant prickly perennials, sterilize the soil you'll be planting in to eliminate existing weed seeds. Here's how Bob does it. Lay a sheet of black plastic on the ground and cover it with a 2-inch layer of soil—this is the soil you'll plant in. Cover the soil with a sheet of clear plastic and secure the edges of the plastic with rocks to keep it down tight. "After a couple of days, the sun will super-heat and bake that soil and it will be ready to spread on your planting bed," Bob says.

To avoid the onslaught of weeds after planting, cover the finished bed with black plastic or a product like EweMulch (a landscape fabric made from wool). Top the weed barrier with an ornamental mulch of bark or stones. Bob particularly likes a mulch of crushed rock (½ to 1 inch diameter) around succulent perennials such as agave and yucca. The rocks look neat and are easy to clean with a blower.

You can also look for less prickly forms of spiny plants. Two of Bob's favorites are Adam's-needle (*Yucca filamentosa*) and *Yucca flaccida*.

PROVEN PLANTS
FOR FLOWER BEDS UNDER TREES

When tree roots take over parts of your lawn, don't fight them. Use them as an excuse to plant beautiful beds of spreading perennials and forget about mowing. Pick perennials that like the same conditions your trees do, says C. Colston Burrell, owner of the Minnesota-based design firm, Native Landscapes. Use water-hungry perennials around trees that like moist soil and drought-tolerant plants around trees that like drier conditions. That way you won't end up over- or underwatering your trees to meet the needs of your perennials. Any of the spreading perennials listed below make good tree companions that won't need lots of attention from you once they're established.

Astilbes (*Astilbe* spp.)
The handsome ferny foliage and plumes of pink, purple, and white flowers in early summer make this perennial a great choice. Plant it in moist soil. Zones 4 to 8.

Epimediums (*Epimedium* spp.)
Handsome heart-shaped leaves decorate this drought-tolerant plant. Small white, yellow, or red flowers appear in spring. Zones 4 to 8.

Hostas (*Hosta* spp.)
The handsome foliage on this plant ranges in size from larger than a dinner plate to smaller than a teacup. Leaves come in shades of blue, green, and yellow, sometimes with silver or gold variegation. Look for cultivars with fragrant flowering spikes in summer and fall. Zones 3 to 8.

Lenten rose (*Helleborus orientalis*)
This late-winter to early-spring bloomer has large showy flowers and handsome evergreen foliage. Zones 4 to 9.

Lily-of-the-valley (*Convallaria majalis*)
Here's a plant that thrives in moist or dry sites. Broad leaves will quickly cover tree roots, and you'll get plenty of fragrant white bell-shaped flowers. Zones 2 to 8.

Plumbago or Leadwort (*Ceratostigma plumbaginoides*)
Since it likes well-drained soil, this plant makes a good companion under trees. Dark green leaves cover plants all summer and turn red or orange in fall. Blue flowers appear in midsummer. Zones 5 to 9.

Serbian bellflower (*Campanula poscharskyana*)
These flowers don't mind dry spots. The trailing stems spread in a hurry and are covered with starry blue flowers in spring and early summer. Zones 3 to 7.

Speedy Success Starts with a Soak

Drench potted perennials with water before you plant them to give them a good start in your garden. Nancy Ondra, owner of Pendragon Perennials, a nursery in Emmaus, Pennsylvania, credits the survival of many plants to her habit of giving them a thorough preplanting soak.

"The medium that most container plants are grown in is really hard to wet," notes Nancy. "And once they're in the ground, it's nearly impossible to give plants enough water to saturate the root ball." As a result, you can under-water newly planted perennials—with disastrous results.

To make sure her perennials get enough water to sustain them through the stress of planting, Nancy sets each plant's container in a bucket full of water or compost tea, so that the roots and growing medium are completely submerged. "I leave them in there until no more bubbles rise from the medium; then I know it's well moistened," she says. Nancy's simple method makes sure that water gets to where the plants' roots are and saves them from a droughty death surrounded by a sea of well-soaked soil.

Plant Flower Beds That Spread

An easy way to start flower beds under trees is to tuck a few perennials in around roots and let them spread. If you try to dig up the entire area for a flower bed, you'll destroy the tree's feeder roots and it will suffer or may die. C. Colston Burrell, owner of the Minnesota-based design firm, Native Landscapes, uses a hand trowel to scrape away leaves and loose soil from around big roots and make small planting holes. He tucks in small starts of perennials that spread prolifically by seed or by runners and fills the holes with leaf mold or compost. "Water the plants frequently until they're established," Cole says. "Then let them find their own way to cover the area." Planting holes save trees and save you the trouble of extra planting.

To save yourself the effort of digging a flower bed and avoid damaging tree roots, dig individual planting holes when you plant under trees. Amend each hole with leaf mold or compost and your trees and plants will thrive.

257

10 Perennials That Fill In Fast

*O*ne gardener's pest can be another's perfect plant. While rapidly spreading plants can be invasive in your carefully planted mixed border, in other situations, the more, the merrier. When you're using perennials as groundcovers, or your budget just doesn't allow the purchase of a whole lot of plants, perennials that either spread rapidly by runners or self-sow abundantly can be a real boon. For these situations, choose from the speedy solutions below.

Spreading Perennials

BEE BALM (*Monarda didyma*)

Densely packed heads of tubular flowers appear from June to July in white and shades of pink, purple, or red (a hummingbird favorite). You can use the pointed aromatic leaves to make a pleasant tea. Choose the mildew-resistant cultivars 'Gardenview Scarlet', 'Marshall's Delight', and 'Purple Mildew Resistant', and plant them in moist soil for quick care-free growth in sun or light shade. Zones 4 to 8.

CATMINT (*Nepeta × faassenii*)

Spikes of small blue-violet flowers bloom heavily in June, then on and off through the summer and fall. The silvery gray foliage is aromatic but not a favorite of cats like catnip. This drought-tolerant plant looks lovely on a dry bank in either full sun or light shade. The flowers attract butterflies. Zones 3 to 8.

GOOSENECK LOOSESTRIFE (*Lysimachia clethroides*)

Spikes of small white flowers bloom in June and July. They make excellent and interesting cut flowers since the flower spikes dip all in the same direction. The lance-shaped leaves grow on 2- to 3-foot-tall stems. The plants thrive in moist or wet soil and like full sun to light shade. Zones 3 to 8.

JAPANESE ANEMONE OR GRAPE-LEAVED ANEMONE (*Anemone tomentosa* 'Robustissima')

This is one of the finest late-blooming perennials. The clear pink single saucer-shaped flowers have yellow centers that appear on 3-foot-tall stems from August to October. Their deep green divided leaves are covered with silvery down when they first come out. These plants like a sunny or lightly shaded site with moist soil. Zones 3 to 8.

QUEEN-OF-THE-PRAIRIE (*Filipendula rubra* 'Venusta')

Here's a choice native prairie plant that's also a great cut flower. You'll get fluffy flower plumes the color of raspberries and whipped cream in late June to July on 3- to 6-foot-tall stems. The leaves are lime green, divided, and crinkled. It thrives in moist soil with full sun or light shade. Zones 3 to 9.

Self-Sowing Perennials

COLUMBINE (*Aquilegia* species and cultivars)

These delicate spurred flowers bloom in blue, red, white, pink, purple, and yellow, and they're often bicolored. Most plants grow 1 to 3 feet tall and have pretty blue-green lobed leaves. The seedpods are interesting enough to leave until the plants have seeded themselves for next year. Plant in sun or partial shade in moist but well-drained soil. Zones 3 to 9.

GOLDEN MARGUERITE (*Anthemis tinctoria*)

Bright or light yellow daisies flourish all summer on 1- to 3-foot-tall stems in full sun. These drought-tolerant plants make great cut flowers, but leave some flowers to go to seed for next year. The finely cut gray-green leaves are aromatic. Zones 3 to 8.

LADY'S-MANTLE (*Alchemilla mollis*)

Clouds of tiny chartreuse yellow flowers appear from May until June on 1-foot-tall plants. Creeping roots spread slowly, but self-sown seeds will spread your planting fast on a moist site in sun or partial shade. The leaves are especially nice with their scalloped edges and gray-green color. Zones 3 to 8.

LANCE-LEAVED COREOPSIS (*Coreopsis lanceolata*)

The seed heads of this native prairie plant attract birds, which gives you another reason to leave the spent flowers in the garden. Enjoy the bright yellow daisylike flowers in a sunny spot all summer. They like moist soil but are drought-tolerant. Bright green lance-shaped leaves grow on 2- to 3-foot-tall plants. Zones 3 to 8.

ROSE CAMPION (*Lychnis coronaria*)

Seedlings will pop up outside your original planting to give you pleasant surprises. Jewel-like fuchsia or white flowers bloom in June on open-branched stems. The silvery gray-green leaves look velvety—they're a real contrast to the bright flowers. Plants grow 2 to 3 feet tall in full sun or partial shade if they have moist, well-drained soil. Zones 4 to 8.

PROVEN PLANTS
FOR NIGHT GARDENS

Do summer heat, chores, and fun keep you out of your garden all day? Extend your garden time with this simple color trick and you'll find out how pleasant your garden can be when the moon is out and the crickets are singing. Instead of filling your garden with colorful flowers, plant silver-leaved and white-flowered perennials—they'll reflect all the available light so you can see and enjoy your garden long past dusk. Brightly colored gardens just disappear at night.

"I have to work such long hours during summer that I never have time to just enjoy the gardens by day," laments Donna Iarkowski, owner of Nature's Way Herbary in Muncy Valley, Pennsylvania. The time crunch and heat convinced Donna to plant "moon gardens" to extend the hours she can spend with her plants. Here are some great perennials Donna recommends for evening enjoyment.

Black snakeroot (*Cimicifuga racemosa*)
Long flower spikes decorate these plants in summer and fall. Use them in sun or light shade. Zones 3 to 8.

Goat's beard (*Aruncus dioicus*)
Fuzzy flowers bloom in late spring and early summer in sun or partial shade. Zones 3 to 7.

Silver artemisias (*Artemisia* spp.)
This silvery-leaved foliage plant thrives in full sun. Zones 3 to 8.

White astilbe (*Astilbe* × *arendsii* 'Avalanche' or 'Bridal Veil')
Fluffy plumelike flowers bloom in late spring and summer in sun or shade. Zones 3 to 9.

White bleeding heart (*Dicentra spectabilis* 'Alba')
Grow plants in sun or shade for heart-shaped flowers in spring and summer. Zones 2 to 9.

White-edged hostas (*Hosta fortunei* 'Albo-marginata' or *H. sieboldii*)
Lilac-colored blooms appear in summer above white-edged leaves. Line shady paths with hostas to outline the walkway. Zones 3 to 8.

White-flowered lavender (*Lavandula angustifolia* 'Alba')
Spikes of flowers bloom in summer in sun or light shade. Zones 5 to 9.

White-flowered purple coneflower (*Echinacea purpurea* 'Alba')
Big daisylike flowers last all summer in sunny gardens. Zones 3 to 8.

White irises (*Iris cristata* var. *alba, Iris* bearded hybrid 'Lacy Snowflake', or *I. sibirica* 'White Swirl')
Large ruffled petals appear in spring and summer. These plants prefer sun or light shade. Zones 3 to 9.

White lilies (*Lilium candidum* or *L. speciosum* var. *album*)
Large trumpet-shaped flowers appear in spring and summer. Plant bulbs in sun or partial shade. Zones 4 to 9.

White peonies (*Paeonia officinalis,* any white cultivar)
You'll get lots of large fluffy blooms in spring and early summer if you place plants in sun or light shade. Zones 3 to 8.

White phlox (*Phlox paniculata* 'David' or *P. carolina* 'Miss Lingard')
Large rounded flower heads bloom in spring and summer in sunny or shady sites. Zones 3 to 8 for *P. paniculata;* Zones 4 to 9 for *P. carolina.*

Beef Up Perennial Gardens with Bulbs

Stretch your garden's color show by interplanting your perennials with bulbs—it's a neat way to get more color without adding maintenance chores. Bulbs like crocuses, daffodils, and tulips make great companions for perennial flowers because they willingly share the same space. The bulbs lie low and emerge early, so they won't disrupt your perennials' performance, and they make good location markers for slow-to-show perennials.

When the bulb foliage starts fading, the perennials bush out and hide tattered bulb leaves so you don't have to trim them. Perennials also help protect bulbs from too much heat and rain. "Spring-flowering bulbs like to be cool and dry when they are dormant in summer," says Brent Heath, co-owner of The Daffodil Mart in Gloucester, Virginia. Perennials shade the bulbs to keep them cool and use up excess moisture so the bulbs stay dry.

Brent recommends planting perennials between or on top of bulbs. For example, if you're planting daylilies 12 to 18 inches apart, plant daffodils 6 inches apart in between the daylilies. Or you could plant daylilies over a daffodil planting. Just don't plant the daylilies too close together, or the bulbs will come up for a few years and then the daylilies will grow too thick and crowd them out. It's easy to tuck bulbs in and around existing perennials too.

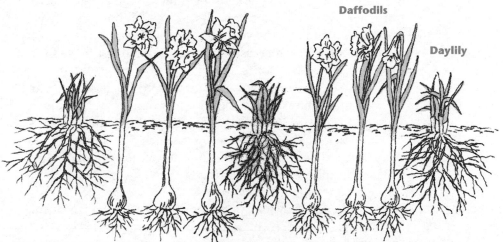

Fill spaces between perennials like daylilies with daffodils or other bulbs to add more spring color to your garden.

POTATOES

Presprout for Faster Potatoes

Knock two weeks off your wait for homegrown potatoes by using a simple method called "chitting." Certified seed-potato producer Megan Gerritsen of WoodPrairie Farm in Bridgewater, Maine, explains how. "About a month before planting time, store the seed potatoes in a dark room at about 65° to 70°F. Once they sprout—and the sprouts should only be ¹⁄₁₆ to ⅛ inch long—lower the temperature to between 50° and 55°F and provide light."

The light doesn't have to be strong, Megan says—just enough so the sprouts don't stretch trying to find it. She keeps her potatoes in her garage and the light coming through the open door is plenty. Megan stacks her potatoes two deep in 8-inch-tall plastic trays with legs, then she stacks the trays 13 high. You can use single or stackable containers, depending on how many potatoes you want to start. Check discount stores for stackable trays and milk crates, or build your own homemade trays out of wood.

Potato sprouts shouldn't get more than about ½ inch long with adequate light. But "some cultivars, like 'Green Mountain', sprout violently," notes Megan. To keep them in check, either increase the amount of light or move them to a cooler spot.

When you're ready to plant, cut the potatoes into block-shaped chunks that weigh 1½ to 2 ounces each (1 ounce for fingerling potatoes). Each piece should have at least two eyes, which are easy to see because they've sprouted. The eye will become the plant, and the chunk of potato will provide energy for the growing eye until it can make its own food through photosynthesis.

You can buy seed potatoes at garden centers or through seed catalogs. If you want to buy organic seed potatoes, order early—they sell out fast. (See "Sources" on page 412 for companies that carry seed potatoes.)

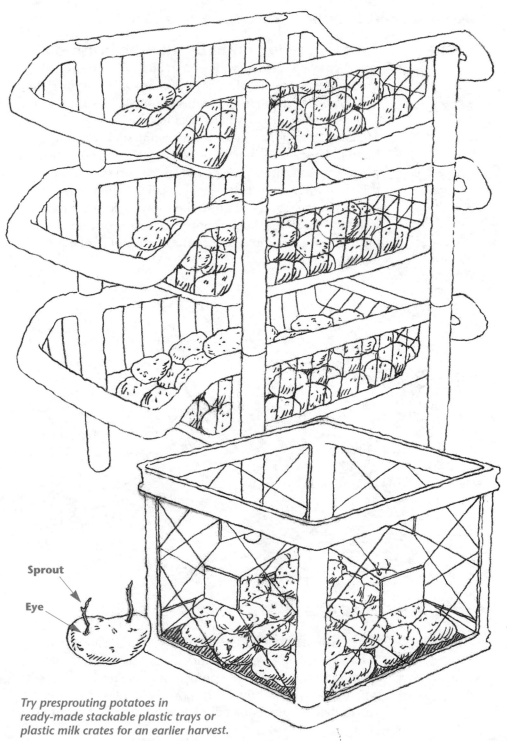

Sprout

Eye

*Try presprouting potatoes in
ready-made stackable plastic trays or
plastic milk crates for an earlier harvest.*

Make a Clean Sweep of Potato Pests

Give Colorado potato beetles the brush-off

and they won't damage your potato crop. All it takes is mulch and a broom. "Mulch your potatoes with straw right after planting, or when the plants are small," instructs Ken Muckenfuss, owner of Mill Creek Organic Farm in Medford, New Jersey. Then use a broom, stick, or your hand to knock the pinkish-colored beetle larvae off the plants into the straw. "The beetle larvae curl up and fall off the plant when disturbed," Ken explains. "Then they get lost in the straw and can't find their way back to the plant." Ken says you should sweep your plants three or four times during beetle season to reduce the chance of beetle damage.

Confuse Colorado potato beetles by knocking their larvae off plants into a maze of straw mulch. The larvae will get lost trying to climb back to your plants.

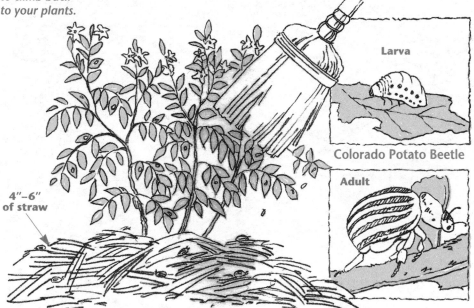

4"–6" of straw

Larva

Colorado Potato Beetle

Adult

No-Dig Spuds Spurn Blight

Fight blight the easy way by growing your potatoes in baskets of compost set on top of your garden soil. "When I moved from Missouri to Pennsylvania, the drainage was so much better that I thought my potato troubles were over," says Rodale garden book editor Joan Benjamin. It wasn't so.

The well-drained soils in the Northeast kept her potatoes dry but didn't keep them from rotting when late blight (*Phytophthora infestans*) fungus invaded. That's when Joan resorted to growing potatoes above ground.

You can use any kind of container that's handy, Joan says. She plants in bushel baskets, but knows people who use 5-gallon buckets or plastic garbage cans with holes poked in the bottom for drainage.

GROW YOUR POTATOES BY THE BUSHEL TO BEAT DISEASES

Here's what to do: Half-fill each container with compost—homemade or from a community recycling site. (Compost helps suppress diseases, so it's an extra measure of safety against the dreaded blight.) Set seed potatoes on the compost, add more compost to completely cover them, and let them grow. As the potato leaves come up, add more compost so the tubers always stay buried. Joan fills her baskets three-quarters or more full of compost once the plants grow up above her containers.

Plant one seed potato in a 5-gallon bucket and two or three in a bushel basket or garbage can. Come summer, you'll have a fine crop of new potatoes. Stick your hand in the compost and pull out what you need. Or for an instant fall harvest, wait until the leaves start to turn brown, then tip your containers over. You'll avoid digging and get perfect potatoes without the cracks or broken pieces that you get when you use a potato fork.

You can avoid disease problems and plant early even in a wet spring when you grow your potatoes above ground in containers filled with compost.

265

PROPAGATION

Make a Rooting Kit for the Road

When visiting a friend's garden, you never know when you'll see a plant that you must have for your own yard. It helps to be prepared, in case you're invited (or decide to invite yourself) to take a cutting. "I never go anywhere without my plastic bags and a pocketknife," proclaims Tony Avent, owner of Plant Delights Nursery in Raleigh, North Carolina. "You never know when a 'gotta have' pops up, and you need to move fast to keep a cutting alive until you get home." Having your own supplies at hand, rather than imposing on your friends, may make them more inclined to share the riches of their gardens.

Besides a sharp knife and plastic bags, other supplies for a "rooting kit" include a bag of coarse sand, sharp clippers, rooting hormone, plastic vials, and a jug of water.

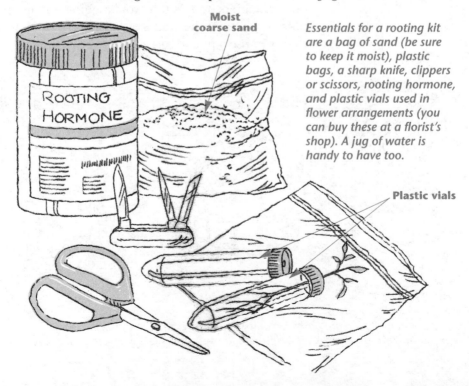

Moist
coarse sand

Essentials for a rooting kit are a bag of sand (be sure to keep it moist), plastic bags, a sharp knife, clippers or scissors, rooting hormone, and plastic vials used in flower arrangements (you can buy these at a florist's shop). A jug of water is handy to have too.

Plastic vials

Now's the Best Time to Take Root Cuttings

YOU CAN

RUSTLE UP ROOT

CUTTINGS ALL

SEASON LONG

When's the best time to divide a plant? The standard answer is "in the season opposite its bloom." However, Tony Avent, owner of Plant Delights Nursery in Raleigh, North Carolina, says the best time to divide a plant is "when you're near it. You usually can't go back later." Often, dividing is the fastest and easiest way to propagate a plant. But when dividing isn't an option, taking root cuttings is a good alternative.

Dividing plants out of season is done all the time, says Tony. Many perennials can survive the stress of division if they're healthy and weather conditions aren't extremely hot and dry. However, trying to divide plants that are in full bloom can be disastrous—the divisions frequently die.

Tony's discovered a trick that allows him to take root cuttings to make new plants from perennials, such as butterfly weed (*Asclepias tuberosa*), even when they're in full bloom. All Tony does is slice into the soil next to one side of the plant and cut a few sections of root. He then cuts each section into pieces that are 2 to 3 inches long. He buries these pieces in sandy potting soil, where they'll quickly begin to sprout.

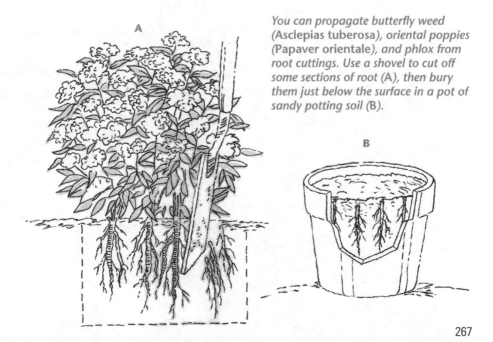

A

B

*You can propagate butterfly weed (*Asclepias tuberosa*), oriental poppies (*Papaver orientale*), and phlox from root cuttings. Use a shovel to cut off some sections of root (A), then bury them just below the surface in a pot of sandy potting soil (B).*

267

2 Tricks for Faster Rooting

Some plants root no matter what you do to them, but others require special coaxing to form roots quickly. Philadelphia gardener Libby J. Goldstein has tinkered with ways to get cuttings to root faster. Here are two of her discoveries.

Keep your shrub cuttings warm and moist. "I've used this trick with crepe myrtle and citrus plants," Libby explains. "In some cases, it speeds up rooting by three weeks. Sometimes it makes the difference between rooting and not rooting at all."

The secret is to take the cuttings before they get too woody. To take semihardwood cuttings, remove 3- to 6-inch-long cuttings from new shrub shoots in summer. Remove the bottom leaves, keeping two or three leaves at the top of each cutting. Put the cuttings in a pot, add a label with the name of the plant and the date you took the cuttings, and cover the pot with a plastic bag. Seal the plastic around the

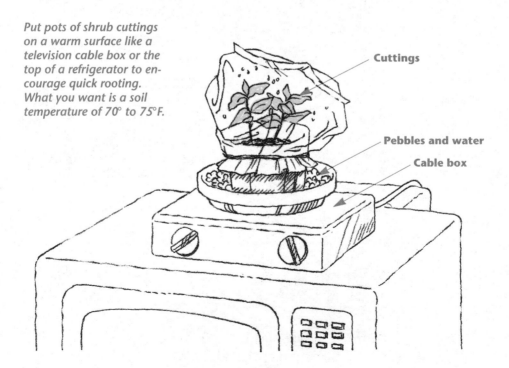

Put pots of shrub cuttings on a warm surface like a television cable box or the top of a refrigerator to encourage quick rooting. What you want is a soil temperature of 70° to 75°F.

Cuttings

Pebbles and water

Cable box

rim with a rubber band or tape to keep moisture in. Place the pot on a pebble tray filled with water to keep the humidity high. Put just enough water in the tray to reach the top of the pebbles—you don't want the pot to sit in water. Put the tray and pot on a warm surface, such as a heating cable, propagating mat, or even the cable box for the television. "The center of a gas stove might also work, or the top of a water heater if it's not too hot," Libby says.

Cut herbs by the light of the silvery moon. Libby says that this tip for rooting pineapple sage "was whispered to me in a library by a famous herb lady who didn't want people to think she was nuts." The secret, which Libby attests works, is to cut the blooming plant anytime between the last quarter and the new moon and put it in water.

❧ QUICK FIX MIX

Homemade Rooting Hormone

Brew your own rooting hormone for woody plant cuttings and they'll root faster and with greater success. Sure you can buy synthetic commercial brands, but it's easy to make your own natural mix from willow shoots. And it's free! William Welch, Texas author of *Antique Roses for the South*, uses this concoction and says a number of other growers use it too.

1 handful of 1-inch-long sections of cut willow branches (any *Salix* species)

cuttings from shrubs, trees, roses, or woody perennials that you want to root

Bring a saucepan of water to a rolling boil and turn off the heat. Split the willow pieces with a knife and add them to the hot water. Steep the willow pieces in the water overnight. In the morning, the water should look like weak tea.

Soak cuttings in the solution for several hours, and then water them with it after you stick them into planting medium.

Note: For convenience you can prepare the willow water ahead of time and store it in the refrigerator.

Save Plants—It's Simple

TENDER PLANTS
ROOT HAPPILY IN
GOOD OLD H₂0

When the first frost threatens, you may panic because there's not enough time to protect tender plants or move them inside. Solve the dilemma by taking cuttings. Just stick them in cans and glass jars of water to root right on the steamy windowsill of your kitchen or bathroom.

John Harris, the horticulturist at New Orleans's Longue Vue Gardens, uses high-tech propagation systems at work but cuts corners when it comes to doing it around the house. "I stuck a bunch of my wife Jodi's heartleaf philodendron in a bottle of water and every bit rooted," John says.

Philodendrons are notoriously easy to root in water, and so are many other tropical and bedding plants. It's a handy way to keep them over the winter as well. When spring comes, the rooted cuttings are ready to set in pots or outside. If you have a couple of glass jars and a warm window, you won't have to worry about storage space or winter protection for plants like dragon tree (*Dracaena marginata*), dumb canes (*Dieffenbachia* spp.), and philodendrons.

Urban gardeners in "Alphabet City"—the infamous Lower East Side of Manhattan, where "make do" is the watchword—find that many of their best groundcovers root quite readily in water as well. Euonymus, ivy, pachysandra, and vinca are popular passalongs because they are evergreen and can be jammed into a bucket of water nearly anytime and they'll root. Even timid newcomers learn quickly that they don't have to know anything about rooting compounds or complicated techniques. Just change the water when it gets murky and before long—three or four weeks—you'll have enough of a start to get growing.

Track Down This Tool

The perfect tool for planting cuttings from roses and other shrubs is free for the taking out along the railroad tracks.

"I've found that the hole made by a railroad spike is just the right depth for starting a rose bush from a cutting," observes William Allen, a gardener in Jonesboro, Arkansas. The spikes (which are used to hold railroad ties in place) are discarded along railroad tracks as part of track maintenance. They look like fat four-sided nails and are about 7 inches long.

For woody cuttings, hammer the spike all the way into the ground, pull it out, then insert the cutting. Next, push the spike into the soil a few inches away from the cutting. Repeat in several spots around the cutting to press the soil against the stem.

Coddle Cuttings with Homemade Covers

Protect cuttings from frost with a quick cover made from a plastic soda bottle. "Grandmother always covered cuttings of roses and other flowers with mason jars," relates Felder Rushing, coauthor of *Passalong Plants*. He remembers how she had to scurry back and forth to uncover them on warm or sunny days, or they'd quickly overheat. Felder found a modern-day equivalent to Granny's mason jars in discarded plastic drink bottles (the liter size or larger). To turn them into minigreenhouses, cut off the bottom, Felder explains. Avoid Grandma's extra work by leaving the cap on loosely, so you can take it off on extra-hot days and replace it at night.

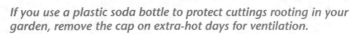

Plastic milk jugs with the bottoms cut out also make good protective coverings for cuttings and newly transplanted seedlings. Or, for protection from cold winds or blowing sand, wrap some plastic around wire tomato cages or just around some sticks stuck in a circle in the soil around the cuttings.

If you use a plastic soda bottle to protect cuttings rooting in your garden, remove the cap on extra-hot days for ventilation.

Mist-ifying Cutting Secret

Fogging cuttings with fine mist is a modern technique that's dramatically upped the percentage of cuttings that "take." Keeping new cuttings covered with a nearly continuous superfine mist of water reduces wilting, keeps leaf temperatures low, and generally helps a higher percentage of cuttings survive and root in record time—weeks instead of months. And you can take advantage of this technological breakthrough by building your own mist system.

Bob McCartney, who propagates over a thousand species of plants each year at Woodlanders, an Aiken, South Carolina, native plant nursery, says that he has found that "many plants are impossible to root otherwise. And on average, I can save a third of the time it would take without mist."

The most expensive part of a home mist system is an electric timer, which can cost $100 or more. The timer operates a special valve called a solenoid valve, feeding water from a faucet into PVC pipes that have mist nozzles mounted on

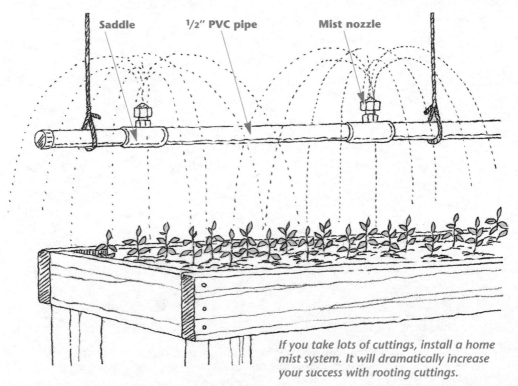

Saddle   ½" PVC pipe   Mist nozzle

If you take lots of cuttings, install a home mist system. It will dramatically increase your success with rooting cuttings.

them. Look for used solenoid valves (they're used on dishwashers) at an appliance repair shop. Mist nozzles are available through nursery supply companies; your local garden center should have catalogs that include mist nozzles.

To set up your system, suspend the PVC pipe from above (for example, from the rafters of a greenhouse). Cut small holes in the PVC pipe, glue a "saddle" over each hole, and screw a mist nozzle into each saddle. Hang the system 1 to 2 feet above the cuttings. Program the timer to turn the mist on for a few seconds every four or five minutes.

Using a system like this, you can make dozens of cuttings nearly any summer month, in an area no larger than a dining room table. You'll save time and have a higher success rate.

Refrigerator Heats Up Cuttings

GIVE PLANT
PROPAGATION
PRIORITY ON THE
FRIDGE TOP

Cuttings respond quickly to gentle bottom heat. You can set up a bottom-heating system fairly inexpensively using heating cables, which are widely available through garden centers and mail-order garden suppliers. (Thermostat-controlled water-bed heaters, set on 70°F, will also work for bottom heat.) Cuttings root faster when heated, and many seeds germinate more quickly in flats put over heat too.

But Felder Rushing, coauthor of *Passalong Plants,* has found a no-cost source of heat right in his kitchen: the top of his refrigerator. First, Felder helps his children sow seed in flats and wrap them with plastic food wrap to conserve humidity. (Another favorite technique in the Rushing household is to insert cuttings in moist sandy soil mix and cover them with minigreenhouses made from glass jars or cutoff plastic bottles.) Then they set them on the refrigerator, where temperatures usually hover in the upper 70s, even in the winter.

Pepper seeds, which normally take up to two weeks to sprout, often germinate in six or seven days on top of the refrigerator, Felder says. Rose cuttings callus and begin rooting within weeks instead of months. Once new growth appears, move plants into natural light, so they'll grow stocky and tough.

PRUNING

Cut Pruning Time in Half

TIPS FOR
FINDING AND
KEEPING TIP-TOP
PRUNING TOOLS

You'll speed through pruning jobs if you choose good tools and keep them clean, sharp, and well oiled. It sounds obvious, but this advice is worth more than you think. Kris Medic, city landscape manager and arborist for Columbus, Indiana, estimates that poorly maintained low-quality tools can double or triple your pruning time. Kris and Mike Ferrara, former equipment editor of *Organic Gardening* magazine and a tool industry consultant, give these suggestions for selecting and caring for your tools.

Buy the best. Top-quality tools have the extras that let you work quickly without tiring. Look for pruners and loppers with shock absorbers. You'll speed through pruning tasks when the tool bears the brunt of each cut, instead of your hands, arms, and shoulders.

Padded or vinyl-coated grips protect your hands from blisters and keep pruners and loppers from slipping while you're making a cut. Try loppers with ash handles instead of metal ones—they'll absorb more of the force of each cut and reduce the impact on your arms.

Mind the metal. Whether you're shopping for loppers, hand pruners, or saws, it pays to choose tools that are made to stay sharp. Look for loppers and hand pruners with heat-hardened steel blades—labeled forged, drop-forged, or tempered. Avoid inexpensive pressed metal blades, warns Mike. Cheap metals may look good new, he notes, but they'll quickly get dull and hard to sharpen.

Buy pruners with removable blades, Mike adds. They make sharpening simpler, and you can replace bent or broken blades instead of buying a whole new set of pruners.

Get a (good) grip. Hand pruners and pruning saws should fit comfortably in your grip without forcing you to hold your hand or wrist in an awkward position. Make sure handles aren't too big or small for your hands. Loppers should feel balanced—not extra-heavy on the blade end.

Pick the lock. The handier a lock is, the less time you'll spend locking and unlocking the blades as you prune, says Mike. Choose pruners with a locking mechanism that you can operate with your *gloved* hand. But make sure the lock isn't under your hand or fingers while you work, or it can rub uncomfortably.

Keep it clean. When you prune, sap builds up on the blades and collects dust, dirt, and moisture. It all adds up to corrosion unless you clean your pruning tools after you use them. Wipe away sap and soil with an old cloth. Then apply a thin layer of oil to protect the blades from moisture and to keep moving parts functioning smoothly.

Stow your gear. After cleaning your tools, store them in a dry protected place. Dew, rain, and snow will turn your tools dull and rusty, and that can really slow you down.

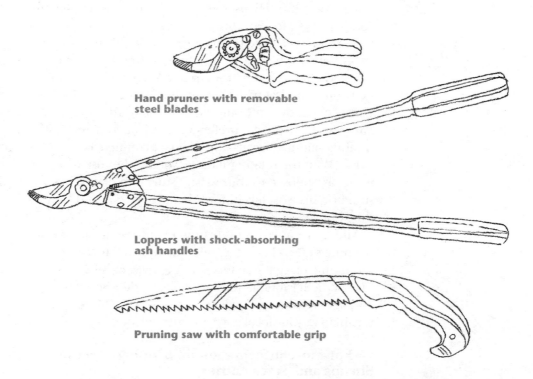

Hand pruners with removable steel blades

Loppers with shock-absorbing ash handles

Pruning saw with comfortable grip

Tools with padded handles or well-shaped wooden handles are most comfortable to use. Save your hands, arms, and shoulders by using pruners and loppers with built-in shock absorbers.

Try the Tools Picky Pruners Choose

LET A PRO POINT

YOU TO

PRECISION

PRUNING TOOLS

To find pruning tools that do the job with speed and ease, ask somebody who does a lot of pruning. That's the advice of Mike Ferrara, former equipment editor of *Organic Gardening* magazine and a tool industry consultant. Professional landscapers and lawn maintenance workers "make their bread with those tools, and you're not going to see them with cheap stuff," he says. "Ask them what kind of pruners they use; they're usually very opinionated about it for a good reason—they can't have the thing break on them while they're working."

As someone who does a fair bit of pruning in the course of a year, C. Colston Burrell, owner of the Minnesota-based design firm, Native Landscapes, has definite preferences about tools. He prefers Felco hand pruners, loppers, and pruning saws. "With these three together, you can tackle anything," Cole says. He uses Felco #2 pruners, which he says cost a lot ($40 to $50), but are well worth it. They're made from solid steel, Cole points out, and they'll still be going strong when you've worn out three or four cheaper pairs.

Good tools save time for curator Murray Kereluk when he prunes the 184 fruit trees in the Food Garden in the University of British Columbia Botanic Gardens in Vancouver. He says he prefers Felco #7 hand pruners with a rotating handle, because they make pruning easier on his wrist. "With the rotating handle, you tend to use your hand more, as opposed to your wrist," Murray explains. Less strain on his wrist lets him work more quickly and with less time out.

Murray rounds out his pruning equipment with a Felco pruning saw. By having a good-quality saw, Murray says he's saved time on maintenance—in the five years he's owned his saw, he hasn't had to sharpen its blade. (See "Sources" on page 412 for mail-order sources of Felco tools, or look for them at your local garden center or nursery.)

❧**For more information on pruning, see the Shrubs and Trees entries.**

JUST SAY "NO" TO EARLY EVERGREEN PRUNING

Ignore your evergreens when you're doing fall cleanup in your landscape—you have plenty of other chores to do then. Instead, start pruning when December rolls around. The timing's perfect for turning your evergreen trimmings into fresh and festive holiday decorations. When the holidays are over, use the branches for garden mulch.

Kris Medic, city landscape manager and arborist for Columbus, Indiana, offers these pruning tips to get good-looking plants and decorations at the same time.

• Prune entire branches back to ground level or a main stem or trunk, rather than snipping off little pieces. Taking off little bits of branches ruins your plant's shape.

• When you prune needled evergreens like fir, hemlock, pine, and spruce, leave the central leader (the top of the tree) alone—cutting it will destroy your tree's nice pointed shape.

• Keep in mind that broadleaf evergreens, such as boxwoods or hollies, grow back faster than needled evergreens. If you need lots of trimmings, prune the broadleaf plants hardest.

• Don't get carried away. You can cut off one-quarter of an evergreen's growth at one time, but less is better. If you need more greens, it's cheaper to buy them than a whole new tree or shrub.

Keep your evergreens in shape and get Christmas decorations too by pruning entire branches in December, as shown in this cross section.

RAISED BEDS

Soil-Sided Beds Save Steps

Skip the sides on raised beds if you've done a good job of soil preparation. When you build a raised bed, add plenty of organic matter and mulch well, says Kim Hawks, owner of Niche Gardens nursery in Chapel Hill, North Carolina. Then your beds won't need to be supported by boards, cinder blocks, or rocks.

Kim simply presses on the sides and ends of her beds to form slopes. She edges the beds by going around their boundaries and digging out a V-shaped section of soil. That cut gives the beds a clean edge that doesn't need wood or stone supports. Kim uses a garden rake to round corners and smooth the edges. The soil settles over a few weeks, stabilizing the beds, and the mulch protects it from erosion during hard rains.

Low Beds—Less Watering

Don't go overboard when you're building raised beds in hot or dry climates. In balmy South Carolina, cold soil isn't as much of a hindrance to gardeners as wet soil, so raise beds high enough for good drainage but not so high they overheat. Raised beds that are too high will dry out more quickly in hot conditions, so they'll need more watering than a bed that's raised up just enough to provide drainage in rainy seasons, points out PBS's *Victory Garden* guest host Jim Wilson of Donalds, South Carolina. "I don't like to stoop over any more than anyone else if I don't have to," Jim says. "Still, it's a waste of time and material to build a bed more than a few inches or a foot high. Any higher, and you'll have to water a lot more often.

"If you need a place to rest when working a lower bed, put a 1-by-4 facer board around the rim to set your knee on," Jim suggests.

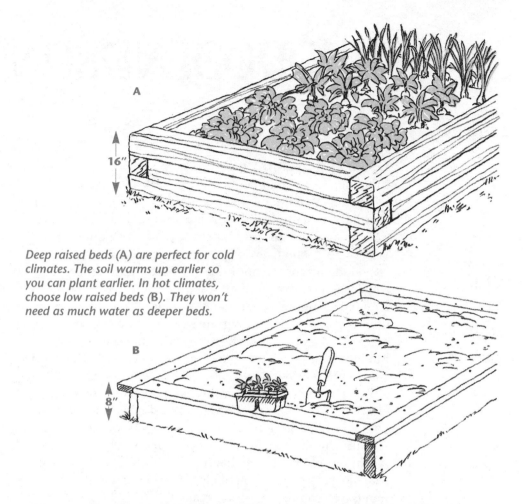

Deep raised beds (A) are perfect for cold
climates. The soil warms up earlier so
you can plant earlier. In hot climates,
choose low raised beds (B). They won't
need as much water as deeper beds.

Deep Beds Boost Northern Harvests

Build deep beds to get more from your raised bed
garden more quickly, says Murray Kereluk, Food Garden
curator at the University of British Columbia Botanic
Gardens in Vancouver.

In cold climates, the soil in raised beds warms up more
quickly in the spring and drains better than in-ground beds,
so you can plant earlier. An earlier start on the season
means an increase in the number of crops your beds can
produce. "If you have a good soil depth—at least 16
inches—you can plant more intensively and get a much
higher crop yield," says Murray, who has tended the Food
Garden's raised beds for over 14 years.

RHODODENDRONS

Chip Away at Black Vine Weevils

Use a cedar-chip mulch to keep weevils off your rhododendrons. Your landscape will look a lot neater, too, and you'll cut down on weeds and watering.

"I have a small rhododendron nursery hacked out of the woods," says Bob Eliot, a Master Gardener with the Washington State University Cooperative Extension Service. "Rhododendrons are notorious for harboring weevils, which eat the leaves at night. I started using cedar chips for a mulch to suppress weeds and found it makes a tremendous difference in repelling the weevils." Bob applies the chips in a 3-inch layer each year. (Make sure the chips you buy are made from true cedar trees, not junipers, which are sometimes referred to as cedars.)

Bob got his cedar chips from a sawmill, which produces chips that are bigger than sawdust but smaller than a wood chipper would produce. He cautions against getting cedar sawdust chips from a furniture manufacturer, because the sawdust would be so fine that it could form a crust over the soil, blocking penetration of air and water. If a mill isn't handy, you can buy cedar chips at garden centers.

PUT WEEVILS ON THE RUN WITH CEDAR-CHIP MULCH

Since black vine weevils feed on rhododendron leaves at night, you won't often see them. If weevils are bugging you, use cedar chips to keep them away.

Black vine weevil   **Cedar chips**

Simple Steps to Rhododendron Success

Rhododendrons are woodland shrubs, growing naturally in rich woodsy soil beneath the dappled shade of tall trees. By giving them the same conditions in your landscape, you'll have attractive, healthy plants that will need mere minutes—rather than hours—of care.

Start your rhododendrons off right with good planting techniques, recommends Tom Ahern, past president of the Lehigh Valley Chapter of the American Rhododendron Society. Tom likes to give his rhododendrons and azaleas planting holes "large enough for the roots to grow into over five years." He refills each hole with a mixture of 1 part peat moss, 1 part pine bark, and 2 parts topsoil, then mulches after planting with 3 to 5 inches of wood chips. This gives his rhododendrons the drainage and acid soil they need, while the mulch keeps the roots cool and moist, like in a forest setting.

Tom stresses that filtered shade keeps rhododendrons healthy and problem-free year-round. He notes that rhododendrons he's planted in the sun are more often attacked by lace bugs during the summer than the ones in shady sites. In the winter, light shade helps protect leaves from moisture loss.

THERE'S NO PLACE LIKE SHADE FOR HAPPY RHODIES

Too much sun (top) means stress, pests, and diseases for rhododendrons and azaleas, so keep plants shaded (bottom).

ROSES

Don't Give Up on Roses

Tough, beautiful, low-maintenance roses are now available. You can order many of these roses through specialty nurseries from coast to coast—and say good-bye to endless rose care.

After tending to thousands of these hardy beauties at the Antique Rose Emporium in Independence, Texas, the last thing production manager Glenn Schroeter wants to do is fuss with his own. "I don't have time for roses at the house, but there are a few out there," says Glenn. "One I really enjoy is 'Caldwell Pink', because it blooms well in our heat but is hardy just about anywhere in the country.

"I rarely prune my roses, because they just don't need it," says Glenn. Modern roses, especially hybrid teas, have been bred for tall straight stems with a single bud at the top for cutting. As a result, they need to be cut way back to stay compact. Old garden roses, especially Chinas, teas, and polyanthas, keep branching freely and retain their shape without all the pruning. "They're landscape-quality plants without all the fuss," Glenn notes. If you'd like to try these old roses, choose the ones that suit your space and climate best. China roses have delicate twiggy branches that grow 3 to 6 feet tall and are hardy to Zone 7. Tea roses are tall and slender, growing 4 to 6 feet tall and 3 to 4 feet wide. All are hardy to Zone 7 and some to Zone 6. Polyanthas are short bushy plants, just 2 feet tall that are hardy to Zone 5.

"When it comes down to it, lots of gardeners are intimidated by roses, thinking they have to do all that soil preparation and pruning and root spreading and spraying," Glenn continues. "I try to get across that you don't have to have a rose garden, just roses in a garden. Group them or plant them in masses, or use them as specimen plants—just like any other shrub or perennial. Plant them 'green side up', get them established with water and mulch, and let 'em rip."

Root Roses Right—On Site

Here's a foolproof way to make more roses.

Michael Shoup, owner of the Antique Rose Emporium in Independence, Texas, grows thousands of roses each year in commercial-size propagation houses. But in his own garden, he's found a super-easy way to get plenty of cuttings to share with friends, using the plant's own energy. Instead of removing pieces of stems and sticking them in sandy soils—which leads to loss and takes time to tend—he uses what he calls a "modified layer." It's a technique that works best in early spring or mid-fall.

"I can't help myself," Michael confesses. "As I wander around the yard, sometimes I grab one or two pliable branches on favorite plants and just bend them down and bury them in the ground. Making a V in the stem doesn't break it, but damages it just enough to start the rooting process. I cover the bent part in about 3 inches of good roughed-up dirt, leaving the tip sticking out of the ground. Then I cover it with a brick or rock or whatever's handy to keep it from popping out. After a couple of months or so, I just lift the rock and tug on the stem to see if it's rooted yet." Once the stem has rooted, Michael severs the stem from the parent plant and moves the rooted cutting to its new site.

Propagate your roses using the "modified layer" technique shown here. Once the stem tips root, cut them from the parent plant and move the rooted cuttings to a nursery bed or your yard or garden.

This Trio of Tips Stops Blackspot Short

Stop blackspot before it starts with preventive measures. "Once blackspot occurs, nothing is very effective in controlling it," says Pam Allenstein, former section gardener of roses at Longwood Gardens in Kennett Square, Pennsylvania. Pam recommends the following tactics for avoiding problems with this disfiguring fungus.

Choose resistant roses. Pam cites cultivar selection as the #1 way to control blackspot—grow roses that aren't susceptible to it. She recommends checking with local growers and your Cooperative Extension office for the most blackspot-resistant roses in your area.

Clean up your act. Blackspot spores overwinter on fallen leaves and prunings left near your roses. When you prune in late winter, give your rose plantings a thorough cleaning to remove any debris where spores might hide.

Spray early and often. If you're too attached to your blackspot-susceptible roses to replace them with more resistant selections, Pam recommends a preventive spray of horticultural oil and baking soda.

❧ QUICK FIX MIX

Anti-Blackspot Baking Soda Spray

Keep blackspot off your roses with this simple spray.

1¼ tablespoons baking soda
½ cup warm water
1 gallon water
2½ tablespoons horticultural oil

Dissolve the baking soda in the warm water, then add enough additional water to make a gallon. Stir the horticultural oil into the baking soda solution. Begin applying this preventive spray in April and spray susceptible roses every two weeks.

Note: To avoid injuring the foliage, it's important to use lightweight horticultural oils, called superior or summer oils, rather than heavy dormant oils. Superior oils have fewer impurities than dormant oils so you can apply them in summer without injury, as long as the temperature stays below 85°F and your roses aren't drought stressed.

Healthy Roses in Hot Climates

Where winters are warm, hybrid tea roses will just keep growing and growing. Without a chance for the plants to go dormant so they can rest and rejuvenate, they tend to get weak. Then flowering drops off and problems begin to arise. You'll end up pampering them just to keep them going. If this happens, stop everything! Cut them back hard and your problems will stop.

"We force our roses into dormancy by pulling the leaves off and cutting the stems back to about 12 inches above the ground," said Ray Guerra, lead groundskeeper for the Las Vegas, Nevada, Desert Demonstration Garden. "They need that rest period to be able to sprint like a short-distance runner, which is what we expect of hybrid tea roses. If they are forced to grow and grow, like running a marathon, they won't perform as well."

Ray cuts back his roses in January, when the weather is cool but not cold. You can do the same during your coldest season of the year. Rake up any fallen leaves and stems to eliminate spores of blackspot or other fungal diseases and pests such as borers. Trash or destroy these old rose prunings to eliminate these problems; don't compost them. In Las Vegas, Ray's roses will resprout in just a couple of weeks, ready for another blooming season.

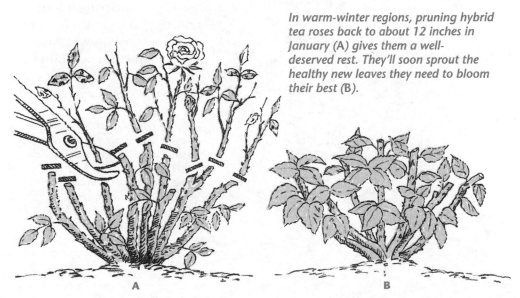

In warm-winter regions, pruning hybrid tea roses back to about 12 inches in January (A) gives them a well-deserved rest. They'll soon sprout the healthy new leaves they need to bloom their best (B).

A   B

285

Protect Tender Plants with Plastic

If you overwinter roses or other tender plants where they're not reliably winter-hardy, you've probably tried several methods for protecting them. Popular choices include bushel baskets, Styrofoam rose cones, and wire cages filled with leaves. Each method has drawbacks—baskets and cones blow away, cones break down, wire is hard to wrestle with, and all three are bulky to store. But now there's a plastic plant protector that solves all of those problems.

Easy Plant Protectors are thick flat panels of high-density plastic with large holes punched all over the surface. You just bend them into a circle around your plants, then fill them with leaves, compost, soil, straw, or some other loose mulch.

"They are the perfect item for rose gardeners," says Penny Nirider of Wilmarc, manufacturers of Easy Plant Protectors. "They hold the leaves in place so they don't blow away, and they're easy to store because they lie flat." The plastic protectors are also easier to install and take down than other methods, they don't blow off, they don't rust or break down in sunlight, and they don't interfere with ventilation and drainage.

You can purchase 16-inch-tall Easy Plant Protectors for about $7 per set. See "Sources" on page 412 for ordering information, or check garden centers and discount stores for one-piece plastic compost bins that are similar and work pretty much the same way.

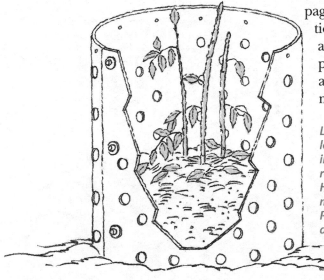

Leaves, compost, straw, or other loose mulch materials make good insulators to shelter your favorite roses against cold winter winds. Hold that warm "blanket" of mulch in place with an Easy Plant Protector or a similarly designed plastic compost bin.

Potted Roses Outside and In

DOUBLE POTS
KEEP ROSES
PORTABLE AND
UNPARCHED

If you grow your roses in pots, you'll get two bene-fits—convenience and low maintenance. Michael Shoup, owner of the Antique Rose Emporium, often entertains in his Independence, Texas, home, and has found a helpful tip for bringing the beauty of his garden indoors. He keeps miniature and small shrub roses growing outdoors in pots, which are set into other pots sunk into the ground. When Michael wants roses indoors for a few days, he simply lifts the potted roses from their in-ground container, washes the pots, and brings them inside.

This is a great benefit, but the real reason Michael double-pots the roses in the ground is to keep roots cool and protected from the hot Texas sun and drying winds. This eliminates several extra waterings over the summer and fall.

Some Roses Aren't Cut Out for Drying

Red means stop when it comes to drying roses—unless you want black blossoms to add to your dried arrange-ments. To get good red color in dried roses, start with flowers that have orange tones in them rather than deep reds, recommends Ellen Spector Platt, owner of Meadow Lark Flower and Herb Farm in Orwigsburg, Pennsylvania. Deep red roses turn black when dried, she cautions. "Don't use 'Mr. Lincoln'—you'll get black every time."

When she dries roses to use in arrangements, Ellen favors a few cultivars that she knows will give her good results when dried. She likes 'Mercedes'—"fire-engine red with an orange cast to it"; 'Tropicana'—"no question about it, it's definitely orange"; coral-flowered 'America'; and 'Double Delight'—"creamy with a reddish flush, sometimes suffused with rosy red."

If you want to go beyond these few in your drying efforts, Ellen recommends looking for roses with flowers that might be described as coppery or outright orange. To accent them, dry some yellow roses. Ellen suggests seeking flowers with golden tones. "The pale yellows tend to fade," she says.

SEASON EXTENSION

Easy Cold Frames and Plant Warmers

So what if you're not mechanically inclined.

These tips for making cold frames and plant covers are so simple and quick, you won't need fancy tools or any building experience. They come from Helen and Fred Brassel, garden writers based in Redington Shores, Florida. And if you happen to be handy, the Brassels say these tips will still save you time and money.

Skip the hammer and nails. To make a quick cold frame and avoid measuring and squaring corners, use hay bales to make three sides of a square, with the open side facing south. Put an old window or sheet of clear Plexiglas on top, and close the open edge with another piece of glass or Plexiglas set at an angle. Remove the front glass on sunny days so plants don't overheat.

Raise the roof. Rig your cold frame lid so you can open it as much or little as you like, and you won't have to look for sticks to prop it up on hot days. Just drive a sturdy stake into the ground behind both back corners of the frame—the

When you need a cold frame fast, build a three-sided straw bale enclosure and make sure the open side faces south. Cover the bales and the open side with sheets of Plexiglas or glass. Slant the cover on the open side back to let in more light.

South

stakes should be about 2 feet taller than the frame. Then screw a hook into each stake, near the top on the side that faces the frame. Attach screw eyes to the two front corners of the cold frame cover. Attach one end of a length of lightweight chain to each screw eye and the other end to the corresponding hook. You can raise the cover to any height you wish just by slipping the appropriate link over the hook.

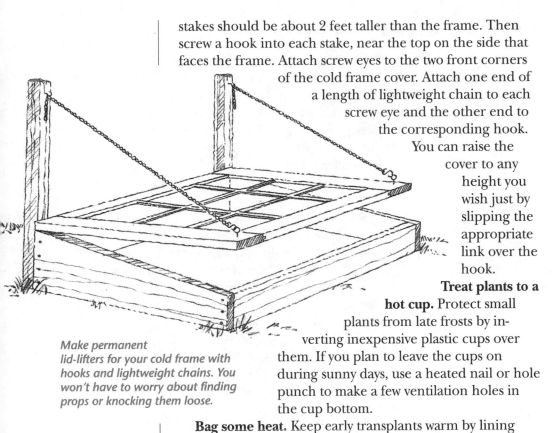

Make permanent lid-lifters for your cold frame with hooks and lightweight chains. You won't have to worry about finding props or knocking them loose.

Treat plants to a hot cup. Protect small plants from late frosts by inverting inexpensive plastic cups over them. If you plan to leave the cups on during sunny days, use a heated nail or hole punch to make a few ventilation holes in the cup bottom.

Bag some heat. Keep early transplants warm by lining plant rows with dark plastic bags filled with leaves. Cover the rows at night, bags and all, with cloth or plastic sheeting. The dark bags absorb heat during the day and release it under the cover at night.

Set bags of leaves alongside transplants when frost threatens. Cover the bags and plants with a tarp or blanket at night to hold in the heat the bags give off.

Wells Give Veggies a Warm Start

SUNKEN POTS
SPEED GROWTH
OF SPRING
TRANSPLANTS

Go underground to give heat-loving vegetables an early start where summers are too hot and dry for raised beds. In Phoenix, where Leva Mevis gardens, spring nights are cold and summers are brutal. So she plants her tomatoes and peppers in "wells" to get them started quickly in the spring and conserve water in the summer.

"I use the cheap black plastic 1-gallon pots that shrubs and perennials come in to make the wells," Leva explains. She cuts out the bottoms of the pots with a beat-up pair of pruning shears, then buries the pots in the ground, leaving an inch above the soil surface. (Leva says the clearance helps keep soil from washing in and keeps cutworms out.) Then she digs a hole in the soil at the bottom of the pot and sets in her transplant. When Leva plants tomatoes, she buries the stems deep—up to the lower leaves—since the covered stems will form roots.

Leva says her original goal was to save water by sinking the roots deeper below the surface of the ground. But she discovered that tomatoes planted in the pots grew incredibly fast. "Three weeks after I transplanted them, they were about a foot tall and blooming, with strong vigorous stems and big healthy leaves. On the other hand, the ones I planted the usual way the same day were the same size they were when I set them out," she says.

The combination of extra heat from the black plastic, plus a little extra trapped humidity and protection from drying winds, seems to do the trick. As the plants grow up out of the wells, Leva fills the pots with sand. Roots will form along the newly buried stems, and the sand will insulate the roots from summer heat.

Give tomato, pepper, and eggplant transplants a head start in hot, dry climates by planting them deep in bottomless plastic pot "wells."

Dig Deep against Cold and Heat

Spare your early vegetables from spring's temperature fluctuations—and from too much summer heat—by planting in trenches. You'll get quicker harvests and have less watering to do, especially in arid southern regions.

"I garden in Phoenix and in Gila County, Arizona," explains Mike Horton. "In Gila County, where we are in the mountains with all kinds of vicissitudes in the spring weather and only about 20 inches of rainfall a year, trench planting gives us a jump on the season and conserves water. In Phoenix, trench planting helps keep the soil cooler during the summer."

To start, Mike digs a 4- to 6-inch-deep trench and works an inch or two of compost and fertilizer into the bottom. He direct-seeds crops like beans, melons, and squash into the compost, and sets a piece of opaque white plastic row cover over the top of the trench. The cover creates a mini-greenhouse, so the seeds germinate days sooner than in aboveground plantings, Mike says. If he's putting out transplants, Mike covers the trench when frost threatens.

Potatoes are another crop that works well with the trench method, Mike says. Plant them in compost at the bottom, then as they leaf out, fill the trench in gradually. Just toss the excess soil from digging the trench back in as needed. In the heat of the summer, filling in a trench sure beats digging to hill up your potatoes.

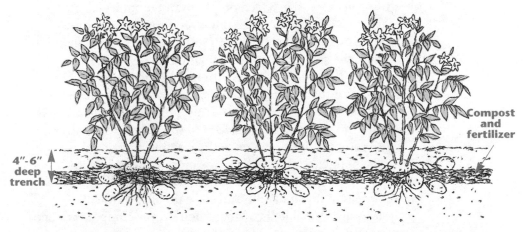

Compost and fertilizer

4"-6" deep trench

If your climate is dry, plant seed potatoes in compost in a 4- to 6-inch-deep trench. But don't try this in wet climates because your potatoes will get waterlogged and rot.

Warm Up Fast with the Layered Look

MIX CLEAR AND
BLACK PLASTIC
FOR WARM SOIL
AND NO WEEDS

Lay down a double layer of plastic to warm your soil fast in spring and control pesky weeds. "Here in the maritime Northwest, it seldom gets real hot, so it's hard to grow warm-season crops," explains Bob Eliot, a Master Gardener with the Washington State University Cooperative Extension Service. Bob's solution is to cover his garden with clear plastic early in the spring to warm the soil, then top it with black plastic to shade out weeds. Here's how to do it.

Cover your garden with clear sheets of plastic—the wider the better. Overlap each sheet 6 to 8 inches to help keep the plastic from blowing around, then peg the sheets in place with 20-penny spikes with washers. Once the soil is warm, put a layer of black plastic over the clear sheets to control weeds. Bob says, "I could take up the clear plastic, but I'm lazy." It's easiest to follow his example. When both layers of plastic are in place, cut an X through both sheets wherever you want to set a plant.

Vented Row Covers Handle Heat and Cold

If you want early spring or late fall crops, save your plants (and time) with slitted row covers instead of solid ones. You won't have to pull the covers on and off your plants when the heat goes up or down a few degrees. To protect his plants, Ted Stephens of Stephens Farm in Sussex, New Jersey, creates minigreenhouses by covering metal- or PVC-pipe hoops with slitted row covers. "When it's warm, the slits open up and let air circulate," Ted says. "When it's cold, the plastic stiffens and the slits close."

On unusually hot spring days, Ted has to pull the covers off to avoid cooking his plants. But he gets earlier harvests using the slitted row covers for less work than solid covers. Ted removes the covers once the weather warms up, then puts them back on in the fall for more frost protection.

Ted says you can use the slitted row covers for more than one season if you handle and store them carefully. The covers are available through garden supply companies. (See "Sources" on page 412 for ordering information.)

Easy Cloche Keeps Out Cold

DO-IT-YOURSELF
A-FRAMES
PROTECT PLANTS

If you have $5 and a screwdriver, you can build a simple A-frame cloche that will protect two rows of low-growing plants from spring or fall cold. "I devised this cloche to be easy to assemble, strong, easily repaired (a real consideration when dealing with winter winds), and inexpensive," explains Jeff Ashton, owner of Hard Core Garden Supply, a company that specializes in season-extension devices. (See "Sources" on page 412 if you'd like to order a catalog.)

Jeff makes his cloche from two 2- by 14-foot frames of inexpensive 1- by 3-inch spruce furring strips, but you can make them any size you need. To make the frame, simply butt the end of each 2-foot furring strip against each 14-foot strip. To make sure the boards are perpendicular, measure diagonally from corner to corner—when the distances are the same, the corners are square.

Join the boards with bent framing plates, which you can buy—unbent—from building supply centers for less than 25¢. Screw the plates into place on both sides of the board, using ⅝-inch Phillips head screws.

Next, cover the top side of the frames with inexpensive 6-mil plastic sheeting, stapling it in place. Finally, attach hinges to a long edge of each frame, so that the frame folds flat for easy storage.

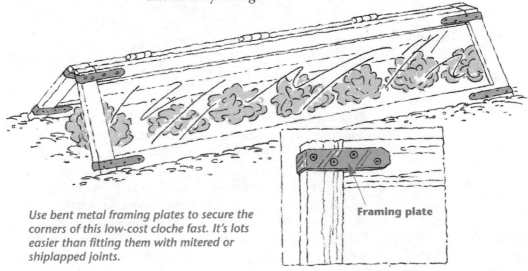

Use bent metal framing plates to secure the corners of this low-cost cloche fast. It's lots easier than fitting them with mitered or shiplapped joints.

Framing plate

3 Quick Covers for Raised Beds

BE PREPARED

FOR FROST WITH

MAKE-AHEAD

SHELTERS

Get frost covers ready when it's warm and you won't have to scurry around when cold weather threatens plants in your wood- or timber-sided raised beds. Whether you're dealing with short or tall crops, or planting in spring or fall, one of these frost covers will make your life easier.

Lay a lightweight cover over little crops. Gardener Vincent Wolfe of Lafayette, Colorado, quickly covers seedlings and low-growing crops with Reemay (a lightweight spunbonded fabric). "I fasten the material to the edges of the bed with an inexpensive 1- by 2-inch furring strip. I just nail the strip over the cover at either end of the bed, so it doesn't take long to install it or pull it off." Because Vincent uses Reemay, which lets light and water through to the plants, he doesn't have to remove the cover until the plants bump the fabric.

A raised bed makes it simple to protect small plants from frost. Lay floating row cover across the bed and hold it in place with furring strips, nailed down at each corner.

Make a minigreenhouse for medium-size crops. For fast frost protection in fall, use long pieces of PVC pipe to turn your raised bed into a hoop house. PVC pipe is flexible so you can bend it from one side of your raised bed to the other to form a support hoop. You'll need a hoop at the front, middle, and back of your raised bed. Use metal brackets to attach the pipe to the long sides of the bed.

The easiest way to install a hoop is to attach the brackets to your beds first (two per side), then slide the end of one PVC pipe into the brackets on one side of the bed, bend the pipe over to the opposite side, and insert the end into the opposite brackets to hold the pipe in place. When you've finished all three hoops, cover them with clear plastic or Reemay whenever frost threatens. You can tie the cover to the frame or hold the ends down with rocks.

Build a PVC shelter over tall crops. Vincent makes a stronger PVC structure to keep his tallest plants from getting frosted. Here's how to do it: Place ⅜- by 8-inch lag screws (large hex-head screws) at 4-foot intervals along your raised bed timbers. Screw them halfway into the tops of the timbers, making sure that they line up exactly across from each other on opposite sides of the bed. Then make a 4-foot-tall flat-topped frame from ¾-inch PVC pipes and connectors. (See the illustration on this page.)

To install the frame, slip the PVC legs over the lag screws, then use clear plastic to make a quick cover. (Vincent doesn't use Reemay over the frame because it doesn't insulate large air spaces well.) Staple the long edges of the plastic to 2- by 2-inch boards so you can easily drape it over the frame. You can roll the plastic up partway when you need to harvest or increase ventilation—just rest the boards on the flat top of the frame. If strong winds are a problem, nail the strips to the edge of the bed.

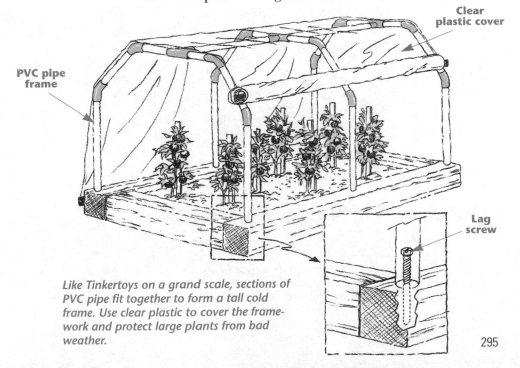

Clear plastic cover

PVC pipe frame

Lag screw

Like Tinkertoys on a grand scale, sections of PVC pipe fit together to form a tall cold frame. Use clear plastic to cover the framework and protect large plants from bad weather.

Electrify Your Soil for a Quick Start

Get a jump start on spring by heating your soil with electric heating cables. "I use a self-regulating heating cable, the kind that's used to keep exposed water pipes from freezing," reports gardener Fred Schenkelberg of Morgan Hill, California. Here's how you can set up your own system.

Till the soil in early spring, then lay out the cable, snaking it throughout your planting area and spacing it about a foot apart. The cable is quite flexible, Fred says. But you may need to pin it down with tent stakes or wire pins if you make sharp curves with it. Because the cable is self-regulating, it won't overheat, so you don't have to worry about it burning out if it crosses over itself.

Push the cable a few inches into the soil, then plant in the foot-wide area between the rows of cable. Fred turns on the cable at night to keep the soil from cooling down, but says it would also work to run the heating cable all day.

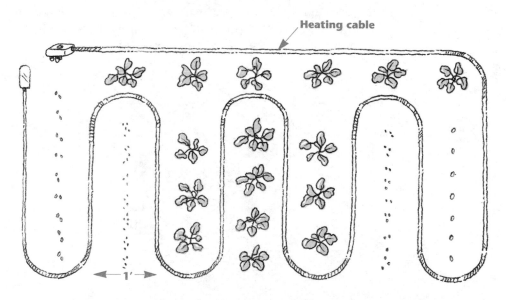

Heating cable

When you're ready to garden in spring but your soil is too cool, give it a warm-up with electric heating cable. Snake the cable along your crop rows, and push it a couple of inches into the soil. Turn the cable on at night to keep sun-warmed soil toasty. The extra heat will give early plants a growth boost.

Once cold weather is over, pull up the cable gently to avoid damaging nearby roots, clean it, and store it until the next year. That way you don't have to worry about damaging it while poking around in the garden during the growing season.

Fred bought his cables at a hardware store—the brand he uses is called Frostex. He says it comes either in a box that holds a 100-foot cable or on a big roll from which you can cut the length you need. You'll also need a fused plug and an end seal, but don't worry about installing them—instructions come with the components.

Buying and assembling a cable, plug, and seal may seem like a lot of effort, but the durability is worth it. "I tried the constant-wattage kind of cable that comes in various lengths and already had a plug connected," Fred says. "But it quit working after a few days. If the cable overheats, the wire in it melts, and that's it." The do-it-yourself cable saves a lot of work in the long run.

"Raincoat" Keeps Soggy Soils Dry

Cover clay soils with plastic in spring and you'll get a jump on the growing season. Usually, just when you want to start planting, spring rains turn clay soils soggy. If you work the soil before it dries out, you'll ruin the soil structure, but waiting for dry weather can delay planting for weeks. You can dodge that setback simply by covering your beds with plastic during heavy rains.

"I have heavy soil that can't be worked when wet without damaging its structure," says gardener Beverly Erlebacher of Toronto. Beverly solves the planting problem by covering her raised bed with a plastic sheet during long rains. The soil in her protected bed dries out a lot faster than in uncovered beds and she can plant significantly earlier. Beverly lets the plastic dry off completely after the rain, then removes it and stores it indoors. Since the plastic doesn't stay outside very long, it isn't damaged by sunlight and lasts a long time.

Bare-Bones Protection for Fall Crops

A HANDY

METHOD FOR

SAFEGUARDING

HARDY GREENS

You can harvest well into winter if you protect cold-hardy vegetables like lettuce and spinach with a few wires and a sheet of clear plastic. In her urban Toronto garden, Beverly Erlebacher grows those leafy greens long after the first frost, along with arugula, baby carrots, bok choy, chicory, endive, escarole, green onions, leeks, and parsley.

To cover her plants through the early winter, Beverly makes a mini-hoop house out of several long pieces of stiff scrap wire and a sheet of plastic. Here's how. Bend both ends of each wire down at 90-degree angles to form flat-topped hoops. Push the ends of the wires into the ground until the flat tops of the hoop are just above the plants' tops, then cover the hoops with plastic. "I've picked lettuce as late as New Year's Eve with this method," Beverly says.

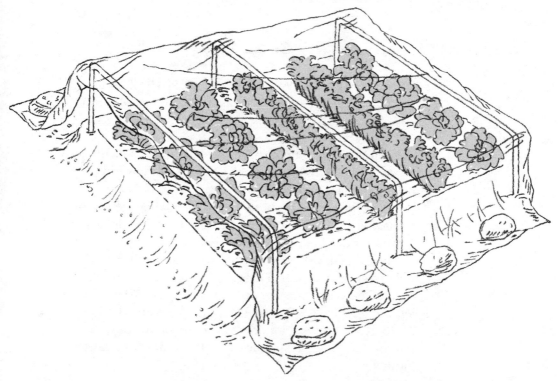

Hoops made of scrap wire and a plastic cover are all you need to keep cold-hardy crops green well into winter. If snow threatens to collapse your hoop house, support the wires with a few short sticks.

Tricks for Stretching Your Growing Season

Here's a trio of time- and money-saving tips that will help you stretch your growing season in spring and fall. The tips come from Jeff Ashton, owner of Hard Core Garden Supply, who explains that he sells "high-performance, low-budget components for cold frames and season-extension contraptions." (See "Sources" on page 412 if you'd like to write for a catalog of Jeff's products.)

• Cover your tomato cages with bubble wrap (packing material) to extend your harvest in fall. You can also wrap cages with 6-mil clear plastic and hold it in place by sealing the side with clear tape. The top stays open. "It's great," Jeff says. "It gives protection, it's cheap, and the cage is already in place."

• "Plant on a 5-degree southern slope—it's like planting 300 miles south of where you are." That's the advice Jeff got from Eliot Coleman, author of *Four-Season Harvest*. If you don't have a slope, make one in your cold frame.

• Grow winter squash in your compost pile for earlier and bigger harvests. Jeff recommends that you cover your compost pile with 3 or 4 inches of soil, then plant squash seeds in it three to four weeks earlier than usual. The heat from the compost helps the plants survive cold weather and makes them grow faster. Plus, the compost provides nutrients for these heavy feeders.

Regrade your cold frame soil to create a 5-degree, south-facing slope. Your crops will grow stronger because they'll receive more of the sun's rays.

SEEDS AND SEEDLINGS

Seed Records Save Time

You can't remember everything about the seeds you plant in your garden from one year to the next. Save yourself the frustration of forgotten names and know-how by recording your successes and failures each season. A few minutes spent writing down what you've learned will pay off in hours of time saved over the long run.

"I grow over 1,700 varieties of perennials. I can't possibly remember them all!" says Nancy McDonald, managing editor of *The American Cottage Gardener* magazine. "So when I get a new seed packet, I attach a 4 × 6 file card with a paper clip. I fill in any important information the seed company didn't supply, like the year and the botanical name."

Nancy uses colored paper clips to code her seed packets—red for seeds that need heat, black for seeds that need dark, blue for those that need cold treatment. On the back of each file card she notes important dates, like when the seed was sown, when it germinated, when she transplanted it to the garden, bloom time, and harvesttimes for vegetables.

"At the end of the garden season, I update my records while my memory is still fresh, noting problems with pests or exciting discoveries," Nancy says. "I store the file cards in a box as permanent records, and believe me, it's one of the things I would grab if my house was on fire."

Part of what makes Nancy's system work is that you can do a lot of the record keeping during the armchair-gardening months. If you can't keep up with the cards during the growing season, jot your observations on a calender or notepad. Come winter, transfer your notes to more permanent records.

Sow Your Own Volunteer Seedlings

Plant volunteer flowers and vegetables where you want them. It's easier than transplanting volunteers that sprout in the wrong place or trying to work around them, says Tina James, a landscape consultant in Reisterstown, Maryland.

"Volunteers always seem to have a jump on the seeds I sow myself, but they don't always come up in a handy spot," she says. So each fall, Tina choses where she wants early-sprouting "volunteers" and sows the seeds herself. She's found that arugula, lettuce, mizuna (a Japanese mustard), and other cool-season greens like fall planting particularly well. Tina also has good luck with fall-planted annual flowers and suspects tomatoes would work just as well.

Tina plants in raised beds to give the seedlings good drainage. And she covers her seedbeds with a couple inches of shredded leaves for good winter protection.

Sort Seeds for Speedy Spring Planting

Use a system to store seeds and you'll find what you need fast in spring. Nino Ridgway, owner of Squeaky Green Organic Produce in Mequon, Wisconsin, sorts her seed packages so she can set a quick planting pace. To make sure she doesn't overlook seeds when the spring rush hits, Nino keeps her seeds in different boxes according to when they need to be started and what kind of germination conditions they need.

"This is just simple organization," she admits. "But it saves me from having to search through one big box of seeds every time I go to plant. Plus I don't have to worry about missing the cycle of an important crop. That's time you don't get back."

Plastic storage boxes and cardboard dividers make it easy to sort (and find) new and leftover seed packages.

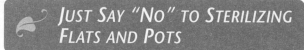

JUST SAY "NO" TO STERILIZING FLATS AND POTS

As long as you haven't had disease problems, sterilizing containers just isn't necessary, says Wendy Krupnick, who manages the trial gardens for Shepherd Seeds Company in Felton, California. She avoids the mess of washing pots and dipping them in bleach solution with a quick solar cleanup.

Wendy empties used pots and flats and lets them sit out in the sun for a few days (she sets them out in the greenhouse if it's rainy). "Most fungus organisms will not survive in hot dry conditions," says Wendy. Once the containers are completely dry, she simply shakes out any soil debris, then stacks and stores them.

Shiny Shoe Box Gives Seedlings Extra Sun

To start sturdy vegetable seedlings, all you need are a shoe box and some aluminum foil says gardener Lyn Belisle of San Antonio. For early seed starting, Lyn lines a shoe box with foil, placed shiny side up.

She pokes drainage holes through the foil and cardboard, then fills the box with potting mix and plants her seeds. Lyn says the top of the soil should be a few inches below the top of the box, so the foil can magnify the heat and light of the sunshine onto the seedlings. You can set the box outside in the sun on nice days.

Fill a foil-lined shoe box part way with potting mix to create a bright and cozy spot for raising heat-loving tomato and pepper seedlings.

Save $ with Homemade Soilless Mix

DO-IT-YOURSELF
MIX MAKES
SEED STARTING
SIMPLE

You'll save a bundle when you bypass overpriced seed-starting mixes and mix up your own instead. That's what Nancy McDonald, managing editor of *The American Cottage Gardener* magazine, does. Nancy starts hundreds of seeds indoors every year so she's worked with lots of different seed-starting mixes. "There's no need to buy the overpriced prepackaged mixes, as it's ludicrously simple to make your own," she says.

To make Nancy's mix, combine equal parts milled peat moss and fine (horticultural grade) vermiculite. Seed starting is the only time Nancy uses peat moss, a nonrenewable resource, and vermiculite, which must be mined. "If you reserve the soilless mix for seed starting, you won't need much," she says.

When you're ready to sow seeds, add enough water to make the mix stick together, but not so much that it's muddy. Fill your flats full so seedlings grow above the flats and get good air circulation.

Help for Seed-Starter Hands

Save your skin from that red-raw chapped look and the abrasions that can result when you spend lots of time with your hands in soil- or peat-based potting mixes. Before you dive into the seed-sowing season, buy yourself a box of thin latex surgical gloves, recommends Steve Frowine, vice president of horticulture for White Flower Farm in Litchfield, Connecticut. They're inexpensive and available at pharmacies in boxes of 50.

Surgical gloves will protect your hands and wrists from the unpleasant aftereffects of otherwise enjoyable tasks like seed sowing and transplanting. And unlike heavy garden gloves, they're specially designed to give your fingers extra sensitivity and a no-slip grip even when they're wet.

"These gloves give you great dexterity for fine work like transplanting annual seedlings or sowing seed," says Steve. He adds that they're also great for keeping your hands clean when you're doing other messy jobs like spreading fertilizer or blending fish emulsion. When your work is done, rinse the gloves if you plan to use them again.

Grow Super Seedlings with Deluxe Potting Soil

Give your seedlings a nutrient boost by growing them in microbe-rich homemade potting soil. You'll get better growth and spend less than you would if you bought lesser prepackaged potting soils.

Ken Muckenfuss, who owns and operates Mill Creek Organic Farm in Medford, New Jersey, uses a two-part process to whip up a mix that keeps his plants in tip-top shape. What makes Ken's mixture deluxe is that he moistens the dry ingredients with manure tea instead of plain water. The manure tea is loaded with microbes that help make the minerals in the dry mix more available to plants. And, Ken says, those beneficial microbes inoculate the soil, giving his plants protection against harmful bacteria and fungi.

To follow Ken's recipe for deluxe potting soil, start by brewing up a batch of manure tea, following the instructions in "Quick Fix Mix" on this page. Proceed from there

❧ QUICK FIX MIX

Muckenfuss's Manure Tea

Ken Muckenfuss, who owns Mill Creek Organic Farm in Medford, New Jersey, brews manure tea by the barrelful to supply moisture and microbes to his Deluxe Potting Soil. (See "Quick Fix Mix" on the opposite page for Ken's special potting soil recipe.) He places the following ingredients in a 55-gallon drum in a well-ventilated area.

10 to 15 gallons manure
5-gallon bucket chickweed
   and/or stinging nettle
water to fill drum

Put the manure in the bottom of the drum. Add chickweed and/or stinging nettle, both of which are rich in trace elements, then fill the drum with water.

Once a week, Ken stirs his "tea" and adds water to replace any that's evaporated. He recommends a brewing time of at least 3 weeks before using the manure tea in the potting soil mix.

Note: Ken combines horse, chicken, and cow manure to get a better balance of nutrients. Don't use manures that have been treated with pesticides or that are from animals treated with hormones or antibiotics.

QUICK FIX MIX

Deluxe Potting Soil

To make his super potting mixture, Ken Muckenfuss, who owns Mill Creek Organic Farm in Medford, New Jersey, combines the following.

9 gallons peat moss

3 gallons vermiculite

3 gallons perlite

1 pound blood meal

1 pound bonemeal

1 pound greensand

1 pound lime

1 pound rock phosphate

pinch of boron (borax is an
   inexpensive source)

Ken blends these ingredients in a 15-gallon cement mixer, which he claims every good gardener has somewhere out back. If you don't own a mixer, make the mix in a compost tumbler or a large barrel with a tight-fitting lid that will let you roll it around to mix the contents. If you have to stir the ingredients in an open container, moisten them slightly with water to avoid breathing in clouds of dust as you work.

Don't use more than a pinch of boron, warns Ken. It encourages rooting, but its levels can quickly go from helpful to harmful in the soil.

Once the ingredients are mixed, Ken adds his Muckenfuss's Manure Tea (see the recipe in "Quick Fix Mix" on the opposite page). He notes that the lime in his mix helps to neutralize the acidity of the manure tea.

to the "Quick Fix Mix" on this page, where you'll find Ken's instructions for mixing up the dry ingredients he uses in his potting soil. As with other recipes, you can reduce the size of the batch to suit your needs.

Once the manure tea is brewed and the dry ingredients are assembled and mixed, it's time to combine them into a nourishing potting mixture for your plants.

Wet the dry materials with 4 to 5 gallons of the manure tea. Use your stirring stick to knock the crust off the surface of the tea, then fill a bucket by sliding it carefully down the inside wall of the brewing drum, suggests Ken. Stir the manure tea into the dry ingredients until they're well moistened. Because the mix contains peat moss, which sheds water, it will take the manure tea a little while to soak into the mix.

Treat Touchy Transplants Tenderly

Put an end to transplant shock by planting tough-to-transplant vegetables in the little plastic mesh baskets that berries or cherry tomatoes are sold in. The baskets are perfect for giving cucumber, melon, and squash seedlings an early start since they have plenty of room for their long roots. When the seedlings are grown, you can set the basket directly in the ground so these touchy plants won't even know they've been moved.

To get started, line each basket with two or three thicknesses of newspaper or paper towel and fill it with potting mix, recommends Yvonne Savio, gardening education coordinator for the Los Angeles County Cooperative Extension Service. Sow four or five seeds per basket and put them in a well-lit spot.

Once warm weather arrives, plant your seedlings, basket and all, making sure the basket and lining are buried. "There'll be no transplant shock, and the roots will grow through the paper and mesh into the surrounding soil. At the end of the season you can lift the baskets, clean them, and store them for future use," Yvonne says.

Keep root systems of squash-family transplants intact by starting them in plastic berry boxes. Set the transplants out, box and all, in your garden, and they'll thrive. Snip off extra seedlings before planting to avoid crowding. You can cut the box bottom off too, or let roots grow through it.

A Quick Seed-Starting Setup

So you want to start seeds indoors, today. It's not a problem if you use this easy and inexpensive seed-starting system. Pauline Neilson, an avid seed starter in Birmingham, Alabama, made the efficient unit shown on the opposite page out of store-bought metal shelving and fluorescent light fixtures. Pauline says to look for shelf units that are wide enough to hold seed flats. She says "18-inch-wide shelves work well for this design."

Pauline doesn't bother bolting the lights to the shelves. Instead she uses rope from a travis rod (the sturdy cord used to open and close curtains) to hang the lights. She ties the rope to one end of a light, pulls the light up tight against the shelf, runs the rope across the top of the shelf, and ties it off to the other end of the light. Then Pauline attaches a multi-strip power outlet to one of the upright posts of the shelving unit with duct tape. She runs the cords from the light fixtures to the multi-strip, plugs the multi-strip into a timer, and plugs the timer into a wall outlet.

Mount fluorescent lights on metal shelf units to give your indoor seedlings a strong start. With this system, you adjust the position of the plants to the lights, instead of adjusting the lights to the plants. Use shoe boxes, phone books, or stacks of newspaper to position seed flats so they're the proper distance away from the lights.

Containers Simplify Small-Seed Planting

It's easy to start tiny seeds if you sprout them in recycled plastic containers. "The sealed container creates such a perfect growing environment that germination has been faster and more complete than anything I've tried before," says Kristl Walek, owner of Gardens North in Ontario. "I learned about this method from a colleague in our local Rock Garden Society and I'm thrilled with it." Here's how Kristl starts dustlike seeds like those from astilbes, lobelias, and petunias.

YOGURT CUPS
HELP LITTLE
SEEDLINGS
COME UP

Fill plastic yogurt or deli containers two-thirds full with soilless mix. Mist the mix until it's moist, not soggy. Then sprinkle the seeds on top, snap on a clear lid (most seeds need light to germinate so use lids that let light through), and attach a label or write the name on the container. Since the lid holds in moisture, the seedlings never need water until you transplant them out of the containers. That means there's no danger of drowning them.

Kristl puts the plastic pots under her plant growth lights, then turns to other tasks until her seedlings grow to the top of the container lids. Then she transplants the seedlings into cell packs or flats.

Plant and Soak Big Seeds in 1 Step

"It's no secret that big, hard seeds, like morning glories, sweet peas, and blackberry lilies, sprout faster when they're soaked overnight in water," says Marlene Cavano, president of Cavano's Perennials in Kingsville, Maryland. But you don't have to soak seeds then wait to plant them—do it all at once.

Marlene used to put big seeds in a small dish of water and then plant them out once they were waterlogged. But it was hard to handle wet seeds and soil, so now Marlene plants the seeds in individual cell packs, places the cell packs in a tray with no holes, and adds water to the tray. She lets the whole flat soak overnight, then empties out any excess water in the morning. The seeds soak up water just as well planted as they do sitting in a dish or cup of water, and Marlene gets out of an awkward, wet planting job.

Speedy Germination Test Seals Seeds' Fate

Leftover seeds are like money in the bank when they sprout reliably, but they're no bargain if you have to re-plant a poor stand. Use this at-a-glance germination test from Nancy Bubel, author of *The New Seed-Starter's Handbook,* and you'll know right away if you'll get a reliable stand or if you'll need to place that seed order.

"All you need are some paper towels and cookie sheets," Nancy says. Use one paper towel for each type of seed you want to test. Lay the towel flat on a tray or cookie sheet. Use a ballpoint pen and ruler to draw a grid of 1-inch squares on the towel, and write down the plant name and the date, too. Use a mister to dampen the towel until it's moist but not soggy and then place one seed in each square. Cover the seeds with two layers of damp paper towels or news-papers and slide the whole works into a large plastic bag. Tie the bag shut loosely with a twist tie so some air can still reach the plants.

Place the bagged seeds in a warm place, such as on top of the refrigerator, and mist them whenever they seem dry. Check for growth daily and count how many seeds sprout.

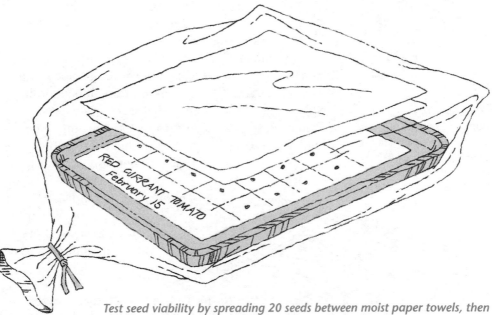

Test seed viability by spreading 20 seeds between moist paper towels, then sealing them in a plastic bag. If 16 or more seeds sprout, plant them at normal rates. If less than 10 seeds sprout, buy new seeds.

Seeds Flourish in Free Seed Containers

Take a look in your fridge for great seed-starting containers you already own. They'll not only save you money, but some can save you transplanting time as well. Here are two tips from gardener Greg Haas of Houston, Texas, for turning your food containers into seed flats.

Make salad containers into minigreenhouses. Greg says you can reuse the hinged plastic salad containers from fast-food restaurants and grocery store salad bars for starting seeds or rooting small cuttings. Place small paper ketchup cups or cupcake liners in the bottom of the containers to serve as minipots. Fill the cups with potting soil, plant seeds in them, and water them. Close the lids of the trays to keep the soil moist and place them on the windowsill. "They're more attractive than egg cartons, and the paper cups can be planted right into the garden," Greg says.

Sprout seeds with ease in egg cartons. Clean and dry empty Styrofoam egg cartons, then punch a little hole in the bottom of each cup for drainage and fill it with soil. Plant at least one seed in each of the 12 sections and water them in.

You can cut off the top of the egg carton and use it as a tray—seal the closing tabs with duct tape so the tray is watertight. "The carton-top trays fit beautifully on almost any windowsill," Greg says.

You can use paper egg cartons too, but you'll need to put a waterproof tray beneath them, Greg notes. When you're ready to plant, cut apart the individual cups of the paper cartons and plant them directly

Paper cupcake liners or ketchup cups make handy seed pots. Put several in a clear plastic salad container to make a perfect growing environment.

Use the bottom half of a Styrofoam egg carton as a seed-starting container—the lid serves as a drip tray.

into the ground. They'll break down so you don't have to take the plants out first.

Unique Products Ease Seedling Care

SEEDLINGS
THRIVE UNDER
REEMAY AND
ON TOP OF
CHAMOIS CLOTH

Keep your eyes open for items that make growing seeds and seedlings easier and you're likely to find them. "I'm not one to keep my head in the sand," says Alton Eliason, a veteran organic gardener in Northford, Connecticut. "When something useful comes along, I use it!" Here are two of his best discoveries for growing seeds and seedlings.

Save seeds and seedlings with row covers. "I think the single greatest thing to arrive on the agriculture scene in my lifetime are the poly-spun fabrics like Reemay that are used to cover crops in the field," Alton says. These super-light fabrics keep pests out but let water and sunlight in. For the first time, you can grow vegetables that are virtually insect free.

Pest protection isn't the only benefit of row covers. Alton uses them to boost seed germination too. When he sows seed in the field, he covers them with Reemay immediately. "Seeds that failed 100 percent, replanted under Reemay, germinated almost 100 percent. The very same seeds," Alton says. It may be that the row cover protects the seeds from extreme temperature changes; Alton isn't sure. But whatever effect the row cover has, Alton is sure it works!

Keep seedlings moist with chamois cloth. Another product Alton raves about is artificial chamois cloth (one trade name is Water Sprite). The material holds a tremendous amount of moisture but doesn't mold or mildew. It's usually sold in small packages as a cleaning cloth for cars and boats, but you can buy it in rolls, Alton says. He uses it to line the bottom of planting flats. Once the flats are planted and watered, the chamois stays moist for days—the soil wicks up water from the cloth as needed.

Alton uses the chamois to water his homemade soil blocks too. If you've ever tried planting seeds in soil that's molded into blocks, you know how easily the blocks crumble. It's lots easier to set them on a chamois in a flat and let them wick up water from the bottom.

Perfect Do-It-Yourself Seed Mixes

BLEND SEEDS
FOR CUSTOM
SALAD AND
FLOWER MIXES

You can get great results from seed mixes if you make them yourself and start them indoors. Premade flower and vegetable mixes are wonderful for blending colors or flavors but only if they have the plants you want. Often times you'll get premade mixes that don't match your growing area or your taste.

That's why Shepherd Ogden, author of *Step by Step Organic Vegetable Gardening,* makes his own mesclun salad mixes. Shep starts by blending the seeds of his most desirable greens. Then he drops a generous pinch of the salad mix into each cell of several four-pack pots filled with a premoistened seed-starting mix.

What comes up in each cell is a tight clump of five or six greens, growing almost as a single plant. Shep sets the clumps or plugs into prepared garden beds, leaving 6 to 8 inches between each one. As they grow, each cluster of plants becomes an instant mixed salad, ready for harvest with a single cut.

To try the same trick to create a custom wildflower planting for your landscape, buy seeds of the individual wildflower species you want in bulk. Then make your own mixture of three or four species and sow a pinch per plug.

Mix seeds of several kinds of greens, then drop pinches of the mix into cell packs filled with soil mix. The seedlings grow to produce "instant salad" transplants.

Quick Seedling Cover-Ups

Pamper newly transplanted seedlings with berry basket hats. Moving outdoors can be a shock for young plants, so save them from stress by shading them with an upside-down basket. "With just a little bit of protection from the sun and wind, baby plants can make their entrance into the big world without a sneeze," says Nancy Bubel, author of *The New Seed-Starter's Handbook*. Nancy likes overturned berry basket plant covers because they nest easily for storage and can stay in place for days. She removes wooden ones after a few days, since they don't admit light, but leaves plastic ones in place for up to ten days.

Berry baskets protect small plants from too much sun and wind. Weight each basket with a small stone so it won't blow away.

Save Seeds from Crusty Soil

Give newly sown seeds a break by topping them with a light, noncrusty material like vermiculite instead of soil. Your seeds will sprout better since they don't have to struggle through a hard soil surface says B. Rosie Lerner, Purdue University consumer horticulture specialist and state Master Gardener coordinator. "The seeds come up just beautifully through vermiculite," says Rosie. "And, because it's a very different color from the soil, it marks the rows for me, so I know exactly where I've planted everything."

Vermiculite's moisture-holding ability makes it a better choice than perlite, Rosie adds. Perlite doesn't hold as much moisture as vermiculite, so it dries out and blows away more quickly.

If marking rows isn't important to you, finished compost and potting soil make good noncrusty seed coverings. But don't use peat moss—it tends to repel water once it dries out.

313

Follow Nature's Lead for Seed Starting

CHILL
PRE-PLANTED
SEEDS
OUTDOORS IN
WINTER

Set seeds outside to chill when they need a cold treatment to sprout. That way you can use Nature's refrigerator instead of cramming your fridge with messy peat-filled pots and flats.

The seeds of many trees and shrubs need a certain number of "chilling hours" (below 45°F, but above freezing) before they'll sprout. By chilling seeds in protected outdoor sites, you can take advantage of the plants' natural cycles and avoid the hassle of having them in your refrigerator.

Russell Studebaker, horticulturist for the Tulsa Zoo, says you'll get better germination if you chill seeds according to Nature's timing. When you gather seeds, store them, and then chill them later, the results aren't as good. Here's how Russell recommends you chill seeds. Sow seeds in the fall in flats filled with a mix of half sand and half sterile compost or peat moss. Cover the surface with a thin layer of whole-fiber milled sphagnum moss. Wrap the flats in plastic bags, and place them in a safe outdoor spot where the seeds will be exposed to naturally occurring cold temperatures. When the warm days of spring arrive, most of the seeds will sprout. As soon as they do, remove the plastic.

Be sure to protect your seeds from squirrels and mice that will dig up and eat acorns, nuts, and other large seeds during the winter. Russell covers his flats with ¼-inch-mesh hardware cloth to keep critters out but says to be sure to take the cloth off in the spring when the seeds sprout.

Chilling seeds outdoors works particularly well for native trees. "It's amazing, especially on some of the oaks, like white oak, how fast they'll sprout," Russell says. For these trees, he uses cans instead of flats to give the long roots plenty of room to grow. "I take the caps off the acorns and push one or two into a juice can full of soil from the garden, covering them an inch or so. They'll come right up in the spring," he says.

Most native trees, shrubs, and fruit trees need a cold treatment. Seeds of annuals and perennials are less likely to have a chilling requirement in order to germinate, but you can check seed-starting books to be sure.

SHRUBS

Give Your Foundation Planting a Face-Lift

Hate your homely foundation planting? If you've inherited or become dissatisfied with an overgrown or chopped-up foundation planting, try removing some of the shrubs. It's the easiest, most inexpensive way to give your foundation planting a face-lift.

Landscape architect Jim Perry of Starkville, Mississippi, often suggests to his clients that removing plants can be more effective than adding more. "Do you really need an overplanted foundation planting?" he asks. "Won't moving some shrubs make more sense and save in several ways in the long run?"

Jim notes that, architecturally speaking, both older and contemporary homes tend to be interesting, and don't need dressing up with a lot of plants. "There are lots of lines and detail in the structure itself, in which rows of shrubs simply disappear," Jim says. "All you really need—which can save lots of money up front and maintenance down the road—is an accent here, some anchor plants there, and an interesting paint job."

When it comes to foundation plantings, fewer shrubs mean lower expenses. Pull some shrubs out of overgrown plantings, or save money on new plantings by using fewer shrubs. Surround one large shrub with a few smaller ones for a finished look fast.

315

Seeds Give Your Shrubs a Head Start

A CORNY WAY

TO IMPROVE

SHRUB GROWTH

Bet you've *never* heard of this technique! But your shrubs will get established faster after planting if you try this simple tip from Lavern Houston, who describes herself as "just a country gal" in Meridian, Mississippi. It's actually an old custom—throwing a handful of seed into the bottom of planting holes. "I don't know why it works, but let me tell you, it *does*," says Lavern.

"You put a handful of corn or bean seeds down in the bottom, and they swell up for a few days, then make air for roots to grow," according to Lavern. Besides adding air pockets to the soil, seeds are chock-full of nutrients, enzymes, and hormones to feed your shrubs. And as they break down, the seeds are a great source of protein for earthworms. So try it—your shrubs will like it!

Slash Shrub Care by 75%

Unshear your shrubs! That's the battle cry of Cass Turnbull, president of Plant Amnesty, an organization that promotes good pruning practices. Cass is fighting for a better way to prune shrubs than clipping them into tight green gumdrops and overgrown meatballs. As she points out, "If you prune properly to begin with, the work gets less every year, and plants look more natural."

Cass suggests a drastic but effective way to get a "meatball" back into shape. "Cut it close—waaaay back," she says. Then let the shrub grow for two or three years before you selectively prune out undesired branches. Use her technique for young, healthy deciduous shrubs like burning bushes (*Euonymus alata*), forsythias, privets, and spireas. (For older shrubs or evergreens, use the more gradual approaches described in "Give Overgrown Shrubs the Heave-ho" on page 318.)

Kris Medic, city landscape manager and arborist for Columbus, Indiana, is a big believer in selective pruning too. Instead of pruning her plants formally—which means shearing them several times a year—she prunes only once a year when the shrubs are dormant. During that one pruning, Kris thins out broken and unhealthy branches and selectively prunes out crossing branches, as shown here.

You'll get beautiful, naturally shaped plants in a quarter of the time you'd spend on repeated shearings, she says.

For a free pruning guide, send a stamped, self-addressed legal-size envelope to Plant Amnesty, 906 NW 87th Street, Seattle, WA 98117.

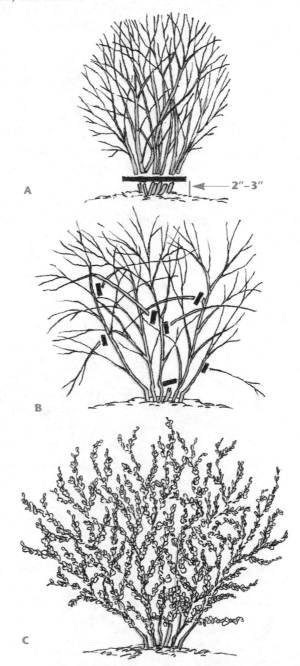

A

2"–3"

You can rejuvenate a lollipop-shaped forsythia by cutting it to the ground (A). After two or three years of regrowth, cut out crossing, rubbing, or diseased branches (B). You'll be rewarded with a healthy forsythia with a graceful vase shape (C).

B

C

Give Overgrown Shrubs the Heave-ho

REJUVENATE OR
GET RID OF
SHRUBS THAT
GROW TOO BIG

Maybe you need exercise, but there are better ways to get it than climbing ladders and trying to prune overgrown shrubs into shape. It's easier to just tear them out and start over. "If you bought an old house, you wouldn't keep the old furniture, would you? Then why feel obligated to keep old shrubs?" asks Cass Turnbull, president of Plant Amnesty, an organization that promotes good pruning practices. "If it's outgrown or out of shape, either prune it, move it, or kill it. And we don't do enough of the last two."

If you can't quite let go of your plants or your pruners, try this easy shrub rejuvenation method, pictured on the opposite page. When your shrub is dormant, remove one-third of the old growth. Use a saw or loppers to cut the branches to the ground—new branches will sprout and take their place. The next year, remove another third of the old growth, and the following year, take out the final third of the old branches. There's less stress on the plant when you prune it gradually like this, and less stress on you since you only do a small part each year.

Once you've removed all the old growth, all you have to do is prune out "bad" branches once a year to keep your plant looking good. Just remove broken, diseased, and crossing branches while the shrub is dormant. As the plant grows bigger, take out two or three of the largest branches each year to keep it from getting overgrown.

Don't try this technique on evergreens—just deciduous shrubs (the ones that lose their leaves in fall). Evergreens can't take drastic pruning, so you'll have to let them grow out slowly. If they've been formally pruned, stop shearing and start selectively pruning branches once a year in early spring. Take out diseased or injured branches, plus any crossing branches or limbs that spoil the plant's shape. If you're not sure if a branch helps or hurts the shrub's appearance, wait. After another year of looking at it, you'll know if it should stay or go.

Once your overgrown shrubs are back in shape—or disposed of—make sure you don't get into the same situation again. Check the mature size of shrubs before you buy—those cute little green balls can turn into towering monsters before you know it. Choose dwarf shrubs like those listed in "Shrubs That Never Need Pruning" on page 320 and kiss your pruning chores good-bye.

To refurbish an overgrown shrub, cut one-third of the oldest branches off at ground level or at a main stem. Repeat yearly until all old growth is gone. Then, each year, prune selectively, cutting out crossing or rubbing branches to enhance the shrub's natural shape.

Shrubs That Never Need Pruning

*P*lanting a large-scale shrub in a small-scale situation is one of the most common landscaping mistakes. It means you have to prune whether you want to or not. And pruning techniques that require more skill than it takes to buzz-cut a plant with hedge trimmers can be intimidating—not to mention time-consuming. So shortcut the pruning process, and let your pruning shears and manuals gather dust by planting these naturally compact or dwarf shrubs.

'COMPACTUM' OREGON GRAPE HOLLY (*Mahonia aquifolium* 'Compactum')

At 1½ to 2 feet tall, this cultivar is half the size of the native Western species, making it ideal for a shady foundation planting or woodland garden. Fragrant, showy bright yellow flower clusters in early spring are followed by blue-black bird-attracting fruits in summer. Evergreen glossy hollylike leaves turn purplish in winter. Plant your shrubs in light shade to protect them from winter burn in cold climates. Zones 5 to 9.

DWARF FOTHERGILLA (*Fothergilla gardenii*)

This refined, mounded, 3- to 4-foot-tall Southeastern native shrub makes a wonderful accent plant or foundation planting—it won't obscure your windows. Sweetly scented 1- to 2-inch-long bottlebrush-like clusters of white flowers appear as the leaves unfurl in spring; pleated, scalloped medium green leaves with silvery undersides turn flame orange, yellow, and scarlet in autumn (the color is best in sunny sites). It prefers moist but well-drained soil. Zones 5 to 8.

'GREEN GEM' HYBRID BOXWOOD (*Buxus* 'Green Gem')

If growing boxwoods is a struggle in your climate, try this hardy evergreen globe-shaped shrub with windburn-resistant foliage. At 1½ to 2 feet tall, it's perfect for a compact formal hedge or gumball-shaped accent plant. It has tiny flowers in early summer and lustrous glossy 1-inch-long leaves. Space plants 1 to 1½ feet apart for a solid hedge. Zones 4 to 9.

'HANCOCK' CHENAULT CORALBERRY
(*Symphoricarpos* × *chenaultii* 'Hancock')

This dwarf 2- to 3-foot-tall cultivar spreads to 10 feet wide, making it an excellent ground-cover shrub for banks. Clusters of pink flowers in summer appeal to hummingbirds and are followed by ½-inch-diameter pink to raspberry red fruits in fall and winter. The leaves are small and blue-green. It tolerates a wide range of soil, moisture, and light conditions. Zones 4 to 7.

'HENRY'S GARNET' VIRGINIA SWEETSPIRE
(*Itea virginica* 'Henry's Garnet')

Arching, fountain-shaped branches add grace to this 2- to 4-foot-tall dwarf cultivar. The plant spreads to form large multistemmed clumps. It's covered with 3- to 6-inch-long spikes of fragrant white flowers in early summer when little else is in bloom. The glossy dark green leaves turn rich burgundy red for 8 to 10 weeks before they drop in autumn. It blooms in shade and tolerates wet soil. Zones 5 to 9.

'IVORY HALO' TATARIAN DOGWOOD
(*Cornus alba* 'Ivory Halo')

This mounded 3-foot-tall cultivar is less than half as tall as the species. Plant it where you will be able to enjoy the oxblood red bark in winter. Flat cream-colored flower clusters in early summer are followed by white fruits that are enjoyed by birds. The foliage is light green with creamy margins. This plant tolerates wet soils. Zones 3 to 8.

'NORDIC' INKBERRY (*Ilex glabra* 'Nordic')

This compact 2- to 3-foot-tall cultivar of the taller native Eastern inkberry makes an excellent evergreen foundation plant or hedge. It resists winter burn better than most boxwoods, so it's a good replacement plant. It also tolerates wet soil and is less prone to chlorosis than other evergreen hollies. You may not notice the inconspicuous flowers that are followed by blue-black fruit, but you're sure to admire the very dark green, lustrous, oblong leaves. Space plants 1½ to 2 feet apart for a dense hedge. Zones 4 to 9.

'PALIBIN' MEYER LILAC
(*Syringa meyeri* 'Palibin', also known as *S. palibiniana*)

Here's an attractive rounded 5- to 8-foot-tall shrub that's a natural in flower or shrub borders. It has all the beauty of common lilacs and none of their drawbacks. In late spring, fragrant 5-inch-long violet flower clusters cover the plant from top to bottom, well within reach for sniffing and cutting, unlike their taller cousins. Lustrous dark green mildew-proof leaves form a solid mound from the ground up—no bare stems here. Zones 3 to 8.

Barrier Fabrics Block Weeds around Shrubs

WEED BARRIER
PLUS MULCH
MEANS LOW
MAINTENANCE

Whether it's hand-pulling or hoeing, weed control around new shrubs is a real chore. But weed-barrier fabrics are an easy way to make this waste of time and effort a thing of the past. Just make sure you buy the new spunbonded weed barriers, not the old knitted ones.

Usually made of polyester or a similar plastic material, the spunbonded barriers, like Reemay's Typar, really keep the weeds out. "They feel like cotton candy," says John Cretti, the "Rocky Mountain Horticulturist" in Golden, Colorado. John tried the older types of barriers but found that they didn't do the job. "Weeds come right through the old knitted kinds," he says. The new products are easy to install and conceal under a more natural-looking mulch like wood chips. They're porous enough to allow air, water, and nutrients to pass through to the soil. And most of them are tough and durable enough to resist punctures, mildew, and rot.

Shepherd Ogden, author of *Step by Step Organic Vegetable Gardening,* uses them under new paths between raised beds. He covers the fabric with 4 to 6 inches of bark mulch for

Stifle weeds around shrubs and hedges with weed-barrier fabric. Roll out the fabric, cut slits in it for plant stems, arrange it around your shrubs, and cover it with mulch.

322

zero maintenance. "Also, they're great for establishing new hedges," Shep says. "Just lay them down, making slits to fit around stems, and cover them with bark mulch. There's no weeding to speak of the first couple of years, and by then, my shrubs have gotten large enough to shade out the weeds on their own."

Landscape fabrics have lots of benefits in addition to weed control. You can use them to add stability to landscape areas that tend to erode. Use them around drainage ditches and behind retaining walls, and to prevent heaving or uneven settling under patios or walkway materials.

JUST SAY "NO" TO PRUNING AND FERTILIZING NEW SHRUBS

Conventional wisdom is that, when you dig and move a plant, you should prune it to balance the topgrowth with its reduced root system. Supposedly this helps plants that have been recently dug and are beginning to wilt. The roots don't have as many leaves to support, so they have a chance to catch their second wind.

However, Carl Whitcomb, a woody plant specialist and researcher in Stillwater, Oklahoma, found that pruning plants at transplant time can actually set them back. Apparently, root-stimulating hormones are produced in the stem tips, which are removed when plants are trimmed. Unpruned plants set into good soil and watered sufficiently have more root mass a year later than those that are pruned to "save" them.

In addition, it's usually not necessary to fertilize newly transplanted shrubs or trees their first season in the ground. Fertilizer, especially nitrogen, stimulates green growth at a time when plants need to be sending new roots into the soil. Let plants get established for a few months or an entire growing season before pushing topgrowth with fertilizers.

For more information on shrubs, see the **Hedges, Fences, and Screens entry.**

SLUGS

Slug Trouble Brewing? Try Beer Bait

LURE SLUGS TO
THEIR DOOM
WITH FRESH
BREW

Nobody likes stale beer, not even slugs. If you want to use beer to trap slimy garden marauders, freshen your bait daily, recommends *Organic Gardening* magazine's editor-in-chief Mike McGrath.

"Beer will only attract slugs for 24 hours," Mike explains. "What we've learned at the magazine about beer is that slugs are actually repulsed by stale beer." He notes that what slugs *really* like is yeast, which makes "really cheap yeasty beers" good slug bait.

In addition to keeping the beer fresh for maximum slug-trapping success, Mike advocates using beer traps responsibly in the garden to avoid injuring beneficial insects. "Some of our readers recommend leaving a little lip protruding above the soil surface to keep ground beetles from falling in," he says.

Spray Snuffs Out Slugs

Zap slugs safely—all it takes is a spray bottle and diluted ammonia. "It's organic, clean, quick, and cheap," says Stephanie Feeney of Bellingham, Washington, author of *The Northwest Gardener's Resource Directory.* For years, Stephanie has patrolled her garden with a squirt gun or spray bottle filled with a solution of 1 part nonsudsing ammonia and 2 parts water. When she sees a slug, she sprays it. "The slug dissolves in milliseconds," Stephanie explains.

"The stream from the gun or spray bottle can reach teeny-tiny slugs, monster slugs, and slugs at the very back of the border," she adds. It won't harm the soil or most plants, like salt, another slug-dissolving standby. Stephanie does caution against using the solution on delicate flower petals. "In that case," Stephanie says, "I use the bottle to whack the offender to the ground before dispensing with it."

Slug It Out with Scrap Copper

Copper shocks slugs, so they keep away from it as though it were an electric fence. Garden centers and catalogs sell strips of copper for repelling slugs and snails, but it can be expensive to encircle plants with the pricey material. You can get the same benefits by using scrap copper.

For an effective slug barrier, surround plants with copper strips set half above and half below the soil.

"Copper tape sold by gardening catalogs is too expensive," points out Earl Rand, a gardener in Culver City, California. "A much cheaper source is a sheet metal shop that makes air-conditioning ducts, flashing, rain gutters, and the like. These shops frequently have strips left over from jobs. They'll sell it for scrap, by the pound—it's very inexpensive."

The strips Earl buys are 4 to 6 inches wide and can be quite long. They're also a heavier gauge than the foil strips sold for gardens. Earl sticks the copper into the ground so that about half is above the soil level and half is below.

Slugs: Hair's the Answer

Don't tear your hair out at the first sign of slug damage in your garden. Instead, get a big bag of hair clippings from a local barbershop, recommends *Organic Gardening* magazine's editor-in-chief Mike McGrath.

Inspired by the Marvel Comics superhero, The Punisher, Mike reacted naturally when he saw the damage slugs were causing in his beloved gardens. "I wanted to inflict pain and suffering," he says. "So I went to the woman who cuts my hair and said, 'Margaret, you got any hair?'" He explains that "when slugs try to crawl across human hair, they get all tangled up, and they strangle and die."

In addition to its slug-stopping abilities, Mike touts human hair for its other garden benefits. "It's a great fertilizer—it contains a lot of nitrogen. It may keep away some mammalian critters as well, and it's free."

Soil Preparation

Free Wood Chips Lighten Up Your Soil

FOR MULCH OR
BETTER
DRAINAGE, TRY
WOOD CHIPS

Your electric company can be the source of free wood chips, a great material for mulching and soil improvement. "Fresh wood chips are readily available to me," says garden designer Stan Beikmann of Niles, Michigan. "I get the electric company, with its routine trimming services, to dump four or five yards at a time from their chipper trucks right on my driveway for nothing." Stan uses the wood chips as mulch, and sometimes as a soil amendment to improve drainage. He works the chips right into the soil and finds that their coarse texture helps improve water absorption and drainage.

As wood chips break down, the nitrogen level in the soil may drop temporarily, because the bacteria decomposing the wood chips are using the nitrogen to create more bacteria. You can compensate by adding a light topdressing of fish meal, blood meal, or cottonseed meal once or twice during the first season after digging in the wood chips. The only other problem Stan has found when using wood chips is mushrooms sprouting up in the beds. However, he says the foliage of his plantings usually hides the mushrooms from view.

Take Small Bites Out of a New Garden

To ease the burden of digging a garden for the first time, break the task into small chunks. If you try to dig it all in a day, you may give up partway through because of frustration and aching muscles—especially if you're dealing with sod or heavy clay. To preserve a positive attitude toward your garden, plan to dig it up over a week or so. Felder Rushing, coauthor of *Passalong Plants,* puts it this way: "It's like eating an elephant—take it one bite at a time, and it ain't so bad."

Felder has a simple system for breaking a garden into bite-size pieces. First, outline the garden with a flat-edged spade by slicing straight down to a spade's depth. Then make parallel cuts 6 or 8 inches apart across the bed. When you're done, the surface of the bed will look like a piece of lined notepaper.

To dig the bed, turn small chunks of soil over, one at a time, staying between the cuts. Do as much as you can at one time, then rest. You'll make steady progress.

Once the entire area is turned completely over, chop up the exposed bottoms of the soil chunks, and spread organic matter over the planting area. Then wait a day or two, mix the organic matter and the soil together, and you're ready to plant.

When you prepare a new site for a garden, use a spade to cut the area into 6- or 8-inch-wide strips before you start digging. Turn the soil over a few strips at a time to divide your task into manageable pieces.

Turn Soil in Fall for a Fast Start in Spring

Start your vegetable garden sooner and with a lot less work next spring by preparing your soil in the fall. Fall digging and tilling save time, especially for gardeners in cold climates, says Paul Pfeifer, coordinator of the Chicago Botanic Garden's GROW (Gardening Resources On Wheels) program. "If you wait until spring, you'll have to let the soil dry out before you can dig, and that can mean a big delay in some areas."

After you remove old crop debris in fall, Paul recommends tilling the soil shallowly to break up the surface. Then add a thick layer of compost to enrich the soil and prevent weeds from springing up. You can also lay down a 2-inch-deep mulch of fallen leaves. Maple leaves are great for this job because they curl as they dry, making a light, fluffy mulch. Oak leaves, on the other hand, stay flat and mat together, which can smother the soil.

Check the garden several weeks before you want to plant in spring. If the leaves have decayed, you can plant right through them. Otherwise, rake them off into a pile to decompose. You'll find the soil below is loose, fertile, and ready for seeds.

JUST SAY "NO" TO BUYING A TILLER

Owning and maintaining a rotary tiller large enough to do the job right can be a costly investment. Stan Beikmann, a garden designer in Niles, Michigan, has discovered several easy alternatives that are cheaper—and better for the soil too.

"I hand-weed, trying to disturb the soil as little as possible, and I avoid walking a lot in the garden. And I mulch," says Stan. By following this regime, Stan avoids compacting his soil, so there's little or no need to till. "If I do need a tiller," Stan continues, "why own one for several hundred dollars and have to store it as well, when I can rent one for 20 or 30 bucks once every year or two?"

Sunken Beds Stay Cool and Save Water

BELOW-GROUND
BEDS ARE BEST
IN HOT, DRY
SITES

Beat the heat in arid climates by growing crops in sunken beds. Native Americans of the Southwest planted their crops close to river floodplains to take full advantage of moist soil for as long as possible. By digging beds into the moist soil, they lengthened their growing season even more. If you garden in a hot, dry climate, you can use this technique of digging sunken beds to save time and water. Sunken beds will also extend your growing season into hotter weather.

Garden writer and teacher George Van Patten of Portland, Oregon, used this technique early in his gardening career, when he lived in eastern Oregon. "We learned quickly that in that high desert with 100° temperatures and only 10 percent humidity, digging sunken beds and lining them with the excess soil protected our plants from extreme heat. And we could water easily by simply flooding the garden beds," George explains.

Of course, if you plan to garden in a sunken bed, you'll have to be sure your topsoil is deep enough to allow good growth. So before making beds, dig a few sample holes; you need good topsoil that's at least a foot deep for this technique to work well.

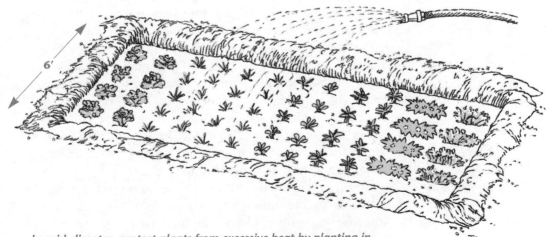

In arid climates, protect plants from excessive heat by planting in sunken beds that are up to 6 inches deep and 6 feet wide. Scrape the extra soil off to the edges of the bed to give plants extra heat protection.

Let Coffee Make New "Grounds" for You

Convert terrible soil into great gardens with ease by drinking lots of coffee. That's the tongue-in-cheek advice of Phil Tietz, an urban gardener and a member of New York City's "Green Guerillas," a nonprofit group that converts abandoned building sites into local community gardens.

Phil found that most community garden sites were on top of filled-in demolished buildings. "There was no dirt, just highly alkaline, pulverized concrete rubble," says Phil. "I had to turn my garden with a pickax and a sledge-hammer." Rather than buying topsoil and having it delivered, Phil decided to "grow my own soil."

After rounding up sawdust from carpenters, Phil arranged for local coffee shops to save leftover coffee-bean burlap bags and used coffee grounds. Layered over the top of the smoothed-out site, these became his major soil amendments. The natural acidity of the coffee grounds neutralized the alkalinity of the rubble, and its nitrogen helped compost the sawdust and burlap. Surprisingly, earthworms began to appear. Phil also added compost as it became available.

While few suburban gardeners have to deal with concrete rubble, they often have alkaline, compacted soil around building foundations. Phil's sawdust-and-coffee-grounds formula can work for these garden sites as well.

The moral of this story is to look for soil-building materials that are inexpensive and readily available to you. If coffee shops aren't plentiful in your neck of the woods, check with your place of business, local cafeterias, airports, hospitals, or other institutions—anywhere where coffee is popular. If you provide food service employees with containers for storing the coffee grounds and pick the grounds up reliably, they'll be likely to help you out.

For other sources of sawdust, check riding or boarding stables or lumber mills if any are nearby. If you gather sawdust from carpenters, check with them first to make sure the lumber they're cutting isn't pressure treated. The chemicals used to make pressure-treated lumber last a long time include arsenic, chromium, and copper—not the kind of ingredients you'd want in an organic garden.

Holy Garden Bed, Batman!

Dig holes instead of a whole bed to save time and effort when planting shrubs and perennials. If you want to start a garden without working up the soil in the whole bed, simply prepare individual planting holes. Then cover the rest of the garden area with a thick layer of mulch, recommends horticulture instructor Gail Barton of Meridian, Mississippi. Gail uses leaves and pine needles because they are readily available in her area.

Before mulching, she sprinkles a little cottonseed meal over the bed—about a pound for every 100 square feet—to add natural nitrogen and protein for earthworms and lets it go at that. Within a year or so, the entire bed will be enriched by the natural activity of the earthworms as they break down the mulch.

JUST SAY "NO" TO DOUBLE DIGGING

When should you double dig? The answer is: Maybe never. Double digging is a labor-intensive soil-improvement process. You need to dig a series of trenches, removing the top layer of soil, loosening the subsoil, and returning the topsoil, mixed with extra organic matter, to each trench.

Texas gardening guru Neil Sperry of Dallas said he hasn't "seen anyone use a shovel to dig more than a 2-by-2 area in years." Neil recommends renting or borrowing a rear-tine rotary tiller, and using it to work organic matter into the soil.

Rosalind Creasy, a garden designer in Los Altos, California, says, "It's unrealistic to think average gardeners will actually double dig—it's very hard work." Ros advocates a passive improvement method instead. "I just add a couple or 3 inches of compost every time I work my garden—once or twice a year—and then I mulch. I used to have adobe-house clay—now you can put your hand in elbow-high or more."

SPINACH

Quick Cover-up Gives Spinach a Smooth Start

FOR MORE
SPINACH, START
SEEDS UNDER
CARDBOARD

Throw a piece of cardboard over newly planted spinach seeds to get better germination. Even experienced seed sowers like Philadelphia community gardener Sally McCabe have been heard to complain about their so-so luck with spinach. But Sally, outreach coordinator for Pennsylvania Horticultural Society's Philadelphia Green Program, says that covering the seedbed with cardboard has improved her spinach success rates.

"Just sow your seeds, water them, then put a piece of cardboard over them," she explains. Keep tabs on your undercover crop to avoid growing a lot of long, pale spinach sprouts that Sally says are good for eating as sprouts, but not much help in producing a crop of spinach. Remove the cardboard when sprouts begin to appear, "but don't take it off on a sunny day or you'll kill everything," Sally warns.

The Earliest Spinach Starts in Fall

Pick spinach in February by sowing seeds in late fall in a cold frame. "That's the best shortcut I know for growing spinach," says Deborah Bertoldi, owner and operator of Cedar Hill Gardens in Reading, Pennsylvania. Deborah says she can usually harvest cold-frame spinach by mid-March in her southeastern Pennsylvania gardens, and adds that sometimes she picks as early as late February.

Deborah recommends planting seeds in a cold frame in October: "Let them come up, then thin out your plants. By February or March, the soil in the cold frame is covered with spinach." Besides giving you a very early spinach crop, the cold frame makes it easier to keep spinach growing when the weather warms. "Since you have the frame in place, it makes it easy to put shade cloth over the spinach to keep it from bolting [going to seed]," she says.

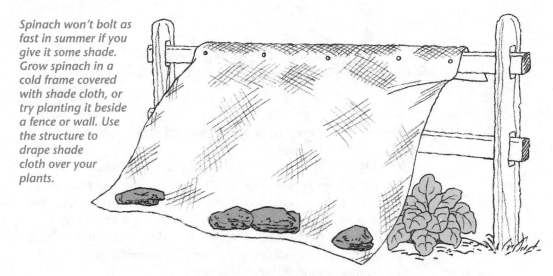

Spinach won't bolt as fast in summer if you give it some shade. Grow spinach in a cold frame covered with shade cloth, or try planting it beside a fence or wall. Use the structure to drape shade cloth over your plants.

If you don't have a cold frame, sow a crop of spinach in late summer for your usual fall harvest. In late fall, mulch the plants with a thick cover of leaves or straw and harvest spinach throughout the winter, suggests Sally Roth, coauthor of *Rodale's Successful Organic Gardening: Companion Planting*. Either way, you can enjoy fresh spinach at times when not much else is growing.

JUST SAY "NO" TO GRITTY SPINACH

Ugh! There's nothing worse than chomping down on a piece of gritty spinach. But start with smooth-leaved spinach like 'Nordic' and 'Space', which don't hold dirt the way crinkled leaves do, and you'll end up with grit-free spinach without a lot of washing.

"Cultivars with flatter leaves are easier to wash, so they don't take as much time to clean," says Sally Roth, coauthor of *Rodale's Successful Organic Gardening: Companion Planting.* Sally uses scissors to harvest each leaf. It's quicker than picking the leaves, she says, and "you don't get dirt on the spinach from roots you've accidentally pulled up."

David Chambers, manager of Mr. Cason's Vegetable Garden at Callaway Gardens in Pine Mountain, Georgia, recommends mulch as another way to reduce the time you spend cleaning spinach. "If we cultivate around the spinach and leave the soil bare, then rain or irrigation splashes the soil onto the leaves, and it's hard to get them clean," he says.

SQUASH

Skip Sprays with Squash Succession

Don't fight pests and diseases. Instead, plant squash every two weeks in late spring and early summer to have a steady supply at harvesttime. When a plant falls prey to common problems such as squash bugs, squash vine borers, wilt disease, or powdery mildew, just pull it out, says Deborah Bertoldi, owner and operator of Cedar Hill Gardens in Reading, Pennsylvania.

"As soon as a plant wilts and starts looking bad, I pull it out," Deborah says. "That way you have good healthy plants that are producing well in the garden, instead of sickly ones." What's more, you remove problems before they spread to other plants.

At Callaway Gardens in Pine Mountain, Georgia, David Chambers, manager of Mr. Cason's Vegetable Garden, agrees with Deborah. Squash growing is easy in the long,

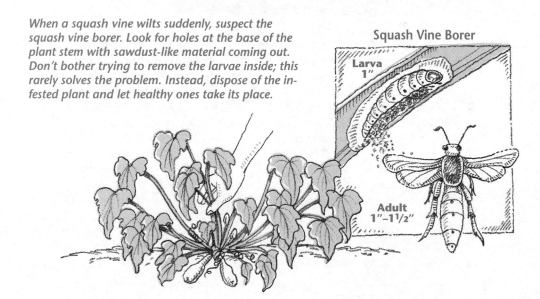

When a squash vine wilts suddenly, suspect the squash vine borer. Look for holes at the base of the plant stem with sawdust-like material coming out. Don't bother trying to remove the larvae inside; this rarely solves the problem. Instead, dispose of the infested plant and let healthy ones take its place.

Squash Vine Borer

Larva
1"

Adult
1"–1¹/₂"

warm Georgia growing season, and David uses successive sowings to keep squash coming from mid-June until frost. "We don't really spray," he says. "We can just start another planting when the plants start to deteriorate."

David recommends growing bush-type squash cultivars: "For both winter squash and summer squash, definitely try the bush types. You'll have fewer problems with disease, and flavor and production will be just as good."

Raised Beds Speed Squash Success

SUN AND WELL-
DRAINED SOIL
ARE KEY TO
QUICK SQUASH

Give your squash plants a lift by sowing seeds in raised beds. "Grow them in raised beds and full sun," recommends Deborah Bertoldi, owner and operator of Cedar Hill Gardens in Reading, Pennsylvania. "That's the quickest way to get squash."

Because the soil in raised beds drains more quickly and warms up earlier in the spring than in a traditional garden bed, it makes them ideal for growing squash, Deborah explains. She says she can plant her squash seeds in early to mid-May in raised beds, rather than waiting until the end of May or early June. As a result, she has squash ready to harvest a few weeks ahead of the normal squash season.

Stop Squash Pests with Radishes

Radishes can protect your squash from squash borers. "For the past eight years, I've planted radishes around my squash plants to protect them from vine borers," says Forrest Arnold, former president of the Austin (Texas) Organic Gardeners Club. "In the spring, when I plant zucchini, white scallop, yellow crookneck, or other types of squash, I plant radish seeds in a 1-foot-diameter circle and plant the squash in the center of the circle. As the radishes mature, I harvest some, but I always leave enough in the circle so that their leaves still touch."

Forrest says he's used 'Champion', 'Early Scarlet Globe', and 'Long White Icicle' radishes, and all have worked. "At the end of the season I do autopsies on the spent squash vines, and I haven't found any sign of borers," Forrest says.

STRAWBERRIES

Stretch Your Strawberry Season

Enjoy strawberries longer by pinching some of your day-neutral berry buds later. "When you grow day-neutral strawberries, you usually pinch the buds off for the first four to six weeks after planting, taking off all the buds as soon as they appear," explains Susan McClure, author of *The Harvest Gardener.* That's so the plants will grow healthy roots and leaves instead of wearing themselves out producing flowers.

Day-neutral berries produce fruit in the summer in mild climates. They'll keep bearing until frost farther north. The first harvest is heavier and the berries are larger—often twice as large—than in later harvests. So to keep from being inundated by berries, and to enjoy the bigger berries longer, spread that first harvest out by pinching some of the plants longer than you normally would. If you just pinch

Stagger the peak production time of day-neutral strawberry plants with a pinching trick. Pinch the flowers off some of your plants longer than the standard four weeks. They'll bear large berries (right) when your less-pinched plants (left) are declining.

the buds for the first four to six weeks, the berries will be big and plentiful, but as time goes on they start to peter out and get smaller.

To prolong the harvest of prime berries, keep pinching the buds in one section of your garden—a third or a fourth of the planting—for an extra two weeks. Or just experiment with a few plants. (Stop pinching three to four weeks before you want ripe fruit, to give the plants enough time to bear heavily before frost.) When your first crop of berries starts getting small, the second flush (the pinched plants) will be coming on with full-size berries.

Quick Tip for Bigger, Faster Berry Yields

You can get more berries on each strawberry plant, and harvest them earlier, with a little undercover work. "Strawberries set fruiting buds in the fall, as the days get shorter," explains David Batchelder, an organic strawberry grower in Stratham, New Hampshire. "I cover my plants with floating row covers made from spunbonded polyester—Agryl and Reemay are two common brands. The covers protect the plants from frost, so they set buds longer." Longer bud setting means more buds, which translates to higher yields the next year.

COVER STRAW-

BERRIES IN FALL

FOR MORE

SPRING FRUIT

David mulches between the strawberry rows with straw before laying the covers on top of his plants, so he doesn't have to mulch in the spring. He anchors the edges of the row cover with soil. David prefers to cover his plants before the first light frost, but since one or two light frosts won't stop bud production, he doesn't worry if the plants aren't covered by then. Just make sure you cover your strawberry plants before the first killing frost.

In the spring, David pulls the covers off when the plants start to bloom. He leaves the covers in the rows between the plants until all danger of frost has passed so he can quickly cover them when a late frost threatens. (For these short-term cover-ups, he just uses rocks or whatever is heavy and handy to anchor the edges of the covers.) David reports that the covered plants bear strawberries 10 to 14 days earlier than uncovered plants. He warns that the covers only last one winter.

Top Tip for Watering Strawberry Jars

Plants in strawberry jars can be hard to water. Sometimes the water doesn't reach the lower levels, or so much soil runs out the sides that small plants are dislodged. What to do? At planting time, insert a homemade watering tube in the center of the jar.

"Take some hardware cloth and shape it into a cylinder," suggests Lyn Belisle, a gardener in San Antonio. "The cylinder should be about 3 inches in diameter and about 2 inches shorter than the height of the strawberry jar. Close the open side of the cylinder with twist ties, stand the cylinder in the middle of the jar, and fill it with pea gravel."

When you fill the rest of the jar with soil, cover the top of the cylinder, then add plants. When you water, pour the water in the center of the pot so it flows down through the cylinder. The cylinder will dispense the water evenly to all layers without flooding the planting pockets.

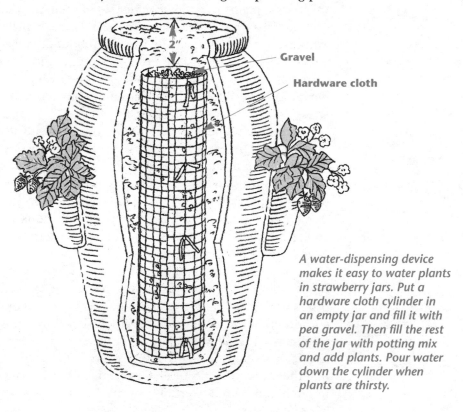

Gravel

Hardware cloth

A water-dispensing device makes it easy to water plants in strawberry jars. Put a hardware cloth cylinder in an empty jar and fill it with pea gravel. Then fill the rest of the jar with potting mix and add plants. Pour water down the cylinder when plants are thirsty.

Compost Mulch for Fungus-Free Strawberries

Here's a simple tip for cleaner strawberries. If botrytis is turning your strawberries to fuzz, the solution may be as simple as a compost mulch. "The fungal spores that cause botrytis generally come from old leaves left in the field," explains David Batchelder, an organic strawberry grower in Stratham, New Hampshire. "It also grows in organic matter in the soil and splashes up onto the blossoms when it rains."

BEAT BOTRYTIS
FRUIT ROT WITH
A BLANKET OF
COMPOST

To keep the spores from reaching the plant, David uses a thick layer of compost mulch. (Make sure it's at least 1 inch thick; 2 to 3 inches is even better.) It can be applied anytime, although in his operation David finds it most economical to do it when he renovates the strawberries. "After I mow the plants and rototill, I spread the compost right over the row," David says. "It forms a solid cover." (If you'd like to try this simple renovation technique, mow off all the leaves on your strawberries with the mower blades set at 2½ inches high. Rake up the leaves, then till the sides of the bed, leaving a 1-foot strip of strawberries down the center. Runners will root into the tilled soil.)

In addition to acting as a barrier to keep spores away from new growth, the compost may house microorganisms that compete with spores for nutrients, thus reducing the number of spores, David says. He estimates that the compost mulch reduces the incidence of botrytis by 50 to 75 percent, depending on how wet the weather is. "It's one of the easiest ways to control botrytis," David says, "and it adds nutrients to the soil."

If you're not sure if botrytis fruit rot is the problem affecting your strawberries, look for these symptoms. A fluffy gray, tan, or whitish mold appears on infected fruit. If you touch or disturb the mold, you'll see a puff of gray spores float up in the air. Your strawberry fruits will look water-soaked and will quickly rot. It's not a pretty sight, but it's easy to solve with compost.

TOMATOES

Covered Cages Keep Tomatoes Cozy

CUSTOM-MADE
SHELTERS BRING
ON A TOMATO
BONANZA

Save your tender young tomatoes from chilly spring weather with easy-to-make plastic-covered cages. Ray Wheeler, a gardener in cold and windy Dickinson, North Dakota, makes tomato cages of sturdy wire fencing to give his plants season-long support. Then he wraps each cage with plastic to keep out the still-icy winds of early spring. "These covered cages reduce wind chill, and the tomatoes grow like nothing I've witnessed in my 40 years of gardening," Ray says.

Ray uses 7½-foot lengths of 12-gauge horse fencing to make round cages that are 48 inches tall and about 28 inches in diameter. Horse fencing is similar to dog pen fence except it has narrow openings at the base and larger openings at the top. For his cages, Ray turns the fencing upside down. He fastens the ends of the fencing together with baling wire and uses the smallest openings (3 by 6 inches) as the top of the cage, where plants need the most support. Then he snips the bottom row of horizontal wires off the base of each cage, leaving wire "legs" to anchor the cage in the ground. To make sure his cages don't topple in strong winds, Ray drives a steel fence post into the ground next to each cage and wires the cage to it.

Once the cages are in place, Ray covers them with plastic sleeves covered with tiny holes. He says the sleeves protect his tomatoes from frost, as well as help retain heat and moisture. "The plastic holds a lot of heat around the plants but doesn't allow them to cook. Also, it confuses bugs—a lot of them just won't go in there," says Ray.

To make tomato sleeves, buy an 8-foot-wide roll of clear 3-mil plastic and cut it into 5½-foot-long pieces—one for each cage. Pull the sides of each piece together to form the sleeve and seal them with duct tape. Punch holes in the sleeve for air circulation; Ray suggests ½-inch-diameter holes, spaced every 8 inches vertically and horizontally.

Slip the sleeve over the cage, leaving 12 inches of plastic at the top for twisting closed during bad weather and 6 inches at the bottom for anchoring with soil. Ray adds a single strip of duct tape around the center of each sleeve to keep it from flapping in the wind.

When reliably nice weather arrives, Ray pulls the sleeves down to the ground so they look like kneesocks that have fallen down to the ankle. And, like socks, he pulls them up again when it turns cold and windy.

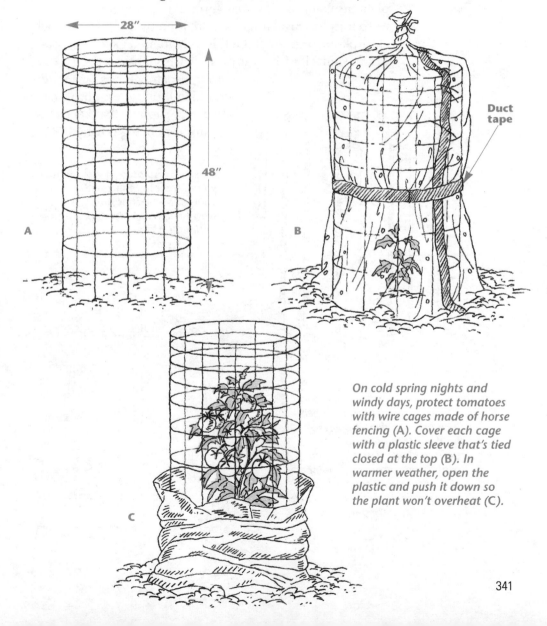

28″

48″

A

B

Duct
tape

C

On cold spring nights and windy days, protect tomatoes with wire cages made of horse fencing (A). Cover each cage with a plastic sleeve that's tied closed at the top (B). In warmer weather, open the plastic and push it down so the plant won't overheat (C).

Water Bags Speed the Season

Plant your tomatoes six weeks sooner. By draping a large water-filled plastic bag over your transplants, you can put them in your garden over a month earlier than usual. "With the bags, plants can survive a 10°F night," says Sligo, Pennsylvania, farmer John Saylor. He got the idea for this method after listening to a farming friend complain about how time-consuming it was to set up a water-holding plant insulator in his tomato-growing operation.

To form his insulating cocoon, John uses a 20- by 48-inch clear plastic bag, which he fills with about 3 gallons of water. (Try it yourself with clear plastic garbage bags.) Each tomato transplant gets its own water bag, which John lowers onto a circular wire support that keeps the plant from being crushed.

Make an insulated shelter for your young tomato plants with a do-it-yourself frame that supports a water-filled bag. Here's one frame option (left) made from a circle of wooden stakes.

12"

12"

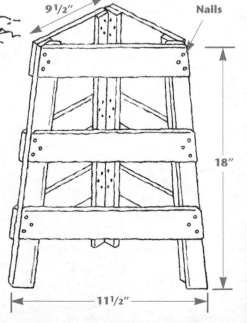

9 1/2"

Nails

18"

You've got lots of choices when it comes to making frames to hold water bags over tender tomato plants. Try this tripod (right) made from scrap lumber, or a wire tomato cage that's a little smaller than the usual cage (top of opposite page).

11 1/2"

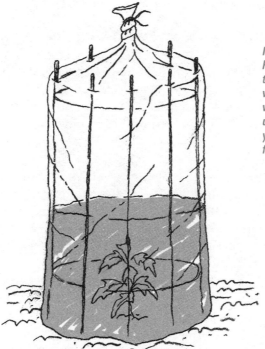

If you want an extra-early harvest, fill a clear plastic trash bag with 3 gallons of water and drape it over a wire cage support. This unusual shelter will protect your tomato transplants from spring cold snaps.

John lowers the bottom of the bag onto the top of the support, and the weight of the water pulls the sides of the bag down to form an insulating doughnut around the plant. Tie the top of the bag to close it, or tuck it in around the top of the support like John does.

"We played around with the design for the support for several years," John says, noting that supports that proved impractical for commercial growers will work fine for home garden use. The first model was a circle of eight 1½-foot-long wooden stakes, driven into the ground to form a 1-foot-diameter ring around the plant. The next workable version was a three-sided wooden frame.

He finally created a 1-foot-diameter stackable wire cage. The 18-inch-tall cage has 4-inch legs below the lowest horizonal wire. It's smaller than a standard tomato cage, but John thinks it works better. When the tomato transplants reach the top of the support, John slits the plastic to let the plants grow through. Then he sets a tall stake beside each cage, and the tomatoes are off and growing!

Faster Tomatoes with Grass Clippings

Warm up the soil with grass clippings to give your tomatoes an edge in early spring. Fresh grass clippings heat up the soil mix that Mary Gruver, a Master Gardener with the Washington State University Cooperative Extension Service, gives her early tomatoes. Her method lets her set tomatoes outside about two months earlier than usual.

CLIPPINGS KEEP EARLY-TOMATOES' ROOTS TOASTY

In Shelton, where Mary gardens, the summers are short and cool so tomatoes grow slowly and bear late in the season. To heat up the soil around her early-planted tomatoes, Mary transplants them into large containers filled with a mixture of grass clippings and soil. Mary says she mixes about 4 parts soil with 1 part fresh grass clippings, then transplants tomatoes into the pots. As the clippings break down, they release heat. "You can feel it when you touch the side of the pot," says Mary. Another benefit is the nitrogen the clippings release into the soil as they break down.

Once she's transplanted her tomatoes into the pots, Mary sets tomato cages over them. She protects her tomatoes from wind and cold snaps by covering their cages with plastic.

The clippings release most of their heat by May. If the summer stays cool, as it often does in her part of the Pacific Northwest, Mary pokes additional grass clippings into the soil to heat things up again.

Mulch Away Tomato Troubles

Diseases won't trouble your tomatoes if you keep the soil around them mulched. Anytime plants get dirty and stay wet—whether it's from heavy splashy rains or overhead watering—diseases such as bacterial spot and Septoria leaf spot can cause a heavy loss of plants and tomatoes. Shepherd Ogden solved this problem by using a layer of mulch in his tomato patch to keep soilborne diseases off of his plants.

Shep, author of *Step by Step Organic Vegetable Gardening*, says using thick layers of organic mulches prevents many bacterial and fungal diseases from causing problems in his garden. "I cover the ground completely, so there is no soil splash whatsoever. The biggest mistake I can make is not putting it deep enough."

How much mulch is enough? Shep says he agrees with the estimate of Felder Rushing, coauthor of *Passalong Plants*: "Whatever mulch material you use, put down enough to completely cover the soil surface," says Felder. "Then add that much more again." This allows for settling and disturbance.

While he finds that bark lasts the longest in his garden, Shep also uses leftover round bales of hay from nearby farms. "It's basically weed-free, and farmers want to get rid of it. A round bale unrolls about 3 feet wide and a solid inch thick."

Shep also warns that, although plastic mulches are easier to install, they require more labor in the long run. The edges tend to catch in the wind and blow around, and you can't plow them under at the end of the season the way you can an organic mulch. Besides, plastic mulch doesn't improve your soil's health the way organic mulch does.

To use a large round hay bale to mulch tomatoes, unroll the bale, then make openings where you want to plant.

Simple Steps to Seed-Saving Success

Saving your own tomato seeds is gross! That's because you have to ferment the seeds in their own pulp to kill seed-borne diseases. It's a disgusting process, but it's a shortcut to a healthy disease-free crop. And it's simple to do. "Saving seeds is easier than most people think," says David Cavagnaro, a seed-saving expert in Decorah, Iowa. "By saving the seeds of your favorite tomato varieties, you won't have to buy seeds for next year's crop. And you won't have to worry about hunting down a source of the special tomato that Grandma always grew."

For seed-saving success, David recommends following the steps perfected by researchers at the Seed Savers Exchange to kill seed-borne diseases and prepare the seeds for planting. Here's what to do.

1 Squeeze the pulp and seeds of a bursting-ripe tomato into a cottage cheese container. To make sure you'll have a good selection of healthy seedlings to choose from, save seeds from more than one tomato and from more than one plant of the same tomato cultivar. Let the open container sit on the kitchen counter for a few days. After three to five days, a layer of fungus will form over the seeds. Once the fungus completely covers the surface of the mixture, you're ready to clean the seeds.

2 Tip the container slightly and use your fingers to rake out the layer of fungus. While you're at it, toss out the larger chunks of tomato and pour the remaining seeds and liquid into a sieve.

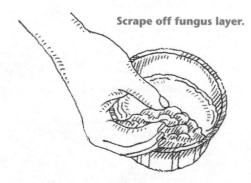
Scrape off fungus layer.

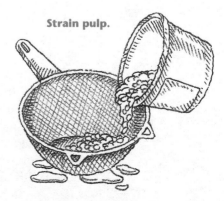
Strain pulp.

Wash seeds.

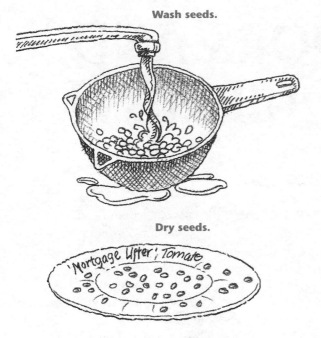

Dry seeds.

'Mortgage Lifter' Tomato

3 Hold the sieve under a stream of running water. Use your fingers to rub the remaining tomato pulp through the sieve.

4 Spread the seeds on a paper plate, label the plate with the date and kind of tomato, and put it somewhere safe to dry. When the seeds are completely dry, store them in labeled paper envelopes in a cool dry place. To tell if your seeds are dry, press down on one with your fingernail. If it's dry, it will break, not bend.

"Seed saving is not only fun," says David, "it's critical to preserving genetic diversity." The key is to make sure you're growing open-pollinated rather than hybrid tomatoes. Since a hybrid is the result of a specific cross, if you save the seed of a hybrid, you won't get the same kind of tomatoes when your next crop ripens. With an open-pollinated tomato, you'll get the same tomatoes year after year, and you can feel good about keeping that variety going. It's easy to get hooked on seed saving since, with most vegetables, you just have to dry the seed!

If you're interested in seed saving, David recommends joining the Seed Savers Exchange, a nonprofit organization dedicated to saving endangered food plants. As a member, you can swap seeds with hundreds of gardeners from across the country and around the world. (For more information, write: Seed Savers Exchange, 3076 North Winn Road, Decorah, IA 52101.)

Tools and Equipment

Small Tools Handle Big Jobs

Bigger is not necessarily better when it comes to gardening tools, says Les Manns, a Master Gardener in Lehigh County, Pennsylvania. He maintains that small-scale tools that are suited to specific tasks can make the best garden time-savers. This is especially true in small spaces where full-size tools won't fit. In these tight spaces, kid-size tools let you work with speed and ease.

SCALED-DOWN
RAKES AND
SHOVELS FIT
TIGHT SPOTS

Les uses a scaled-down version of a conventional rake to clean out leaves and debris beneath his azaleas and rhododendrons. The rake's small size—about 8 inches across the broad end of the tines—makes it handy for getting into limited spaces, while its long handle lets him reach beneath bushes without kneeling on the ground.

Organic Gardening magazine's research editor Cheryl Long is another small-tool advocate. Her favorite shovel has a full-length wooden handle and a blade that's about 6 inches wide and 8 inches long—some 3 inches smaller in both dimensions than a heavy-duty model. "It's much more convenient to work with in permanent beds," Cheryl says. "I like it a lot for planting and moving perennials. You can control it better because it's smaller, so you can get it right where you want." Cheryl adds that she rarely sees shovels like hers in hardware stores, but that it's worth the trouble to ask a store to special-order one for you; hers is made by Ames.

Another benefit of children's tools is that they're lighter weight than standard-size tools, reducing the risk that you'll tire out before your work's done. And that's an important consideration when there's lots to do and little time to do it in. (See "Sources" on page 412 for mail-order companies that sell child-size garden tools.)

Hoes to Help You Weed with Speed

Wipe out weeds quickly and easily using a hoe that fits both you and your garden. Matching your hoe (or any tool) to the task at hand makes it easier for you to get the job done faster—and more comfortably too.

At the University of British Columbia Botanic Gardens in Vancouver, Food Garden curator Murray Kereluk works amid raised beds and graveled paths that help limit weed invasions. Where weeds sneak in, Murray makes short work of them with his stirrup hoe, a tool that's sharp on both sides of its narrow, stirrup-shaped blade. "It's amazing what you can do with a hoe, as opposed to a very expensive herbicide," he says.

Stirrup hoe

With two sharpened edges, the blade of a stirrup hoe cuts weeds on both the push and pull strokes. Stirrup hoes are also called oscillating, hula, swing-head, or action hoes.

With her Winged Weeder Junior, Cheryl Long rarely needs to make time in her schedule for weeding her perennial beds. "You just carry it around as you're enjoying the garden in the evening," recommends Cheryl, *Organic Gardening* magazine's research editor. "If you see a stray weed, you just take the little weeder and cut it down, and you're done.

"It's good for working around perennials where you normally wouldn't think of hoeing. You can get in there and snip all sorts of weeds out, and you don't even have to bend over," says Cheryl.

See "Sources" on page 412 for mail-order companies that sell these hoes and others that may suit you and your garden.

Winged Weeder Jr.

The long handle and sharp arrow-shaped head of the Winged Weeder Jr. make it an efficient tool for tackling weeds in tight spots. It's great for hoeing around established perennials or plants in a rock garden.

349

Big Tires Save Time

BIG WHEELS AREN'T JUST FOR KIDS ANYMORE

Buy a new set of wheels to replace the small standard-issue plastic wheels on your lawn and garden tools. You'll cut the time you spend mowing or fertilizing *and* make your work easier. "Most implements have undersized wheels because they're cheaper," says Mac Cheever, owner of a landscape design and maintenance company in Milton, Wisconsin. "Think about the contour of what you're pushing the tool over; if the wheel is the same size or smaller than the dips and holes, it's going to get caught all the time, and it's hard to push."

For Mac, wheel size became a $1,000 decision when he decided to buy a new front-deck riding mower for his lawn maintenance business. He'd encountered problems with the small wheels that supported the decks on two previous mowers—they tended to catch on sidewalk edges and tree roots, sometimes bending the shaft that held them. "Very aggravating," says Mac, noting that the wheels on his new mower are probably twice the diameter of those on his old ones. "It's just made an incredible difference," he says. "This mower, which in essence is identical to the other one, cut about 15 percent off my time this year. Those wheels were the reason I spent $1,000 more and bought this mower instead. And it made that much difference."

Lehigh County, Pennsylvania, Master Gardener Les Manns is equally enthusiastic about wheel size. Les swears by a wheeled trimmer he owns that is supported by two bicycle-size tires. "It's one of the easiest things to push around," he says. "Any tools that have larger wheels are usually easier to manage than those that have only small wheels. That's a real handy thing for people who are looking to eliminate effort."

Big wheels have uses beyond mowers and trimmers, notes Mac, who says he prefers big wheels on his walk-behind fertilizer spreader, too: "When you've got 50 pounds of fertilizer in a spreader and you're pushing it across a bumpy lawn, the last thing you want it to do is hook a wheel and make the thing stop and dump or twist and mess up your pattern."

But wheel size isn't the only consideration—durability is just as important. Mac says that his spreader originally had

12-inch-diameter plastic-spoked wheels. "It would hold about 50 pounds of fertilizer, and of course, you're turning it and pushing it, and eventually the wheels caved in. Bad news." Mac replaced the plastic wheels with wider pneumatic tires that improved the spreader's stability so it was less likely to tip and spill.

If your local hardware store doesn't carry replacement wheels in a size you like, try recycling old bicycle tires or wheels from the kids' wagon. Check with equipment manufacturers too—sometimes they'll offer upgraded wheels for their products for an additional cost. You can also check with mail-order tool suppliers. See "Sources" on page 412 for ordering information if you'd like to replace the wheels on your lawn equipment.

Ready-to-Wear Boots Best Bet

Keep your boots in the garden and you won't track mud back inside. Barbara Donnette, manager of Seattle's P-Patch Community Gardening Program, reports that gardeners there use a simple technique to keep their garden footwear nearby. "Most gardeners simply drive a couple of stakes into the ground at the end of the garden, then leave their garden boots upside down on the stakes when they're not working in the garden," says Barbara. There's another big benefit to on-site boots: You won't have to go back for the boots if your plot's muddier than you thought.

Upend your rubber boots on stakes when you're through gardening. They'll stay dry inside and be ready to slip on when your garden's wet but needs tending.

351

Crazy Cart Keeps Tools Close

You *can* take it with you—to your garden, at least. If you hate running back to the garage each time you discover that you need the pruning shears or a garden spade, consider this amusing step-saver.

Erin Hynes, author of *Rodale's Successful Organic Gardening: Improving the Soil,* recalls the morning her family awoke to find that a friend (and practical joker) had left a giant homemade tool caddy on the patio during the night. The contraption had a long, narrow frame set on casters, brackets for holding both large and small garden tools, a basket for seed packets and other small items, and a cord for pulling the cart. For decoration, a shiny pinwheel was affixed to one end and a rubber Jolly Green Giant doll to the other.

The funny-looking cart got a few laughs, but it also worked! Before he'd head out to the garden, Erin's father would load the cart with all the tools he might need. Then he could work for hours without having to return to the garage for something he forgot.

If you don't happen to have a caddy-building friend, avoid the left-behind-tool-blues with one of the many commercially available tool belts or caddies sold in garden centers and mail-order catalogs.

CADDIES AREN'T JUST FOR GOLF; THEY'RE FOR GARDENS TOO

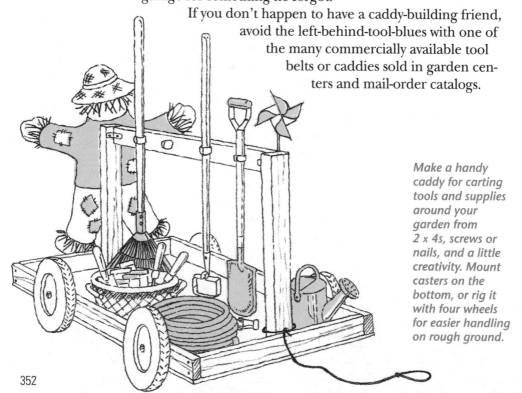

Make a handy caddy for carting tools and supplies around your garden from 2 x 4s, screws or nails, and a little creativity. Mount casters on the bottom, or rig it with four wheels for easier handling on rough ground.

Help for Heavy Loads

Get a grip on large loads—you'll save time *and* your back. Making several trips from the compost pile to the garden with a tippy, overloaded wheelbarrow can strain your muscles and take up your gardening time. Jill Jesiolowski, senior editor at *Organic Gardening* magazine, found a way to breeze through heavy lifting and moving tasks when she discovered her WheelAround Garden Cart. (See "Sources" on page 412 for information on ordering your own cart.)

Although Jill initially was skeptical when she saw the low three-wheeled cart, she quickly discovered how versatile it was. "I was swept away," she says. "I have a wheelbarrow, and I almost always use this instead."

By adding a #2 galvanized tub (sold separately) to the cart's flat, round bed, Jill is able to move large bulky loads with ease. She uses it to carry loads of weeds from her garden to her compost pile and makes fewer trips because of its ample capacity. The cart's low center of gravity lets her fill the tub with heavier materials like rocks, too. Jill says she prefers the ease of pulling the cart to lifting and pushing a wheelbarrow. "I can put much more in this little cart than I ever could in a wheelbarrow, and move it around by myself," she says.

A WheelAround Garden Cart makes moving large container plants or tubs full of weeds, compost, or even rocks, a simple task. The handle folds down, so the cart is easy to slide into a small storage space.

353

TREES

Size Trees to Your Site

Make sure new trees fit the size of your yard and house for a lifetime of beautiful landscaping—without pruning. "The biggest mistake homeowners make when planting a tree is disregarding how tall it will grow," says Sam Jones, owner of Atlantic Star Tree Nursery in Forest Hill, Maryland. "There's nothing worse than seeing a huge hemlock blocking an entrance or a maple that someone has topped off in a futile effort to change the scale."

BASE PLANTING PLANS ON YOUR TREES' MATURE SIZE

If you don't want to spend time hacking away at over-grown trees or replanting your landscape in 10 or 15 years, take the tree's height into account *before* you plant it. Sam says that for most homes on small lots, a small tree—that's one that reaches 15 feet tops—is the right size. Small disease-resistant crabapples are good choices, and so are small maples like Amur maple (*Acer ginnala*), Japanese maple (*A. palmatum*), or paperbark maple (*A. griseum*). You can also plant large shrubs and use them just as you would a small tree. Try planting flowering shrubs like viburnums and limb them up into a single- or multitrunked tree form. They often look better and grow faster than trees.

It's hard to picture the mature size of a tree when you're looking at a sapling in the nursery, so Sam suggests that you do a little homework first. Visit a park, botanic garden, or arboretum with mature trees and see exactly how tall they can get. Talk with your local park service or look through tree books to find out how big trees grow. (See "Recommended Reading" on page 418 for a selection of good books on trees.) Check with your local extension service, nurseries, and utility companies—they'll all have recommendations and maybe even brochures and handouts that list good small trees.

"Planting a tree is a long-term decision," Sam points out. Do it right, and you'll have a tree that fits your landscape for a lifetime.

5 Terrific Trees for Quick Shade

*S*mall trees are great for small lots, but if you've got a large home and yard, big trees have a place. Maybe you've got a new home on a barren lot, or your sunroom gets so much sun it's like an oven. You need shade in a hurry, but you don't want to spend top dollar for a large shade tree. These trees shoot for the sky in no time, giving you quick shade even if you're starting from a modest 4- or 5-foot size.

AMUR CHOKECHERRY (*Prunus maackii*)

Plant this densely branched round-headed tree if you want to draw birds to your yard. After it produces small white flowers in May, black fruits appear, then disappear as feathered friends eat them. The highly glossy cinnamon- or russet-colored bark is attractive in all seasons. This tree grows 35 to 45 feet tall. Zones 2 to 6.

CUCUMBER TREE (*Magnolia acuminata*)

This magnolia has a beautiful pyramidal to rounded shape and bold tropical-looking dark green foliage. Large yellow-green flowers bloom from May to June, and the fruits that follow resemble cucumbers—split open to show dark pink seeds. The cultivar 'Elizabeth' has stunning primrose yellow flowers. If you need a large-scale tree, this one grows 50 to 80 feet tall with a similar spread. Zones 3 to 8.

JAPANESE PAGODA TREE (*Sophora japonica*)

You'll feel cool under the wide spreading canopy of this tree. It has lustrous dark green compound leaves and lovely creamy white fragrant flower clusters in July and August, when little else is blooming. It grows 50 to 75 feet tall. Zones 4 to 8.

JAPANESE ZELKOVA (*Zelkova serrata*)

The vase shape of this tree gives it an elm-like look. It has dark green, rough, pointed oval leaves with variable autumn color ranging from yellow through reddish purple. The bark is shiny on young plants and peels away as the tree ages. 'Village Green' is an excellent very-fast-growing cultivar that will reach 50 to 75 feet tall. Zones 5 to 8.

RIVER BIRCH (*Betula nigra*)

Here's a graceful tree that changes shape from pyramidal while it's young to rounded at maturity. It has lustrous medium green leaves and pink to cinnamon-colored bark that peels away from the trunk and looks especially stunning in winter. 'Heritage' has almost white bark. This is the very best birch for hot summer areas, though it likes moist soil. It's resistant to birch borers and grows 40 to 70 feet tall. Zones 4 to 9.

Small Trees Make a Better Buy

Bigger is not better when it comes to planting trees. "A 2- or 3-foot tree will catch up with a 6-footer in two seasons," Bob Brzuszek states flatly. As curator of the Crosby Arboretum in Picayune, Mississippi, Bob doesn't have time or money to waste, so he routinely sets out small trees.

Smaller trees cost less and weigh less than bigger ones, so you not only spend less money buying plants, you also spend less time and effort planting. Since small trees have small root systems, they don't need a lot of care. "From a watering and fertilizing perspective, it's the only way to go," Bob says. Plus, they survive better than large plants, so you avoid the cost of replacing big expensive trees that die from transplant shock.

If you need to plant new trees near existing plantings, small trees are easy to tuck between the roots of other plants. Since you don't have to disturb the soil much to get them in the ground, the existing plants don't suffer.

When they buy their small trees, the staff at Crosby Arboretum selects tough species that are adapted to their local soils and conditions. They go with species that have a history of growing well in harsh conditions, like urban areas where the soil is compacted, and winds and sun are harsh.

John Cretti, the "Rocky Mountain Horticulturist" in Golden, Colorado, recommends that high-country gardeners do the same, using plants that are adapted to their area, "not just the fast growers that are often short-lived or need frequent trimming."

Kim Mulcahy goes for quality, not instant effect when he chooses trees. He's an urban gardener and a member of New York City's "Green Guerillas," a nonprofit group that converts abandoned building sites into local community gardens. Kim says that by choosing young trees, you can afford good features like disease resistance, improved flowers and fruiting, attractive foliage and habit. Really young trees won't give you instant results like large ones, but the years go by so fast you'll hardly notice the wait. That's because young trees grow faster than older ones—planting isn't as stressful for them, so they get established faster. And, since young trees aren't as stressed from moving as older trees, they're likely to have fewer disease and insect problems too.

Dig Wide, Not Deep

Most tree roots don't grow deep, so dig your tree holes wide and shallow. Bob Brzuszek, curator of the Crosby Arboretum in Picayune, Mississippi, found that digging deep holes for trees is a waste of time and good compost. "Except in the rare patches of deep, moist, well-drained riverbank soils, roots in our wet climate are generally shallow, where they can breathe," Bob says. For the best results, he digs wide, shallow holes for his trees and plants them in the native soil. Bob says he saves time by not adding soil amendments and the trees do just fine—unless he's setting out a really fussy one.

For finicky trees, Bob recommends using peat moss as a soil amendment rather than compost, because the compost compacts a little too much and doesn't last very long. He says a combination of peat moss and compost would probably be the best way to amend soil, but he doesn't have the time. And since most trees thrive without any additions, Bob finds planting in native soil is the easiest way to go.

Make your planting hole only as deep as your tree's existing root system. Use the soil line on the trunk to find the depth the tree grew at in the nursery, and replant it at the same level.

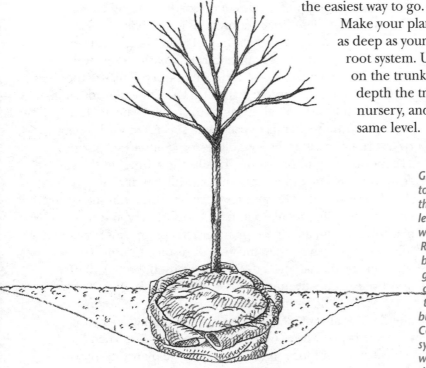

Give tree roots room to spread by making the planting hole at least five times as wide as the root ball. Remove any rope or binding that might girdle the trunk, and cut off and remove the top half of the burlap wrap. Completely remove synthetic burlap wrap—it doesn't decompose.

357

Boost Tree Growth with Soil Organisms

TREAT YOUR

NEW TREES

WITH MIGHTY

MICROBES

Give your trees a jump start with compost or a few shovelfuls of fresh, moist woodland soil at planting time. (Compost is the best choice unless you have your own woods—and a spot where you can dig up a little soil, without disturbing existing plants.) These materials are rich in worms, beneficial bacteria and fungi, and other soil organisms, which help soils come alive and make roots thrive.

Use fresh material that hasn't dried out or baked in the sun. Simply mix the compost or woodland soil lightly into the top layer of your planting area and quickly cover it with an organic mulch. The mulch protects the microbes by keeping them cool and shady, and it will soon begin to compost itself, feeding the soil organisms you've added.

How do these organisms help your trees grow? "It's long been known that forest fungi form symbiotic relationships with tree roots," explains Dr. Donald Marx, chairman of Plant Health Care, a Pittsburgh company that provides products and services that correct plant health problems. Dr. Marx's pioneering studies of mycorrhizal fungi earned him the Wallenberg Prize (equivalent to the Nobel Prize) and may have a big impact on tree planting in the future.

Mycorrhizal fungi occur naturally in healthy forest soil, but they're difficult to grow in the laboratory. Because the fungi are so important to tree health, Dr. Marx is producing off-the-shelf forest fungal products for homeowners. He's come up with inoculants to use on all species of yard trees (plus ornamentals and vegetables); see "Sources" on page 412 for ordering information. To add these fungi to the soil around plants, mix them into the backfill soil during planting or mix them into the soil before you plant seeds. Or try a root-dip inoculant to treat roots when you transplant. When you add these plant-specific organisms to your soil, you'll get really dramatic growth results. Compost won't make as dramatic a difference by itself, but it will help improve the effectiveness of these beneficial fungi.

Dr. Marx believes inoculants will eventually be recommended for almost all planting situations. That's because you usually plant trees (and other plants) in disturbed soil—instead of forest soil where there are plenty of mycorrhizal fungi present.

Stop Staking Trees

New trees grow better without stakes. "It's not always necessary or even advisable to stake a newly planted tree," claims Michael Hollins, president of the Ecosystem Recovery Institute and Sylvan Native Nursery and Seed Company in New Freedom, Pennsylvania. "In fact, when treetops are allowed to move with the wind, they develop a larger root system and a stronger, thicker trunk."

Michael points out there are some situations where you still have to use stakes—but they're the exception. Stakes are important on sites that are so windy that roots can't take hold in the surrounding soil. Plus, there are some big-headed, top-heavy trees like maples and oaks that may need stakes to get them through their first growing season. And, you may have to stake trees in sandy soil if it's so loose it won't hold them upright.

"Something else to consider is whether the tree is bareroot or container grown. It's easier to make strong soil contact with bareroot trees," Michael says. "So I stake them only if they'll be up against a lot of wind."

When you do have to stake a tree, use the method pictured on this page. It's recommended by Dr. Alex Shigo, former chief scientist and Pioneering Project Leader for the United States Forest Service. It supports the tree but lets it move enough to develop a strong trunk and roots.

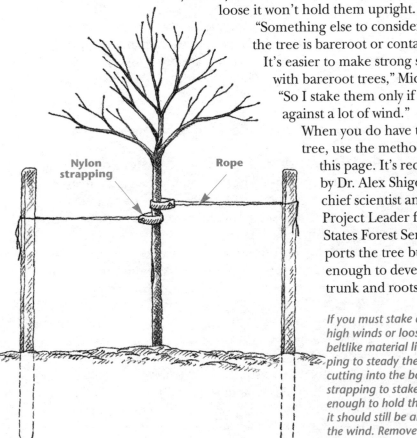

Nylon strapping

Rope

If you must stake a tree because of high winds or loose soil, use broad beltlike material like nylon strapping to steady the tree without cutting into the bark. Tie the strapping to stakes just tight enough to hold the tree upright— it should still be able to sway in the wind. Remove the stakes as soon as the tree can support itself.

Planting Trees without Water

IT DOESN'T
HURT TO PRAY
FOR RAIN

You can save time and trouble hauling buckets of water and hoses around if you plant trees when they don't need water. If you time planting right, you don't need to haul water—an important consideration when you plant trees a long distance from a water source or plant lots of trees at one time.

"Plant dormant trees in the seasons when temperatures are cooler and precipitation is more abundant," says Bonnie Lee Appleton, a tree specialist at Virginia Tech. In most areas, late fall to early spring is the best time, depending on when the soil is thawed enough to dig holes. Freezing temperatures generally won't damage dormant trees, Bonnie says. She points out that you're more likely to have enough soil moisture to get roots established during spring and fall. And once the trees have strong root systems, they're more likely to survive dry spells later in the season.

Here's another tip from Bonnie. "The night before planting, soak the roots in a bucket of water so they can take up extra water. Then pray for rain."

Sound Watering Practice Means Big Savings

A little water makes a lot of difference in how fast your trees grow. Why does their growth rate matter? Because, according to Sam Jones, owner of Atlantic Star Tree Nursery in Forest Hill, Maryland, "A mature landscape tree can enhance property values by $20,000." That's a pretty strong incentive to get your trees growing and keep them growing. Here's Sam's simple summertime watering technique to protect your investments the easy way.

Sam says, "The best way to water is slowly so that the feeder roots can take up the moisture as it's provided." That way the trees get every drop of water you give them, so there's no waste or runoff. Pull your hose up to a tree and turn it on to a slow drip. Leave the hose on for a few hours or overnight. Put it on a timer if you're afraid you'll forget to turn it off. Move the hose to a different tree every night—it takes only a few minutes—and keep at it until you water all the trees in your yard, or until the rains come.

Double-Quick Watering Technique for New Trees

Deep watering can cut your watering time in half. Balled-and-burlapped trees don't handle drought well and that means lots of time with a hose, unless you know this quick watering technique. It comes from Rose Vincent of Vincent Landscapes in Austin, Texas, who says it's the method she recommends to her clients.

Push a hose down into the soil where the root ball meets the hole you dug for it, until it won't go any further. Then turn the hose on so the flow is a little more than a drip or trickle but much less than a full-force gush. Let it run until water freely bubbles up out of the hole. Then remove the hose and fill the hole with soil.

Rose says that this method cuts watering time in half for trees and large shrubs and ensures that there are no dry pockets around the root ball. How often you water depends on the weather; during a typical year, she suggests watering a newly planted tree or shrub twice a week. Use this treatment for just the first year; after that the roots should be well enough established that you can water the soil surface during dry weather.

Make watering go better and faster by pushing the end of your hose down into the loosened soil around newly planted trees. This method brings water right to the root ball and eliminates wasteful surface runoff.

Trees That Make Fruit Cleanup a Breeze

So you like the look of fruiting trees but not the cleanup. Here's how to get the look without the raking. "People ask me to recommend varieties of trees that don't have messy fruit," says Bonnie Lee Appleton, a tree specialist at Virginia Tech. "Since fruit is important for wildlife, I try to steer them to varieties that have smaller fruits." Bonnie says smaller fruits stay on the tree longer and are so attractive to birds that they never end up on the ground.

One tree Bonnie is very enthusiastic about is the crabapple. She says people avoid it because of problems with rust and scab, but there's no need to. There are excellent disease-resistant cultivars available with beautiful small fruits. Bonnie suggests you check with your local extension service to find the best selections for your area. New cultivars come out every year so you can pick trees with better disease resistance, more flowers, and small or large heights.

Leaf Yourself More Free Time

Rake leaves under the rug, so to speak, and you'll have a clean yard and a weed-free zone wherever you choose. "I used to have a backyard with humongous trees, which generated prodigious mounds of leaves, which overwhelmed my compost pile," says David Daulton, who gardens in Columbus, Ohio. His solution was to create a "leaf garden."

On a day when the wind was in his favor, David would rake the leaves into a bed of low-growing fragrant sumacs that grew along his fence. The combination of the wind, the fence, and the sumac branches kept the leaves from blowing away. Much of the pile would shrink by spring, but enough would remain to smother weeds.

Erin Hynes, author of *Rodale's Successful Organic Gardening: Improving the Soil,* used a similar method, raking leaves under the row of tall evergreens that grew in front of the fence at the back of her property. She found that 2- and 3-foot-high leaf piles would break down within a few months. It's a great way to avoid bagging leaves and beautify a weedy row of trees or shrubs.

5 No-Fuss Crabapples

Crabapples add pizzazz to your landscape with beautiful flowers and small fruits that attract birds. You'll find there are hundreds of cultivars to choose from. Most leave a lot to be desired because they are susceptible to diseases that result in lots of lawn litter. You can avoid disease problems and lawn raking if you pick disease-resistant trees like those below. All are hardy to at least Zone 4 and are resistant to the diseases scab and fire blight.

'ADAMS' CRABAPPLE (*Malus* 'Adams')

This broad-headed tree has a rounded form and grows 25 feet tall. It has crimson flowers and oblong ½-inch fruits that turn deep red in July, maroon by August, and last until spring. Leaves are bronze to red in early spring, green with red veins in summer, and bright orange in autumn. This is an older cultivar that has stood the test of time.

'DONALD WYMAN' CRABAPPLE
(*Malus* 'Donald Wyman')

This tree has a rounded to upright-spreading crown that reaches 20 feet tall. In spring, its red buds open into white flowers that are followed by ½-inch fruits. The crabapples turn bright scarlet in September, oxblood red by November, and persist until birds eat them just before flowering the following spring. Leaves turn yellow to bronze in fall.

'PRAIRIFIRE' CRABAPPLE (*Malus* 'Prairifire')

Here's a rounded tree that grows 20 feet tall. It has rich rose pink flowers and glossy foliage that emerges red and turns green with red veins. The ½-inch fruits turn deep red by July and maroon by November. They last until hungry birds claim them in March.

'SENTINEL' CRABAPPLE (*Malus* 'Sentinel')

Young trees have a columnar shape but grow upright-spreading as they reach a mature height of 18 feet. Its red buds open to pink-edged flowers that fade to white. The ⅜-inch fruits turn crimson by August, oxblood red by November, and stay on the tree until April.

'WALTERS' SIBERIAN CRABAPPLE
(*Malus baccata* 'Walters')

If you want vigorous growth and a rounded form, 'Walters' is your tree. It grows 20 to 50 feet tall and has glossy dark green leaves. Its rose red buds open into pink-flushed flowers that fade to white. The ⅜-inch fruits turn gold with an orange blush in September and light cider color by November. Fruits decorate the tree until birds devour them in April.

5 Trees That Need No Cleanup

Some trees such as sycamores and willows will have you cleaning up after them all year long. Give yourself a break and leave messy trees for parks and wilder settings. Near your home choose trees with neat habits like those listed below.

BALD CYPRESS (*Taxodium distichum*)

This graceful deciduous conifer has a pyramidal shape and grows 50 to 70 feet tall. Its needles are soft green in summer and turn warm russet in late fall. The needles grow only ½ inch long—they're so small you don't have to rake them. Rounded cones stay on the tree for a year. Bald cypress can take wet or dry conditions and is pest-free. Zones 4 to 9.

GINKGO (*Ginkgo biloba*)

Depending on the cultivar, ginkgos grow narrowly pyramidal to wide spreading and can reach 50 to 80 feet tall. Fan-shaped leaves turn bright yellow in fall and drop all at once after a freeze, so you only have to rake once. They tolerate urban conditions and are pest- and disease-free. Plant male cultivars since females have vile-smelling fruits. Zones 4 to 9.

SWEET BAY MAGNOLIA (*Magnolia virginiana*)

The multi-stemmed trunk and oval shape of this tree add variety to plantings. It grows 10 to 25 feet tall and has long, lustrous, evergreen or semi-evergreen leaves that hang on late and drop gradually so you don't notice them fall; creamy yellow flowers appear in May and June. It grows in heavy and wet soils and will tolerate a little shade. This plant has no significant pest or disease problems. Zones 5 to 9.

WHITE FRINGE TREE (*Chionanthus virginicus*)

This tree grows 15 to 20 feet tall and may be open and spreading or bushy. White dangling flower clusters appear in May and June and are followed by dark blue fruits—there's no fall cleanup since birds eat the ripe fruit. It likes moist soil but can handle most sites. It's relatively free of insect and disease problems and tolerates air pollution. Zones 3 to 9.

'WINTER KING' GREEN HAWTHORN (*Crataegus viridis* 'Winter King')

This round-headed tree grows to 25 feet tall. Its showy white flowers bloom in May and are followed by clusters of bright red fruits. The lustrous medium green leaves turn scarlet to purple in fall. The leaves are small and the fruits stay on the tree most of the winter so you can forget about fall cleanup. This is the least thorny and most disease-resistant hawthorn. It has a neat growth habit that looks shapely without pruning. Zones 5 to 9.

Cut Out 2 Tree Pests

The more you know about pests, the easier it is to foil their plans to destroy your trees. Here are some tips about tree caterpillars from extension entomologist Dr. Philip Nixon at the University of Illinois Cooperative Extension Service that will help you get the most out of pest control techniques.

Destroy eastern tent caterpillars. You can cut out the nests of worms that spin webs in trees, but for best results do the cutting at the right time. Eastern tent caterpillars feed outside their nests during the day, so cut them and their nests out of your trees when they return from feeding in the evening.

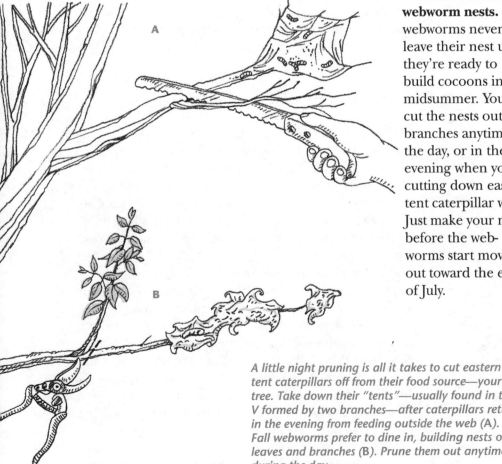

Whack out fall webworm nests. Fall webworms never leave their nest until they're ready to build cocoons in midsummer. You can cut the nests out of branches anytime of the day, or in the evening when you're cutting down eastern tent caterpillar webs. Just make your move before the webworms start moving out toward the end of July.

A little night pruning is all it takes to cut eastern tent caterpillars off from their food source—your tree. Take down their "tents"—usually found in the V formed by two branches—after caterpillars return in the evening from feeding outside the web (A). Fall webworms prefer to dine in, building nests over leaves and branches (B). Prune them out anytime during the day.

Pruning by the Pictures

Know what you want your tree to look like before you haul out the pruning shears. "Most nonfruit-bearing trees need little pruning," claims Bonnie Lee Appleton, a tree specialist at Virginia Tech. Before you start cutting on any of your trees, look at a picture of a mature specimen of your tree. You'll find photos in tree encyclopedias or field guides, or take your own photos when you visit parks or botanic gardens. "This will remind you of the natural shape of the tree and give you a direction to aim for if the tree is wayward," Bonnie says.

She adds that one of the biggest mistakes you can make is to prune the bottom branches off of trees like hemlock, holly, or spruce. This kind of pruning destroys the way the trees look and their landscape value too. When you're tempted to do some pruning, a quick glance at a picture will remind you to put the loppers down!

Make the Cut While It's within Reach

FOR SHAPELY
TREES, NIP
PROBLEMS IN
THE BUD

"It's a lot easier to prune a small tree than a tall one," notes Sam Jones, owner of Atlantic Star Tree Nursery in Forest Hill, Maryland. Sam manages to avoid lots of ladder work by cutting out potential problems while trees are young and easy to reach from the ground. There are two areas to concentrate on, Sam says. Here's how he prunes his small trees so they don't need pruning work when they're tall.

Weed out bad branches first. Start by removing the weaker branch of any interior branches that cross or rub. While you're at it, remove any spindly or damaged branches. When you cut out a branch, cut to the trunk leaving a slight shoulder. Cut on an angle that will slant away from the trunk. "If you cut right to the trunk, you're exposing a larger area than necessary," Sam explains. The smaller the wound you make, the faster the tree can seal it off against diseases and pests. See the illustration on the opposite page for the best way to make a pruning cut.

Shape new branches next. When the cleanup work is done, "Stand back and look at the tree," Sam says. "Are the branches well spaced? Are there more on one side than the other?" If your tree looks off balance, you can redirect some of the branches by cutting them back to buds that point in the direction you want.

Always prune just above the bud you want to keep. Buds that point away from the tree will become branches that grow out and let air and light into the tree. Buds that point in toward the tree will become branches that fill in the tree's center. In most cases, you'll want to prune to buds that point away from the tree so you'll open it up and get good air circulation. Too many branches on the inside crowd each other which stresses the tree, gives insects places to hide, and looks bad.

"As far as when to prune, just before bud swell in early spring is right for just about everything," Sam says. So get an early start while your trees are small.

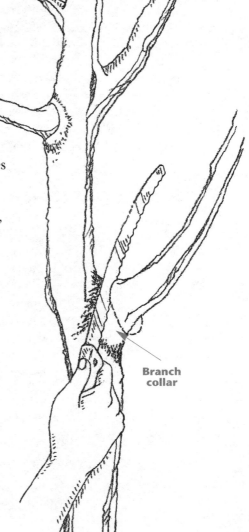

Branch collar

When you prune a branch back to the trunk of your tree, make the cut where the branch and branch collar (swollen area) meet. By pruning your trees right while they're young, you'll avoid a lot of care and pruning as they mature.

Simple Stump Removal

Sometimes you're stuck with a stump you can't landscape around or transform into a birdbath. Short of calling in a stump removal service, what's the fastest way to make it disappear?

LET BENEFICIAL MICROBES TURN TREE STUMPS INTO SOIL

"Here's what I do," says Sue Bloodgood, owner of Happy Hollow Nursery in Cockeysville, Maryland. "Cut the stump as close to the ground as possible." That's pretty straightforward, but what Sue suggests next makes all the difference. Make some cuts into the wood with an ax or use a drill and bore holes. Dig up a bucket of soil from the woods—the woodland soil contains wood-digesting microbes that lawn and garden soils don't have. (If you don't have a woods, substitute fresh compost.) Add a few handfuls of blood meal for extra nitrogen and cover the stump with the mix. Within a year, your stump will be gone and you'll have a great pocket of soil for a choice new plant. (If you'd like a nicer look while the stump breaks down, plant a vine like ivy or vinca on top of the woodland soil mix.)

Turn an Old Stump into a Work of Art

Tree stumps make great additions to your landscape. You've just got to know how to transform them from an eyesore into a thing of beauty. If you've ever tried to dig up the old stump of a large tree, you know that it's a backbreaking job. Fortunately, you can leave the stump where it is and incorporate it into the design of your garden. That's the advice of C. Colston Burrell, owner of the Minnesota-based design firm, Native Landscapes. Here are some simple ways Cole deals with stumps.

• Cut the top of the stump off to make it level, and use it as a pedestal for a birdbath, sundial, or sculpture.

• If the stump is a hardwood such as oak, carve it into a garden statue with a wood chisel.

• Hollow the stump out and fill it with water to serve as a birdbath, or fill it with soil and make it into a planter.

Cole has turned a number of stumps into planters and found they work just great. "I have one stump in my yard right now that's planted with woodland flowers like dwarf coral bells and partridgeberry," he says.

Other nice plants for a stump garden include creeping groundcovers such as euonymous and periwinkle, and ferns and wildflowers such as wood ferns (*Dryopteris* spp.) and foamflower (*Tiarella cordifolia*) for shady areas. For sun, try ornamental grasses, foliage plants such as bergenia (*Bergenia cordifolia*), or trailing annuals such as lantana, lobelia, and vining nasturtiums.

Turn an old stump into a birdbath—just hollow out a shallow depression and fill it with water. Your feathered friends will drop by to sip and splash. Birds prefer shallow water, so if you dig too deeply, fill the stump with soil instead and make it a planter.

VEGETABLES

Try Trouble-Saving, Self-Sown Vegetables

Take it easy in fall and you'll be amazed at the bounty of young vegetable plants that sprout voluntarily in your garden in spring. All you have to do is let your spent crops go to seed and hold off on turning your garden soil until late spring. Many vegetables will reseed to give you another season's harvest.

Alan Kapuler, director of research for Seeds of Change, a national organic seed company in Santa Fe, New Mexico, says "Just wait to see what comes up and use them as a transplant." The freebies save you from buying or growing transplants and make a nice spring surprise. Amaranth, peppers, and tomatoes all reseed reliably and Alan has also had success with the following crops.

- Beets

- Chinese greens

- Fava beans

- Lettuce

- Shungiku or chop suey greens (*Chrysanthemum coronarium*)

- Sunflowers

A   B   C

When your lettuce bolts (goes to seed) in summer (A), don't pull it out. Let a few plants sow their seeds in your garden for next year's crop. Self-sown seeds are ready to sprout as soon as good weather comes along in spring (B). You'll get a head start on planting without setting foot in your garden's cold, wet soil. Plus you'll enjoy an extra-early harvest (C).

JUST SAY "NO" TO PULLING WEEDS

If you have a lovely crop of weeds growing in your vegetable garden, you may want to celebrate! Some wild plants make tasty greens, says Roger Swain, host of PBS's *Victory Garden.* And they're about as easy to raise as a vegetable can get. Just let them grow and harvest them when they reach the right stage.

Roger harvests the spring greens on dandelions before they bloom by using a penknife to cut dandelion roots off below the ground. He calls them "Exquisite!" and enjoys sautéing them in bacon fat and dressing them with a splash of vinegar.

Two other prolific delicacies are lamb's-quarters and purslane, both common garden weeds. "I make sure to get both of these wild edibles when they are young and tender," Roger says. "I nip off the top 3 to 4 inches of the plant for steaming or salads, then cut the rest of the plant down." How easy can vegetable growing get?

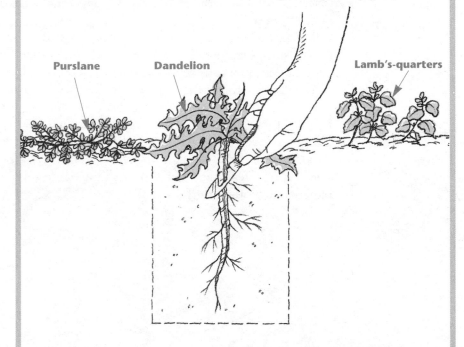

Purslane   Dandelion   Lamb's-quarters

Edible weeds make great additions to salads and side dishes—why fight them when you can eat them! Gather the tender top 3 to 4 inches of purslane or lamb's-quarters before cutting off the rest of the plant. Use a knife to harvest dandelion greens by cutting the roots off below soil level.

Presprout Seeds for a Speedy Harvest

Get heat-loving crops off to a good start the easy, early way by presprouting seeds. It's a great way to get a jump on the season with crops like corn and squash—without spreading sheets of plastic to warm the soil. Presprouting also eliminates thinning, and it can save space since you won't need to start flats and flats of seeds.

Nancy Bubel, author of *The New Seed-Starter's Handbook*, says "Starting the germination process takes only a few minutes." Here's her technique.

Use one paper towel for every type of seed you want to start. Write the plant name on the paper towel with a ballpoint pen. Dampen the paper towel, smooth it out, and spread the seeds on it so they're not touching. Then roll up the paper towel with the seeds in it. When you're finished, place the rolled up towels in a plastic bag. You can put several rolls in one bag.

The next step is to incubate the seeds. Close the bag loosely since seeds need oxygen to germinate. Place the bags of seeds in a consistently warm (70° to 80°F) place. Nancy uses the top of the refrigerator or hot water heater.

Check your seeds for sprouting every day, misting them lightly if they seem a little dry. You want to catch the seeds after they have begun to form roots but before they are so far along that the roots grow into the paper towels. (If that does happen, tear the towel and plant the damp shred of paper right along with the seed.)

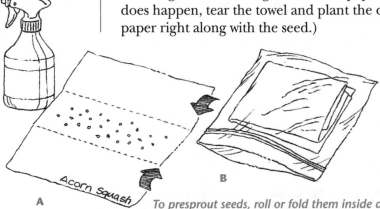

A   B

To presprout seeds, roll or fold them inside a damp paper towel. Rolling lets you start more seeds per towel. Folding keeps seedling roots from getting tangled up. To use this technique, fold a paper towel in thirds, place seeds in the middle, then fold the ends over the seeds (A). Fold the towel in half and place it in a plastic bag (B). Gently unfold the towel to check on seeds.

When the seeds sprout, plant them with the little tail, or radicle, going down—use tweezers to handle small seeds. You can transplant the sprouts into pots or plant them directly into your garden.

Nancy pots up her melons for extra growth but sets pre-sprouted corn, cucumbers, and squash right into the garden. "For the small amount of set-up time, harvests are at least two weeks earlier," Nancy says. She adds that pre-sprouting seeds also makes sense if you have expensive, scarce, or heirloom seeds that you don't want to risk losing.

You can presprout all kinds of seeds. Just remember that some seeds like lettuce need light to germinate—in that case, lay the towels flat instead of rolling them up.

Furrow-Free Method Speeds Seed Sowing

"FINGER PLANTING" CUTS SEED-SOWING TIME IN HALF

Who needs furrows? Fern Marshall Bradley, a Rodale garden book editor, doesn't waste time making furrows when she sows beans, peas, and onion sets. "I just prepare my soil so it's nice and loose, and then poke the seeds down into it," Fern says.

If you sow seeds the traditional way, you'll have to make a furrow, set the seeds in it, then cover the seeds, she says. Plus there's the added step of fixing the furrow if it caves in while you're sowing. Fern estimates that her method of poking seeds into the soil with her fingers saves her about ten minutes per 50-foot row. "I'd even go so far as to say you could cut your seeding time in half," she says. Fern adds that all her plants come up just as well getting poked into the ground as they do planted in a furrow.

For even greater time savings, use this method to plant onion sets. When you poke onion sets into the ground, they don't get knocked over the way they do when you set them in a furrow, so you don't have to straighten and rearrange them.

To get the proper planting depth, Fern uses a handy tool—her hand. She tucks beans and peas into the soil to about the depth of her thumb; onion sets go in just so their tips are covered. Then she lightly firms the soil over the planting area. When she feels like being precise, Fern lays a yardstick on top of the soil to keep her spacing even.

Pick Fast-Producing Vegetable Crops

For an extra-quick harvest, plant vegetable cultivars that mature fast. Check the number of days until harvest listed with plant descriptions on seed packets and in catalogs. Choose the cultivars that mature earliest. They don't take any more effort than growing later-maturing vegetables, but you'll get fresh produce several days to two weeks earlier.

When you taste the first fresh tomato or bean of the season, you'll see why Howard-Yana Shapiro, Ph.D., director of agriculture for Seeds of Change, a mail-order seed company that sells organic seeds, recommends these early-producing cultivars. (For information on ordering early cultivars, see "Sources" on page 412.)

PLANT SHORT-
SEASON CROPS
FOR HURRY-UP
HARVESTS

Bush Beans

'Provider' snap	(50 days)
'Roc D'Or' yellow wax	(52 to 60 days)
'Golden Lumen' wax	(54 to 60 days)
'Royalty Purple Podded' snap	(55 days)
'Beurre de Roquencourt' wax	(55 to 60 days)

Pole Beans

'Oregon Giant' snap	(55 to 60 days)
'Black Seeded Blue Lake' snap	(55 to 63 days)
'Cascade Giant Stringless' snap	(58 days)

Summer Squash

'Round French' zucchini	(45 days)
'Caserta' zucchini	(50 to 57 days)
'Cocozelle' bush zucchini	(55 days)
'Golden Scallopini' bush	(55 days)

Sweet Peppers

'Ecuadorian Sweet Relleno'	(62 to 65 days)
'Earliest Red Sweet'	(70 days)

Tomatoes

'Oregon Spring'	(55 to 70 days)
'Stupice'	(60 to 70 days)
'Orange Queen'	(65 to 70 days)
'Early Red Chief'	(70 days)

Outsmart Vegetable Pests

Get to know the insect pests that bug you and you'll have an easier time controlling them. When you know their habits, it's simpler and cheaper to arrange your garden and control measures to keep them out. Extension entomologist Dr. Philip Nixon at the University of Illinois Cooperative Extension Service shares these tips.

Play keep-away with spud and squash pests. Colorado potato beetles and squash bugs overwinter near where their victims grew. You can reduce next year's infestation by moving susceptible crops to a different part of the yard—the farther away, the better.

Grow squash that borers don't like. If squash vine borers make mush of your squash plants, grow butternut squash—it's not as susceptible as other winter squashes. And grow vining rather than bush summer squash; because the vines root at leaf nodes, a borer in one part of the stem isn't likely to cut off the water supply to the whole plant.

Eat corn before corn earworms do. Because corn earworms usually attack corn late in the summer, you can avoid damage by planting a short-season cultivar. Look for cultivars that mature in 70 days or less.

Knock off tomato hornworms in the morning. Check your plants for these big green caterpillars early in the day. That's when they perch at the top of tomato plants and are easy to find, pick off, and squish.

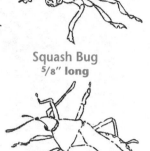

Colorado Potato Beetle
1/3" long

Squash Bug
5/8" long

Squash Vine Borer
1" long

Corn Earworm
1"–2" long

Tomato Hornworm
4" long

Vines and Trellises

Quick Trellises from Trees

Pick up sticks when you want a trellis in a hurry. Harold Greer, owner of Greer Gardens in Eugene, Oregon, got the idea for using tree branches as trellises on a trip to England. "And they're so easy," he says. "Just stick an interesting-looking forked branch in the ground or rest it against a wall." They make great trellises for lightweight vines like clematis (*Clematis* spp.) or passionflowers (*Passiflora* spp.).

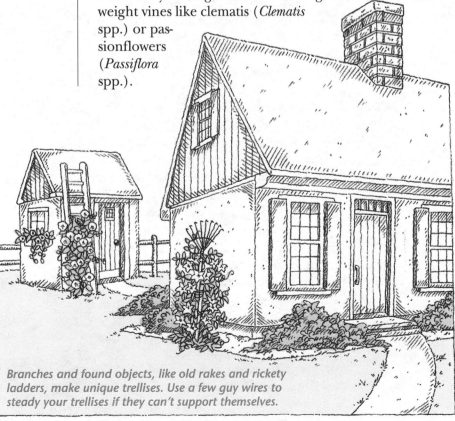

Branches and found objects, like old rakes and rickety ladders, make unique trellises. Use a few guy wires to steady your trellises if they can't support themselves.

PROVEN PLANTS
FOR QUICK COVER-UPS

To beautify your home in a hurry or quickly hide an unpleasant view, plant fast-growing flowering vines that also have great-looking foliage. "Vines are fast, easy, inexpensive, and remarkably beautiful, too," says C. Colston Burrell, owner of the Minnesota-based design firm, Native Landscapes, who recommends the following plants for decoration or screens.

Clematis (*Clematis* spp.)
Even when its flowers aren't in bloom, this perennial plant looks handsome, thanks to an abundance of bright green or blue green leaves. The showy star- or bell-shaped blooms appear in summer and fall in shades of white, pink, red, purple, and blue. Zones 3 to 9, depending on species.

Dutchman's-pipe vine (*Aristolochia durior*)
Try this perennial vine where you need the shade of its overlapping heart-shaped leaves. Look for the unique yellow and purple pipe-shaped flowers in spring. Zones 5 to 8.

Five-leaf akebia (*Akebia quinata*)
This perennial vine's soft blue green five-leaflet leaves are evergreen in warm areas. In spring, unusual purplish flowers dangle under the newly emerging leaves—they're not showy but are fragrant. Zones 5 to 8.

Scarlet runner bean (*Phaseolus coccineus*)
Soft green bean-type leaves set off this creepers brilliant scarlet flowers. Hummingbirds like the flowers—you'll like the tasty, edible beans. This vine is perennial in South America, where it's native. It's treated as an annual farther north.

Trumpet honeysuckle (*Lonicera sempervirens*)
In warm climates, this perennial vine's shiny oval leaves stay evergreen. Clusters of bright orange or red flowers put on a spectacular show from late spring through summer. Zones 4 to 9.

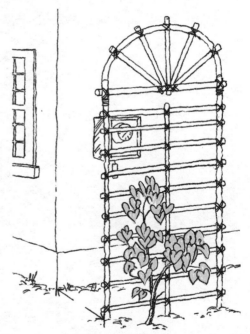

Keep electric meters, air conditioners, and other unsightly necessities out of sight but still accessible. Install a freestanding trellis and plant it with a flowering vine such as Dutchman's-pipe vine. Place the trellis 2 feet out from the item you want to hide.

Plastic Trellis Provides Prompt Privacy

Create a portable privacy screen that will let you grow vines wherever you want them, by using inexpensive PVC pipes and a few 5-gallon buckets. You'll have time to spare for planting the vines if you use this simple design from gardener Pauline Neilson of Birmingham, Alabama.

"We were facing the loss of privacy on our deck with the construction of a new house next door, so we decided to construct a trellis and grow vines and climbing things on it," recalls Pauline. Here's how they did it. First, she and her husband built the base. They capped three 2-foot lengths of 2-inch-diameter PVC pipe on one end, filled three 5-gallon plastic buckets halfway with Redi-Mix cement, and set each capped end into one of the buckets of cement.

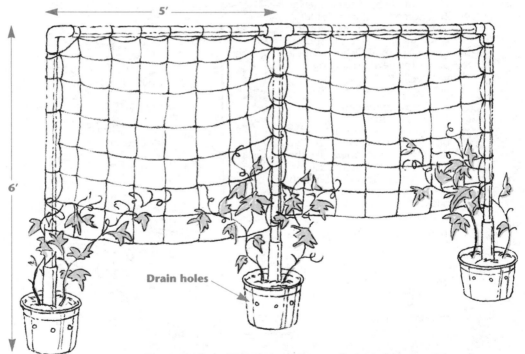

5'

6'

Drain holes

Plastic buckets, PVC pipe, netting, and plants form a quick and easy-to-move privacy screen that you can adjust to fit any size site. Use quick-growing annual vines like those listed on page 380 to turn your homegrown structure into a lush, living screen.

Then they made a trellis frame to insert into the 2-inch pipes. They used three 6-foot lengths of 1½-inch-diameter PVC pipe for the vertical supports and two 5-foot lengths of pipe for the horizontal support. They connected the two vertical supports at either end of the trellis to the horizontal pipes with L connectors and to the center vertical support with a T connector. Pauline says they found the PVC pipe surprisingly easy to work with.

PIPE IN A LITTLE PRIVACY WITH A PVC TRELLIS

When the frame was finished, they draped trellis netting over the whole thing to support the plants. Since the support buckets were only half full of cement, Pauline and her husband drilled drainage holes just above the cement level and filled each bucket with soil. Then they planted vining plants into the soil.

Pauline says they store the trellis when winter comes—it's easy to remove from its cement-bucket supports.

Support Vines with Stakes of Steel

Use a strong stake right from the start and you'll have no worries when your prized vine matures. "If you have vining plants, and you need to give them a little trellis, don't use bamboo," warns Cheryl Long, research editor at *Organic Gardening* magazine. She uses plastic-coated steel stakes to build custom-size trellises for her container-grown vines. Cheryl lays three or four stakes parallel and then wires another stake across the top of the others to hold them together.

Cheryl explains that bamboo or wooden stakes are risky because they can rot. It's heartbreaking to spend a couple of years training and nursing a perennial vine, she says, only to have a stake rot out and the whole thing snap off. There's not a lot you can do to fix broken stakes—vines twine around them so you can't get at them or remove them.

Sturdy stakes are important for standards (plants trained to a single treelike stem) too, Cheryl notes; you don't want to see years of training wasted because a support rots away.

Annual Vines for Quick Color and Cover

*F*or plenty of striking foliage and nonstop, all-summer bloom, there's no substitute for the tropical look of annual vines. They can cover a fence or climb up a porch post in a jiffy, providing quick shade and screening. These vines are easy on the pocketbook, too, since most of them are easy to grow from seed. You can try a new one each year or switch to perennial vines when you're sure you've found the look you like. Most of the vines listed here are true annuals, but a few are tender perennials that are grown as annuals. Start all of these vines indoors for earlier bloom.

BALLOON VINE (*Cardiospermum halicacabum*)

Small single white flowers are followed by 1-inch-long, pale green, three-sided balloonlike seedpods that are fun to pop. The pods hold black seeds that are marked with a heart-shaped spot. Attractive, finely cut leaves cover the vines that twine to 12 feet in sun to partial shade.

CHILEAN GLORY FLOWER (*Eccremocarpus scaber*)

Grow this vine by a window where you can see the hummingbirds feed on its clusters of tubular orange, yellow, or cream flowers. Plant it in full sun for flowers all summer until frost. The vines twine to 15 feet, creating a lacy curtain of fine leaves and tiny tendrils.

CREEPING GLOXINIA (*Asarina erubescens*)

It's hard to resist a summerlong display of showy, tubular, rosy pink blooms. But that's what you'll get in sun or shade. The leaves are bright, blue-green, and arrowhead shaped on vines that twine to 15 feet.

CUP-AND-SAUCER VINE (*Cobaea scandens*)

This vine gets its name from its flowers that look like showy violet cups set on green saucers. It blooms from midsummer to frost in sun to partial shade. The flowers have stems long enough to make them useful as cut flowers. Oblong leaves cover this fast-growing 10- to 30-foot plant.

CYPRESS VINE (*Ipomoea quamoclit*)

Small, tubular, crimson flowers bloom all summerlong and attract hummingbirds to your garden. Extremely delicate lacy foliage covers these vines that grow to 20 feet in sun to partial shade.

FLAG-OF-SPAIN (*Mina lobata*)

Graceful arching sprays of tubular flowers open red and turn orange, yellow, then cream as they age—you'll see all of the colors on a single spray. The flowers bloom from mid-summer to frost in full sun. Vines twine to 6 feet with pretty fleur-de-lis-shaped leaves.

HYACINTH BEAN (*Dolichos lablab*)

For food and decoration, it's hard to beat this tender perennial. It has purple-veined three-leaflet leaves and purple stems. Spikes of white or purple pealike flowers are 15 inches long and bloom from midsummer until frost. They're followed by shiny flat purple pods that you can use as snap beans, shell beans, or dry beans. Vines twine to 20 feet.

MOONFLOWER (*Ipomoea alba*)

Light up summer evenings with large, fragrant, trumpet-shaped, white flowers that open before your eyes at sunset. These flowers stay open until dawn. Grow them in a sunny spot with morning glories for a round-the-clock flower combination. Heart-shaped leaves cover vines that grow to 12 feet.

MORNING GLORY (*Ipomoea tricolor*)

Abundant, sky blue, funnel-shaped flowers open in the morning, then fade and drop by afternoon. You'll get blooms all summer in sunny sites. Lush heart-shaped leaves adorn 15- to 20-foot vines.

PURPLE BELL VINE (*Rhodochiton atrosanguineum*)

Showy, maroon-purple, bell-shaped flowers stay attractive from midsummer to frost if you set plants in sun to partial shade. The vines twine to 8 feet and have delicate, red-tinged, heart-shaped leaves.

TWINING SNAPDRAGON (*Asarina scandens*)

You'll enjoy the violet, blue, pink, or white snapdragon-like flowers that bloom on this vine from midsummer to frost in sunny to shady sites. Bright green arrowhead-shaped leaves cover the vines that twine 4 to 8 feet.

VARIEGATED JAPANESE HOP (*Humulus japonicus* 'Variegatus')

Grow this vine for its attractive foliage and you won't be disappointed. Showy five- to seven-lobed leaves are splashed with white and cover vines that twine to 20 feet. Clusters of light green flowers are attractive but not particularly showy. A related plant, golden European hop (*H. lupulus* 'Aureus'), is a perennial and grows to 30 feet. It has pretty golden leaves and ornamental conelike fruits that are great for dried arrangements and for brewing beer.

Easy Maintenance Hinges on Trellis Design

A simple hinge can save you from wrestling with vines and reaching around trellises when it's time to paint your house. When you install a trellis next to a wall that needs painting or other maintenance, hinge the bottom of the trellis to let it drop out from the wall, says Mary Ann McGourty, co-owner of Hillside Gardens in Norfolk, Connecticut. "During painting or pruning, tie a rope to the trellis to hold it away from the wall without damaging the vine," she explains. The rest of the time you can keep the trellis upright by attaching it to the wall with a galvanized hook and eye.

Mary Ann adds that you should always leave 4 to 6 inches of dead space between a trellis and wall—you can do this by nailing a block of wood to the top of each trellis support post to act as a spacer. That keeps the vine healthy since it gets good air circulation, and it also keeps the vine from damaging the wall.

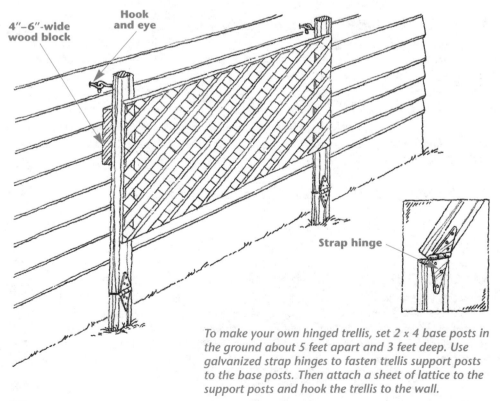

4"–6"-wide wood block

Hook and eye

Strap hinge

To make your own hinged trellis, set 2 x 4 base posts in the ground about 5 feet apart and 3 feet deep. Use galvanized strap hinges to fasten trellis support posts to the base posts. Then attach a sheet of lattice to the support posts and hook the trellis to the wall.

5 Vines That Need No Trellis

*H*ere's a group of vines that climb with no visible means of support. They don't need a trellis or training help since they climb with aerial rootlets or suction-cup-like adhesive disks. Because of their clingability, you'll want to restrict these vines to surfaces such as brick, stone, or siding that won't need painting later.

BOSTON IVY (*Parthenocissus tricuspidata*)

Pests don't bother this deciduous vine and it's pollution tolerant. It has glossy dark green three-lobed leaves that turn orange red in the fall. The flowers aren't showy but they're followed by blue black fruits that add autumn interest. It grows at a medium-to-fast rate and may climb to 50 feet or more. Zones 4 to 8. A good related plant, 'St. Paulii' Virginia creeper (*P. quinquefolia* 'St. Paulii'), is a better climber than its species, Zones 3 to 9.

CLIMBING HYDRANGEA
(*Hydrangea anomala* subsp. *petiolaris*)

Beautiful exfoliating cinnamon-colored bark and strongly horizontal branches lend winter interest to this deciduous vine. Glossy medium green leaves set off the flat clusters of showy white lacy flowers that bloom in late spring to early summer. This slow-growing plant may climb to 50 feet. Zones 4 to 7. Japanese hydrangea vine (*Schizophragma hydrangeoides*) is an attractive relative of climbing hydrangea that grows in Zones 5 to 7.

ENGLISH IVY (*Hedera helix*)

An evergreen vine for shady sites, English ivy features dark green, glossy, lobed foliage. Only very mature vines produce inconspicuous flowers that are followed by blue black fruits. Plant it in partial to full shade in well-drained soil, and the vines will grow at a moderate rate to 25 feet. Zones 4 to 9.

TRUMPET CREEPER (*Campsis radicans*)

Hummingbirds love the red, apricot, or yellow trumpet-shaped flowers that adorn this deciduous vine in midsummer. Handsome, doubly compound, dark green leaves cover fast-growing vines that climb to 30 feet. This plant isn't troubled by disease or insect problems. Zones 4 to 9. For larger flowers, try *C.* × *tagliabuana* 'Madame Galen', Zones 5 to 9.

WOOD VAMP (*Decumaria barbara*)

A deciduous vine native to southeastern United States, wood vamp has glossy dark green foliage and white lacy flowers that bloom in the spring. The vines grow slowly to 30 feet and prefer moist soil. Zones 6 to 9.

WALKWAYS AND PATHS

Shells and Stone Make a Durable Path

Create a quick path that holds up well without the trouble or expense of pouring concrete or laying brick. Garden designer Phillip Watson of Fredericksburg, Virginia, makes paths using his trademark mixture of crushed oyster shell and stone dust.

"After excavating a few inches, I edge the path with steel or iron bands, like you can get through landscape companies," says Phillip. "Then I fill the area with a mix of equal parts crushed oyster shell and stone dust—sand just doesn't seem fine enough. You can get stone dust from quarries or building supply centers and crushed oyster shell from chicken feed stores. I mix in 10 or 15 percent mortar and wet it down. As it dries, it sets up like concrete but still percolates water. Sometimes I add a little crushed brick dust to pick up the color, but I love the way the usual mix all but glows in the dark."

Turf-Saving Steps for Grass Paths

Grass paths are gorgeous, and they're so comfortable to walk on. But they can get threadbare if you use them a lot, and they can become soggy, muddy, and torn up during wet weather. Instead of spending time reseeding barren areas, plan ahead to keep your grass paths looking good. Here's how.

Walk on the far side. One simple way to keep grass paths from developing bare patches is to take the pressure off the center of the path. Whenever you can, walk on the edges of the path, where other people usually don't, to minimize traffic wear and tear.

Put in paving. If you need all-weather access, or find that varying your walking pattern isn't enough to keep the grass growing well, put a strip of paving down the center of the path. It will provide all-weather footing and make it easier to push a wheelbarrow. Use natural-looking stone or old brick. Let the grass creep in around them to help them blend in.

"People take the path of least resistance," says Bobbie Schwartz, a garden designer in Cleveland. "They will make paths where they don't exist if that's the quickest way to get from point A to point B."

Where traffic is heaviest, Bobbie recommends setting 2-foot-square stepping-stones flush with the soil surface and 6 inches apart. Set them in a straight or curved line (whichever looks best) and mow right over them.

Staining Makes New Concrete Look Better Fast

Bright white concrete—it just doesn't look natural. If you've ever been blinded by the glare of a new concrete walk or driveway, try this simple solution from Rick Griffin, a landscape architect in Jackson, Mississippi: "Paint it."

"I've used this technique successfully for years, but still hear of salesclerks at paint stores telling my clients it won't work," says Rick. "The trick is to use 1 part latex paint to 4 parts water, which makes a stain, not a paint. Apply it in light coats soon after the concrete has been poured—within days, if possible—and the effect can last a long, long time." Rick uses a garden sprayer to apply the stain evenly.

"Play around with color combinations to create, say, a muddy look or a dull sheen, anything to knock down the glare and pick up some of your garden colors," says Rick. "A light dash of pink or yellow in the mix can cause the paved area to glow when your flowers are in bloom."

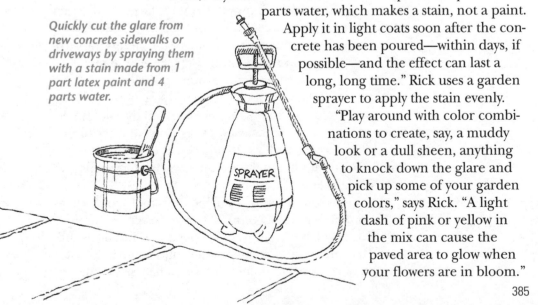

Quickly cut the glare from new concrete sidewalks or driveways by spraying them with a stain made from 1 part latex paint and 4 parts water.

SPRAYER

Narrow Paths Just Right for Small Spaces

USE PLAZAS TO
ADD WORK
SPACE TO SMALL
GARDENS

Downsize your garden paths to play up your garden—and save money and space. Traditional design wisdom says that garden paths should be wide enough—at least 4 feet—for two adults to walk side by side. While this "people first" approach makes for comfort (and elbowroom for maneuvering a wheelbarrow), it takes up a lot of space—space that many yards don't have to spare. And the wider the path, the more it costs to pave it.

Phillip Watson, a garden designer in Fredericksburg, Virginia, has found that "in small spaces, small gardens, there's just no way to make paths wide enough." His solution is to add wider places along narrow paths. "You can create plaza areas along the way for work, or for visitors to turn around or stop and talk," says Phillip.

Holly Shimizu, chief horticulturist of the United States Botanic Garden in Washington, D.C., agrees, saying that "Designing pathways that require people to travel single file means visitors are more likely to focus on the garden, especially if they have to step over something like a root or rock."

Lock Pavers in Place to Reduce Weeds

Nestle your walk or patio pavers together with metal to keep them from popping out of the ground. Then weeds won't grow between them, causing a lot of work and frustration. Aluminum strips are one of the easiest ways to keep paving tight and hold pavers in place. These metal restraints form a secure edging around paving.

"Years down the line, your paving will still look good if you use restraints to hold it all in place. And that definitely helps to keep down weeds," says Doug Cole, nursery foreman for Katerberg Verhage Landscape Services in Grand Rapids. Restraints also help to keep grass from growing from the lawn into the paving.

Aluminum restraints are available from tool supply catalogs and building supply centers. Doug uses PermaLoc restraints. Available in several thicknesses, including ⅛ and ³⁄₁₆ inch, restraints are 1½ inches high and come in 8-foot lengths. It's easy to cut them to fit with a hacksaw or shears.

To use restraints, build a solid base of crushed stone and sand before you install your walk or patio. Start with a 3- to 4-inch-deep layer of small gravel (crushed stone), then put a 1-inch layer of sand on top, tamping them down firmly. Then lay the pavers in place. Set the metal restraint strips snugly beside the pavers and spike them down into the firm stone-and-sand base. Insert the spikes through a flap in the edging—no screws or drills are necessary. Add sand to fill in between and layer over the pavers, and use a compactor to vibrate and push the pavers down into place.

Get the Edge on Messy Walks

Do you spend too much time raking mulch or shoveling soil off the walk? Keep these chores to a minimum by edging the walk with a slightly raised row of bricks, stones, or lengths of specially made metal or plastic edging material (available at most garden supply stores). Wooden boards can work too, but they won't last as long.

If you want to try a really eye-catching edging, use glass. According to George Striticus, a member of the Southern Garden History Society, who lives in Birmingham, Alabama, it was common until the late 1800s to edge garden paths with rows of ceramic ale bottles stuck in the ground neckfirst! To create a modern version of this edging, set sturdy glass bottles in the ground neckfirst.

Place them at a 45-degree angle, close enough to touch each other. Set the bottles half in the ground and half out of the ground to hold them in place. You may need to add cement on each side, as you would with bricks to hold them steady when they're bumped.

Glass bottle edgings work best for walkways in garden beds. They're not too practical beside a lawn since the bottles can get broken if they're hit with a lawn mower.

387

WATER GARDENS

Fast Flowers for Water Garden Color

Don't wait for your water lilies to bloom to have flowers in your water garden. You can brighten your water garden anytime during the growing season by sticking in a pot of whatever's in bloom, says Lucinda Mays, curator of Callaway Gardens in Pine Mountain, Georgia. (And she means *whatever's* in bloom—annuals, perennials—ordinary garden plants.)

"Get out there and play," urges Lucinda, noting that it's much easier to add color from flowers to a water garden than most people realize. Just buy potted plants that are in full bloom and set them in the water so the pot lip sticks 2 inches above the water level. Pull the plants out of the water after a few days when they start showing signs of stress and move them to your flower garden, Lucinda says. They'll thrive despite their dip in the water.

Black Is the Color of a Well-Kept Pond

Don't sing the pond-cleaning blues when you look at your water garden. If you paint it black or use a black liner, and sink your plants in black pots, you won't see the algae and debris that can make a water garden look dirty. "You won't feel like you have to clean it out every time you look at it," says Lucinda Mays, curator of Callaway Gardens in Pine Mountain, Georgia.

If you want to slow algae growth, add harmless black vegetable dye, available from water garden supply companies, to the water. (See "Sources" on page 412 for companies that sell water garden supplies.) The dye not only makes your water look cleaner, it also makes it look deeper.

Read All about It—Mosquito-Eating Plants!

BLADDERWORTS
CONTROL PESKY
MOSQUITOES

Water gardener wipes out mosquitoes! If your water garden is a breeding ground for mosquitoes, try this unorthodox—but effective—solution. "If you are concerned about mosquitoes in a small water garden, you should consider putting in floating bladderwort," recommends gardener Carl Strohmenger of Tampa. "These things are carnivorous and have a huge appetite for tiny critters in the water. You shouldn't have a mosquito problem if you have a healthy bladderwort."

Carl explains that there are many species of bladderworts (*Utricularia* spp.) "Bog floating bladderwort, little floating bladderwort, and common bladderwort have yellow flowers. Purple bladderwort has purplish flowers," he says. "Bladderworts are found across the country in bodies of freshwater. There are even one or two species in Alaska."

If your local nursery can't supply bladderworts, Carl says to contact the International Carnivorous Plant Society, which has a seed bank for many carnivorous species. Contact the society in care of the Fullerton Arboretum, California State University, Fullerton, CA 92634.

You won't see the leaves of bladderwort plants since they float beneath the surface of the water. But bladders among the leaves will be hard at work, catching mosquito larvae. Flowers appear above the water in spring and summer.

WATERING

Weary of Watering? Unhand That Hose!

TURN LEAKY
HOSES INTO
TRICKLE
IRRIGATION
SYSTEMS

Don't waste another minute holding a hose! Instead, make some extra holes in your old hoses, and use them as a simple irrigation system, says B. Rosie Lerner, Purdue University consumer horticulture specialist and state Master Gardener coordinator.

"Trickle irrigation, as a time-saver, is just fabulous," Rosie notes. "If you have old hoses around that have become brittle, or you let them stay out too long and they've frozen and cracked, go ahead and poke a bunch more holes and let them become soaker hoses. It doesn't have to be something expensive." You can snake your homemade soaker hose through a garden bed, attach it to a length of good hose, and turn the water on at low pressure. Water will trickle out through all the holes and gradually soak the soil. Attaching a timer to the system frees you from having to monitor the watering process.

Switching to some type of irrigation system will benefit your plants as well, Rosie says, because you probably wouldn't really spend *enough* time hand-watering to give your plants the water they need.

Suit Your Water System to Your Site

Don't get soaked by buying more irrigation equipment than you really need. Before you invest time and money in an irrigation system, consider your garden's water needs and the features of your site, recommends Cyane Gresham, a gardener at the Rodale Institute Experimental Farm in Kutztown, Pennsylvania. "Irrigation is almost like clothing," she notes. "It needs to be matched to a person's garden setup and their goals for an irrigation system."

Take a look at how much water you have available (and its cost), your water pressure, how clean your water is, and

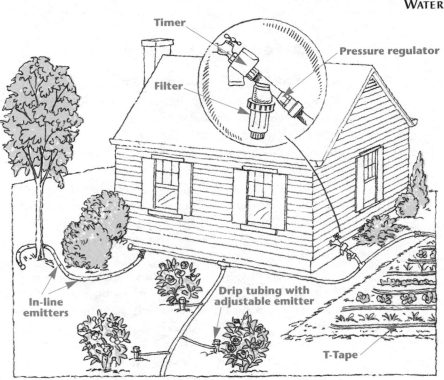

Timer

Pressure regulator

Filter

In-line emitters

Drip tubing with adjustable emitter

T-Tape

You can create an irrigation system that delivers the right amount of water to different parts of your garden and landscape. Use different types of emitters (like spaghetti tubing and mini-sprinklers) and valves that allow you to water some areas and not others.

the cost and availability of irrigation equipment, suggests Cyane. And think about how much time you spend watering by hand or moving hoses around, and compare that expenditure of time and effort to the cost of a more permanent system. An easy way to shop before you buy is to request catalogs from irrigation equipment dealers and suppliers, Cyane says. (See "Sources" on page 412 for mail-order companies that sell irrigation supplies.)

If you have different types of plantings around your yard, you may need to use more than one kind of drip equipment. "Perhaps the hardest thing is balancing a system," says Eric Glassey, who provides technical assistance to customers at DripWorks in Willits, California. "Where you have some trees or big plants in one area and some smaller plants in another, you want to make sure that the big plants get a greater amount of water." Every system must have a filter, Eric says. He also recommends a flush valve so you can drain the system after waterings to keep algae from growing in it and to prevent damage from freezing.

Trust T-Tape to Water Your Vegetables

TRY A T-TAPE

WATER SYSTEM

AND STOP

HAULING HOSES

For an efficient, low-cost system for watering vegetables, try T-Tape. T-Tape is a flattened black plastic hose about 1 inch wide that looks like black tape. But when attached to a water source, T-Tape puffs up, reaching a diameter of about ¾ inch. Regularly spaced holes in the tape let water gently drip out at the base of plants.

Using fittings and valves, you can design a T-Tape system that will water all of your vegetable rows, as shown in the illustration on page 391. T-Tape is available with a variety of hole spacings and flow rates. You can bury the tape or leave it on the soil surface.

Ken Muckenfuss, owner of Mill Creek Organic Farm in Medford, New Jersey, prefers the ease of using T-Tape compared to soaker hoses. "You don't have to move it like a soaker hose," says Ken. "And the waste is minimal."

He buys ¼-mile-long rolls of T-Tape for about $100. Shorter lengths are available for a higher cost per foot, but Ken believes the large rolls are economical even for home gardeners, who can keep the unused portion on hand to replace lines that tear. Another option is to purchase a roll with a few of your gardening friends. (See "Sources" on page 412 for mail-order companies that carry T-Tape.)

Keep Costs Low with a Homemade System

Combine ordinary garden hoses, sprinklers, and connectors to fashion a semipermanent irrigation system that doesn't require digging trenches or spending thousands of dollars.

"This sounds funny, but we run garden hose in various spots throughout the yard, add pulsating sprinklers, add a timer, and set our lawn mower to a higher height to roll over the hoses," reports gardener Mary Ann Casey of Medfield, Massachusetts. "It works wonderfully." At the end of the gardening season, Mary Ann picks up and stores the hoses to save them from damage during the winter.

Judi Colver serves in the Army and has to move about every three years. She's also devised an aboveground irrigation system—one she can take with her from home to home.

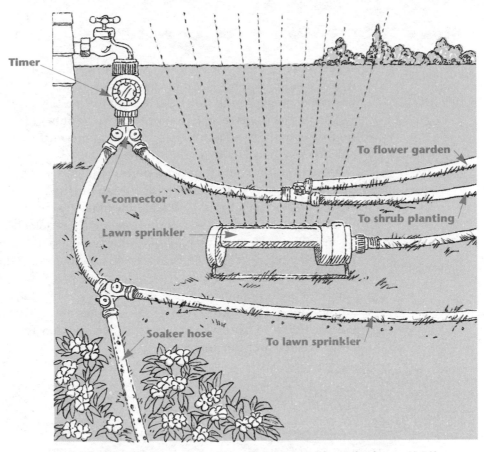

Timer

To flower garden

Y-connector

To shrub planting

Lawn sprinkler

Soaker hose

To lawn sprinkler

Build a portable aboveground irrigation system with garden hoses. Use Y-connectors to add as many hoses as you need to cover your yard. Watering is easy—just turn on the water, set the timer, and open the Y-connectors to the areas you want to water.

"I purchased inexpensive hose, Y-connectors, multiple male and female repair couplings, and an inexpensive timer," Judi explains. "We placed the timer at the spigot and the first Y-connector at the timer overflow. Then we attached hoses to each side of the Y-connector and proceeded to cut and splice hose as needed, putting a repair coupling at the ends of the spliced hose." Every time Judi splices a hose, she uses a Y-connector to expand her system: one side of the connector attaches to another length of hose, and the other to an oscillating sprinkler head. All this, Judi says, for a total cost of under $100. Not only does she save money on the system, she saves time watering because she doesn't have to move hoses or sprinklers around.

Timers Take the Worry Out of Watering

Save water and money by using a timer to control your irrigation system. The most inexpensive timer you can buy is a manual windup timer. To use it, attach it to your irrigation system, and set the timer dial to the number of hours you want the system to run. Windup timers are available for less than $10 at discount centers.

More expensive automatic timers give you more control over when and how you water. Jerry Jordan of DripWorks in Willits, California, advises, "Look at how much diversity you need." If you have separate watering systems for vegetables, lawn, and roses, for example, design your system to use more than one valve, so you can have separate watering "stations." Most automatic timers have at least two programs, so you can water one station once a week for two hours, for example, and another twice a day for 15 minutes. Jerry prefers electric timers to battery-operated ones because they're more reliable over the long run.

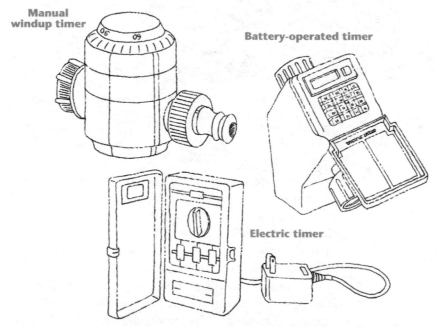

Manual windup timer

Battery-operated timer

Electric timer

Choose the water timer that fits your budget and lifestyle best: a manual windup timer is the least expensive, but you have to reset it each time you water. Automatic timers come in a range of prices and can operate your water system while you're away. An inexpensive electric timer costs about as much as a middle-of-the-line battery-operated one but should last much longer.

Good Measurements Make for Better Watering

GAUGES MEAN
NO GUESSING
WHEN IT COMES
TO WATERING

How good are you at gauging your plants' water needs? Chances are a moisture gauge is better. One inch of water per week is the standard rule of thumb for watering. But that rule doesn't take into account different soil types, some of which hold water longer than others. Also, widely varying relative humidities and temperatures in different regions of the country affect how quickly soils lose moisture. To keep more accurate tabs on soil moisture, use a moisture gauge.

A moisture gauge is a small instrument that monitors evaporation, rainfall, irrigation, and soil moisture content, and provides a guide to follow for watering your plants. All you do is stick the gauge in the ground near the plants you want to monitor, and then follow the instructions that come with the gauge to determine when and how much to water.

If you have a very expensive plant that you want to monitor, you may want to consider investing in a more sophisticated piece of equipment called a tensiometer.

"A tensiometer is a plastic tube with a ceramic tip on one end and a gauge on the other that measures the availability of water in the soil," explains Dr. E. Thomas Smiley, a researcher with Bartlett Tree Research Laboratories in Charlotte, North Carolina. Tensiometers are not cheap—they run about $100. Nor are they very portable; they need to be set up and equilibrated each time they're moved. But they are more accurate than moisture gauges. For gardeners who habitually overwater, they can significantly reduce water bills. And, as Dr. Smiley points out, for someone who has spent $1,000 moving a large tree, they are a worthwhile investment.

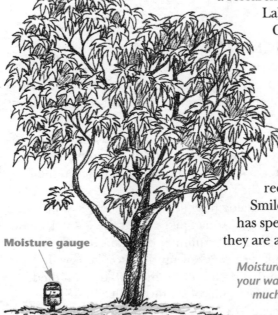

Moisture gauge

Moisture gauges can help you get a grip on your watering needs. They'll keep track of how much water plants get and guide you to more accurate watering practices.

Tired of Tangled Hose? Try This

Roll your hose inside a holder made from an old tire and you'll never waste time wrestling with a tangled hose again. Felder Rushing, coauthor of *Passalong Plants,* thinks used tires are the best thing since half whiskey barrels. He uses them as planters, coffee tables, swings for his kids, and as a perfectly shaped garden hose holder.

USE OLD TIRES
TO ORGANIZE
HOSES

"All it takes is about five minutes and a kitchen knife to cut a tire into a pleasing holder," Felder says. "Lay the tire down flat, and carefully stick the knife into the soft sidewall. Then cut all the way around, close to the tread (where the tire curves around). You'll end up with a round doughnut-shaped piece of rubber to discard.

"Turn the cut tire over, and do the same thing on the other side, but make the cut in a zigzag shape, like a piecrust," says Felder. "Cut from near the tread to near the rim hole, back and forth, all the way around. You'll have a multi-pointed star-shaped piece to discard. I hang them on the fence sorta like artwork."

After cutting both sides, Felder inverts the tire, pulling one side through the other. The finished product looks very much like a crown with flared-out points. You can wrap up to 75 feet of hose inside it.

Give Your Plants a Spiked Drink

Try an Aqua Spike to send water straight to the root zone of your plants. Aqua Spikes are carrot-shaped hollow spikes that are inserted into the soil beside plants. For a water source, fill an ever-handy 2-liter plastic soda bottle with water, invert it, and stick it into the opening of the spike. The water slowly seeps out through holes in the base of the spike into the surrounding soil.

Frank Oliver, catalog director for Gardener's Supply Company, which sells Aqua Spikes, tried these watering devices in his garden in the summer of 1993. "It was a wicked drought," Frank recalls. "Only my tomato plants with Aqua Spikes survived that dreadful summer. All the rest died."

The spikes come in sets of six for about $10. (See "Sources" on page 412 for ordering information.) You'll need one spike per mature large plant, such as tomatoes, and one for every two small plants, such as cabbage, lettuce, and patio tomatoes. Gardener's Supply recommends putting sand into the bottom of the spike to slow the flow of water to about 2 liters of water per two hours.

Easy Way to Water? Coke Is It!

Put soda bottles to work watering your vegetables and flowers. You probably have plastic soda bottles in your recycling storage can, and you can easily use them to save time hand-watering or the expense of buying a drip irrigation system.

One method is to punch small holes in the bottoms of 2-liter bottles, then bury the bottles up to their shoulders next to vegetables or flowers. Rodney Barton, who gardens in Hickory Creek, Texas, recommends punching a ¼-inch-diameter hole in each of the five "feet" on the bottom of the bottle. Rodney uses an X-Acto knife with a punch attachment to make the holes. If you have sandy soil, use fewer holes, not smaller ones, because smaller holes are more likely to clog.

"Filling the bottle once a day is enough for most plants, even in our hottest, driest weather," says Rodney. He fills the bottle by slipping a garden hose (with the end cut off) into its neck. "I use the filling time to pull weeds. I know the bottle is full when I get sprayed!" Rodney says.

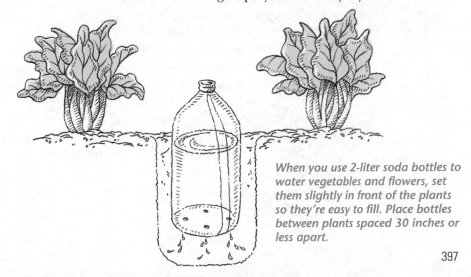

When you use 2-liter soda bottles to water vegetables and flowers, set them slightly in front of the plants so they're easy to fill. Place bottles between plants spaced 30 inches or less apart.

WEEDS AND WEEDING

Shallow Soil Work Keeps Weeds Down

Let sleeping weeds lie and you'll spend less time fighting them. If you stick to shallow tilling, you'll avoid unearthing buried weed seeds and, over time, you'll reduce weed problems in your garden. That's the conclusion of John Ehrlich, manager of West River Farm. He's been experimenting with shallow-till methods on the 100-plus raised beds on the community-supported farm he operates near Annapolis, Maryland.

When you use a rotary tiller to prepare a new bed or turn in a cover crop, John recommends that you use the lowest gear possible and set the blades on the highest setting. If you're in the market for a new tiller, look for a European model. "They've been using shallow-till methods for years, and their tools are designed accordingly," John says. If you'd prefer using a manual cultivator, try a wheel hoe (see the illustration on page 404) or broadfork (see the illustration on this page).

Cultivate shallowly—no deeper than 1 or 2 inches—and you'll kill off newly sprouted weed seedlings without unearthing the thousands that are buried more deeply. Keep weeds from going to seed in your garden and each year there will be fewer weed seeds in the upper layers of soil. Eventually, the top soil layer will be virtually weed-free.

Use a broadfork to prepare garden beds without bringing up lots of weed seeds. Hold one handle in each hand, press your foot on the crossbar, and pull back on the handles to gently lift the soil without turning it over.

JUST SAY "NO!" TO DEEP-DIGGING WEEDS

Go easy with your tools when it comes to hand-weeding. "The more soil you churn up when you weed, the more weed seeds you bring up to the light where they can sprout," says Janet Britt, who operates a community-supported farm in the Hudson River Valley in New York. It doesn't matter what kind of hand-cultivating tool you use, she explains, as long as you try not to stir up more than 1½ inches of soil in the process.

Fred Hoover, a market grower in Phoenix, agrees and recommends that you choose a tool that just skims the surface. "Some people use a scuffle hoe or a stirrup hoe," he says. "But I use a lettuce knife, which is something like a machete, but shorter. Keep it sharp and you can zip through the rows in a flash."

Use a lettuce knife or another favorite hand tool or hoe to slice weeds off at the soil surface. Digging deep is too much work and it only brings up more weed seeds.

Compost Cuts Weeding Chores

Banish weeds from your garden and boost plant growth simply by applying a 2-inch layer of compost around your plants. It sounds too good to be true, but the proof comes from researcher Stephanie Allen at the Center for Urban Horticulture in Seattle. Stephanie tested compost as a mulch for the Seattle Solid Waste Utility.

"The results were dramatic," Stephanie says. "Especially since I was working with poor soil." Compost mulch reduced weed-seed germination in Stephanie's test plots by seven to nine times and increased vegetable and herb plant growth by six to ten times.

Any mulch will discourage weeds, Stephanie says, but compost works harder. It acts like a fertilizer for plants, improves drainage in poor soils, and helps hold moisture in sandy soils. Rich soils won't show as big a jump in production, but the compost will still provide great weed control.

Sheet Compost for Weed-Free Flowers

Imagine that you never pull a weed, but you still have a beautiful flower garden. The secret to this "miracle" is sheet composting (spreading compost materials on the soil instead of in a bin). It's a technique usually reserved for vegetable gardens, but it's equally effective for flower beds, according to Veet Deha, a horticulturist in Ithaca, New York.

"Sheet composting works, as long as you are willing to set up the bed in the fall and delay planting until spring," says Veet. "And believe me, it's worth the wait." Just follow Veet's simple steps:

WEEDS WON'T SURVIVE, BUT FLOWERS THRIVE IN COMPOST

1 Lay out the shape of your bed right on the sod. There's no need to till.

2 Put a layer of mulch or compost over the entire bed—as much as you can rustle up. "There's no way you can use too much," says Veet. It doesn't even have to be finished compost. You can use leaves and grass clippings—even pulled weeds.

3 Place a layer of newspapers—10 to 12 sheets thick—on top of the compost or mulch. Wet down the paper with a hose to keep it from blowing away.

4 Cover the wet paper with a 2- to 3-inch layer of mulch, grass clippings, shredded leaves, or wood chips. Use whatever is available and looks nice to you. Make sure all of the

To keep the edges of a sheet compost bed neat, use an edger to make a trench around the bed. Cut out sections of sod (3 inches deep and as wide as the edger) around the bed. Toss the cutout pieces into the bed, roots up, before adding a layer of newspaper. Make sure the paper extends into the trench to control weeds. When your bed is finished, trimming the edges is easy—just set your mower wheel in the trench and mow.

paper is covered, because it will wick moisture away from your plants if it's exposed.

When the pile is done, wait at least six months for the material under the newspaper to break down. To plant, use a sharp knife or trowel to dig through the mulch and paper layers—avoid tearing the paper a lot. The roots of the plants should be in contact with the soil, not just sit in the mulch.

Veet claims that this method results in a virtually weed-free garden that will remain trouble-free as long as you don't dig it up and expose a lot of weed seeds.

Swipe Soil to Keep Weeds Out of Your Path

"Scalp" the topsoil from garden pathways to stop them from becoming weedways. After you dig your garden beds, remove the topsoil from the paths, says Holly Kennell, a Washington State University Cooperative Extension Service agent in Seattle. "You don't want the paths to grow anything," she points out. "You don't want them to have good soil." Pile the swiped topsoil on your beds, add some organic matter, and you'll have ready-to-plant raised beds.

Once you've stripped the good soil off your paths, top them with a thick layer of wood chips. You'll never have to worry about weeding again, Holly says. To get chips for your paths, she suggests checking with local arborists, who often give away the chipped prunings their work creates. "Just call them up and tell them that when they're working in your neighborhood, you'd be happy to have a load of chips," says Holly. Stress that you only want *one* load, she cautions, or you might end up inundated by chips.

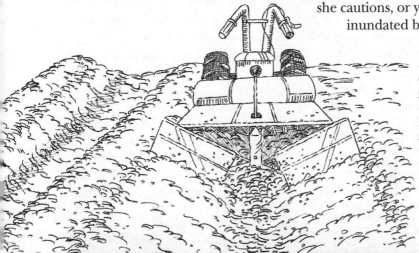

Strip off the topsoil, and weeds won't grow in your paths. Move topsoil from your paths to your garden beds with a tiller-and-hiller attachment to save lots of shoveling.

Why Weed Pathways?

CLOBBER WEEDS
WITH CARD-
BOARD AND
WOOD CHIPS

There's no need to weed garden pathways if you've got cardboard on hand. Veet Deha, a horticulturist in Ithaca, New York, came up with this zero-maintenance weed barrier. It couldn't be easier or cheaper. Just lay cardboard on the paths, then cover the cardboard with wood chips.

Waxed produce boxes, available from grocery stores, are Veet's favorite source of cardboard. Recyclers don't want them because they slow down the recycling process, but they're great for the garden because they're long-lasting.

When you install the cardboard, make sure you generously overlap the adjoining pieces. Any cracks—or even near-cracks—allow weeds to grow sideways and sneak through. When you've got the area completely covered with cardboard, use mulch to keep it in place. The waxed boxes are slippery, so you'll need about 7 inches of wood chips to make the paths comfortable to walk on. With regular cardboard, 3 inches of chips will do.

"Newspaper can also serve as a barrier instead of cardboard," Veet says. "I figure 1 sheet lasts one month, so if I want a three-year mulch, that's 36 sheets. Use what you've got. We even recycle pizza boxes this way."

Weed Early, Weed Easy

Want to get a jump on weeds? Pick an unseasonably warm day in February—it's too early to plant, but it's a great time to pull perennial weeds. In fact, it's the best time.

"Taprooted perennials are much easier to pull out early in the season than later," says Mary Jane Else, an integrated pest management weed specialist at the University of Massachusetts. "And perennial grasses are especially vulnerable to pulling in early spring. By late spring, grasses have a robust, spreading root system, and the only way to get rid of them is to dig them up."

Tina James, a landscape consultant in Reisterstown, Maryland, modifies this system to suit her needs. She routs out all the tough grasses before planting time, but leaves taprooted weeds alone. Tina waits until fall to dig out dandelions, chicory, and curly dock, because that's when the roots have the most vigor for making herbal preparations. "There's a season to everything, depending on your objectives," she says.

Try This Sure-Fire Swiss Secret

Swiss gardeners prevent weed problems by letting their beds go "stale" before planting. "The Swiss are famous for their time-and-motion studies, and they've documented many ways to prevent weeds," says Veet Deha, a horticulturist in Ithaca, New York. "The 'stale bed' method saves me from some particularly tedious weeding jobs." Here's how to let your beds go stale.

Prepare your garden beds as usual. Before planting, wait until the first flush of annual weeds sprout (ten days to two weeks). When you see the first leaves on the weeds, make a furrow and plant your crop right in the weedy beds.

Now wait again, this time for your seeds to send out a radicle—the little tail that becomes the root. Peek in the soil about the time seeds should be germinating. When you see the radicle, use a tool called a flamer to burn out the weeds. (Flamers are available in garden supply catalogs.) Because the seeds haven't sent up leaves yet, they won't be hurt, but the weeds will be history. Your seedlings will emerge in a few days. With this technique, your crop will come up in clean soil and, since you didn't disturb the soil, there won't be many more weed seeds at the surface ready to sprout.

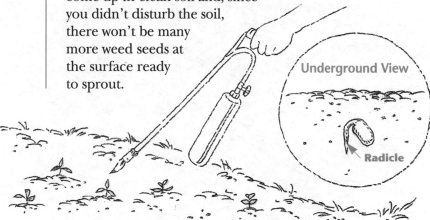

Flamers work great, but only when weeds are small. If you don't want to invest in one, use the back of a rake to gently knock out weeds. It works almost as well.

Favorite Tools Make Short Work of Weeding

**WEEDS DON'T
STAND A
CHANCE WITH
THESE TOOLS**

No matter which weeds invade your garden, someone, somewhere has a tool to make them disappear. Check this list of favorites for the tools that will make your weeding job easiest. (For other tools, see "Hoes to Help You Weed with Speed" on page 349.)

Machete makes mincemeat of large weeds. When weeds threaten to go to seed, it's important to get rid of them fast to head off an explosion of future weeds. For example, a single fleabane (*Erigeron canadensis*) plant can produce over 200,000 weed seeds! Janika Eckert, research assistant at Johnny's Selected Seeds in Albion, Maine, uses a machete to chop down large weeds quickly. Janika says that she tries to incorporate weeding into whatever else she's doing, whether it's thinning, sowing, or transplanting, so that she doesn't have to deal with large weeds. But for the occasional weed that gets by her, her machete is a powerful and effective weed-stopper.

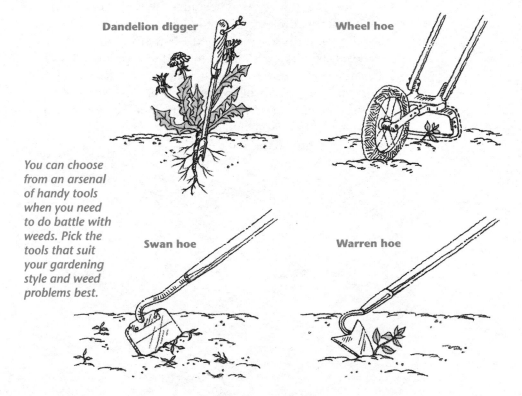

Dandelion digger

Wheel hoe

Swan hoe

Warren hoe

You can choose from an arsenal of handy tools when you need to do battle with weeds. Pick the tools that suit your gardening style and weed problems best.

Utility scissors cut annual weeds to the quick. Wendy Krupnick, who manages the trial gardens for Shepherd Seeds Company in Felton, California, uses utility scissors to clip off annual weeds like lamb's-quarters, pigweed, and purslane below the soil surface. The scissors hardly disturb the soil, and whatever bits of root remain just break down and add more organic matter to the soil.

Dandelion digger destroys taprooted weeds. "A dandelion digger is great for routing out dandelions, dock, thistles, and other weeds with a long taproot," claims Maggie Melnick, a market grower in Fiddletown, California. Maggie's technique is to thrust the dandelion digger into the soil next to the weed root and then break the root loose by pushing the blade of the tool under it. This technique allows you to pop the weed and root out without disturbing the surrounding soil, so you unearth fewer weed seeds than you would if you dug the root out with a shovel or trowel.

Wheel hoe wipes out weeds in big gardens. Janet Britt, who operates a community-supported farm in the Hudson River Valley in New York, uses a wheel hoe to fight weeds in her fields. "Since I have 3½ acres under cultivation, I need a very efficient tool," Janet says. She recommends small-wheeled hoes fitted with oscillating blades because they are much more efficient than large-wheeled models.

Swan hoe scuttles weeds. The lightweight, razor-sharp blade of a swan hoe suits Cyane Gresham, who tends many gardens at the Rodale Institute Experimental Farm in Kutztown, Pennsylvania. "You can skim through the rows with little effort and without tearing up the soil," Cyane says.

Warren hoe works where the soil's compacted. Cyane also likes a Warren hoe when she's weeding in compacted or heavy soil. "The point of the triangular blade makes it easier to get under weeds growing in tough soil," she says.

Lawn mower grinds up tall weeds. "I rely on mulch for most of my weed control," says Tina James, who gardens in a median strip near Baltimore, Maryland. "But sometimes the weeds have gotten so tall it's hard to put mulch down." That's when she brings out the big gun—her lawn mower. In 15 minutes, her weed problem is flattened. The mowed weeds act as a base layer of mulch, which she can then top with more mulch of her choice.

WILDFLOWERS

Carpet Your Yard with an Instant Meadow Garden

PREPLANTED
FLOWERS TURN
LAWNS INTO
MEADOWS

A carpet of flowers? You've probably seen someone installing a carpet, rolling it out, tacking it down, and—presto—like magic, you have a finished room. Now you can do the same thing outdoors with Wildflower Carpet that will grow into a beautiful meadow garden.

You can buy Wildflower Carpet from local nurseries, garden centers, and sod farms. (See "Sources" on page 412 for ordering information.) These preplanted strips of flowers work great if you want to cover a lot of ground or don't have time to wait for a seeded meadow to fill in. Peter Milstein, national manager for Wildflower Carpet in Denver, describes his company's carpet as 5-square-foot slabs of perennial wildflowers grown like sod in a peat-based mix. The slabs arrive at your house with about 3 inches of foliage and a full root system—all ready to begin growing. You're in luck if you have a sandy loam soil, which the wildflowers prefer. But they'll also tolerate other soils—with the exception of pure clay. And they are hardy enough to grow in all of mainland United States, except subtropical Zone 10.

"I've planted about 300 square feet of Wildflower Carpet on the east and west sides of my house. Let me tell you, it's easier than planting annual flowers," Peter says. "My meadows have been in for two summers now, and the flowers have returned quite nicely."

Peter says that there are several species of flowers in bloom at any given time during the growing season, which creates an ever-changing sea of color in his yard. In spring, purple, gold, blue, and pink predominate, with dame's rocket, Johnny-jump-ups, rockcress, and wallflowers. Early summer brings a chorus of white and yellow with lance-leaved coreopsis and Shasta daisies. In fall, the earth tones of black-eyed Susans and blanket flowers finish the meadow display for the year.

Starting and maintaining your Wildflower Carpet is simple, Peter explains. Here's how to do it.

1 Till the soil about 3 to 4 inches deep and remove all turf, weeds, rocks, and clods before planting. If your soil is very poor, amend it with organic matter before planting. Work a balanced organic fertilizer into the top 2 or 3 inches of soil.

2 As soon as you receive your Wildflower Carpet, remove the fabric backing, and piece the sod sections together on the prepared bed. Firm them into place.

3 Water well after planting, and keep the area moist for the first four weeks. Provide an inch of water a week through the rest of the growing season, irrigating if rainfall is limited. (You should also water occasionally through winter in dry climates.)

4 Knock down the brown stems in fall with a weed wacker to form a natural mulch over the flowers.

5 Fertilize lightly in spring with a slow-release fertilizer or compost.

Plant a meadow garden fast using preplanted mats of flowers called Wildflower Carpet. Prepare the soil, then lay down the "carpet" pieces just as you would pieces of sod.

It's Not a Mess, It's My Garden!

Wildflowers make good neighbors. Gardener Evelyn Connors of Tulsa had to prove this truth to City Hall when she was told to clean up her yard, or else: Or else the city would do it and bill her for it. She took the city to task, pointing out that her garden was not a mess—it was a carefully planned collection of low-maintenance, self-sustaining native prairie wildflowers. She and all her fellow garden club members decided to fight to preserve what is becoming known as a valid garden style.

The city pretty quickly decided to back off the fight after an outpouring of public outrage, and to this day Evelyn and hundreds of visitors enjoy her collection of hardy, drought-tolerant, wildlife-attracting flowers and grasses.

If you plant a wildflower garden of your own, avoid battling City Hall by showing passersby that your yard really is a garden. Do this by adding a section of split rail or picket fence, a bench, a gate—anything that looks visitor-friendly and conveys a garden feeling to the scene. Use garden features like birdbaths too, and plant lots of flowers.

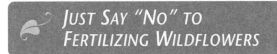

JUST SAY "NO" TO FERTILIZING WILDFLOWERS

Too much of a good thing is bad for your wildflower garden—and it's unnecessary work and expense for you. So don't make the mistake of adding too many nutrients—especially nitrogen—to the soil where you want to grow wildflowers, says Hank Bruno, the trails manager at Callaway Gardens in Pine Mountain, Georgia.

"Wildflowers are generally found on poorer soils," Hank notes. Instead of thriving when you give them a generous feeding, your wildflowers may respond by producing lots of lush, floppy foliage and fewer flowers—probably not what you had in mind!

Hank says moderation is the key when he prepares the soil for wildflowers at Callaway Gardens. He uses a little bit of lime to modify the local soil's acidity, and he adds organic matter to help retain soil moisture and fertility. "What we're not doing is putting in a lot of nutrients," he says. "As a result, we get stiffer stems and more flowers than we would if there's more available nitrogen."

Quick Tips Maximize Meadow Success

MEADOWS
THRIVE WITH
GOOD PLANTING
PRACTICES

To make the most of your meadow, keep in mind that it's still a garden and it needs some care. That's the advice of Hank Bruno, the trails manager at Callaway Gardens in Pine Mountain, Georgia. While an established meadow planting needs less care than a typical lawn, your new wildflower meadow will need your help to get off to a strong start. Hank offers these tips to help you speed your wildflower meadow to showy success.

Check your mix. If you're buying a seed mix, look for a good balance of annuals for quick color and perennials for long-term growth. "The perennials will be the real strengths of the garden, but they may take two or three years to get going," Hank points out.

Sow sensibly. Mix your seed with sand to help you distribute small seeds evenly. "A little bit of these tiny seeds goes a long way," warns Hank. "Make sure you don't overseed it, to avoid creating intense competition among plants, or some species will shade out others."

Pop in plants. "If there's a particular flower that you want in the meadow, it's worth it to set a few plants into the planting," says Hank. Planting rather than seeding gives your favorite plants a head start on the competition and makes your meadow showy sooner.

Plug in grasses. Grasses are an important part of a successful meadow, because they make it look more natural and they fill in between the flowers. But it's easy to add too much grass seed to your mix and crowd out your flower seedlings, says Hank. Tucking in a few plugs of the grasses you want is an easy way to add grass while keeping it under control.

Add a few drifts. You'll get a nice, harmonious effect if you include drifts of color in your meadow by planting sections with a single kind of plant. Drifts give your meadow a unified look that's more effective than the spotty pattern you'll get if you simply sow all the different plants and colors together. Hank suggests sowing a few of your favorite flowers in bands to create a meadow with more to offer than a multitude of mixed blooms.

USDA PLANT HARDINESS ZONE MAP

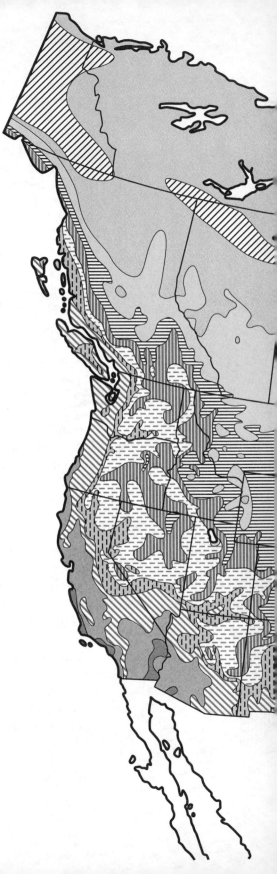

Average annual minimum temperature

Temperature (°F)

Zone		Temperature
Zone 1		Below -50°
Zone 2		-40° to -50°
Zone 3		-30° to -40°
Zone 4		-20° to -30°
Zone 5		-10° to -20°
Zone 6		0° to -10°
Zone 7		10° to 0°
Zone 8		20° to 10°
Zone 9		30° to 20°
Zone 10		40° to 30°

411

SOURCES

The following companies carry products mentioned in *Great Garden Shortcuts* tips. To find a specific product, look under the topic it's listed under in the book. For example, for deer fencing, look for "Fencing" under "Deer."

Animal Pests

Bird-Control Devices

Modern Agri-Products
322 Main St.
Lynden, WA 98264

Walt Nicke Co.
P.O. Box 433
36 McLeod Ln.
Topsfield, MA 01983

Peaceful Valley Farm Supply Co.
P.O. Box 2209
Grass Valley, CA 95945

Mole-Med

Gardens Alive!
5100 Schenley Pl.
Lawrenceburg, IN 47025

Annuals

Seeds for Cut Flowers

W. Atlee Burpee & Co.
300 Park Ave.
Warminster, PA 18974

Park Seed Co.
P.O Box 31
Cokesbury Rd.
Greenwood, SC 29647

Thompson & Morgan, Inc.
P.O. Box 1308
Jackson, NJ 08527

Apples

Scab-Resistant Apple Cultivars

Adams County Nursery, Inc.
P.O. Box 108
Aspers, PA 17304

Bear Creek Nursery
P.O. Box 411
Northport, WA 99157

Hilltop Nurseries
P.O. Box 578
Hartford, MI 49057
15 trees minimum order.

Raintree Nursery
391 Butts Rd.
Morton, WA 98356

Rocky Meadow Orchard
  and Nursery
360 Rocky Meadow Rd. NW
New Salisbury, IN 47161

St. Lawrence Nurseries
325 S.H. 345
Potsdam, NY 13676

Stark Bro's Nurseries & Orchards Co.
P.O. Box 10
Louisiana, MO 63353

Beneficial Insects

A-1 Unique Insect Control
5504 Sperry Dr.
Citrus Heights, CA 95621

Gardens Alive!
5100 Schenley Pl.
Lawrenceburg, IN 47025

Harmony Farm Supply
P.O. Box 460
Graton, CA 95444

The Ladybug Company
8706 Oro-Quincy Hwy.
Berry Creek, CA 95916

M & R Durango Insectary
P.O. Box 886
Bayfield, CO
  81122

Broccoli
Floating Row Covers
Gardener's Supply Co.
128 Intervale Rd.
Burlington, VT 05401

Gardens Alive!
5100 Schenley Pl.
Lawrenceburg, IN 47025

Harmony Farm Supply
P.O. Box 460
Graton, CA 95444

Bulbs
Bulb Drills
Langenbach
P.O. Box 453
Blairstown, NJ 07825

Plow and Hearth
P.O. Box 5000
Madison, VA 22727

Bulb Planters and Bulbs
White Flower Farm
Litchfield, CT 06759

Heirloom Tulips
The Daffodil Mart
Rt. 3, Box 794
7463 Heath Tr.
Gloucester, VA 23061

Old House Gardens
536 Third St.
Ann Arbor, MI 48103-4957

Southern Bulb Growers
Louisiana Nursery
Rt. 7, Box 43
Opelousas, LA 70570

Ty Ty Plantation Bulb Co.
Box 159
Ty Ty , GA 31795

Carrots
Seeds for Short Carrots
Johnny's Selected Seeds
310 Foss Hill Rd.
Albion, ME 04910

Pinetree Garden Seeds
Box 300
New Gloucester, ME 04260

Shepherd's Garden Seeds
30 Irene St.
Torrington, CT 06790

Composting
Plastic Barrel Composter
Gardener's Supply Co.
128 Intervale Rd.
Burlington, VT 05401

Deer
Fencing
Benner's Gardens, Inc.
P.O. Box 875
Bala-Cynwyd, PA 19004

Eggplant
Seeds for Oriental Eggplant
W. Atlee Burpee & Co.
300 Park Ave.
Warminster, PA 18974

Johnny's Selected Seeds
310 Foss Hill Rd.
Albion, ME 04910

Park Seed Co.
P.O. Box 31
Cokesbury Rd.
Greenwood, SC 29647

Shepherd's Garden Seeds
30 Irene St.
Torrington, CT 06790

Fruit Trees
Chickens and Ducks
(for weeding fruit trees)
Marti Poultry Farm
P.O. Box 27
Windsor, MO 65360-0027

Stromberg's Chicks & Gamebirds
  Unlimited
P.O. Box 400
Pine River, MN 56474

Columnar Apple Trees
Stark Bro's Nurseries
  & Orchards Co.
P.O. Box 10
Louisiana, MO 63353

Dwarf Fruit Trees
Bear Creek Nursery
P.O. Box 411
Northport, WA 99157

Raintree Nursery
391 Butts Rd.
Morton, WA 98356

Grapes

Sticky Tape

Entosphere
4623 N. Blythe
Fresno, CA 93722

Walt Nicke Co.
P.O. Box 433
36 McLeod Ln.
Topsfield, MA 01983

Green Manure

Seeds

Johnny's Selected Seeds
310 Foss Hill Rd.
Albion, ME 04910

Peaceful Valley Farm Supply Co.
P.O. Box 2209
Grass Valley, CA 95945

Ronniger's Seed Potatoes
Star Rt.
Moyie Springs, ID 83845

Groundcovers

The Primrose Path
R.D. 2, Box 110
Scottdale, PA 15683
Catalogs cost $2.

Bareroot Groundcovers

W. Atlee Burpee & Co.
300 Park Ave.
Warminster, PA
 18974

Mellinger's Inc.
2310 W. South Range Rd.
North Lima, OH 44452-9731

Prentiss Court Ground Covers
P.O. Box 8662
Greenville, SC 29604

Clematis

Milaeger's Gardens
4838 Douglas Ave.
Racine, WI 53402-2498

Wayside Gardens
1 Garden Ln.
Hodges, SC 29695

White Flower Farm
Litchfield, CT 06759

Ice Plant

W. Atlee Burpee & Co.
300 Park Ave.
Warminster, PA 18974

Park Seed Co.
P.O Box 31
Cokesbury Rd.
Greenwood, SC 29647

Netting (for cleaning groundcovers)

Benner's Gardens, Inc.
6974 Upper York Rd.
New Hope, PA 18938

Harvesting

Apple-Picking Bags

Harmony Farm Supply
P.O. Box 460
Graton, CA 95444

Raintree Nursery
391 Butts Rd.
Morton, WA 98356

Breathable Bags

Evert-Fresh
P.O. Box 540974
Houston, TX 77254

Hedges, Fences, and Screens

Redleaf Rose

Bear Creek Nursery
P.O. Box 411
Northport, WA 99157

White Flower Farm
Litchfield, CT 06759

Herbs

Nichols Garden Nursery
1190 N. Pacific Hwy.
Albany, OR 97321

Richters
P.O. Box 26, Hwy. 47
Goodwood, Ontario L0C 1A0

Sandy Mush Herb Nursery
316 Surrett Cove Rd.
Leicester, NC 28748

Well-Sweep Herb Farm
317 Mt. Bethel Rd.
Port Murray, NJ 07865

Insects
Diatomaceous Earth and Pyrethrum Products

John Dromgoole's The Natural
  Gardener
8648 Old Bee Caves Rd.
Austin, TX 78735

Peaceful Valley Farm Supply Co.
P.O. Box 2209
Grass Valley, CA 95945

Hot Pepper Wax
Territorial Seed Co.
P.O. Box 157
20 Palmer Ave.
Cottage Grove, OR 97424

Worm's Way
3151 S. Hwy. 446
Bloomington, IN 47401

Kiwi
David Kuchta
R.D. 1 Tippets Rd., Rt. 54
Nesquehoning, PA 18240
*Send SASE for price list and planting
information.*

Raintree Nursery
391 Butts Rd.
Morton, WA 98356

Lawns
Ecolawn Seed Mixes
Hobbs & Hopkins Protime
  Lawn Seed
1712 S.E. Ankeny St.
Portland, OR 97214

Nichols Garden Nursery
1190 N. Pacific Hwy.
Albany, OR 97321

Pennmulch Pellets
Agro-Tech 2000
666 Plainsboro Rd.
Bldg. 200, Suite 2B
Plainsboro, NJ 08536

Moss
Mostly Moss
168 Old Bethel Rd.
Jackson, GA 30233

Tripple Brook Farm
37 Middle Rd.
Southampton, MA 01073

We-Du Nurseries
Rt. 5, Box 724
Marion, NC 28752

Mulching
Electric Leaf Mulcher
The Alsto Company
P.O. Box 1267
Galesburg, IL 61401

Ornamental Grasses
Plants
Kurt Bluemel, Inc.
2740 Greene Ln.
Baldwin, MD 21013

Greenlee Nursery
301 E. Franklin Ave.
Pomona, CA 91766

Limerock Ornamental Grasses
R.D. 1, Box 111-C
Port Matilda, PA 16870

Plant Delights Nursery
9241 Sauls Rd.
Raleigh, NC 27603

Seeds
Johnny's Selected Seeds
310 Foss Hill Rd.
Albion, ME 04910

Pinetree Garden Seeds
Box 300
New Gloucester, ME 04260

Thompson & Morgan, Inc.
P.O. Box 1308
Jackson, NJ 08527

Potatoes

Seed Potatoes

Johnny's Selected Seeds
310 Foss Hill Rd.
Albion, ME 04910

Ronniger's Seed Potatoes
Star Rt.
Moyie Springs, ID 83845

Pruning

Felco Pruning Tools

The Alsto Company
P.O. Box 1267
Galesburg, IL 61401

Harmony Farm Supply
P.O. Box 460
Graton, CA 95444

Langenbach
P.O. Box 453
Blairstown, NJ 07825

The Urban Farmer Store
2833 Vicente St.
San Francisco, CA 94116

Roses

Easy Plant Protectors

Wilmarc, Inc.
Dept. GPG
5266 E. 65th St.
Indianapolis, IN 46220

Plants

Antique Rose Emporium
Rt. 5, Box 143
Brenham, TX 77833

Roses of Yesterday and Today
802 Brown's Valley Rd.
Watsonville, CA 95076

Season Extension

Row Covers

Peaceful Valley Farm Supply Co.
P.O. Box 2209
Grass Valley, CA 95945

Season-Extension Devices

Hard Core Garden Supply
P.O. Box 118
Asheville, NC 28802

Spinach

Seeds for Smooth-Leaved Spinach

W. Atlee Burpee & Co.
300 Park Ave.
Warminster, PA 18974

Johnny's Selected Seeds
310 Foss Hill Rd.
Albion, ME 04910

Pinetree Garden Seeds
Box 300
New Gloucester, ME 04260

Shepherd's Garden Seeds
30 Irene St.
Torrington, CT 06790

Tools and Equipment

See the Pruning heading for a list
of companies that offer Felco
pruning tools.

Child-Size Gardening Tools

Let's Get Growing!
1900 Commercial Way
Santa Cruz, CA 95065

Walt Nicke Co.
P.O. Box 433
36 McLeod Ln.
Topsfield, MA 01983

Replacement Wheels for Lawn Mowers

Northern Hydraulics, Inc.
P.O. Box 1499
Burnsville, MN 55337-0499

Stirrup Hoes

Kinsman Company, Inc.
River Rd.
Point Pleasant, PA 18950

Langenbach
P.O. Box 453
Blairstown, NJ 07825

A. M. Leonard, Inc.
P.O. Box 816
Piqua, OH 45356-0816

WheelAround Garden Cart

WheelAround Corporation
241 Grandview Ave.
Bellevue, KY 41073

Winged Weeders

Creative Enterprises, Inc.
P.O. Box 3452
Idaho Falls, ID 83403

Harmony Farm Supply
P.O. Box 460
Graton, CA 95444

Trees

Inoculants

Plant Health Care Inc.
440 William Pitt Way
Pittsburgh, PA 15238

Vegetables

Early-Maturing Vegetables

Johnny's Selected Seeds
310 Foss Hill Rd.
Albion, ME 04910

Seeds of Change
P.O. Box 15700
Santa Fe, NM 87506-5700

Reseeding Vegetables

The Cook's Garden
P.O. Box 535
Londonderry, VT 05148

Water Gardens

Supplies

Lilypons Water Gardens
6800 Lilypons Rd.
P.O. Box 10
Buckeystown, MD 21717-0010

Paradise Water Gardens
14 May St.
Whitman, MA 02382

William Tricker, Inc.
7125 Tanglewood Dr.
Independence, OH 44131

Watering

Aqua Spikes

Gardener's Supply Co.
128 Intervale Rd.
Burlington, VT 05401

Drip Irrigation Supplies

Misti-Maid
909 E. Glendale Ave.
Sparks, NV 89431

Drip Irrigation Supplies, including T-Tape

DripWorks
380 Maple St.
Willits, CA 95490

Harmony Farm Supply
P.O. Box 460
Graton, CA 95444

Wildflowers

Wildflower Carpet

Wildflower Carpet, Inc.
1325 S. Colorado Blvd.
Suite 404
Denver, CO 80222
For ordering information, call (800) 247-6945.

RECOMMENDED READING

Annuals and Bulbs

Proctor, Rob, and Nancy J. Ondra. *Rodale's Successful Organic Gardening: Annuals and Bulbs.* Emmaus, Pa.: Rodale Press, 1995.

Companion Planting

McClure, Susan, and Sally Roth. *Rodale's Successful Organic Gardening: Companion Planting.* Emmaus, Pa.: Rodale Press, 1994.

Composting

Martin, Deborah L., and Grace Gershuny, eds. *The Rodale Book of Composting.* Emmaus, Pa.: Rodale Press, 1992.

Fruits

Reich, Lee. *Uncommon Fruits Worthy of Attention.* Reading, Mass.: Addison-Wesley Publishing Co., 1991.

Smith, Miranda. *Backyard Fruits and Berries.* Emmaus, Pa.: Rodale Press, 1994.

Garden Supplies

Ettlinger, Steve. *The Complete Illustrated Guide to Everything Sold in Garden Centers (Except the Plants).* New York: Macmillan Publishing Co., 1990.

General Gardening

Books

Bartholomew, Mel. *Square Foot Gardening.* Emmaus, Pa.: Rodale Press, 1981.

Benjamin, Joan, and Barbara W. Ellis, eds. *Rodale's No-Fail Flower Garden.* Emmaus, Pa.: Rodale Press, 1994.

Bradley, Fern Marshall, ed. *The Experts Book of Garden Hints.* Emmaus, Pa.: Rodale Press, 1993.

Bradley, Fern Marshall, and Barbara W. Ellis, eds. *Rodale's All-New Encyclopedia of Organic Gardening.* Emmaus, Pa.: Rodale Press, 1992.

Ellis, Barbara W., ed. *Rodale's Illustrated Encyclopedia of Gardening and Landscaping Techniques.* Emmaus, Pa.: Rodale Press, 1990.

Ellis, Barbara W., Joan Benjamin, and Deborah L. Martin, eds. *Rodale's Low-Maintenance Gardening Techniques.* Emmaus, Pa.: Rodale Press, 1995.

McRae, Bobbi A. *The Frugal Gardener, More Than 200 Ways to Save Resources (and Money) by Recycling in Your Garden.* Austin, Tex.: Fiberworks Publications, 1992.

Miller, Crow. *Let's Get Growing.* Emmaus, Pa.: Rodale Press, 1995.

Powell, Eileen. *From Seed to Bloom, How to Grow Over 500 Annuals, Perennials, and Herbs.* Pownal, Vt.: Garden Way Publishing, 1995.

Magazines

Organic Gardening, Rodale Press, Inc., 33 E. Minor St., Emmaus, PA 18098.

The American Cottage Gardener, Inchmery Press, Marquette, MI 49855.

Fine Gardening, The Taunton Press, Inc., Newtown, CT 06470.

Horticulture, Horticulture, Inc., 98 N. Washington St., Boston, MA 02114.

National Gardening, National Gardening Association, 180 Flynn Ave., Burlington, VT 05401.

Herbs

Kowalchik, Claire, and William H. Hylton, eds. *Rodale's Illustrated Encyclopedia of Herbs.* Emmaus, Pa.: Rodale Press, 1987.

Michalak, Patricia S. *Rodale's Successful Organic Gardening: Herbs.* Emmaus, Pa.: Rodale Press, 1993.

Landscaping

Ball, Jeff, and Liz Ball. *Rodale's Landscape Problem Solver.* Emmaus, Pa.: Rodale Press, 1989.

Cox, Jeff. *Landscaping with Nature.* Emmaus, Pa.: Rodale Press, 1991.

Hynes, Erin, and Susan McClure. *Rodale's Successful Organic Gardening: Low-Maintenance Landscaping.* Emmaus, Pa.: Rodale Press, 1994.

Kourik, Robert. *Designing and Maintaining Your Edible Landscape—Naturally.* Santa Rosa, Calif.: Metamorphic Press, 1986.

Roth, Susan A. *The Four-Season Landscape.* Emmaus, Pa.: Rodale Press, 1994.

Ornamental Grasses

Greenlee, John. *The Encyclopedia of Ornamental Grasses.* Emmaus, Pa.: Rodale Press, 1992.

Perennials

Bradley, Fern Marshall, ed. *Gardening with Perennials.* Emmaus, Pa.: Rodale Press, 1996.

McClure, Susan, and C. Colston Burrell. *Rodale's Successful Organic Gardening: Perennials.* Emmaus, Pa.: Rodale Press, 1993.

Phillips, Ellen, and C. Colston Burrell. *Rodale's Illustrated Encyclopedia of Perennials.* Emmaus, Pa.: Rodale Press, 1993.

Pest and Disease Control

Books

Carr, Anna. *Rodale's Color Handbook of Garden Insects.* Emmaus, Pa.: Rodale Press, 1983.

Ellis, Barbara W., and Fern Marshall Bradley, eds. *The Organic Gardener's Handbook of Natural Insect and Disease Control.* Emmaus, Pa.: Rodale Press, 1992.

Michalak, Patricia S., and Linda A. Gilkeson. *Rodale's Successful Organic Gardening: Controlling Pests and Diseases.* Emmaus, Pa.: Rodale Press, 1994.

Smith, Miranda, and Anna Carr. *Rodale's Garden Insect, Disease and Weed Identification Guide.* Emmaus, Pa.: Rodale Press, 1988.

Magazines

The IPM Practitioner, Bio-Integral Resource Center (BIRC), P.O. Box 7414, Berkeley, CA 94707-0414.

Plant Propagation

Hill, Lewis. *Secrets of Plant Propagation.* Pownal, Vt.: Storey Communications, 1985.

Preserving the Harvest

Hupping, Carol, et al. *Stocking Up III.* Emmaus, Pa.: Rodale Press, 1986.

McClure, Susan, and the Staff of the Rodale Food Center, eds. *Preserving Summer's Bounty.* Emmaus, Pa.: Rodale Press, 1995.

Pruning

Medic, Kris. *Rodale's Successful Organic Gardening: Pruning.* Emmaus, Pa.: Rodale Press, 1995.

Roses

McKeon, Judith C. *The Encyclopedia of Roses.* Emmaus, Pa.: Rodale Press, 1995.

Seed Saving and Starting

Ashworth, Suzanne. *Seed to Seed.* Decorah, Iowa: Seed Savers Exchange, 1995.

Bubel, Nancy. *The New Seed-Starter's Handbook.* Emmaus, Pa.: Rodale Press, 1988.

Reilly, Ann. *Park's Success with Seeds.* Greenwood, S.C.: Geo. W. Park Seed Co., 1978.

Still, Steven M. *Manual of Herbaceous Ornamental Plants.* 4th ed. Champaign, Ill.: Stipes Publishing Co., 1993.

Soil

Gershuny, Grace. *Start with the Soil.* Emmaus, Pa.: Rodale Press, 1993.

Trees and Shrubs

Dirr, Michael A. *Manual of Woody Landscape Plants.* 4th ed. Champaign, Ill.: Stipes Publishing Co., 1990.

Shigo, Alex L. *100 Tree Myths.* Durham, N.H.: Shigo & Trees Associates, 1993.

Vegetables

Jeavons, John. *How to Grow More Vegetables Than You Ever Thought Possible on Less Land Than You Can Imagine.* 5th ed. Berkeley, Calif.: Ten Speed Press, 1995.

Michalak, Patricia S., and Cass Peterson. *Rodale's Successful Organic Gardening: Vegetables.* Emmaus, Pa.: Rodale Press, 1993.

Ogden, Shepherd. *Step by Step Organic Vegetable Gardening.* Rev. and updated. New York: HarperCollins Publishers, 1992.

Watering

Kourik, Robert. *Drip Irrigation for Every Landscape and All Climates.* Santa Rosa, Calif.: Metamorphic Press, 1992.

Weeds

Hynes, Erin. *Rodale's Successful Organic Gardening: Controlling Weeds.* Emmaus, Pa.: Rodale Press, 1995.

INDEX

Page references in **boldface** indicate illustrations.

A

Acer ginnala, 142
Achillea millefolium, 197, 252
Aconite, 44
Actinidia
    arguta, 180, **181**
    deliciosa, 178–79, **179**
    kolomikta, 180
Aeration, 201
Aesculus parviflora, 142
Agryl (floating row cover), 337
Ajuga, 219
Akebia, five-leaf, 377
Akebia quinata, 377
Alchemilla mollis, 259
Alfalfa meal, 96
Allium schoenoprasum, 155
Alyssum, sweet, 13
Amelanchier, 35
American Cottage Gardener, The, 183, 300, 303
American Society of Landscape Architects (ASLA), 187
Anemone, Japanese (grape-leaved), 258
Anemone tomentosa, 258
Annuals
    for all-summer bloom, 12–13
    for cutting, 10–11
    for flowering screens, 102
    hardy, 7, 8–9
    in landscape design, 192, **192**
    planting techniques for, 6–7, 10
    seeding techniques for, 10–11
    self-sowing, 7, 8–9
    vine types, 380–81
Anthemis tinctoria, 259
Antique Roses for the South, 269
Antirrhinum majus, 7, 13

Aphids
    control of, 27, 30, **30**, 116, 163, 164
    description of, 166
Apple maggot flies, 15, **15**
Apple-picking bag, 136, **136**
Apples
    apple maggot fly traps for, 15, **15**
    dwarf, 16–17, **16**, 104, **105**
    harvest of, 18, **18**
    pollination of, 14, **14**
    pruning techniques for, 16–17, **16**
    scab-resistant cultivars of, 17
Apple scab, 17
AQ10 (fungal parasite), 81
Aqua Spikes, 396–97
Aquilegia, 259
Arctostaphylos uva-ursi, 126
Arid climate, 285, 290–91, 329
Aristolochia durior, 377
Artemisia, 260
Aruncus dioicus, 260
Asarina
    erubescens, 380
    scandens, 381
Ash, mountain, 35
ASLA (American Society of Landscape Architects), 187
Asparagus
    cultivars, 21
    growing tips for, 20–21
    harvest of, 21
    planting depth of, 19, **19**
    thickness of, 20, **20**
Association of Natural Biocontrol Producers, 29
Asteromoea mongolica, 252
Astilbe, 124, 256
    white, 260
Astilbe × arendsii, 260
Avena sativa, 110, 119
Azalea, 281, **281**

OTHER BOOKS FROM RODALE PRESS

If you've enjoyed *Great Garden Shortcuts,* you may be interested in these other garden books from Rodale Press.

The Experts Book of Garden Hints

Over 1,500 Organic Tips and Techniques from 250 of America's Best Gardeners

Fern Marshall Bradley, Editor

For more great gardening advice, turn to this exciting collection of new ideas and techniques for every part of your yard and garden. You'll find step-by-step directions, tips, and projects from professional horticulturists, garden designers, and organic growers.

Rodale's Low-Maintenance Gardening Techniques

Shortcuts and Time-Saving Hints for Your Greatest Garden Ever

Barbara W. Ellis, Joan Benjamin, and Deborah L. Martin, Editors

Here's a no-sweat, no-strain guide to planning and planting a beautiful, bountiful garden. Whether you're growing fruits and vegetables, flowers or vines, trees, shrubs, or lawn grass, this book shows you how to do it with less effort and better results.

Rodale's Garden Answers— Vegetables, Fruits and Herbs

At-a-Glance Solutions for Every Gardening Problem

Fern Marshall Bradley, Editor

When you need to solve gardening problems fast, here's the place to look. You'll find problem-solving tables with organic solutions for more than 400 insect, disease, and cultural problems. Plus, you'll get complete instructions for more than 200 gardening techniques, and the best planting and harvesting tips for all of your favorite crops.

Rodale's All-New Encyclopedia of Organic Gardening

The Indispensable Resource for Every Gardener

Fern Marshall Bradley and Barbara W. Ellis, Editors

With over 400 entries, ranging from Abelia and Composting to Shade Gardening and Zucchini, you'll find all the plant information and techniques you need to garden organically. This complete, practical, up-to-date guide contains gardening information collected from garden experts and writers nationwide.

The Best of Organic Gardening

Over 50 Years of Organic Advice and Reader-Proven Techniques from America's Best-Loved Gardening Magazine

Mike McGrath, Editor

Here's the best of the best—a collection of articles from the pages of *Organic Gardening* magazine to give you advice on composting, mulching, pest control, growing better vegetable crops and flowers, and much, much more. Plus, you'll find articles by favorite garden writers such as Ruth Stout, Euell Gibbons, and Helen and Scott Nearing.

Rodale's Pest and Disease Problem Solver

A Chemical-Free Guide to Keeping Your Garden Healthy

Linda Gilkeson, Pam Peirce, and Miranda Smith

Identify and solve all of your pest and disease problems with this handy guide. A-to-Z coverage of over 180 plants lets you find both the problem and the cure, fast. You can also look up symptoms, individual pests and diseases, organic controls, and even which pests and disease are most common in your area. Color photos and up-to-date instructions make it easy to solve plant problems.

Rodale's No-Fail Flower Garden

How to Plan, Plant and Grow a Beautiful, Easy-Care Garden

Joan Benjamin and Barbara W. Ellis, Editors

If flowers are what you fancy, here's a collection of sensational ideas, designs, and techniques that guarantee gardening success. Now you can avoid every kind of flower garden problem and get beautiful blooms every time. You'll find 16 gorgeous garden designs that you can easily adapt to your yard, plus 20 full-color plant combinations to mix and match as you please.

For more information or to order one of these books, call 1-800-848-4735 or fax us anytime at 1-800-813-6627.